TWILIGHT
OF
THE GODS

'The heroes of Valhalla are scattered, hordes of giants are killed, and the field is wet with blood. In Heaven there is disaster. So is the sun darkened at high noon, the heavens and the earth are turned red with blood, the seats of the mighty gods drip gore. So is the moon lost in blackness, while the stars vanish from the skies. Now there is naught but thick blackness and silence unbroken. The end hath come – Götterdämmerung, "the Twilight of the Gods"!'

Extract from 'The Song of the Vala'
Teutonic Myth and Legend
by Donald A. Mackenzie

David Stone

TWILIGHT
OF GODS
THE
THE DECLINE AND FALL OF THE GERMAN
GENERAL STAFF IN WORLD WAR II

CONWAY

First published in Great Britain in 2011 by Conway,
an imprint of Anova Books Company Ltd,
10 Southcombe Street,
London W14 0RA
www.anovabooks.com
www.conwaypublishing.com

British Library Cataloguing in Publication Data:
A catalogue record for this book is available from the British Library

ISBN 9781844861361

Editing and design by DAG Publications Ltd
Printed and bound in Great Britain by TJ International Ltd, Padstow, Cornwall

A number of the photographs used in this work are from the author's
private collection and the Conway Picture Library (CPL) of Anova Books
Ltd. However, the author also wishes to acknowledge the extensive use of
the images provided by the Bundesarchiv, Germany, at pages 2, 3, 4, 5, 6, 7
(top only), 8, 9, 12, 13, 14, 15, 16, 17, and 18; all page references refer to the
three sections of illustrations. Anova Books Ltd. is committed to respecting
the intellectual property rights of others. We have therefore taken all reasonable efforts to ensure that the reproduction of all content is included
with the full consent of copyright owners. If you are aware of any uninten-
tional omissions, please contact the company directly so that any necessary
corrections may be made for future editions.

To receive regular email updates on forthcoming Conway titles,
email conway@anovabooks.com with 'Conway Update'
in the subject field.

Contents

Introduction

This book tells the story of the progressive demise of the German general staff and its eventual downfall during the final years of the war fought by Hitler's Third Reich between 1939 and 1945. While it deals primarily with this remarkable but ultimately ill-fated organization, it also examines many other important aspects of the German high command during the war years. No historical subject can truly be understood or appreciated in isolation, so I have included a necessarily brief account of the origins and heritage of the Prussian and German general staffs and the post-1919 development of the Reichswehr in order to set the main text properly in context. Similarly, in order that the trials and tribulations of the general staff and of a number of senior commanders during the war may be properly comprehended, an account of the often bizarre relationship between the army and the rising National Socialist movement during the 1930s has also been included. Crucially, it was during these pre-war years that the foundations of all that later transpired were laid.

Despite the apparently inexhaustible interest in any and all aspects of the Third Reich, within the much broader history of Germany and its army, the relatively short period from Hitler's attainment of power in 1933 to his death and the total collapse and military defeat of the nation in 1945 was an historical aberration, a curiosity. This is one of the reasons why the period still attracts such extensive debate and interest worldwide. Even the army that fought for Germany from 1939 to 1945 was in many ways quite different in nature, composition and motivation from that of Prussia, then of imperial

Germany, and finally of the Weimar Republic prior to 1933. Certainly the 'Hitler years' – the rise of National Socialism and the Nazis, the Holocaust, the SS state and so on, and indeed every aspect of World War II itself – all merit study, not least because such analysis provides a plethora of salutary warnings from history, with lessons for future generations. One aspect particularly worthy of consideration is the command and control of the army by the high command and the general staff, without which Hitler's war could not have been prosecuted. Traditionally the army general staff supported, and was therefore an integral part of, the army high command. This organization was almost entirely populated by officers who were members or former members of the army's general staff corps, the principal source of candidates for the most senior and prestigious operational-level command and staff appointments.

While the army and the general staff owed much of its restoration in the mid-1930s to Hitler, the support of army officers for the Nazis in the 1930s was at best naïve and at worst perverse. And while that support might be seen – with the benefit of hindsight – as ill-judged, in 1930s Germany such attitudes were perfectly understandable. For all his flaws, Hitler was an accomplished propagandist and a charismatic and convincing leader of the masses, appearing on the political scene when Germany's fortunes and future were uncertain, with its population very receptive to strong leadership and the prospect of restoring economic and social stability. Accordingly, I have attempted to follow two overlapping and interdependent strands in this account. First of all, in setting the scene for the story of the general staff during World War II, I have necessarily dealt with the circumstances and key events that produced the situation in which the army high command felt constrained to support the National Socialists and by so doing placed itself under an obligation to Hitler. This part of the story includes the increasingly flawed 'unholy alliance' that existed in the pre-war years between the general staff and Hitler and the Nazi leadership. Next, I have tried to highlight the way in which this 'unholy alliance' became ever more strained and deteriorated as the army high command and its general staff tried to continue its business as usual during the war years, while at the same time Hitler pursued a policy of reducing their power and taking ever more command authority to himself. The outcome of this divergence of aims and objectives was inevitable, although the violent manner of its eventual manifestation in July and August 1944 was certainly not anticipated by Hitler or by those officers of the general staff who paid the ultimate penalty for their ill-fated attempt to rectify a situation that had been set in train almost a decade earlier.

Throughout, reference is made variously to the army general staff (Generalstab des Heeres), the general staff (Generalstab) and the high command. In various contexts these terms may be interchangeable. By way of clarification, therefore, it should be explained that the army general staff was the supporting staff organization that advised and directed the policies and activities of the army high command, which comprised the most senior military commanders, virtually all of whom were also Generalstab officers. As such, the general staff was an inseparable part of the army high command. From 1935 the armed forces high command was the Oberkommando der Wehrmacht (OKW) while that of the army was the Oberkommando des Heeres (OKH), and the term 'OKH' is also indicative of the 'army general staff' wherever it is used. Meanwhile, the term 'general staff' was widely used to describe those specially selected and trained officers who filled the most important command and staff positions throughout the army (not just within the army general staff). In practice, these 'general staff officers' were the officers of the general staff corps (Generalstabsoffiziere), an elite body of specially trained officers, originally selected for their professional and intellectual abilities, who embodied the principles, ideals and ethos of professional excellence that had characterized the old Prussian general staff in the nineteenth century. Generalstabsoffiziere were trained to the highest standards through a combination of formal instruction, service with troops and in major headquarters, and the widest possible experience of all arms and services, military history, science and technology. Once trained, they were earmarked to fill the most demanding and important command and general staff appointments throughout the army. A regime of continuous assessment was overlaid upon each phase of the general staff training process. Failure, with the officer's consequent return to non-general staff employment, was possible at any stage. The special qualifications and abilities of these officers and their membership of the general staff corps were immediately distinguishable by the crimson (Karmesin) 'arm of service colour' (Waffenfarbe) distinctions borne on the tunic shoulder straps, collar lace and the trouser stripes of their service uniforms.

With regard to the use of German vis-à-vis English in this work, in a number of cases I have chosen to use German words rather than their English equivalents – although I have usually indicated both versions where appropriate. I have adopted German rank designations wherever they are linked to a specific officer's name, while using the English version where a rank is referred to in more general terms. Where an officer's rank is shown, it reflects the rank held at the time of the action or event in question, which may not necessarily be the highest or final rank achieved by that officer. In some cases I have used the broader term 'General' to describe officers of 'general officer rank' rather than specifying the rank as 'Generalmajor', 'Generalleutnant' or 'Generaloberst'. Where I have omitted the rank of a frequently mentioned officer (such as von Rundstedt, von Brauchitsch, Guderian or Halder), it should be assumed that his rank is unchanged from that indicated when that officer's rank was last shown. Although it would be strictly correct to show those officers holding the rank of 'General' as 'General der Infanterie', 'General der Panzertruppe', 'General der Kavallerie', 'General der Artillerie' and so on, for clarity I have in most cases chosen simply to show them as 'General' without such amplification (which would normally have been included on official documents, nominal rolls, signature blocks and so on). The index entries show the highest final rank that an individual officer achieved in the Wehrmacht as well as his full rank title where appropriate.

Whereas an officer's rank in the US or British army usually reflected the appointment held, this was not so in the German army, which applied a system of relative seniority, time served and performance assessment. Consequently, a German army lieutenant general might be found commanding a division, a major general might command an army corps, and a general, colonel-general and field marshal could as readily command an army corps, an army or an army group in various situations. The German concept of officer employment and promotion involved selecting the right man for the task, irrespective (within reason) of his rank, and it was therefore well understood that promotion was not necessarily implicit in that selection. Despite being fully qualified as a general staff officer and with an impressive professional track record, Hauptmann (later Generalfeldmarschall) Erich von Manstein spent no less than thirteen years as a captain before his promotion to major in 1928 at the age of forty![1]

Throughout this work, I have referred to the three levels of military command and war-fighting activities: strategic, operational and tactical. While these terms will be familiar to many readers, a word of clarification may nevertheless be appropriate at this stage. Today it is generally understood that 'strategy' is the province of the commander of a theatre of operations, working within established political parameters. As such, 'strategic' activities are usually conducted by army groups and armies. The activities conducted by corps and divisions are at the 'operational' level, with those by brigades (or regiments), battalions and below being at the 'tactical' level. However, such categorization can be over-simplistic, as the activities conducted by a corps or division where it is the only formation in a theatre of operations may well be 'strategic' in reality (arguably, the campaign fought by Rommel's Afrikakorps in North Africa being a case in point). Similarly, by the final year of the war, the strength of many German army divisions was frequently closer to that of a regiment or even battalion (especially on the Eastern Front), even though their allocated tasks might still – theoretically – have been 'operational' in nature. The lesson here is that these terms provide an indication of a level of command rather than a definitive categorization – especially in the case of the operational and tactical levels, where activities frequently blurred and overlapped.

Mindful of all this, and of the fact that this work deals not with war-fighting today but with that carried out by the German army in the mid-twentieth century, I have adopted the level of command definitions used by the German army of the 1939–1945 period. These were originally based upon the Prussian experience of war-fighting in much earlier times, having been finally developed, refined and applied by Generalfeldmarschall Helmuth Karl Bernhard Graf von Moltke, chief of the general staff during Prussia's, and finally Germany's, brilliant successes against Austria, Denmark and France in the nineteenth century and the principal architect of those victories. Under von Moltke, 'operational' activities were primarily the province of armies, corps and divisions, all of which were to be regarded as 'operational manoeuvre units': capable of moving, striking and achieving outcomes often significantly greater than their actual size or theoretical strength might imply. However, what may be extrapolated from von Moltke's definition or concept of the 'operational' level of command is that not only is this the most vital level of military activity but also that it can in certain circumstances also reflect the capability and mission of a unit or formation rather than simply its nominal size or designation. From this concept, the Germans coined the term 'Bewegungskrieg', which implied, involved or called for decisive movement or manoeuvre at the operational level. The attitude of mind that routinely accorded such large formations this 'operational' or 'manoeuvre' status was undoubtedly one of the factors that imbued German officers and the general staff with the ability to imagine, conceive and conduct the sorts of offensives and manoeuvres that characterized the Blitzkrieg years of 1939–41, together with some of the operations conducted in Russia after June 1941 and in the Ardennes in 1944. Whether entirely deserved or not, the doctrine of Bewegungskrieg was also an important contributor to the reputation for military superiority and professionalism that the German army and the general staff acquired in the nineteenth century and retained well into World War II. It complemented the German doctrine of Auftragstaktik, the concept of directive- or mission-led operations and delegation. This pragmatic concept has been misunderstood and misapplied by some other armies in the post-1945 period, and the extent of its application in the 1939–1945 conflict has often been overstated. Indeed, even within the Wehrmacht, the combination of modern radio communications with the very direct and intrusive nature of Hitler's control of the army after 1941 limited the ability of commanders and the general staff to apply the principle of Auftragstaktik as it had been conceived, taught and utilized in earlier times.

An important aspect of any account of the German general staff during the Third Reich period is the story of the German resistance movement against Hitler, within which many members of the army and the general staff – but primarily senior and general staff officers – played key roles. Indeed, the ebb and flow of the various conspiracies against Hitler provided an ever-present backdrop to the story of his often troubled relationship with the army between 1933 and 1945. The growing resistance within the army to Hitler and his policies is a thread that runs through much of this book, and I have included a specific chapter dealing with aspects of the wider story of this movement in order to make the reader aware of some of the broader political-military and civilian-military plotting, activities and agendas within Germany that directly or indirectly influenced very many of the high-level decisions and events affecting the army from the mid-1930s but especially from 1941 to 1944. The full story of the German resistance movement against Hitler would readily fill a book in its own right, and several such specialist works appear as references in this book. Accordingly, this particular chapter can do no more than summarize the story of these conspiracies, while still focusing primarily upon the military resistance rather than its civilian counterpart. It follows that this 'semi-stand alone' chapter does not seek to provide a comprehensive catalogue and explanation of every political and philosophical agenda, policy, sub-group and personality involved in the remarkably widespread and complex but often disparate and disjointed German resistance movement that opposed Hitler and National Socialism until 1944. None the less, the chapter that succeeds and complements it does comprise a fairly detailed account of the events that took place at Hitler's field headquarters at the Wolfschanze and in Berlin on 20 July 1944, during and immediately after the last – and so nearly successful – attempt by the military members of the resistance to assassinate Hitler. Although it could be argued that these details are not absolutely essential to the wider story of the general staff during the Nazi era, the 20 July plot was incontrovertibly a defining moment in that story, one that set the seal on the final demise of that organization, and it is for that reason that the actions that day of Oberst Claus Schenk Graf von Stauffenberg, together with those of a number of other army and general staff officers, have been chronicled in some detail.

Next, I have taken the liberty of using the endnotes not merely to cross-reference particular facts or quotations to other works but also to amplify aspects of the story of the general staff or to explain other matters concerning the war that – if included within the main text – might possibly impede the flow of the principal theme, but which I none the less believe to be essential or of special interest or relevance to the subject in hand. Some endnotes are, therefore, quite fulsome and comprehensive, with several constituting 'stand alone' accounts on a variety of matters. With regard to the appendices, the reader may find the organizational details of the OKW, the OKH and its staff branches, and the Ersatzheer (the 'replacement army', but which may also be referred to as the 'home army' or 'reserve army' in recognition of its wider functions and responsibilities) a useful amplification and clarification of some aspects of the main text. Although these organizations are necessarily shown as they existed at one specific time fairly late during the war, the sheer scale, span of responsibility and complexity of the OKH in particular are very evident from the material shown in these appendices.

I have resisted the temptation to include maps illustrating the overall course of the war or the ebb and flow of specific campaigns or operations. Rather, I have focused upon the planning function that was, of course, a core responsibility of the general staff. Accordingly, I have used a series of sketch maps in the appendices to illustrate and clarify a number of aspects and significant stages of the planning processes that affected the Polish campaign in 1939, the offensive against France and the Low Countries in 1940 and finally that against Russia from 1941. These maps are designed to complement the detailed descriptions of the development of these key campaigns within the main text. Two maps dealing specifically with the events of 20 July 1944 have also been included.

While researching this work I became increasingly struck by the several important factors and influences that affected the reconstituted general staff, not only from its official restoration and revival in 1935 but also those that were the legacy of the post-World War I years during its downgraded and concealed existence during the Reichswehr period. The less than ideal circumstances of its restoration, and the unprecedented political, economic and social situation within Germany with which it had to contend, were factors virtually unknown to its pre-1918 predecessors. However, taken as a whole, it might be argued that these circumstances and influences meant that the general staff that served the army of the Third Reich was fundamentally and unavoidably flawed from the outset. It is also arguable, therefore, whether or not this organization could ever have regained within Nazi Germany the sort of power and status that the general staff had enjoyed prior to 1918. In the course of my own professional military training, I was frequently aware of the regularity with which, during modern-day training courses, study days, battlefield tours and so on, the German general staff was presented as the historical epitome of military excellence. Indeed, the general staff that went to war in 1939 was often cited as exemplifying all that was best in the art of command and control, military analysis and that of planning. Nevertheless, it is probably more accurate to say that the Prussian general staff of the nineteenth century and the German imperial general staff that succeeded it until 1918 were the foremost such organizations in the world at that time, and many other nations adopted the Prussian or German model for their own armed forces. However, the manner in which the general staff was constrained to exist in the shadows from 1919, and the somewhat flawed process by which it was then resurrected in 1935 in Hitler's Germany, mitigated very strongly against that organization ever being able to regain the authority and status that it had enjoyed prior to 1918. This was probably inevitable, despite the consummate professionalism and dedication of a succession of general staff officers who sought to to revive, maintain, develop and apply the best traditions of the German general staff between 1935 and 1945. On a practical level, this was frequently to very good effect, and notwithstanding the obstacles and opposition they had regularly to overcome from elsewhere within the armed forces and the Nazi regime itself. However, the ethos and traditions of the German army and the general staff were fundamentally at odds with much of the ideology and many of the objectives of the Nazis. Accordingly, the growth of the active opposition to Hitler within the general staff from the 1930s and his continued mistrust of the organization were both predictable and understandable. But what was perhaps more of a surprise – given the character of Hitler and the nature of the Nazi and SS state over which he presided – was that Hitler was prepared to tolerate potentially harmful opposition and dissent at the very heart of the Wehrmacht for so long. Only in 1944 did the Führer at last take decisive and devastating action against those who opposed him within the general staff and elsewhere. At that time, events and ill-fortune conspired to seal the fate of the German general staff that had served the army of the Third Reich to the best of its ability in spite of the constraints and sometimes insurmountable obstacles placed in its way not only by the armed forces of the opposing Allies but also by the political leadership of the very country for which it fought.

Preface

Götterdämmerung
('Twilight of the Gods')

Set deep within the dark fir forests of Rastenburg in East Prussia lay the Führer's principal field headquarters in the east, the Wolfschanze[2], an extensive complex of wooden buildings, concrete blockhouses and bunkers sited in a well-guarded, heavily-camouflaged compound. There, on 20 July 1944, a high-level planning conference had been called by Hitler. By 12.30 p.m. some twenty-three senior military officers and civilians had been joined by Hitler in the conference room of the Lagebaracke, a sizeable wooden hut with a large conference room, at the centre of which was a large table covered with situation maps. On that day, as had also been the case on so many of the days preceding it, these maps showed the Third Reich's ever-deteriorating strategic situation on all fronts.

Although not usually an attendee, another army officer was due to be present at this particular conference, Oberst Claus Schenk Graf von Stauffenberg – a 37-year-old cavalry officer from southern Germany who had served with distinction in a Bavarian regiment in Poland, France and North Africa before being severely wounded by an air attack in April 1943. After lengthy treatment and convalescence, he had returned to duty as the chief of staff of the army's department of ordnance and had arrived at Rastenburg shortly after 10.00 that morning in order to provide an update report to the midday conference on aspects of the replacement or home army (the Ersatzheer), of which he was then the chief of staff. However, by July 1944, despite his undoubted courage and loyalty to the Fatherland, he no longer supported the Hitler regime. Amongst the mass of papers, files and reports he carried in his bulging briefcase was a powerful time-bomb. His mission that July day was to kill Hitler, thereby saving Germany from the evil policies and catastrophic incompetence that by then characterized the Third Reich. With Hitler dead, Stauffenberg's co-conspirators intended to negotiate a peace with the Western Allies, hoping to achieve their agreement to Germany's retention of its pre-1939 borders.

Von Stauffenberg entered the conference room a little before the time he was due to give his report. He paid his respects to the Führer while his briefcase was placed under the table close to Hitler, against one of the table's substantial legs. Having done so, he said that he needed to make a telephone call to Berlin in order to obtain a few last-minute details for his report and so left the room. The OKH chief of operations, Generalleutnant Adolf Heusinger, was in the middle of giving his report on the situation on the Eastern Front when, shortly after 12.40 p.m., the bomb detonated with a tremendous explosion that destroyed the conference table, devastated the room, blew out the tarred felt roof and threw at least one man straight through one of the building's three windows. One man died instantly, three later died of their wounds, several sustained severe injuries, and virtually all of the rest received lesser injuries. Hitler was shocked, his right arm was injured, his eardrums were damaged, and he sustained burns to his head and his right leg. Remarkably, however, given his close proximity to the explosion, the Führer was not only still alive, he was also able to walk away more or less unaided from the scene of death and destruction.

However, von Stauffenberg arrived back in Berlin believing that the bombing had been successful. There he found a chaotic situation at the Bendlerstraße building that housed the general army office of the Wehrmacht high command. Orders and counter-orders were fuelled by rumour, but by early evening it became abundantly clear to all that Hitler had survived the attack. With Hitler's survival, the conspiracy and attempted coup collapsed rapidly. Having already shown their hand in the attempted coup, von Stauffenberg and three other army officers were arrested that evening. Later, all four were summarily shot by a firing squad in the courtyard of the Bendlerstraße building, the hastily arranged executions illuminated by vehicle headlights. Those four officers at least were spared the horrors and humiliations that followed in the aftermath of the failed assassination attempt, as an inevitable purge of the officer corps quickly gained momentum and literally tore the heart out of the army, as well as removing many men who might well have contributed positively to the German recovery in the post-war years.

On 7 August 1944, the first session of the so-called People's Court – the Volksgericht – convened in Berlin, with the remit to mete out Nazi justice and retribution to those arrested and held for trial in connection with the bomb attack at the Wolfschanze. The Volksgericht sat in the principal chamber of the former Prussian Court of Appeal within the city's law courts. There, over a six-month period, Judge Roland Freisler, the court's uncompromisingly pro-Nazi president, was in his element. Day after day he directed streams of invective against those accused of any sort of involvement in, or knowledge of, the abortive attempt to kill the Führer. Harsh lights illuminated the courtroom, accentuating the garish colours of the three large red-black-white swastika flags that decorated the wall, dramatically and unequivocally indicating the exclusively Nazi nature of the proceedings. The only other obvious ornaments in the chamber were two prominently displayed busts, one of Frederick the Great and the other of Hitler. The courtroom lights also enabled a concealed camera to film every perverse twist and turn of the unfolding drama, with all of Freisler's condemnatory and prejudicial diatribes recorded. However, the post-20 July Volksgericht hearings were not open to the general public or to any relatives or supporters of the accused, being held *in camera* throughout. In most cases, Freisler's often lengthy tirades concluded with the routine pronouncement of yet another death sentence, against which there was no appeal, the sentence usually being carried out by various forms of hanging or strangulation in the execution shed of Berlin's notorious Plötzensee prison soon afterwards. The court comprised two professional judges and five non-judicial members selected from Nazi party officials, the SS or the Wehrmacht. However, it was a 'court of law' in name only, as the judges were empowered to outvote or overrule the lay members, and in any case Freisler dominated the proceedings as president of the Volksgericht. He knew full well that the Third Reich's 'People's Court' was not about legality or natural justice: it was about Hitler's desire for revenge and retribution, together with the need to create a climate of fear throughout Germany in order to maintain the undisputed authority of the Nazi party throughout the country and to deter any dissent as the nation's strategic situation in east and west became ever more precarious. Freisler knew well his duty to his Führer, and the litany of show trials and savage sentences from 7 August 1944 delivered in very large measure all that Hitler and Heinrich Himmler, the head of the Gestapo and the SS, required of him. These trials also afforded Hitler and the Nazi hierarchy a long-sought opportunity to complete their dis-empowerment of the army high command and the general staff. This in turn would enable the SS to increase its own power and establish its absolute primacy throughout Germany, including control of the country's home-based replacement army, the Ersatzheer.

The succession of two hundred or so defendants eventually arraigned before the Volksgericht during the Gestapo purges that followed the 20 July bomb attack included civilian and military personnel, the latter including senior and junior officers alike. However, while the resistance movement against Hitler had gained much momentum by 1944, with varying levels of military and civilian support for an end to the war and for an alternative to the Nazi government also evident in various parts of Germany, it was largely army officers who had taken leading roles in the conspiracy; very many of these officers were members or products of the renowned German general staff. Indeed, the head of this clandestine group was former chief of the general staff Generaloberst Ludwig Beck, while the actual assassination plot was directed by Generalmajor Henning von Tresckow, with von Stauffen-berg having taken on the principal role.

Consequently, while the story of the decline and fall of the German general staff from 1939 to 1945 chronicles the progressive demise of this organization over the course of a number of years, its eventual end was exemplified by the appearance before the Volksgericht on 7 August 1944 of Generalfeldmarschall Erwin von Witzleben, Generaloberst Erich Höpner, Generalmajor Helmuth Stieff, Generalleutnant Paul von Hase, Oberstleutnant Robert Bernardis, Hauptmann Karl Klausing, and Oberleutnant Peter Graf Yorck von Wartenburg. Just one day later, having been roundly abused, intimidated, humiliated and accused by Freisler of high treason and betraying Germany, all seven of these well-known and (in four cases) very senior officers were found guilty. Their executions were carried out with calculated savagery at Berlin-Plötzensee later that same day. On Hitler's orders, these and the subsequent killings at Plötzensee were filmed, affording the Führer the opportunity later to witness and savour his revenge. Hanging, beheading and garotting were variously employed by the Plötzensee executioners. During the days and months that followed, a further 89 alleged conspirators followed those first seven army officers into the same execution shed, the majority of them serving or retired army officers.

Overall, some 200 people were executed for their alleged involvement in the conspiracy, with many more imprisoned or consigned to concentration camps. The 'intensive interrogation' of some suspects by the Gestapo and SS investigators included forms of torture more reminiscent of medieval times than of the mid-twentieth century. In the meantime, once its origins became all too clear, von Stauffenberg's failure on 20 July and the collapse of the coup brought about the final break between Hitler and the army's general staff. A superlative military organization and institution that had existed for almost one and a half centuries – but with its origins rooted in the Prussian army in much earlier times – which had provided service to the nation and its army with consummate professionalism for so many years, experienced the nadir of its fortunes during the late summer and autumn of 1944, preceding the eventual and inevitable fall of its Nazi masters by little more than six months.

The term 'Götterdämmerung' – the word used to describe the orgy of mayhem and destruction in the 'twilight of the gods' depicted at the end of Richard Wagner's opera *Der Ring des Nibelungen* – is frequently used to describe the final days of the Third Reich and Hitler in Berlin in April 1945. However, during the Blitzkrieg years to 1942 the German army's high command and the general staff had aspired to become 'gods of war' in all but name, and so 'Götterdämmerung' is in many ways a more apt description of the final fall in 1944 of these sometime masters of the German warrior class than of the deeply flawed political leaders who ultimately brought about their demise. During this process of decline and fall, these military leaders and consummate professionals in the art of war first of all regained a measure of their traditional status in the 1930s – largely through their deliberate, misplaced, politically naïve or passive acquiescence in a pact with the perverse devilment of National Socialism and Adolf Hitler its leader. But despite the considerable strategic successes achieved on the battlefield from 1939 to 1941, that opportunistic but unholy military-political alliance in the 1930s laid a flawed foundation upon which all that followed was built. Consequently, the army in due course paid a particularly heavy price, eventually losing everything as Germany's fortunes gradually declined from 1942. This process of decline and fall involved army officers of all ranks – from Generalfeldmarschall to Leutnant – but at its core, and inextricably engaged directly and indirectly in this process from beginning to end, were the members of the German general staff.

1
A Tradition of Excellence
1870–1918

In 1870, Helmuth von Moltke was in his seventieth year. He, above all others, was responsible for the introduction, development, training and refinement of the 'Prussian Great General Staff' system of command and control, building successfully upon the foundations of Prussian martial excellence established during the early years of the nineteenth century by the great military thinkers and practitioners von Gneisenau, von Scharnhorst and von Clausewitz. Von Moltke's own credentials as a professional staff officer were also impeccable, and he had consistently shown outstanding ability during the Danish campaign over Schleswig-Holstein in 1864 and that against Austria in 1866. However, he has been described as 'a remote and dedicated professional'. This remoteness was perhaps indicative of the fact that his particular abilities as a staff officer were not always mirrored by his wider powers of leadership. This included an occasional inability to control some of his more senior subordinate commanders in the field.

The general staff concept originated in Prussia and was carried forward vigorously into the wider German army in the mid-nineteenth century. Although staff systems in their earliest forms could be traced back to the Prussian army of the early eighteenth century, von Moltke had perfected the general staff model in 1857. Members of the general staff were the most competent and intellectually astute officers of the army, and appointment to the general staff was a highly competitive, selective and continuing process. The general staff dealt with all matters concerned with 'the movement, quartering, engagement and mobilizing of the troops, and to warfare in general'. This last area of responsibility effectively provided a right and duty to be involved in all aspects of the conduct of operations. Despite this wide remit, the actual number of general staff officers was relatively small: there were just 200 in 1870, rising to no more than 250 by the end of the war with France in 1871.

Subject to recommendation to do so, officers who had completed three years' service applied to sit an entrance examination that would admit them to the Kriegsakademie (war college for general staff training). There they completed a course of three years, which also included periods of service with units of the field army in order to ensure that their theoretical training and studies were balanced by practical experience. Rigorous assessment of the students continued throughout the course. This first step culminated in a very testing examination that determined the immediate future employment of the officer, either as an instructor at a military school, or as an adjutant (dealing with all aspects of the routine staff work and management of the army), or as a general staff officer. Of an annual Kriegsakademie intake of about 400 officers, only 120 usually reached the final examination point, and of these only the top ten or twelve officers were taken annually for general staff employment.

These few outstanding officers next completed between two and three years attached to the Great General Staff in Berlin, where the training, education, assessment and selection process continued. Finally, the officers who successfully completed this period under the direct supervision of the chief of the general staff were assigned permanently to the general staff; but any subsequent decline in performance could result in an immediate return to regimental duty. Now qualified, these officers were subsequently employed in general staff appointments at all levels of command down to division and thereafter progressed in rank and responsibility within the general staff system. Theirs was a process of continuous personal professional development, which blended service with troops, staff work, travel and all forms of intellectual development to prepare them for the most important appointments and ultimately, if appropriate, for high command. Throughout their service, these officers enjoyed a deservedly privileged position and, when serving as the chief of staff of a formation, they would invariably assume command of that division, corps or army in the absence of its commanding general. Their presence in every major headquarters, installation and organization also guaranteed the chief of the general staff a first-hand view of the activities and performance of every part of the army, together with an ability to exert his influence over these matters very directly. This then was the remarkable military organization that directed the German army during Prussia's wars against Denmark in 1864 and Austria in 1866, culminating in the crushing defeat of France in 1870–1 by an army that was German – albeit led by Prussia – thus enabling the unification of the German states with the proclamation of the Second Reich, headed by Kaiser Wilhelm I, on 18 January 1871.

From its adoption in 1894, the so-called 'Schlieffen Plan' was at the heart of the army's strategic planning for a future war. This compilation of formal documents for operational planning was designed to enable Germany to fight and win a war conducted on two fronts – against France and Russia. Such strategic planning was Germany's response to the succession of international alliances made during the latter part of the nineteenth century which – from Berlin's perspective – had progressively isolated and surrounded Germany with potentially hostile powers: a situation reminiscent of that which had faced Frederick II of Prussia in the eighteenth century. Although it was eventually adopted in 1894, the general staff planning for this conflict had actually been in progress ever since 1871, having been directed at first by von Moltke. He had initially planned for overwhelming force to be deployed against France, with a holding action against Russia. This strategy would allow for the speedy defeat of Germany's traditional foe in the west before the bulk of the army redeployed eastwards to deal with Russia. Later, von Moltke modified the plan to take account of new border defences then being constructed by France, together with an updated estimate of Russia's ability to mobilize more speedily than had originally been assessed. As a result, the plan was fundamentally amended to enable Russia's defeat first of all, then that of France. In 1888 – the year in which Kaiser Wilhelm II became German head of state – von Moltke retired, being followed as chief of the general staff by General Alfred von Waldersee, who left his predecessor's strategic plans largely unaltered. However, in 1891 von Waldersee was in turn succeeded by General Alfred von Schlieffen, who would serve as chief of the general staff until 1906.

Von Schlieffen was the archetypal German general staff officer – dedicated, intellectually astute, professionally most competent, and above all else a pragmatist and an innovator. He was a committed exponent of the Bewegungskrieg concept of wars of manoeuvre or movement and of the primacy of the offensive in operations. However, he also exemplified the extent to which the general staff had become distanced – some would say decoupled – from the international political realities and imperatives of the late nineteenth century. This divergence of military and diplomatic activity and thinking meant that the core strategy upon which the army's planning, doctrine and deployment were based was inevitably founded upon a number of incorrect premises. Early in his time as chief of the general staff, von Schlieffen re-assessed von Moltke's first plan and came to the conclusion that the greater threat still lay to Germany's west, and that in the event of war France should therefore be defeated as quickly as possible, certainly before any major campaign was launched against Russia in the east. Over time he developed a series of operational scenarios and options, from which emerged what became known as 'the Schlieffen Plan', although in practice this 'plan' was more of a living document or collection of documents, to be used on a continuing basis for strategic debate and operational planning rather than as a definitive and final war plan. As such, the Schlieffen Plan exemplified the flexibility of thought and intellectual ideals and principles of the German general staff system. However, von Schlieffen would certainly neither have expected nor advocated its provisions and application to a future war to remain unchallenged and untested by the general staff officers of the day. An example of the general staff's consideration of future combat in the light of earlier conflicts was produced in 1903. Developed under von Schlieffen's auspices, the publication *Der Schlachterfolg: mit welchen Mitteln wurde er erstrebt?* (literally, 'Success in Battle and How Do We Strive for It?') included some 65 maps of past campaigns accompanied by a detailed analysis of their conduct. This historical analysis led to deductions that reconfirmed the importance of the offensive, the desirability of the indirect or oblique attack, and the importance of manoeuvre to achieve this and enable the comprehensive destruction of an opposing force. Such well-considered thought processes and analysis typified the general staff's approach to war planning, and by this means it prepared the army for the next great conflict.

An early version of the Schlieffen Plan envisaged more than 90 per cent of the German army being launched against France, utilizing surprise, mobility and envelopment to defeat it speedily. The army would then turn its attention to the Eastern Front and the defeat of Russia. Over the next fifteen years, von Schlieffen and the general staff further refined the plan, the basic concept remaining largely unaltered. A fundamental pre-requisite of the plan was for Germany to have a sufficiently large army to carry it out, and thus von Schlieffen's work was a key pillar of the general staff's ongoing argument for ever-increasing amounts of manpower and resources. In 1906, Generalleutnant Helmuth Johannes Ludwig von Moltke (von Moltke 'the Younger') succeeded von Schlieffen. He reviewed the plan and made a number of significant changes to it, all of which were in place by the time that the plan was implemented in 1914. Indeed, in the late nineteenth century and during the years leading up to 1914, work bearing directly or indirectly upon the Schlieffen plan was the principal day-to-day focus of the general staff, despite occasional aberrations such as Germany's expedition to China to suppress the Boxer rising in 1900 and the army's colonial campaigns in Africa. However, from 1888 the backdrop to German strategic planning increasingly reflected the imperialistic ambitions of Kaiser Wilhelm II, with his desire to confirm Germany as the foremost military-industrial power in Europe, as well as developing the country's overseas territories and influence on a scale to challenge and ultimately equal or exceed that of the British Empire.

Inevitably, various flaws in the Schlieffen plan were revealed within weeks of the outbreak of World War I – hardly surprising perhaps, in view of the well-worn adage that military plans rarely survive first contact with the enemy (tellingly, this axiom was originally stated by the first von Moltke: 'No plan survives contact with the enemy's main body'). In any event, von Moltke 'the Younger' subsequently felt constrained to resign due to the responsibility he felt for having amended the plan during the years following von Schlieffen's departure. However, it is probably true to say that even the original plan was overly optimistic, both in its assessment of the strength of the French border defensive positions and of the ability of a German general staff, untried in the realities of modern warfare, to control armies on the huge scale at which they were deployed by the empire in 1914 – albeit that von Schlieffen himself had already acknowledged in 1901 that 'armies consist of masses that are ever more difficult to control and ever less manoeuvrable'.[3] However, it would be unfair to blame von Schlieffen for the subsequent failure of the army to achieve a rapid victory in the west in 1914 and to avoid a two-front war, for he had retired almost a decade before the war broke out. Neither should von Moltke 'the Younger' attract such unqualified criticism, as it was he who ensured that the army that went to war in 1914 was the best equipped and best organized in Europe. Rather, it was changes on the international scene (notably those affecting the strategic balance following the creation of the Franco-Russian-British Triple Entente between 1892 and 1904–7) that produced a mismatch between the anticipated French military response indicated in the plan and what the French high command actually did on the day. Despite the inherent professionalism of the general staff, the plan with which it went to war in 1914 failed to take account of issues in a changing and modernizing world that extended well beyond the primarily military-industrial area. Accordingly, there was some evidence that a degree of complacency or over-confidence had been allowed to develop within a general staff that had justifiably gained an unchallenged reputation in 1871, but which had been untested in a major war during the almost half a century that followed.

Irrespective of its validity or otherwise, von Schlieffen's plan depended upon the quality and training of the army, and upon the army having in place an operational doctrine appropriate to support its strategic mission, operational readiness and training. Given that the plan was based almost entirely upon an offensive strategy, it was absolutely essential to sustain a very high level of readiness and training standards on a day-to-day basis. This inevitably placed a significant burden upon a peacetime army whose national strategy required that it should be maintained in a state of permanent readiness for war.

The army's operational doctrine was directed by the general staff, and the process begun in earnest by von Moltke in the mid-nineteenth century continued largely unchanged during the decades that followed. The Kriegsakademie continued its pivotal role of ensuring a common approach and consistency of military thought by those favoured officers selected for membership of the general staff. By 1914 the total number of general staff officers was 625. This represented an increase of only 375 since 1871, despite the significant changes and several significant expansions of the army that had taken place since then. Typically, the course of 1913 at the Berlin Kriegsakademie numbered just 168 officers. It included three young officers who were destined to become celebrated commanders in World War II: Guderian, von Manstein and Höpner. Their training schedule comprised just 25 hours of formal instruction per week during the first and second years of the three-year course.[4] Without the opportunity to revalidate it in the crucible of war, this system always had the potential to become inflexible or over-standardized, while a criticism levelled at the Kriegsakademie during the periods before both world wars was that it concentrated upon operational and tactical matters to the detriment of any time allocated to strategic studies, such as the correlation between military power, diplomacy and economic factors at a national level. This somewhat surprising weakness in the syllabus was despite the intellectual aptitude of the general staff candidates and officers, all of whom were well capable of assimilating such instruction and the discussion of these issues. The emphasis upon operational matters at the Kriegsakademie was also to the detriment of time spent on intelligence, logistics and personnel issues, which reflected the long-standing Prussian preoccupation with what were seen by many as the more glamorous or victory-winning aspects of war-fighting. The modules of academic subjects were either science-based, incorporating mathematics, physical geography and physics, or a combination of general geography and the French, English or Polish language. History also featured prominently in all subject mixes. Sport, private study and individual research were encouraged, and it was an officer's personal responsibility to maintain a satisfactory standard of personal fitness.

Despite this ever-present risk of stagnation of military thinking in the years of relative peace after 1871 and before 1914, it was from the mid-nineteenth century – building upon the thoughts of such eminent military philosophers and soldiers as von Clausewitz, von Scharnhorst and von Gneisenau – that the important concept of what became known as Auftragstaktik (the concept and doctrine of mission-orientated command) was developed[5] by the general staff and then disseminated throughout the army. In simple terms, Auftragstaktik required a commander to allocate a subordinate commander his mission – i.e., what he had to achieve – and the necessary resources, but not to tell him how he was to carry it out. At the same time, the senior commander would make his subordinates fully aware of his own mission so that, in the event that the operational situation changed or commanders became casualties, the overall mission could still be concluded successfully without recourse to issuing further orders. In purely practical terms, Auftragstaktik enabled the effective conduct of mobile offensive operations and the German way of war-fighting; as such its emergence, adoption and subsequent development by the general staff was virtually inevitable. At the same time, the flexibility and tactical responsibility this concept conferred upon junior commanders engendered the initiative, aggression and fighting spirit that were so often the hallmarks of the German army's commanders in combat units during both world wars. Despite this, however, the army's continued obsession with its traditional deployment drills – especially at the tactical level – still attracted accusations of inflexibility and stagnation from some contemporary commentators, as did the repetitious nature and intensity of an annual training cycle conducted against the background of a period of almost fifty years of peace for Germany in Europe. Whether in the high command and the general staff or within the battalions and companies of a regiment, an army that is too long at peace can never be totally ready for the ultimate challenge of war, no matter how much a nation has invested in its preparedness in terms of time, study, resources and training.

Auftragstaktik has continued as a fundamental principle of the German way of war-fighting right up to the present day, and was in evidence during the army's early campaigns in World War II. However, the relative ease with which it could be applied during the wars of Wilhelm I, von Bismarck and

Helmuth von Moltke (when the complete freedom of action of operational-level commanders was taken for granted by the general staff) reduced significantly once wars began to be fought on the scale and at the levels of complexity and operational interdependence seen in 1914–18 and 1939–45. Meanwhile, Auftragstaktik was by no means a risk-free operational panacea – it also attracted its own risks and dangers. Ironically, perhaps, the greatest threat to the concept would prove to be the modernization of warfare, specifically those future advances of communications technology that provided commanders at higher levels with immediate access to commanders at the front line. Far from being a command and control benefit for the army, such capabilities always risked the sort of unprecedented level of 'top down' interference and 'tactical second guessing' that was exemplified by Hitler's actions once he assumed supreme command of the army from the beginning of 1942. In the German army, Auftragstaktik (which was more accurately understood and applied in practice in the twentieth century as the 'independence of subordinate commanders') hardly survived beyond the first two years of World War II, only being resurrected in the post-1945 era during the Cold War.[6] Nevertheless, while Auftragstaktik has generated much analysis and discussion in military and academic forums alike, its interpretation and adoption in various suitably modified forms is generally laudable for any army, where the delegation of operational or tactical command and control, but not of a superior commander's ultimate responsibility for the outcome of events, usually reflects sound training and a high level of confidence in one's subordinates. However, Auftragstaktik in its purest form would never have been able to survive the scale, complexity and technological advances in place by the time that Germany went to war in 1939.

When Germany went to war in 1914 the actions of its army were directed by two particular general staff documents. Its strategic deployment and operational activities were of course based upon the requirements of the Schlieffen plan. However, during the pre-war years, the general staff had also developed the *Kriegsbrauch im Landkriege* – literally 'Customs of Warfare on Land', (usually termed 'War Book of the German General Staff' in the 1915 English-language edition) – which drew upon, updated and amplified many of the principles and philosophical thoughts that had been articulated by von Clausewitz, von Scharnhorst and von Gneisenau in earlier times. First published in 1902, the *Kriegsbrauch im Landkriege* was produced as a general staff publication and issued widely throughout the officer corps. It provided a remarkably clear insight into the German approach to modern war and to the way in which it expected its soldiers to conduct themselves on operations. It also explained some of the actions during the war that were later condemned by Germany's enemies as extreme or contrary to the laws of war. In several cases the provisions of the *Kriegsbrauch im Landkriege* have greater resonance with certain of the the army's conduct and actions during the 1939–1945 conflict than with those during the 1914–1918 period. Throughout, the *Kriegsbrauch im Landkriege* established quite clearly that, provided they were necessary to achieve the objective, any and all actions, activities and methods of warfare were legitimate. Given that this general staff publication set the standards of behaviour for the army at war and was endorsed by the high command, some examples of its provisions provide a revealing insight into the pragmatism and policy-making role of the general staff in 1914–18 and its ability to influence directly the behaviour and actions of the front-line soldier. As we shall see later, in 1939–45 this function became increasingly politicized by the Nazis, and as a result the authority of the general staff was undermined year on year.

Some of the more significant pronouncements contained within the pages of the *Kriegsbrauch im Landkriege* included cautioning against excessive concern with humanitarian issues, including certain of the principles espoused by the Geneva, Hague and Brussels conventions, especially those dealing with the civilian population of an occupied country. It was recognized that by its very nature modern war could not be limited to the combat conducted between military forces and that such warfare would inevitably involve action to achieve, by any and all available means, the destruction of 'the total intellectual and material resources' of an enemy state. Prisoners of war were to be treated as such: humanely and not criminalized, although they could be required to work if necessary. It was recognized that 'prisoners should be killed only in the case of extreme necessity', although 'only the duty of self-preservation and the security of one's own state can justify it'. Meanwhile, the bombardment of those areas that were not by definition 'fortifications' was acceptable in pursuit of the military objective. While churches, schools, libraries and buildings of particular cultural significance should not be bombarded if possible, their exemption from destruction could only be assured where their non-military use was certain. Similar principles applied to the matter of seizing and using any strategic resources from an occupied country. While such action was acceptable, the looting of private property and of cultural collections such as those found in museums and libraries was not condoned. A moral stand was also directed on all forms of subterfuge, faithlessness and fraud, such as misuse of the Red Cross flag, breaking the terms of a parole or armistice and using surrender as a lure to kill the enemy: all of these were condemned, together with fire-raising and robbery. The 'murder of the enemy's leaders' was also condemned. However, the use of enemy and neutral uniforms, flags and identifying symbols was acceptable, although contrary to the Hague conventions on these matters.[7]

Somewhat more controversially, but with the army's experiences of fighting against French North African troops in 1870–1 very much in mind, the use of non-European troops (specifically non-Christian or what were regarded as uncivilized native levies) to fight in a European war was roundly condemned. By implication, such troops were placed beyond any expectation of legitimacy. In similar vein, with the army's experiences of the campaign against the French irregular units of *francs-tireurs* in 1871 very much in mind, the Germans viewed such irregular forces as illegitimate and illegal combatants in 1914. (In 1871 most captured *francs-tireurs* were summarily executed.). The Hague Conventions of 1899 and 1907 were included in the *Kriegsbrauch im Landkriege* as an appendix, while the main text made it quite clear that the general staff did not recognize the right of civilians to resist invasion, thereby indicating that such resistance was beyond the laws of armed conflict, and (by implication) that any reprisals taken by the army in response to such hostile action carried out by civilians would be both inevitable and legitimate.[8]

The great deployment (the Ausmarsch) of the army took place at the beginning of August 1914. Thereafter the plans implemented by the high command in August 1914 provided the Germans with a number of early successes despite various flaws that were revealed in the modified Schlieffen Plan during the following weeks. Foremost among these was the fact that the plan had been based upon the premise that the German army would be much larger than it was – as early as 1905 the plan had called for 94 divisions, while only 60 were actually available. Manpower increases of 300,000 had been sought by the general staff in 1912 and again in 1913, but only 136,000 additional troops had been authorized. On this basis alone, the general staff advice should have been that success could not be guaranteed, especially if for any reason the army's reliance upon speed and mobility as a force multiplier could not be realized.

Next, despite its initial success, the strategic plan depended upon the success of a great right hook through Belgium and into France before sweeping on towards Paris. However, as a clear illustration of the way in which the business of warfare had changed during the decades since 1870, the general staff took insufficient account of the time required for the immense numbers of men and horses that comprised the German army of 1914 to cover the amount of ground involved while at the same time dealing with a multitude of water obstacles, demolished bridges, destroyed railways, and roads blocked by columns of refugees. They also had to overcome the various opposing forces that sought to stop or delay them. In order to maintain its planned schedule, General Alexander von Kluck's First Army on the German right was required to advance an average of more than fourteen miles every day for three weeks – no mean achievement even had the roads been clear, the bridges intact and enemy opposition non-existent. Notwithstanding the professional competence of the general staff, the optimism that attended some of the more fundamental aspects of the plan was undoubtedly more reminiscent of the situation that had faced Prussia and its allies in 1870 than that which faced imperial Germany in 1914. In August 1914 the general staff and the high command quickly learned that its colonial campaigns and imperialist adventures were no substitute for the experience gained from conducting an all-out European war. Also, although they had been as innovative and as realistic as was practicable in peacetime, the army's great pre-war Kaisermanöver training exercises generally fell well short of producing the sort of problems of command and control soon to be encountered on the Western Front. It is difficult to quantify the extent to which the constraints of peacetime training had affected the planning parameters and assumptions applied by the general staff. 1914 soon showed that it had underestimated the difficulties incurred by a single operational headquarters attempting to maintain command and control of large and well-dispersed mobile forces operating on two widely separated fronts while at the same time providing the required levels of logistic support for these forces. In the meantime, the doctrine of Auftragstaktik meant that operational-level (i.e., corps-level and above) commanders embarked upon the war with the expectation that they would be able to pursue their aims and objectives with little or no day-to-day direction or interference from their superior headquarters. At the same time, the sheer scale of the army's operations also meant that the high command's lines of communication with these commanders were extended, frequently problematical and therefore intermittent. As a result, the command, control and coordination of the actions of the army and army corps commanders – and even more importantly their re-direction – became increasingly difficult as the campaign proceeded.

However, while the German general staff was undoubtedly better prepared for the war than were the high commands of the opposing French, British and Russian armies, in the area of intelligence the Germans had made the cardinal error of underestimating their enemy. More than four decades after the débâcle of 1870–1, the French had learnt well the strategic importance of railways and so were able to move their operational reserves by rail to counter the offensive faster than the Germans could advance on foot and horseback. Similarly, von Schlieffen (conducting his planning in the late nineteenth century) had anticipated a fairly supine French defence rather than the major offensive that the French army had planned to conduct immediately on the outbreak of hostilities. The governments, populace and armed forces of nations that lose wars are usually more adept in learning from their defeat and taking appropriate remedial measures, while victorious nations frequently rest upon their laurels, as complacency and stagnation prevail over common-sense. In 1914, the German general staff was reminded of this historical truism as the army's capabilities were found wanting in some areas.

Finally, the political isolation of the general staff from many of the realities of the constantly changing international scene meant that from the outset the plan developed by von Schlieffen had been almost exclusively military, based upon the implicit assumption that international political considerations were secondary or of no importance. One consequence of this was the general staff's underestimation of the level of resistance that would be encountered by the Germans during their invasion of neutral Belgium. In the event, the Belgians' robust if short-lived resistance to the invaders had much wider international consequences, the violation of Belgian neutrality being a key part of the rationale for Britain's early entry into the war. Meanwhile, the widely circulated reports of the killing of Belgian and French civilians (5,521 and 896 respectively) by the Germans during the 1914 campaign provided a welcome gift to the anti-German propagandists. This deliberate distancing of the army from international and even internal political issues would once again be adopted by the high command and actively promoted by the general staff in the post-1918 period, which in due course contributed indirectly to the rise of National Socialism and the achievement of power by Hitler in 1933, as well as to ideological and political issues and pressures that eventually had such a corrosive and divisive effect upon the traditional honour and loyalty of the army. Inevitably, this also contributed to the final demise of the general staff in 1944.

The intended war of manoeuvre on the Western Front ground to a halt on the Marne in late August, precipitating long years of positional warfare (Stellungskrieg) – better known perhaps as 'trench warfare' – for which (as we have seen) neither the army nor the general staff were particularly well prepared. Only on the Eastern Front was the army able to apply its doctrine for a war of manoeuvre, using its access to a superior rail network to move forces rapidly to that vast and largely undeveloped operational theatre, where the general staff out-thought and pre-empted the Russian high command at virtually every turn. It was in the east, following victories at

Gumbinnen, Tannenberg and the Masurian Lakes that Generalfeldmarschall Paul von Hindenburg and General Erich Ludendorff achieved prominence and international renown, subsequently becoming the principal German commanders on the Western Front.

Although the army was mired in the Stellungskrieg on the Western Front in France and Belgium for much of World War I, the officer corps and the general staff never wavered from its belief in the efficacy of the war of manoeuvre and the tenets and conclusions set out in documents such as the seminal study *Der Schlachterfolg* in 1903. The campaign against the Russians in 1914 reinforced the desirability of this sort of warfare and the success that the army might anticipate whenever it was adopted. For the general staff, the Stellungskrieg was an operational aberration that certainly would not be allowed to supplant the tradition of Bewegungskrieg that remained at the core of the army's operational doctrine. Certainly the army successfully adapted to meet the new and unforeseen demands imposed upon it by trench warfare, and it adopted new tactics and technology to counter what was always a distasteful sort of fighting. Indeed, for very many officers the Stellungskrieg situation that had developed on the Western Front was both an anathema and an operational aberration. Unsurprisingly, therefore, throughout the long years of stalemate in the west, the high command and the best minds in the general staff continually sought a means of returning to the oblique attack, of achieving the breakthrough that would immediately confer mobility once again, and of restoring the ability to manoeuvre on what had become a stagnated battlefield.

But neither sheer numbers nor unprecedented levels of firepower could bring about the required change; nor could technological innovations such as poison gas, air power, machine-guns and super-heavy artillery. Even the appearance of the tank produced only limited and local tactical advantages for those combatants who employed them (and the Germans were slower than the Allied powers to exploit the potential of the tank during World War I). However, with a virtually unbroken line of defences from the Swiss border to the North Sea coast, and an approximate equality of army strengths manning those defences, this aspiration was always a vain hope. The conflict degenerated into a war of attrition that Germany – faced by France, Great

Britain and its empire, their allies and finally the industrial might and military potential of the United States – could not win. By the time that Ludendorff launched his final offensives in 1918 – the Kaiserschlacht – the end was inevitable.

Germany had relied and gambled upon concluding a short and decisive campaign against France and then a more protracted campaign in the east; the sort of short war that it had conducted so successfully during the previous century. That it had failed to do so was in part a consequence of its past military experiences, which had steered the high command and the general staff towards a number of understandable but flawed planning assumptions. However, the experience of 1914–18 shaped and hardened the resolve of the general staff and the whole officer corps that never again would the army allow itself to be forced into fighting a Stellungskrieg, and that all of its energy and intellect would henceforth be directed towards restoring the army's Bewegungskrieg capability, while ensuring that any future war would indeed be one of manoeuvre based upon the primacy of the offensive. This then was the mindset, or mission, of the general staff as it considered the ramifications of the armistice of 1918 and pondered the future of what was then widely promoted within Germany as being 'an undefeated army'. The armistice was followed a year later by the Treaty of Versailles, which at once threw any such forward planning into turmoil. By the terms of the treaty, the victorious Allied powers now required nothing less than to dismantle the German general staff – which was viewed by the victors as being the principal architect of Germany's military aggression in 1914 – and thereafter to ensure that it could never be resurrected. Already the seeds of the Götterdämmerung some 25 years later were being sown in Germany and within its defeated army.

2

Progress and Pragmatism

The Reichswehr and General von Seeckt
1918–1926

Germany's defeat in 1918 precipitated almost three decades of civil unrest and military change, much of this a direct consequence of the terms of the post-war peace treaty announced to the German delegation at Versailles on 7 May 1919. The punitive and arguably humiliating requirements exacted by the Allied powers in 1919 became known just as the already shaky government of the post-war Weimar republic was beginning to return a measure of control to the country, albeit that this was mainly being achieved through its ruthless suppression of various revolutionary movements (primarily the communists) by the use of semi-mercenary units of the blatantly right-wing but generally effective Freikorps. But then, with Germany just starting to emerge from the post-war nightmare of a socialist revolution, and even the possibility of the country becoming a communist state, the Allied powers at Versailles promulgated the draft conditions to be imposed upon Germany by the impending peace treaty. Even taking full account of the wholesale death and destruction that had taken place between 1914 and 1918, especially in France and Belgium, a number of these edicts were excessively vindictive and ill-advised. The treaty even required Germany to admit its 'war guilt' and to arraign its military leaders to answer charges of war crimes. For the officers and soldiers of the Freikorps and the regular army, the perceived political betrayals of 1918 were compounded by this treaty. It also added considerable weight to the so-called 'stab in the back' (Dolchstoß) concept actively promoted from 1918 by the old high command led by von Hindenburg, which attributed the blame for Germany's defeat to the politicians, war profiteers and various civilian groups, thus establishing and perpetuating the myth of the 'undefeated German army'.[9] Early on, the Dolchstoß propaganda had been promoted by the deputy chief of the general staff, Generalleutnant Wilhelm Groener, who stated on the eve of the armistice that 'the army stands splendidly; the poison comes from home'. Subsequently this line and the perception it represented was reinforced widely and at the highest level, including by President Friedrich Ebert when he greeted units of the Guards on their return to Berlin with the words, 'We welcome you back home with joyful hearts, the enemy did not defeat you.'[10]

At Versailles the Allies sought to emasculate the German army as well as disbanding the air force and neutralizing the navy. If fully implemented, the treaty would have left Germany defenceless. Specifically, the army was to be manned by no more than 100,000 long-term volunteers, including a maximum of 4,000 officers. This army would be organized into two army groups with a total of seven infantry divisions and three cavalry divisions. Its operational role was to be limited to home defence and border security. Significantly, the German general staff was to be abolished, with a 'military office' or Truppenamt established to oversee day-to-day administrative matters, while all forms of planning and preparation for mobilization were forbidden. Furthermore, all military schools (apart from one arms school maintained for each arm), the Kriegsakademie and all the officer training academies were to be abolished. In theory, Versailles marked the end of the general staff and made the existence of a viable officer corps virtually impossible. The army's planning, officer training and command structure having been effectively neutralized, its operational capability was then to be negated by denying it any heavy weapons (including tanks), heavy artillery of all calibres and combat aircraft. (In parallel, the German navy was reduced to little more than a coastal protection force.) It was no accident that the victorious Allied powers decreed that the principal arm of Germany's post-war army was to be the cavalry: after 1914 this was the arm that had been shown to be the least relevant or effective in a modern war. The authorized scales of all small-arms (such as rifles, pistols and light machine-guns) were set at the absolute minimum essential to provide what the Allies deemed to be a basic military self-defence or policing capability.

The wider provisions of Versailles were no less draconian, fuelling the national sense of anger and betrayal that swept through Germany in 1919. At a stroke the treaty denied Germany secure borders and permitted the Poles – a nation traditionally detested by many Germans – to acquire large areas of territory at Germany's expense. In addition to losing all of its overseas colonies it would be deprived of Alsace-Lorraine along with certain other frontier territory, which would go to Belgium and France. Meanwhile the Poles were to gain large tracts of German territory in the east, including Danzig, which was now categorized as a 'free city'. A plebiscite was to take place to determine whether Silesia should in the future be under German or Polish sovereignty. France was to assume responsibility for the 'protection' of the Saar coal-mining region for at least fifteen years, in compensation for the destruction of the French coal-mining industry, and the Allied powers would occupy parts of the Rhineland for the same period as a guarantee of German compliance with the treaty. To the east of the occupied area a demilitarized zone some 50 kilometres wide was also to be established along its entire length. Finally, an Allied Control Commission would be established to oversee German compliance with all the provisions of the treaty.

Faced with no practicable alternatives, the German government accepted the treaty and duly signed it on 28 June. By so doing it further weakened both its ability to govern and its ability to maintain the already tenuous control it exerted over the military forces of what had by then become the 'Weimar Republic'.[11] Through their understandable but ill-judged desire to exact such telling retribution upon Germany, the Allied powers had created in all sections of the population of Germany a unifying sense of outrage that would in due course be successfully exploited by Hitler and the propagandists of the Nationalsozialistische Deutsche Arbeiterpartei (NSDAP), the Nazis. In the short term, it also provided an energy and impetus within the army to restore its former capability, power and prestige by any means possible; only by doing so could the honour of the Fatherland be restored. At the heart of this movement was the well-concealed work of what was in practice a new general staff in waiting, working under the direction of Generaloberst Hans von Seeckt, the chief of staff and head of the army (Chef der Heeresleitung) responsible for developing the new republic's army, the Reichswehr.

In March 1920, the army's standpoint in the republic's affairs had been clarified by the outfall from an abortive right-wing military-political coup (the Kapp-Lüttwitz putsch). By its measured response, the army had proved its ability both to support the government and to restore order within the state, but at the same time it had demonstrated that it would not tolerate any political direction that did not match its traditional perceptions of duty, honour and the army's core role. In other words, it would not entertain orders or instructions that were predominantly democratic or socialist in nature. Thus it set itself on a potential collision course with the Weimar government, as well as signalling its possible amenability to a less democratic and more reactionary regime in the future. General von Seeckt had been appointed in the aftermath of the putsch and later insisted that by his deliberately detached and even-handed management of the army's involvement in the affair he had safeguarded and maintained the apolitical nature of the Reichswehr, although even such distancing of the army would invite indirect political consequences. In 1920, the Reichswehr was still very traditionalist, while many of its members were overtly right-wing: a situation that presaged the relative ease with which it would in later years achieve an accommodation with Hitler and the National Socialists. In the meantime, much of the officer corps once again began to regard itself and the army it led as an elite, pivotal and independent authority, whose historic destiny was still to influence the direction and conduct of Germany's internal affairs whenever necessary. On the other hand, after the Kapp-Lüttwitz putsch the democratic and political left regarded the burgeoning capability and influence of the Reichswehr with great misgivings and profound distrust.

Although he had more than proved his martial talents during the 1914–18 war, General von Seeckt's particular contribution to the development of the German army was primarily organizational rather than on the battlefield. Between 1920 and 1926, von Seeckt created the Reichswehr as an effective fighting force and (by artfully circumventing many of the constraints imposed by Versailles) established a viable offensive capability for the army. This later became the operational cornerstone of the much-expanded Wehrmacht with which Germany went to war in 1939. He also provided the army with a command and control framework from which a resurrected and reinvigorated general staff arose during the 1930s. Consequently, von Seeckt's contribution to the story of the general staff and that of the wider German army was highly significant. Arguably, it compared in many ways with the work carried out by von Roon and von Moltke in reforming and modernizing the Prussian army during the previous century. Ultimately, his work provided Hitler with the military wherewithal to realize his political ambitions by force of arms.

Von Seeckt came from a traditional Prussian military family and had enjoyed a distinguished military career both at regimental level and as a member of the general staff. His war record was exemplary and included planning the successful German breakthrough at Soissons in January 1915. In the immediate post-war period he served as military expert to the peace delegation, acting chief of the general staff, and then as head of the 'Preparatory Commission for the Peace Army'. A traditionalist, he held many reactionary views, foremost among which was seeing the army's role as a non-political but nation-shaping force and institution vital to the future existence and nature of the German state. In broad terms, his vision was for the republic to have a modern version of the imperial army that had served Germany so well from 1870 to 1918: it was a vision that resonated widely throughout the officer corps. However, unlike so many of his more closely focused professional contemporaries, he also appreciated art, humanity and many of the intangibles of life, being described by one commentator as, 'a man of the world in the best sense of the term, adroit, self-possessed, skilful in the handling of men and affairs, with a great appreciation of the beautiful in every form, music, art, women, nature – he himself in later years said that vanity, sense of beauty, and the cavalier's instinct were the three outstanding traits in his character.'[12] A man of few words, his inscrutability earned him the nickname 'the sphinx', while his reputation as an organizer, innovator and diplomat enabled him to exert great influence upon the politicians and ministers with whom he worked and whose environment he understood all too well. This was despite his personal dislike of politicians and of a republican system that in his view forever threatened the stability and good order of the state during the Weimar era. These views and beliefs led him to direct that, 'political activity of every kind will be energetically kept out of the army. Political strife within the Reichswehr is incompatible with the spirit of comradeship and discipline and can only harm military training'.[13]

The active de-politicizing of the army in the years following the Kapp-Lüttwitz putsch and the traumas inflicted upon Germany by the often extreme left–right influences that had emerged immediately after the war (and continued to varying degrees throughout the Weimar years) was a major objective of von Seeckt's reforms. Participation in political meetings and organizations was forbidden to the armed forces, and even the constitutional right of the soldiers to vote was suspended. However, this deliberate de-coupling of the army from the political process meant that it was also distanced from any real awareness or comprehension of the malign political influences and undercurrents that would emerge within Germany a few years later. This was one of the factors that facilitated the relative ease with which the Reichswehr would in due course be transformed into the Wehrmacht. The daunting task that faced von Seeckt was, therefore, to create an effective post-1920 German army against a continuing background of political unrest, while at the same time not contravening (or at least not being seen to contravene) the potentially crippling terms of the treaty of Versailles. The military reforms he introduced were conceptual, organizational and educational – the last of which included training in all its many forms. All of these overlapped, were interdependent and were implemented progressively over a number of years. Most importantly, however, throughout this process von Seeckt developed and utilized the expertise of the officers of the Truppenamt, who provided the key functions of a 'general staff' that officially did not exist.

Organizationally, von Seeckt and the general staff had two matters to consider. First, he was constrained by Versailles to create an army within the terms of that treaty – or to find ways in which to defeat those terms. Second, given that the constrained army organization would inevitably be much smaller than that which Germany's political and military leaders believed the country actually needed to ensure its security and eventual return to prominence as a major European power, the Reichswehr had to be developed as the professional cadre of a considerably greater national force in embryo, rather than as a complete army. His principal objective was, therefore, to provide for Germany a small, well-trained professional army that was capable of conducting high-tempo offensive operations and achieving decisive results in short order. This was the sort of warfare that Prussian and German leaders had sought to achieve ever since the time of Frederick the Great. But behind and in support of this small professional army there would also need to be a large militia force capable of conducting defensive and security operations. In order to create a viable offensive capability to support the doctrine of Bewegungskrieg it was also necessary to develop an appropriate level of mobility, but with Versailles prohibiting weaponry such as tanks, combat aircraft and heavy artillery, this presented von Seeckt and his colleagues with a considerable challenge. Therefore, a prerequisite for meeting this challenge was the availability of high-grade general staff officers, which in turn depended upon the quality of officer serving in the wider Reichswehr.

Of the 16,000 officers serving in the provisional Reichswehr when the Versailles terms were announced, only 4,000 were permitted to serve in the new Reichswehr. Consequently, only the best and most experienced officers were retained, very many of these having already demonstrated their abilities on the staff and in combat during the war. In order to maintain the strength of the officer corps, no more than 200 new ensigns were required annually. Consequently, neither the numbers nor the quality of those available for officer selection gave von Seeckt special cause for concern.

However, the army was still viewed as a somewhat less than prestigious career by much of post-1918 German society. Therefore those men who did seek a commission were particularly well-motivated. Theirs was a vocation of service and duty to the Fatherland rather than a career embarked upon in the hope of gaining the social advantages and kudos that had characterized the extravagant and often profligate lifestyle of many officers in the old imperial army. Indeed, the Reichswehr officer was now expected to live on his army pay, which was increased appropriately. Such attitudes entirely reflected the ethos of the new Reichswehr, in which the social and class barriers so assiduously maintained between officers and soldiers in the imperial army were now modified; an officer's duty of care for those he commanded was now just as important as his ability as a tactical leader.

In order to enter the officer selection process, an applicant had already to have matriculated successfully. This academic hurdle was followed by four years of training before a young ensign's commission could be confirmed. Failure at any stage could result in his subsequent rejection. More advanced military training courses followed, with regular rigorous testing and assessment at all stages. Even though the officer had by then been commissioned, any subsequent decline in his performance, or a judgement that he lacked the ability to progress further, could still result in the termination of his commissioned service. Such was the nature of a highly selective meritocracy in which every officer was required and trained to command or to operate at least one level above their actual rank and appointment, and frequently at two or even three levels above it. This concept was characterized as the 'leadership-based army' or Führerheer concept and was in many respects a natural extension of the Auftragstaktik doctrine. In the matter of selecting future general staff officers, the competition was particularly hard-fought. With the Kriegsakademie no more, the selection process devolved on to the military districts (Wehrkreise), where potential staff candidates were examined in a wide range of subjects, including languages, history, political science, rail movement and modern communications systems, as well as standard academic subjects. These formal examinations were complemented by assessment of a candidate's character. An indication of the rigorous nature of this selection process was evident in the results recorded for Military District IV in 1922 when, that spring, 164 officers sat the formal examination, but just twenty went on to the next stage that autumn for Führergehilfenausbildung ('commanders' assistants training'). Six of the twenty successfully completed that stage, but of these only one officer of the group was eventually appointed to join the staff of the Truppenamt in Berlin as one of its Führerstabsoffiziere ('command staff officers').[14]

Although the way to a commission was regularized and eased for the well-educated soldier – with success in three examinations providing access to the officer selection system – the officer corps of the late 1920s still came overwhelmingly from the traditional military families and officer class. The army high command was still a very traditional and Prussian-influenced body; numbers of officers who had been promoted from the ranks during the war had been discharged after 1918, irrespective of the distinguished service of many of these men. Consequently, whereas in 1913 only 25 per cent of regular officers came from military families and from the well-established Offizierskaste (literally, 'officer caste' or 'class'), in 1929 no less than 67 per cent did! An analysis of the social status of the fathers of the Reichswehr officers serving in 1930 showed that no less than 95 per cent were or had been of sufficient social standing for their sons to have been eligible candidates for a commission based upon the pre-1914 criteria. Meanwhile, the social status of the remaining five per cent (small farmers, artisans, minor officials, and other workers) would have debarred their sons from gaining a commission prior to 1914. Similarly, of 195 ensigns commissioned in 1929, 164 had entered through the normal officer selection system, with only 31 commissioned from the ranks.[15] Thus, although change was undoubtedly the order of the day, certain long-established traditions still greatly influenced matters where the officer corps and the selection of officer candidates were concerned. This would continue to be so until after the Nazis gained overall power in 1933. The perpetuation of this system during the 1920s meant that the ethos of the officer corps in the 1930s was overwhelmingly traditional in character, and therein lay one of the factors that would inevitably bring it into conflict with Hitler and the ideology of National Socialism in the years ahead.[16]

Under von Seeckt's guidance, there was a new emphasis upon raising the professional standards of the individual officer and soldier to unprecedented levels. To that end, the use of individual initiative was increasingly promoted through applying the already familiar concept of Auftragstaktik, but at much lower levels of command than had been the case in former times. Von Seeckt reaffirmed the concept of Auftragstaktik and the responsibility it placed upon commanders and their subordinates when he stated, 'Mission-type orders means assigning the objective to be reached, providing [the subordinate commander with] the necessary means to do so, but allowing [him] complete freedom of action for the execution of the mission.'[17] At lower levels of command, this doctrine was exemplified by conducting tactical training for small-unit offensive operations, building upon the success of the Stoßtruppen – the highly effective German assault detachments or 'shock' troops that had evolved during the trench fighting on the Western Front. At the higher levels of command it was recognized that Germany would almost certainly be confronted by superior enemy numbers in a future war, and so subjects such as mobile defence, fighting withdrawal, concentration of forces and delivery of a decisive counterstroke were all studied and regularly exercised. Von Seeckt and his general staff colleagues were determined that never again would the army become embroiled in the strategically stultifying kind of warfare it had experienced on the Western Front from 1914 to 1918, and through these operational concepts and superlative training methods they sought to ensure this.

The demise of the military academies abolished by Versailles was largely overcome by the theoretical and intellectual training formerly carried out by those institutions now being conducted within the Wehrkreiskommando (military district headquarters) and separate divisions of the Reichswehr. This included staff training, written exercises, command and control exercises, and exercises carried out by all levels of headquarters both with and without troops, together with all manner of war games. In order to avoid openly contravening the terms of the Versailles treaty, staff training was suitably dispersed, with the general staff tutors (three per Wehrkreiskommando) who were conducting this training now going to groups of candidates in regional locations instead of these young officers attending centralized instruction at a staff training academy as in the pre-1918 era. During 1923, Hauptmann Erich von Manstein was one of these tutors, instructing in tactics and military history, and completing a daily round trip of 200 kilometres by rail in order to meet his training obligations because no accommodation was available for him and his family where he was instructing at Wehrkreiskommando II in Stettin.[18] During the four-year course, the would-be general staff candidate would spend the first two years on part-time academic and theoretical studies at a regional Wehrkreiskommando, this being supplemented by a formidable programme of reading and private study. The third year involved the candidate serving as a trainee staff officer in a division headquarters. Finally, during the fourth year the candidate served in the Reichswehr ministry in Berlin, where he worked with, and was closely supervised and continuously assessed by, selected members of the Truppenamt. As had been so in former times, the professional and personal standards required of the aspiring Führerstabsoffiziere remained very high, and, even though the selection process they had undergone before beginning their staff training had been rigorous, only about one-third of the officers completed the four-year course successfully to become fully qualified staff officers.

At the same time, the Truppenamt continued to act as a general staff in all but name, under the direction of Generalmajor Otto Hasse. This relatively small organization comprised four departments. Department T1 actually dealt with operations and deployments, but in order to obscure this it was officially shown as responsible for 'home defence'. Department T2 worked on organizations and force development; Department T3 covered matters concerning foreign armies (including aspects of military intelligence); and Department T4 had responsibility for training. The traditional general staff functions of mapping, survey and historical research and analysis had passed into civilian hands, although the work of these civilians – all experts in these specialist fields – was in practice closely overseen by general staff officers. The Truppenamt also had within it a small air planning staff for what was (in theory) Germany's non-existent combat air force. Meanwhile, the old 'operational' staff function had ostensibly been removed from the Truppenamt as required by Versailles. However, this task had in reality simply been displaced and concealed within the Reichswehr, so that operational staff planning largely continued as before but within the army groups and army corps or military districts rather than at the more visible Truppenamt. There were also various numbers of staff officers in posts within the army divisions and serving the heads of branches or arms of the service. This resulted unavoidably in the duplication of a number of staff functions, although it also provided a useful reserve of staff expertise and a potentially useful pool of such officers serving beyond the established 'general staff' organization represented by the Truppenamt, or who lacked the necessary qualifications or other attributes required of general staff candidates.

In 1921 von Seeckt published a much-revised and updated edition of army field service regulations. This general staff publication was titled the *Command of Combined Arms Combat*: it encapsulated his vision for the army's offensive capability in the future and provided a forward plan for the future development of the Reichswehr. Although quality was a major consideration, the development of sufficient manpower, weaponry and firepower – together with the resources to sustain them – also occupied the attention of the general staff. In practice, the army managed in various ways to exceed the manpower ceiling that had been imposed by the Allies. Together with various other contrivances, significant numbers of officers and soldiers who would in other circumstances have served in the Reichswehr were placed into the paramilitary Landespolizei. Other would-be Reichswehr soldiers also served with the Grenzschutz-Ost (border troops on Germany's eastern border) in Silesia, where continued friction with the Poles frequently resulted in violent clashes. Meanwhile, the Reichswehr requirements for equipment and higher-level training were largely satisfied by weapons development and production carried out in Sweden and Spain and by Germany's access to large-scale training areas and other facilities in Russia from 1922.[19]

Despite the importance of its work and the fact that it continued as the focus of the traditions and heritage of the old general staff, the Truppenamt established under von Seeckt's direction was necessarily a relatively small organization. This reflected the need for it to be seen by the Allied Control Commission as abiding by the terms set at Versailles. As well as limiting its size, other obfuscation devices included use of terms such as Führerstab and Führerstabsoffiziere ('leader[ship] or command staff' and 'leader[ship] or command staff officer') in place of 'general staff' and 'general staff officer' respectively. Nevertheless, those officers serving in the Truppenamt never doubted that they were in all but name a new German general staff in embryo. This was reinforced by von Seeckt when, shortly after his appointment as Chef der Heeresleitung and while alluding to the situation of the general staff officer and the army in the wake of Versailles, he set out his vision of the nature and duty of the general staff officer: 'The form changes, the spirit remains. It is the spirit of silent selfless devotion to duty in the service of the army. General staff officers have no name. We have now no time either to lament or to accuse – we certainly have no time to be weary. As long as we do our duty, our honour is unimpaired.'[20] None the less, in the Weimar Republic the situation of these officers frequently proved difficult and was always somewhat ambiguous. While maintaining the best traditions and qualities of the Prussian general staff officer of former times, the officers of the Truppenamt had to serve to the best of their ability a republican regime whose nature was fundamentally at odds with the military, political and traditional heritage of its imperial predecessor. At the same time, these officers were required to work to mitigate the effects of the Versailles treaty while concealing their actions from the inspectors of the Allied Control Commission. The unavoidable levels of secrecy and subterfuge that this involved meant that their progress and achievements were largely concealed from much of the army and therefore often went unrecognized by all but the highest levels of command. In addition, the planning and execution of operations, mobilization for war and large-scale manoeuvres – some of the professionally most satisfying aspects of the work of the general staff officer – had either been devolved to the military districts and army group headquarters or temporarily abandoned altogether in the wake of Versailles. In such circumstances, the unique personal qualities looked for in a general staff officer at that time well exceeded a mere consideration of his academic qualifications and proven professional competence.

Between 1920 and 1926 General von Seeckt and the Truppenamt played a vital part in reviving, developing and maintaining aspects of a German military capability that the Versailles treaty had specifically sought to prevent. This was achieved against a background of continuing internal political unrest, which often gave way to violence, and the army's hostility to the Weimar Republic and its political leadership. Von Seeckt generally held similar opinions, despite his own position within the Republic's governing body as military chief of staff, but he successfully sublimated his personal views on the matter for the greater good of the army and the country he served. Nevertheless, true to his belief that the business and everyday social life of the army and that of politicians should never be allowed to converge, he actively discouraged the Republic's first chancellor, Friedrich Ebert, from attending military parades and manoeuvres. This was despite Ebert's well-meant and genuine desire to involve himself positively with the armed forces of the republic he now served. Similarly, von Seeckt opposed any moves by the Republican government to award medals or decorations to members of the army. By the time of his resignation from active duty in 1926 – the activities of the Freikorps and the early stirrings of the NSDAP (notably Hitler's abortive 'Beer Hall putsch' of 1923) notwithstanding – he could not reasonably have foreseen the impending sea-change in Germany's political and economic fortunes in the 1930s or have anticipated the purpose to which the army would eventually be put by Hitler. Despite this, in his capacity as head of the army, von Seeckt had met Hitler privately in Munich in early March 1923 to discuss the possible use of the brown-shirted Nazi Sturmabteilungen (SA) under army control to deal with increasing civil unrest following a French military intervention in the Ruhr area that January, and possibly to confront the French troops directly. Following that meeting, von Seeckt indicated that he had been suitably impressed by the Nazi leader but remained somewhat uneasy about the fervency of his nationalist views and the extent of his aspirations. It follows that it would be disingenuous to suggest that an officer of von Seeckt's intellect and experience was entirely unaware of the nature of the National Socialist movement in Germany, although he (together with so many other officers) probably doubted its true potential.

But whatever his personal assessment of Hitler's possible political influence in the future or of the potential threat posed to Germany by the National Socialist movement, it is undeniable that von Seeckt's own achievements as Chef der Heeresleitung contributed very significantly to all that would be triggered by Hitler's eventual achievement of power. Von Seeckt had directed the resurrection of the army as a viable fighting force and laid down the foundations of its future offensive capability. In parallel with this, he developed and maintained a general staff organization in waiting. Without his work to expand the Reichswehr into such a force during the 1920s, its later transformation into the Wehrmacht would not have been feasible – certainly not in time to go to war in 1939. However, as early as 1923, there was other evidence that this process was already proceeding well. By then, numbers of those middle-grade and more junior officers destined to gain prominence as general staff officers and commanders in the years ahead were already filling various important staff appointments in the Reichswehr. Among the names of the many lieutenant colonels then serving as divisional chiefs of staff were von Rundstedt, von Leeb, von Bock, von Blomberg and von Falkenhausen. Kesselring and von Brauchitsch held staff posts in Department T4 of the Truppenamt, while von Fritsch, Beck and Halder occupied divisional or regimental staff appointments. There was also a young staff captain then serving as an inspector of motor transport in 1923 – his name was Heinz Guderian. For all these officers, their individual date with destiny was fast approaching, together with that of the army and Fatherland they served.

3

An Unholy Alliance

1925–1939

From 1925, the fortunes of the general staff became increasingly and inextricably bound up with much of the political manoeuvring that took place as von Hindenburg dominated the army and the government alike (being viewed by many almost as a new Kaiser). The minister of war from 1928 was Generalleutnant Wilhelm Groener, and the Reichswehr was headed by General der Infanterie Wilhelm Heye following von Seeckt's resignation in 1926.[21] In 1930, Heye was succeeded as Chef der Heeresleitung by Generaloberst Kurt Freiherr von Hammerstein-Equord. From 1932, General Kurt von Schleicher, a man close to, and favoured by, both von Hindenburg and Groener, exerted great influence upon a succession of chancellors, achieving that position himself in December 1932 but then being forced to resign on 28 January the following year.

Despite von Seeckt's apolitical aspirations and policies for the army during his development of the Reichswehr, these were also the years during which many army officers became associated with the National Socialists to varying extents, some indicating their support and collaborating quite openly. Towards the end of the decade, in East Prussia, General von Blomberg and his chief of staff at Military District I, Oberst von Reichenau, actively encouraged links between their Reichswehr command of Grenzschutz Ost and the local SA organization. Such liaisons also extended in some instances to the army providing basic military training for SA units, although von Blomberg's later formalization of this arrangement within Military District I, with Reichswehr personnel being detached to implement it as necessary, was not well received by a number of army officers in East Prussia.[22] It is sometimes suggested that such activities only really took place post-1933 and that until then Hitler and the Nazis were still largely uninvolved with the army and its rising leaders. However, this perception misrepresents the true influence of the Nazis in military circles in the mid- to late-1920s, well before the National Socialists emerged as the strongest right-wing party at the election in 1930. Given the numbers of Freikorps men – ex-soldiers all – who had joined the NSDAP or the Stahlhelm organization, and the preponderance of World War I veterans who had found places in the Nazi Sturmabteilung (the SA) or the Schutzstaffel (literally, 'protection detachment'or 'SS'), it was inevitable that the National Socialist message would be heard by, and find favour with, many army officers and soldiers. Indeed, it would be naïve to deny that a right-wing political movement espousing concepts such as tradition, patriotism and a return to Germany's former international greatness could fail to gain support within a Weimar Republic that was at best tolerated and at worst despised by many army officers.

Certainly the progress of Hitler and the Nazi party towards achieving power was remarkable and in many ways ran contrary to the traditional culture and nature of the German people. However, the rise of the NSDAP was perhaps somewhat more understandable viewed in the wider historical context of the recently ended 1914–18 war and the devastating impact of Versailles soon thereafter, together with the unpopularity of Weimar and the fear of Bolshevism and a perceived Polish military threat. All this was set against the deliberately apolitical or isolationist development of the Reichswehr by von Seeckt. The political process had been so weakened in the post-1918 years that, while the German people yearned for stability and a strong, capable, democratic and (within reason) liberal government, the Reichswehr was probably the only institution that could have delivered and then safeguarded this. But the army was neither a whole-hearted supporter of the Weimar government nor was it involved directly in the political process. Consequently, a political vacuum emerged at the very time when the NSDAP found itself well placed to fill that vacuum without needing to worry about any significant opposition from the Reichswehr.

As the months passed, Hitler and the NSDAP consolidated their political position and power within most of the principal civilian institutions and authoritative bodies of Germany. These included the police, the judiciary, the state civil services and the local administrative bodies. But a constant focus of Hitler's attention was always the army, with the officer corps a prime target of the Nazi political message. Time and again Hitler emphasized his policies of rearming Germany, reintroducing military conscription, dispensing with the constraints imposed by Versailles, saving the state from the evils of communism[23] and restoring Germany to its former greatness – all of which enjoyed considerable support within the Reichswehr. Many officers regarded Hitler's statement that the new German state would be founded jointly upon the Nazi party and the Reichswehr as positively reassuring after the uncertain and turbulent years of Weimar. Many also considered that the Nazis' intended constraints on civil liberties and their openly anti-Semitic policies and measures were of little consequence, being an acceptable price to pay if the army could once again became a real power both within Germany and in the wider world.[24]

However, despite its appeals to patriotism and the particular attraction of a number of these core policies to army officers, the army's enthusiasm for National Socialism was neither universal nor unequivocal. Its relationship with the Nazi party was by no means clear-cut. Indeed, some senior officers, including Generaloberst von Hammerstein-Equord, made their opposition to the movement very plain, taking disciplinary action against officers who actively tried to promote National Socialism in their units. At the same time, Hitler's own actions were sometimes ambivalent. Despite the practical advantages to the Nazis of joint army and SA cooperation in East Prussia, he later forbade this, judging that the possible disadvantages of the party's association with the armed forces of the unpopular Republic outweighed its short-term benefits to the SA. One senior staff officer who sought to negotiate the fine line between the pro- and anti-Nazi groups was Generalmajor Kurt von Schleicher, who as a colonel had been appointed head of the 'political department' within the Reichswehr ministry in 1926 and in 1929 was appointed to a similar but more far-reaching post by minister of defence Groener.

Always a manipulative, politically ambitious, vain, self-serving but professionally competent man, von Schleicher was a reactionary who actively courted Hitler and the Nazis from 1930, although he did so primarily as a means of achieving his goals for Germany and the army rather than from any belief in the merits of the Nazi cause. His particular focus was upon the many former soldiers who now populated the SA and the SS. Both organizations were clearly potential sources of trained manpower on which the army might draw in the future. Indeed, he later tried unsuccessfully to use the Reichswehr and the trades unions together to contain the rapidly growing popularity and power of Hitler and the NSDAP. Consequently, his always dangerous involvement with National Socialism placed him at the very centre of much of the political chaos that ensued from 1930. This chaos included the demise of the minister of war, Generalleutnant Groener, following his unsuccessful attempt to ban the SA, and the fall of chancellor Brüning with the appointment of Franz von Papen – a former general staff officer – in his place. It was at that time that von Schleicher became minister for the Reichswehr. Then, in July 1932, von Papen was forced to call an election. As a result, the Nazis became the largest single party represented in the Reichstag. Hitler refused to accept a coalition government, and von Hindenburg refused to accept him as chancellor. A further election in November 1932 did not alter the situation significantly, and this led von Hindenburg to appoint von Schleicher to this position.

Many changes were taking place within the army's hierarchy during this period. In 1932, the soon-to-be-familiar names of a number of officers holding posts in the Truppenamt included von Manstein, Jodl, Keitel, Krebs, Model and Speidel. Von Brauchitsch was an inspector of artillery. Von Rundstedt, von Bock, von Leeb and von Fritsch were division commanders. Halder was a divisional chief of staff, while the now Oberst Guderian was chief of staff to Generalmajor Lutz, the inspector of motorized troops. General Werner von Blomberg had replaced von Schleicher as minister for the Reichswehr. In October 1933 Generalleutnant Ludwig Beck was appointed head of the Truppenamt and in February 1934 Generalleutnant Werner Freiherr von Fritsch became Chef der Heeresleitung. All of these senior officers now occupied key posts and all were (at that time) committed supporters of the National Socialist cause. However, von Schleicher's time in office as chancellor only lasted just over a month: a coalition government was finally formed early in 1933, with Hitler as chancellor and von Papen as his deputy. Thus von Schleicher enjoyed the dubious distinction of being the last chancellor of the Weimar Republic, while his political machinations and less than wholehearted dalliance with the Nazis prior to 1933 would lead to his violent murder a little more than a year later.

The outcome of several years of political chaos, street violence and economic turmoil (notably the Wall Street stock market crash of 1929)[25] and finally the events of 1932 and 1933 – which culminated in Hitler's appointment as chancellor and the Nazis gaining power as a properly elected government – represented a defining moment for the country and its armed forces. This was especially so for the army and the general staff, who now had to adjust to the fact and implications of Germany having a National Socialist government and Hitler as chancellor. The changed balance of power and political pre-eminence of the Nazis was demonstrated very effectively by the instructions issued on 15 March 1933 for the introduction of the new black-white-red Reichskokarde insignia throughout the armed forces and for the adoption of an eagle and swastika (Hakenkreuz) helmet decal, which incorporated the traditional German eagle with the NSDAP symbol. By the end of 1935 the Nazi emblem was to be seen everywhere, its acceptance and legitimacy being greatly assisted by its use as an integral part both of the badge of the Reichswehr and of the German nation.[26]

In parallel with various measures affecting the armed forces directly, legislation was also being introduced to strengthen the Nazis' hold on Germany. On 28 February 1933, the day after a major fire broke out at the Reichstag building (allegedly having been started by Bolsheviks intent upon fomenting a communist revolution in Germany, although some also suggested that this arson attack had been instigated by the Nazis themselves), the government passed an emergency decree that effectively suspended all significant civil liberties. It also introduced an Enabling Act on 23 March that removed the legislative authority of the Reichstag, placing this into the hands of the government itself (and therefore directly into Hitler's hands as chancellor), thus opening the way for a progressive deconstruction of the country's traditional constitutional and legislative authority during the years that followed. These actions were portrayed as necessary to the 'national revival' and generally attracted little or no criticism in the country as a whole, while in many places the population greeted them enthusiastically. Having finally gained power within, and by manipulating, the legally constituted parliamentary democratic system, Hitler then moved swiftly to ensure that the Nazis did not remain vulnerable to the safeguards inherent in such a system.

March 1933 was also the month in which Hitler and Goebbels took the opportunity to cement the union of old Prussia and imperial Germany with the new National Socialist state, as well as furthering that of the army and the Nazi party. They did so at a carefully orchestrated military, political and religious extravaganza at Potsdam where, on Tuesday 21 March, a service of thanksgiving held at the town's garrison church began with a moving rendition of the traditional chorale *Nun danket alle Gott*. Then, before a large gathering of military, Nazi party and government ministers, officials and other dignitaries, President von Hindenburg stood to endorse publicly the reconciliation of the German nation, its traditional protector the army, and the new National Socialist government. Subsequently, Hitler spoke of this celebration of 'the union between the symbols of the old greatness and the new strength'.[27] Significantly, the service of thanksgiving and its central act of reconciliation were conducted directly above the crypt containing the tomb of Frederick the Great, a setting hugely symbolic for the German people as a whole but particularly so for an army officer corps steeped in the traditions and martial history of its Prussian antecedents.[28] Prior to the service, the German president had inspected a Reichswehr guard of honour, then afterwards he took the salute at a combined parade and march past of Reichswehr, SA, SS and Stahlhelm units. The propaganda impact of these disparate and often rival organizations now being presented as brothers-in-arms was lost on no one who witnessed the event, while neither was von Hindenburg's implied endorsement of the new unity of purpose of these forces.

A significant and particularly violent event in 1934 illustrated the increasing convergence and extent of the interplay between the NSDAP and the army by that stage. This event – the first of two particularly noteworthy portents of future difficulties for the army – was also of special significance for the way in which it established in its wake a working environment and various precedents that would affect very directly the command and control (therefore the general staff) of the army during the coming conflict. However, although its origins and impact were very much wider, this event centred initially upon a former soldier called Ernst Röhm. During the war, Röhm served as a commissioned officer from 1914, and then as an enthusiastic member of the Freikorps in the post-1918 period. By 1923 he was a Reichswehr captain serving in the Munich area. In the 1920s, his openly right-wing views soon drew him into the embryo NSDAP and close friendship with Hitler. Soon Röhm was responsible for organizing the close-protection squads that safeguarded the Nazi leader during the party's political rallies. Röhm had many character flaws, and his hard-drinking, homosexuality, brashness and social indiscretions generated considerable disfavour within the party leadership. Nevertheless, he had the ability to motivate and lead others, while his record as a former front-line soldier was not in doubt. Neither were his enthusiasm for the ideals of National Socialism or his loyalty to the party and especially to Hitler personally. However, in 1923 Röhm's involvement in the so-called 'Beer Hall putsch' resulted in his dismissal from the army, after which he found various employment, including as a military instructor in Bolivia. Then, in 1931, with the Nazis in the ascendant, Hitler invited Röhm to return to Germany and once again take command of the party's brown-shirted protection detachments – by then known as the Sturmabteilung (SA). Under Röhm's leadership the SA increased in size from 70,000 to 170,000 in 1931, and by 1934 it claimed a strength of 4,500,000. This force was considerably larger than the Reichswehr, something already giving cause for concern in the army high command.

In earlier times, von Seeckt had recognized the potential capability of the SA, but by 1934 the Brownshirts represented a formidable paramilitary capability, a capability that Röhm believed should be not only the core of the party but also a formally accredited part of the Reichswehr, with specific responsibility for the defence and security of the German homeland. Indeed, it was his belief that the SA should be the foundation upon which Germany's national army would be built in the future while simultaneously acting as the means and organization through which a continuing National Socialist revolution would be moved onwards into its next phase. In February 1934, these views brought Röhm and the SA into direct conflict not only with the army but also with Hitler and other senior Nazi party leaders, notably Heinrich Himmler, who headed the SS, and Hermann Göring, both of whom were by then convinced that the politically volatile SA should be supplanted by the politically more predictable SS. At the same time, several of the Republic's actively non-Nazi political leaders, such as von Papen, saw the SA as the embodiment of the Nazi excesses of the past. As perceptions of the threat posed by the SA hardened within the army high command and in some political circles, a situation was developing in which Hitler would soon have no alternative but to choose between the army and the SA. In fact, the outcome of that potential dilemma was never really in doubt: he knew that only a properly constituted modern army could realize his strategic ambitions. In June 1934 matters finally came to a head prior to, and during, what became known as 'Die Nacht der langen Messer' – the 'Night of the Long Knives', or the Nazi 'blood purge'.

The Night of the Long Knives, June 1934

On 30 June 1934, the 'blood purge' was launched by scores of SS murder squads. To reinforce the army's disquiet and that of the Nazi leadership about the ambitions of Röhm and the SA, the way for this purge had already been prepared or contrived by several events. These included Hitler's warning to Röhm on 4 June that the SA was not to initiate a second socialist revolution, an anti-Nazi speech by von Papen at the University of Marburg on 17 June, and an attempted shooting incident (allegedly by an SA trooper) against Hitler on 20 June (when Himmler was slightly wounded). The impact of the von Papen speech was considerable, and it is almost certain that its clear condemnation of the violence and extremism exhibited by the SA finally prompted Hitler to take decisive action against the 'Brownshirts'. On 25 June, the 'League of German Officers' expelled Röhm, while the national military intelligence organization, the Abwehr, claimed to have information that the SA intended a coup. With some alacrity, the army commander cancelled all leave in anticipation of civil disorder instigated by the SA – increasingly the army and members of the general staff were becoming drawn directly or indirectly into these events. On 27 June, army headquarters in Berlin authorized weapons and transport issues to the local SS unit, commanded by Sepp Dietrich, when what purported to be an 'SA execution list' was provided to the army staff. The list deliberately included the names of several army officers, and this fuelled a rumour that the SA planned to eliminate the leadership of the 'old army'.

On 30 June the SS acted, confident in the knowledge that the army would not interfere with their murderous intentions. During the few days that followed, some 77 leading Nazis were arrested and summarily executed, together with at least another 100 less prominent party members perceived to be critical of Hitler's policies. Within 48 hours Röhm was dead, having been shot at Stadelheim prison after declining to use a pistol provided for him to commit suicide. In fact, the overall figure for those killed, including SA men, political figures, civil servants, and military officers, was almost certainly much higher – probably exceeding 1,000. Despite his well-known contempt for the SA, the recently retired General von Schleicher and his wife were among those murdered, being shot down by six SS gunmen at their home in Neubabelsberg, Berlin, in front of von Schleicher's fourteen-year old step-daughter. Many of the other 'blood purge' murders in Berlin were carried out in the cellars of the Berlin-Lichterfelde barracks – where no fewer than 40 died – which was shortly to become the headquarters and main barracks of the SS-Leibstandarte 'Adolf Hitler'. Others were killed at the Gestapo headquarters at Prinz-Albrecht-Strasse and at a military detention centre near Tempelhof airport. Tellingly, Hitler and his closest associates were personally involved in the bloodbath despite the fact that numbers of those killed had for many years been their friends, colleagues and comrades-in-arms in the old army, the Freikorps and the NSDAP. The army justified its matériel support for the SS purge of the SA with the argument that the latter's military aspirations had directly threatened the army, while Röhm's revolutionary socialist aims had threatened the stability of the state. Small-scale though this support was, it moved the army much closer to the Nazis. More significantly, the failure of the army to condemn or criticize the murder of von Schleicher and von Bredow – both well-known generals – indicated all too clearly the direction in which the army high command, the general staff and the wider officer corps were inexorably moving by mid-1934. It also underlined the general mood of acquiescence to the Nazi policies that prevailed within the army at that time.

While the sheer extent of the violence and the calculated political pragmatism and disregard by the Nazis for their former comrades of the SA systematically murdered during the 'blood purge' were shocking enough, the attitude of many senior army officers to this event was remarkable. These were men who, almost without exception, were traditionalists, who had served as officers in the 'old army' and followed its long-standing codes of honour and discipline to the letter. The reactions and responses of some of these men in 1934 are instructive, for they provide an insight to the later relationship between Hitler, the Nazi government, the army high command and the general staff. These senior officers were, after all, the same men who went on to direct the work of the general staff during the pre-1939 years and then during the coming war.

On the night of 30 June, the Chef der Heeresleitung, General von Fritsch, and General Beck, the head of the Truppenamt, had together chosen not to enquire too assiduously into reports of a number of shootings at Lichterfelde. Both men were on duty at their place of work in Berlin at the time and all too readily accepted the explanation that this was simply an internal Nazi party matter in which it would be imprudent for the army to become involved. A general rumour that an SA revolt or coup had been pre-empted was actively promoted by the Nazi leadership and the SS. Indeed, reports that the SA leadership was being eliminated were greeted enthusiastically by some senior officers who had regarded the burgeoning strength of that paramilitary organization and its aspirations with increasing concern in recent months. When he was made aware of the killings of SA leaders in his own area, General Erwin von Witzleben, commander of Military District III, was apparently 'delighted and remarked that he wished he could be there'.[29] Von Fritsch apparently sought clarification of what had gone on – prompted by the news of the von Schleicher and von Bredow murders and an awareness that, as head of the army, it was unthinkable that he should be seen to have taken no action at all. But his enquiries were very half-hearted. By and large he took refuge in the well-circulated story of a pre-empted SA revolution, while explaining the army's inaction by the fact that he could in any case do nothing without direction from von Hindenburg. However, the German president had deliberately (and conveniently) remained incommunicado while all these events had been taking place. Similarly, neither the minister of defence, Generaloberst Werner von Blomberg, nor his chief of staff and head of the bureau of ministers, Oberst Walther von Reichenau, felt it necessary to respond to von Fritsch's concerns. Together they took the line that von Schleicher was in any case no longer an officer and that any misdirected killings had simply been an unfortunate incident during the unavoidable suppression of a potentially dangerous revolution – 'collateral damage' in modern parlance. In 1934 both of these influential officers had committed themselves to support the Nazi regime, pragmatically accepting that this might well be at the expense of the more traditional loyalties and principles by which they were bound as army officers. Indeed, von Reichenau's personal satisfaction that, due to the inaction of the senior officers at the ministry of defence and the Truppenamt, the army had been largely shielded from and uninvolved in the Nazi 'blood purge' was illusory, as by their very inaction these officers had signalled the army's passive complicity in the events of 30 June.

Although a talented, pragmatic and resolute officer, von Reichenau exemplified those senior army officers who deliberately distanced themselves from politics while simultaneously seeking to use their support for the Nazis to restore and enhance the position of the army and the country. Naïvely, von Reichenau and others believed that they could forge a close compact with Hitler while simultaneously marginalizing the Nazi party and curbing, then neutralizing the SA. However, von Reichenau was still quite prepared to accept 'an element of terror ... to purge a state of all its rot and decay',[30] but not where such measures were carried out by a paramilitary organization such as the SA. Arguably, von Blomberg's support for Hitler was more personal. He had dallied with democracy, socialism and communism at various times during the post-1918 years, but in 1933, describing his view of Hitler, he stated that, 'he was suddenly filled with feelings that he had never expected to experience again: faith, reverence for a leader, and total devotion to an idea', while, 'according to Blomberg's intimates, a friendly comment from the Führer was enough to bring tears to his eyes'.[31] Whatever their motives or perspectives, the acquiescence of such senior and influential officers simply indicated their broad approval of Hitler and the Nazis as a means to an end, without realizing that they had already lost control of this movement and of the man at its head.

When news of the von Bredow and von Schleicher killings became known, some efforts were made by Generaloberst von Rundstedt, General von Witzleben and the latter's chief of staff, von Manstein, to investigate the allegedly inappropriate or treasonable actions of the two men. However, not surprisingly perhaps, this move was not supported by von Blomberg or von Reichenau; neither was a separate request made directly to Hitler by Generalfeldmarschall August von Mackensen in the wake of 30 June for 'the re-establishment of common decency in public life'. A meeting of the Schlieffen Society, attended by 400 staff officers, passed a resolution to the effect that both the murdered officers had 'fallen upon the field of honour', but this resolution was not allowed to be publicized in the newspapers. In an increasing atmosphere of secrecy and the active promotion of disinformation concerning the two murders, it became generally understood within the army that these men – particularly von Schleicher – had in some way acted contrary to the standards of behaviour expected of a German officer and that they had therefore brought their untimely fate upon themselves.

The events of 30 June 1934 and the few days that followed were undoubtedly a defining moment both for Germany and for the army. However, the satisfaction felt by many senior officers such as von Reichenau at the elimination of the SA and the removal of its threat to displace the army proved short-lived. While the 'blood purge' enabled Hitler to consolidate his power and establish the political course of the Nazi party for the next decade, the mass killings also eliminated the SA and replaced it with the much more effective and ideologically focused SS. It was this organization (now formally established as an independent body configured as 24 corps-size units or districts within Germany) that later spawned the Waffen-SS – the 'armed SS'[32] – many of whose troops would in due course fight alongside those of the army on many of Germany's World War II battlefields. For the general staff, the rise of the Waffen-SS eventually had particular implications: these SS units developed in parallel with those of the army and with almost identical resource requirements. At first, Hitler supported the army high command's lobbying against the SS being equipped with such heavy weapons as artillery, while also authorizing army inspections of SS units to ensure standardization of training. But such concessions were in due course abandoned in response to counter-lobbying by Hitler's closest associate, Heinrich Himmler – arguably, as head of both the SS and the Gestapo, the second most powerful man in Nazi Germany. In future years the Waffen-SS would increasingly compete with the army for all sorts of matériel and (eventually) manpower while (as the favoured elite military arm of the Nazi party) enjoying a distinct advantage over the army. So 1934 marked the point from which the fortunes and fate of the general staff in later years truly began to be shaped, just as the fortunes of the army continued to converge with those of the Waffen-SS.

This process continued apace, when, following the death of President von Hindenburg on 2 August 1934, Hitler assumed the title of 'Führer' instead of 'president' and so took to himself absolute power throughout Germany. A new soldier's oath was imposed upon the armed forces, at which stage the Reichswehr could no longer avoid or deny the influence of the Nazis in its day-to-day affairs. In earlier times, during the Weimar regime, soldiers had been required to swear allegiance to the Reich, to its constitution and lawful institutions, and obedience to the president of the republic and their superior officers. Then, in accordance with a modified and simplified oath introduced by Hitler in December 1933 soon after he gained power, they were no longer required to swear allegiance to 'the people of Germany and the Fatherland'. But on 2 August 1934 the new version of the soldier's oath was promulgated throughout the Reichswehr. President von Hindenburg had died that morning, and shortly thereafter Generalfeldmarschall von Blomberg ordered that every member of the armed forces was to swear the new oath. The text of the 1934 oath was drafted by Generalmajor von Reichenau, the new head of the Truppenamt, and it would continue in use until the end of the coming war. Every officer and soldier was required to 'swear by God this sacred oath that I shall render unconditional obedience to Adolf Hitler, the Führer of the German Reich and its people, supreme commander of the armed forces, and that I shall at all times be prepared, as a brave soldier, to give my life for this oath'.[33] It is noteworthy that by requiring allegiance to a named individual rather than to the office he held this oath violated both the German constitution and the Oath Act of 1 December 1933, and was therefore illegal. It was adopted none the less, as was new legislation that merged the posts of president and chancellor. This move, citing the January 1934 Act for the Reconstruction of the Reich, also violated the constitution by ignoring Article 2 of the Enabling Act of 1933. Thus, at a stroke absolute power was conferred upon Hitler. And at the same time this legislation removed the army's traditional route of final appeal to a president or non-elected head of state separate and distinct from the country's political leadership.

On 16 March 1935, Hitler announced the introduction of compulsory military service; the defence ministry and the high command were only advised of this major policy decision 24 hours beforehand. At the same time, the subterfuge that had accompanied the development of Germany's post-Versailles armed forces was finally abandoned. The existence of an embryo air force was revealed, together with a target army strength of 600,000 men within 36 divisions organized as twelve corps. Then, on 21 May 1935, the Reichswehr was renamed 'Die Wehrmacht' – the national armed forces – comprising 'Die Kriegsmarine' (the navy), 'Die Luftwaffe' (the air force) and 'Das Heer' (the army). Within the Wehrmacht every officer, soldier, sailor and airman now owed his duty, honour and loyalty not merely to the German state but to Adolf Hitler as its Führer.

In the meantime, during March, the Chef der Heeresleitung had been re-designated Oberbefehlshaber des Heeres (supreme commander of the army), while the 'Heeresleitung' had become the Oberkommando des Heeres (OKH) – the army high command. As its 'supreme commander', Generaloberst von Fritsch therefore became the army's commander-in-chief, a powerful appointment but one in which he immediately became vulnerable to the power-plays and aspirations of key members of the Nazi leadership. At the same time, the Truppenamt finally abandoned the innocuous and generally ill-favoured, but pragmatic, title under which it had laboured ever since the creation of the Reichswehr. From March 1935, the title 'general staff' was formally resurrected, with that organization's existence and vital role officially acknowledged throughout the army and the Wehrmacht once again. However, in resuming its status, power and authority, the army general staff also attracted the attention of those Nazi leaders who viewed this organization as a potential threat to their own plans and authority if not curbed. Although few if any general staff officers appreciated the danger in the spring of 1935, the restoration of the general staff would bring them into direct conflict with the aims and aspirations of men such as Himmler and Göring, as well as with Hitler himself. For some, it would also precipitate various crises of conscience that would involve them in a conspiracy leading to accusations of treason resulting in imprisonment or summary execution.

While the 'Night of the Long Knives' and its aftermath had implications not only for the army but also for Germany as a whole, the second indicator of future events affecting the Nazi regime and the command and control of the army – and therefore the general staff – occurred just two years later, towards the end of 1937. By that stage, the rearmament, reorganization and expansion of the Wehrmacht were all proceeding apace, in parallel with many social, economic and security measures instigated by Hitler and the Nazi government. In the case of the army, the much expanded general staff was playing a key role in these developments. However, with its priorities focused primarily upon restoring the strength and combat effectiveness of the army – especially its ability to conduct mobile offensive operations – the high command once again overlooked, or chose to ignore, the political threat posed by a Nazi party that could not countenance a potential alternative power-base in Germany. By and large, most of the actions and programmes necessary to ensure the creation of the Wehrmacht had either been achieved or had been set well in train by the end of 1937, which meant that (in the view of the Nazi leadership, and of Himmler and Göring in particular) the time had come to curtail the power and authority of the army high command and the general staff, and to remind the army where the real power lay in Nazi Germany. In order to bring the armed forces entirely under Hitler's authority, and thus make them an entirely compliant tool for implementing his foreign policies, it was first necessary to weaken the traditional and long-standing system of command and control at the highest levels of government and military authority, so that the Nazi state could then develop in accordance with National Socialist policies and ideology unconstrained by the traditional German values, loyalties and traditions embodied in the army's officer corps.

Many aspects of the National Socialist agenda impacted directly upon the relationship between the government and the high command as the Führer tightened his direct control over the government and its ability to direct the armed forces. This produced an increasingly uncomfortable dilemma for many Wehrmacht officers, especially those in the army. By the mid-1930s, numbers of officers who had originally regarded the Nazis as a useful (but merely temporary) expedient by which the prestige, power and influence enjoyed by the old imperial German army might be restored, finally began to realize that they had lost control of a process they had supported either actively or by their passivity and acquiescence during the late 1920s and early 1930s. The depth of their dilemma was increased considerably by the extent of the military renaissance that had already been achieved by the Nazi government, which in turn suggested all sorts of potentially glittering professional opportunities and chances of promotion for these officers in the future. The broad view expressed by historian Andrew Roberts that 'the German generals were for the most part corrupt, morally debased, opportunistic and far removed from the unideological [sic] knights of chivalry that they liked to portray themselves as'[34] should perhaps be treated with a degree of caution, although at the same time the obsessive ambition, personal drive and excessive competitiveness of a number of these senior officers is a matter of record.[35] So also is the fact that an ethos of competition, a presumption of intellectual superiority and an overriding desire to achieve military excellence and professional fulfilment were nowhere more energetically encouraged, developed and ingrained than within the German general staff. Hitler and National Socialism now appeared to offer many officers the chance to prove themselves and realize their most ambitious career aspirations, as well as to attain a degree of recognition and social status within Germany that would have been impossible for all but a few before 1933.

In late 1937 several senior army officers overcame their reticence and spoke out publicly against Hitler's expansionist intentions. In the case of the general staff, such criticism was little more than their professional duty in advising the high command, as it had noted Hitler's expansionist policies and – with a realistic knowledge of the Wehrmacht capability at that time – it was particularly concerned by the prospect of a new war against France and Great Britain. However, by expressing such doubts these officers played directly into Hitler's hands, ultimately paving the way for him to achieve total control of the armed forces and direct command of the army. Ever since 1935, some officers had even criticized the speed of the rearmament process, correctly identifying that in many cases quantity was being achieved at the expense of quality. Foremost amongst these officers (despite their tacit support for the Nazis in earlier times) were Generaloberst Ludwig Beck, Generaloberst von Fritsch and Generalfeldmarschall von Blomberg. As chief of the general staff, commander-in-chief of the army and war minister respectively, this triumvirate of senior officers wielded considerable power at a time when control of the armed forces and matters of national defence were still the direct responsibility of the ministry of war. However, Hitler and his principal associates were well aware that neither this 'old army' power-base nor the criticism emanating from it could be allowed to continue unchecked. This triggered the second major pre-war clash between Hitler and the military leadership. It came early in 1938 and was a defining moment that ended the careers of von Blomberg and von Fritsch and subsequently reduced the authority of Beck – which in turn adversely affected the status of the general staff.

The Blomberg-Fritsch Crisis, January to February 1938
In December 1937, Germany's second great commander of World War I, General Erich Ludendorff, died. During the old soldier's funeral, von

Blomberg confided to Hitler both his intention to marry again (he was a widower) and that the lady in question had what was coyly termed 'a past'. Neither Hitler nor Göring demurred when von Blomberg announced his intentions, and both were duly present as witnesses at the von Blomberg wedding on 12 January 1938. However, by then Hitler already regarded the general staff and the foreign ministry as increasingly significant obstacles to his foreign policy and expansionist ambitions, as both counselled against the use of military force to achieve these. The general staff was also seen as an obstacle by Himmler, who had a vision of the SS as the principal military force in Germany, and by Göring, who advocated the subordination of all of the Wehrmacht combat forces to the Luftwaffe. Consequently, on 24 January accusations of immorality were made against von Blomberg's new wife, while separate allegations of homosexuality – then still a criminal offence – were simultaneously made against von Fritsch.

As a widower, government minister and field marshal, von Blomberg was ill-advised in his marriage to his secretary Eva Gruhn – it was generally well known within the high command that Gruhn had enjoyed a somewhat colourful and risqué social life. Rather more directly, an anonymous telephone call made to von Fritsch after von Blomberg's wedding inquired whether or not the chief of the general staff was aware that the war minister had 'married a whore'! Police records showing Gruhn to be a prostitute who also had a conviction for selling indecent postcards were quickly brought to Hitler's attention via the Berlin chief of police, enthusiastically prompted by Göring and supported by Himmler. Von Blomberg was accused of bringing the officer corps into disrepute, and his position became untenable. He was dismissed from his post by Hitler on 26 January, his official 'retirement' not being announced until 4 February. During his formal dismissal meeting with the Führer in January, von Blomberg apparently suggested that von Fritsch might succeed him as minister of war. Following Hitler's rejection of this proposal, he then suggested that Hitler might wish to assume supreme command of the armed forces himself. This prophetic suggestion played directly into Hitler's hands as well as illustrating how far von Blomberg's priorities had moved away from more traditional loyalties to the army and the state. It also demonstrated his naïvety and lack of awareness of Hitler's true aims and aspirations. With von Blomberg's dismissal, von Fritsch, as commander-in-chief of the army, now represented the most prominent source of opposition within the army to Hitler's expanding authority over the armed forces.

In the case of von Fritsch, a confirmed bachelor and misogynist, the Gestapo alleged that he had committed a homosexual offence with one 'Bavarian Joe', a 'rent boy', in the goods yards by Potsdam railway station in November 1934. The 'evidence' for this was provided by a man called Schmidt, well-known as a homosexual blackmailer who had previously been convicted and served a prison sentence for that offence. The allegation was laid by Himmler and was entirely false,[36] but von Fritsch's fate was sealed in Hitler's eyes when Schmidt was produced to confront him and stated unequivocally that he recognized him as the man who had committed the offence. Göring was also present at this confrontation; and, while the von Fritsch allegation had been instigated by Himmler, he also had a vested interest in its outcome. Although Hitler had by then been persuaded of the general's guilt, the Gestapo subsequently interviewed von Fritsch. They then followed this up by arresting and interviewing his former soldier servants (batmen) in a vain attempt to substantiate Schmidt's 'evidence' by soliciting evidence of any 'unnatural' behaviour or 'practices'. Apparently, Schmidt was later murdered by the SS, presumably to avoid any risk of his being re-examined and changing his evidence. The allegation was baseless, but Himmler and Göring had prepared their campaign of innuendo and character assassination well enough; although an officers' court of honour subsequently exonerated von Fritsch absolutely, irreparable damage had been done.[37]

Many army officers failed to recognize the true import of Hitler's actions and their effect upon the army and the general staff, but some were not deceived. One such was Oberstleutnant Hans Oster, a staff officer based in the national military intelligence office and working closely with its head, Admiral Wilhelm Canaris. Oster sought the support of the principal military commanders in Dresden, Hannover and Münster for a military show of force to secure von Fritsch's position and continuance as army commander-in-chief. Despite their own distaste for the Nazis, and while variously expressing their outrage and sympathy concerning Hitler's manner of dealing with von Blomberg and von Fritsch, none of these potentially influential generals were prepared to act, however, a fact that again demonstrated the increasing impotence of these men in matters of politics and policy beyond the army itself. Even General Beck, despite his oft-stated opposition to Hitler, felt constrained to issue orders to the general staff that the von Fritsch affair was not to be discussed. Furthermore, Beck was outraged by Generalleutnant Franz Halder's suggestion to him on 31 January that the army should attack the Gestapo headquarters, which was widely acknowledged to be the source of the false and malicious allegations against von Fritsch. Tellingly, and illustrating the sort of misplaced sense of duty and naïve traditionalist mindset of many senior army officers at that time, Beck declared that such action would be 'mutiny, revolution' and that 'such words do not exist in the dictionary of a German officer'.[38]

Eventually, the Blomberg-Fritsch crisis culminated in the forced resignation of both officers, their joint retirements being announced officially on 4 February 1938.[39] General (later Generalfeldmarschall) Walther von Brauchitsch succeeded von Fritsch as commander-in-chief of the army and was promoted Generaloberst on 4 February, while General Friedrich Fromm assumed command of the Germany-based Ersatzheer. During that year no fewer than sixteen generals were relieved of their commands and a further 44 senior commanders were transferred to other duties.[40] Everywhere, officers whose loyalty to Hitler was not in doubt were appointed to replace these men, and, although many of the new appointees were undoubtedly competent, their political reliability generally was of more significance than their military capability. Despite remaining in post as chief of the general staff, Beck became increasingly isolated. After February 1938, with the demise of the traditional war ministry in the wake of von Blomberg's departure and with the power of the army and general staff further weakened by the departure of von Fritsch and the subsequent removal of so many other senior officers, Hitler was finally able to assume overall command of the German armed forces as 'Führer und Oberster Befehlshaber' (leader and supreme commander). His assumption of this role also inevitably diluted the authority of the newly appointed commander-in-chief of the army, Generaloberst von Brauchitsch – an officer destined to play a significant part in the events affecting the general staff and the army during the next three years.

Heinrich Alfred Hermann Walther von Brauchitsch was born in Berlin on 4 October 1881, the fifth son of a Prussian general of cavalry. With his family's illustrious military background and a first-class education at the renowned Französisches Gymnasium, von Brauchitsch was readily accepted into the Prussian 3rd Regiment of Foot Guards as an officer on 22 March 1900, and just a year later he transferred into the 3rd Regiment of Guards Field Artillery. He proved to be an outstanding officer both at regimental duty and in staff appointments, and was appointed to the general staff during World War I, being promoted major in July 1918. Throughout his early service and later as a senior officer, he was described as a most intelligent, approachable and well-educated man. An accomplished linguist, he also maintained a wide-ranging interest in all aspects of politics and economics, while also gaining a reputation as an innovator, particularly in the development of artillery (development of the dual-role capability of the 88mm anti-aircraft gun was largely instigated and carried through by von Brauchitsch) and the arrangements for air–ground cooperation between the army's new motorized units and the Luftwaffe's close-support combat aircraft. Although he excelled as a general staff officer, his genuine concern for the welfare, provisioning and accommodating of the troops he commanded made him a popular and effective leader and commander. He served as a general staff officer in various posts at the Truppenamt from 1922 to 1925 and between 1928 and 1932, in which year he was promoted major general. His principal command appointments included an artillery battalion in 1925 (as a lieutenant colonel), military district Wehrkreis I and the 1st Infantry Division at Königsberg in 1933 (as a lieutenant general), and I Army Corps (also at Königsberg) from 1935. While serving in East Prussia, his distaste for some aspects of Nazism and the SS, and for civilians interfering in military matters, was demonstrated by a personal clash with the local Gauleiter, Erich Koch, and by his removal of SS units from involvement in the army's manoeuvres in the area for which he was responsible. Nevertheless, von Brauchitsch had considerable regard for

Hitler himself, describing him in December 1938 as 'Adolf Hitler, our leader of genius, who has recast the great lesson of our front-line soldier in the form of the National Socialist philosophy, has built and secured for us the new Great German Reich ... the Führer, who combines in his person the true soldier and National Socialist'.[41] While not regarded as one of the true Nazi generals, he certainly supported Hitler and many of his policies, including the persecution of various ethnic groups in Poland and elsewhere as the war progressed, rationalizing these as unavoidable if Germany was to achieve its destiny. On 20 April 1936, von Brauchitsch was promoted General der Artillerie, subsequently taking command of the 4th Army Group in 1937.

Although von Brauchitch's many professional and personal qualities were not in doubt, he displayed a somewhat surprising weakness of character in February 1938, in the wake of the final act of the von Fritsch–von Blomberg saga and just as Hitler announced his expansionist intentions regarding the Sudeten Germans, which later developed into the Czech crisis. In 1920, the then Major von Brauchitsch had married Elizabeth von Karstedt, a wealthy heiress who in due course inherited estates of about 1,200 square kilometres in Pomerania – a marriage that made von Brauchitsch a very wealthy man. However, in February 1938, contrary to his own religious upbringing and to Hitler's personal disapproval of divorce, von Brauchitsch divorced Elizabeth in order to marry Charlotte Rueffer, a renowned beauty and the daughter of a Silesian judge. Significantly, however, Charlotte was also a great admirer of Hitler and totally committed to the National Socialist cause (Ulrich von Hassell, an opponent of Hitler, once commented that she was 'a 200 per cent rabid Nazi'). In light of this, Hitler saw considerable future advantage in the match. Accordingly, he not only encouraged von Brauchitsch to divorce and re-marry, but also lent him 80,000 Reichmarks to enable this by offsetting his loss of income from his first wife's fortune. Already in his late fifties, von Brauchitsch was undoubtedly influenced by his new wife during the months and years that followed, as well as having diminished his moral position as a senior German officer by making himself vulnerable to future innuendo, social stigma and criticism concerning his divorce after 28 years of marriage. By the time that he became commander-in-chief of the army, Generaloberst von Brauchitsch was at the focus of a range of conflicting influences. These included his personal circumstances, with the strongly pro-Nazi views of his new wife, and his own increasing ambivalence regarding Hitler, the Nazis and the role of the army and the general staff in the governance and future of Germany. For von Brauchitsch, as for so many other German army officers, these matters were as ever set against the familiar crises of conscience over honour, duty, loyalty and the obligations set out in the soldier's oath.

The OKW

The events and changes in the high command that took place in early 1938 demonstrated both the power and the modus operandi of the Nazi party and government, as well as showing how isolated the army had become by that stage. Elsewhere within the Wehrmacht, the Luftwaffe was patently in thrall to Göring, while officers and sailors of the Kriegsmarine were generally much less traditionalist than their army comparators, being more politicized and pro-National Socialist in outlook. Meanwhile, Himmler's SS continued to expand its military capability and to consolidate its power and position within the state. Soon after the removal of von Blomberg and von Fritsch, and in light of the uncertainties and concerns occasioned by these enforced resignations, Hitler judged the time right to create an armed forces high command (the Oberkommando der Wehrmacht (OKW)),which was based at Zossen-Wünsdorf to the south of Berlin. This further dissipated the traditional power of the army general staff as the ultimate controller and director of Germany's armed forces. The headquarters of the army general staff was also at Zossen. The former war ministry was dissolved, its functions being subsumed into the OKW and no longer distinguishable from the activities carried out by that organization, while the authority that had been vested in the country's minister of war was thereafter exercised by Hitler himself.[42]

Arguably, the establishment of the OKW upheld the principle of unity of command that had long been central to German thinking on the direction and control of military forces. While routinely applied at all levels of command, at the highest level this fundamental principle was intended to enable the efficient management of all aspects of the national military capability. However, in the German armed forces of the Third Reich, a succession of diverging and competing political and military imperatives and the misuse of the OKW by Hitler, to achieve more parochial objectives, would eventually affect and detract from this worthy principle. The OKW command and control concept reinforced the fact that the army, air force and navy were not separate services in the sense in which they were recognized as such in (for example) the British or US armed forces. Although frequently referred to as 'services' in non-German contexts and publications, these organizations were actually three separate branches of a single service, the Wehrmacht (the national armed forces), with overall command of the Wehrmacht now exercised by the OKW rather than by, or via, the war ministry or general staff as had been so in former times. From its inception in 1938, the OKW became responsible for all aspects of the Wehrmacht's ground, air and maritime warfare policies in peace and war, while also directing and coordinating the activities of the army high command (Oberkommando des Heeres, or OKH), the air force high command (Oberkommando der Luftwaffe, or OKL) and the navy high command (Oberkommando der Kriegsmarine, or OKM) as necessary. Prior to hostilities, the OKW was responsible for the national defence plans, and once war began it would control operations on land, sea and in the air. In order to separate routine administrative actions from the business of war-fighting, on the commencement of hostilities the OKW and the various subordinate high commands divided into forward and rear headquarters. The rear element remained in the Berlin area, dealing with all non-operational and non-urgent matters, while the forward headquarters staff located in the theatre of operations controlled operations in progress. The organization of the OKW again highlighted the unique status of the paramilitary and military SS forces controlled by Heinrich Himmler. Despite the accelerating size and military capability of the SS (that of the Waffen-SS in particular), the absence of any formalized SS representation within the otherwise comprehensive military, paramilitary, civil service, economic and political organization of the OKW emphasized the jealously preserved separateness of the SS and the discrete nature of its command and control arrangements.

In practice, the OKW would fail to achieve the level of effectiveness and authority set out in its terms of reference. This was due mainly to the constraints placed upon its activities by Hitler and by his interference in its work – although General (later Generalfeldmarschall) Wilhelm Keitel was the principal OKW officer (Chef des OKW) from 1938 and throughout the war, his function was always that of a chief of staff, or executive officer, rather than a commander. The other OKW officer of particular note was Generalmajor (later Generaloberst) Alfred Jodl, who succeeded Generalleutnant Max von Viebahn as head of the OKW operations staff branch (Wehrmachtführungsstab) in 1939 and remained in that post throughout the war. Both Keitel and Jodl remained loyal to Hitler and ultimately bore a significant amount of responsibility by their endorsement of Germany's military activities from 1939. However, these two officers were very different from each other. Whereas Keitel was an officer of average ability and limited intellect who simply did Hitler's bidding without question, Jodl (of whom we shall hear more later) was an extremely competent staff officer who deliberately chose to compromise his conscience – together with his wider loyalty and duty to the army, the general staff and the nation – for the Führer and his own advancement. In any event, quite apart from the practical limitations of the OKW, the creation and existence of this new headquarters meant that after 1938 it was no longer possible for the army general staff to regain the power and prestige that it had enjoyed prior to 1918.

The OKH .

However, the OKH continued to be the principal headquarters by, and through, which the general staff organized, directed, regulated and supervised the activities of the army in peace and war. Until 1944, the OKH also had responsibility for command and control of the Ersatzheer. As the army's main source of replacement manpower, the Ersatzheer was charged with training and providing reinforcements and support for the field army (Feldheer). On mobilization, the OKH divided into two parts in much the same way as the OKW, the main headquarters deploying into the field with the principal staff branches dealing with operations, training, organization and force development, and intelligence. Logistical supply matters at the main headquarters were overseen by a quartermaster general who also advised the commander-in-chief. However, the overlapping and intrusive nature of the newly established OKW was evident in the presence of a number of OKW staff officers at the OKH main headquarters, although ostensibly these were to provide advice and to coordinate transport, communications and air support. Meanwhile, the OKH rear headquarters remained in Berlin on general mobilization. There it retained responsibility for the secondary and routine day-to-day staff functions usually carried out by the OKH main headquarters in peacetime, as well as for any functions not represented at the OKH forward main headquarters.

From the start of the war, the OKH forward headquarters in the field was always sited close to Hitler's own field headquarters (the Führerhaupt-quartier) while in due course a discrete element under Hitler's direct control was established within the OKH. Such arrangements enabled Hitler's close oversight and (in due course) direct control of army operations; they also demonstrated the Führer's reservations about the army's traditional conservatism and reliability – especially that of the officer corps – compared with the politically more reliable Luftwaffe and Kriegsmarine. Despite this, the OKH was still the headquarters to which the army groups, corps and other major formations continued to look for operational direction and support. Most of the army's most talented general staff officers and commanders served at the OKH at some stage during their careers. Their practical and professional abilities were usually indicative of staff experience gained during the pre-1938 era, especially during the military revival of the Reichswehr by von Seeckt during the 1920s. Accordingly, although the OKH would eventually become little more than a conduit through which Hitler imposed his will upon the army, this headquarters still managed to perform its routine command functions effectively, but without enjoying the sort of unconstrained thinking and freedom of action that had characterized German army's high command in the past.

Below the OKH in the army chain of command were the various army groups (Heeresgruppen), of which there were six in peacetime. Prior to mobilization each of the Heeresgruppen served as the superior headquarters of various numbers of the nation's fifteen pre-war military districts (Wehrkreise).[43] On general mobilization in 1939 the Heeresgruppen ceased their peacetime training role and formed two operational army group commands and a number of individual army headquarters. Once hostilities commenced, the residual Wehrkreise structure in Germany came under the control of the Ersatzheer, which from that point fulfilled a wide range of functions that were separate from but directly supported those of the Feldheer.

4
Revival and Rearmament
1935–1939

The mismatch between the traditional ideals of the army and the ideological imperatives of the Nazi party were thrown increasingly into contrast between 1933 and the outbreak of World War II in 1939. This was exemplified by the 'Night of the Long Knives' in 1934 and the Blomberg-Fritsch crisis in 1938. However, these were but the most significant of a number of clashes and conflicts of perception or interest that occurred or emerged during these years. Such clashes were perhaps inevitable. It is worth remembering that for the army and the high command, the requirement to serve an elected head of state – from 1918 a president and then from 1934 a Führer – was a relatively new experience for military forces that had been led by the hereditary monarchs of the various states of northern and southern Germany until 1871, then by the German Kaisers until 1918.

The focus must now fall specifically upon the process by which the general staff was formally resurrected with the end of the Truppenamt in 1935, and its subsequent preparation to direct, command and control the army at war just four years later. From 1935, the task of resurrecting not only the organization and capability of the general staff but also of reviving its traditional ethos of military excellence had fallen directly upon General Ludwig Beck. Formerly the Chef des Truppenamtes (adjutant-general) of the Reichswehr from 1933, he became chief of the army general staff at the time of Hitler's announcement, in March 1935, of the rearmament and expansion of Germany's armed forces.

Ludwig August Theodor Beck was born at Biebrich, in the Rhineland to the south-west of Limburg in Hessen-Nassau, on 29 June 1880. He followed a traditional military education and by 1908 was an officer in the 15th Field Artillery Regiment, a Prussian artillery unit. During World War I, Beck proved to be a highly competent officer serving in a range of staff and non-staff appointments, although it was as a staff officer that he excelled. There, his professional ability, administrative and organizational talents, clarity of thought and expression, together with his interpersonal skills, set him apart from many of his contemporaries. After 1918, he commanded a Reichswehr artillery battalion, and later the 5th Artillery Regiment at Ulm. In 1930, during his time as a regimental commander, Beck strongly defended the right of three of his young lieutenants to be members of the Nazi party at a time when the membership of political organizations was illegal for those serving in the Reichswehr. It was while giving evidence at the trial of these officers at Leipzig that Beck first met Hitler, who was also giving evidence on behalf of the three officers. Hitler subsequently indicated that he had been most favourably impressed by the then Oberst Beck. As a major general, Beck assumed command of the 1st Cavalry Division at Frankfurt an der Oder in 1932. Then, just a year later, on 1 October 1933, he was promoted lieutenant general and appointed head of the Truppenamt. In earlier times, Beck had served in a number of appointments within the well-disguised 'shadow' general staff of the Truppenamt and elsewhere in the army during the Reichswehr years, where his outstanding professional abilities and intellect had already been well recognized. While serving at the Truppenamt during 1931–2 he had been the prime mover in the development and adoption of the army's manual of operational and tactical doctrine, '*Truppenführung*',[44] which was promulgated in 1933 and 1934. He also advocated and supported the development of the army's embryo panzer forces, demonstrating a forward-looking approach to such new forms of warfare. By the time he was appointed chief of the general staff, General Beck was generally positive about the rise of the Nazis and the implications of this for the Reichswehr and Germany. He also favoured armed action by Germany to achieve political pre-eminence and military domination in central and eastern Europe, aspiring to levels of power and influence eventually exceeding those of the pre-World War I German empire. However, he considered that such action would not be feasible before the mid- to late 1940s at the earliest. Beck was also absolutely convinced of the need for the general staff to resume its decisive role in strategic decision-making and other matters of national consequence, with the chief of the general staff, rather than the minister of war, being the principal military adviser to the head of state.

The task facing Beck in that March of 1935 was formidable: the restoration of the general staff's authority and influence would be at least as difficult as implementing the physical reorganization and development that were now urgently required. An additional obstacle to his work was Hitler's simultaneous creation of the new OKW. That headquarters not only competed for talented staff officers to fill its own posts, but also drew away some of the power that the army general staff had previously enjoyed. Indeed, a view expressed by a number of general staff officers in 1935 was that, in the leader-focused state that Germany had become, the traditional role of the general staff in peacetime should henceforth be confined simply to studying and anticipating the potential problems of war; once hostilities began, the general staff function would be merely that of assisting the leader to achieve his aims and implement his decisions, rather than actively contributing to the strategic decision-making process and the operational command and control of the forces in the field. Such heretical views reflected the reduced numbers of general staff officers who had qualified or held staff posts in the pre-Reichswehr period. They also exposed the questionable motives of some officers who perceived that it would be politically astute and therefore advantageous to their future careers to support views that would find favour with the Nazi hierarchy. Such thinking was anathema to a traditional general staff officer of the 'old army' – such as General Beck – as was the idea that a German officer would ever compromise his honour and his duty to Germany and the army for political gain or personal advantage.

It was noteworthy that one of the prime movers of the group lobbying for reductions in the size, capability and power of the reconstituted army general staff was the future Generaloberst Alfred Jodl, who in 1935 was an Oberstleutnant. This ambitious, intelligent and very competent officer was openly pro-Nazi and had been a supporter of Hitler ever since he was first introduced to him by Ernst Röhm in 1923. At the same time, his family background was middle-class, and he was resentful of the traditions of the old Prussian officer class and of what he saw as the professional inertia and in-house patronage displayed by many senior officers of the 'old army'. Jodl would in due course become one of the Führer's closest military advisers and strategic planners, serving as chief of the operations staff at the OKW throughout the coming war. His part in the story of the general staff was significant, as his personal vision involved the creation of an all-powerful 'armed forces general staff' that would direct and have precedence over the separate staff organizations of the army, navy and air force. Although this idea was abhorrent for many army officers in a nation in which the army had always enjoyed undisputed primacy in the past, it was not altogether without merit in light of the significant technological advances – especially those affecting aviation, the armaments industry and command and control – since World War I. In any event, and irrespective of any personal motives, as head of the so-called 'department of national defence' within the armed forces office (Wehrmachtsamt)[45] of the war ministry from 1935, Jodl was well-placed to promote his views and aspirations during the years ahead. Indeed, in a number of respects he saw them realized with the creation of the OKW. Undoubtedly there were other professionally competent but similarly politicized pro-Nazi officers who might not have had the good fortune to come from a traditional (preferably Prussian) military background. For such officers, the appeal of what was ostensibly an egalitarian National Socialist military meritocracy was possibly somewhat greater than that of a system dominated by a fully reconstituted general staff in the old mould – especially as this would inevitably include the general staff's time-honoured role of providing officers for key command appointments, a role that could baulk their own career ambitions.

Resurrection of the General Staff

As we saw earlier, from 1920 the Truppenamt comprised just four departments: T1 (home defence, dealing with operations and plans), T2 (organizations and force development), T3 (foreign armies) and T4 (training), with most of the other long-accepted general staff functions having been re-allocated to civilian agencies or delegated downward to be carried out elsewhere within the military chain of command. Manning levels at the Truppenamt had reflected this, with a consequent diminution of the power and perceived influence of the Truppenamt within the army for almost fifteen years. Now, however, the general staff expanded rapidly, with almost 200 staff officers appointed within a matter of weeks, a third of whom were recalled to duty from retirement as an unavoidable short-term expedient. The four-department organization now expanded to twelve, grouped into four divisions each headed by an Oberquartiermeister (literally 'senior general staff quartermaster', and in practice a deputy chief of staff), with the old training and foreign armies departments each divided in two, the organizations and personnel department extensively reorganized, and new departments created to deal with logistics and supply, mapping, transportation, fortifications and defences, and technical or technological matters.[46] This last department incorporated a section to study the impact of new scientific innovations and discoveries and develop the army's response to these. The general staff also assumed responsibility for Germany's military attachés (some nineteen in 1935), army film production and a number of subsidiary offices and organizations dealing with military history, historical document archives and other categories of military records. Only the most talented and professionally outstanding officers were selected to fill the very few Oberquartiermeister posts, of which Oberquartiermeister I was the most prestigious, dealing as it did with operational planning, the incumbent becoming in effect the vice-chief of the general staff.

All of the senior positions within the general staff were held by officers of the general staff corps (Generalstabsoffiziere), those officers specifically selected and trained to fill key command and staff posts throughout the army, but especially at the higher levels of command. However, while Generalstabsoffiziere were to be found in a very wide range of important positions, the army general staff (Generalstab des Heeres) existed specifically to advise and support the army commander-in-chief in peace and war, dealing with matters such as operations, intelligence, logistics, organization and force development and army policy and planning. The headquarters of the army high command was the Oberkommando des Heeres (OKH), within which many general staff officers were employed. Self-evidently, however, not every member of the Generalstab des Heeres could be a professionally qualified Generalstabsoffiziere, although the general staff corps and the army general staff were both headed by the chief of the army general staff (Chef des Generalstabs des Heeres). Consequently, the rapid expansion of the army general staff and the future development of the general staff corps from 1935 were both matters that were the direct responsibility of General Beck.

As in the past, formal staff training was conducted by the Kriegsakademie, shut down in accordance with the Versailles treaty in 1920, but reopened in October 1935. The reopening was also the occasion on which it was officially retitled the 'Wehrmachtakademie', although the familiar former name still persisted in everyday use, certainly within the army and the general staff. During the opening ceremony, which was attended by Hitler and Generalfeldmarschall von Blomberg as well as other senior officers and officials, General Beck's speech contrasted noticeably with that of the field marshal. While von Blomberg used the opportunity to reaffirm his support for Hitler, praising his leadership and policies, Beck (quite properly as chief of the general staff) set out his vision for the general staff and its work in the future, describing what was in many ways a return to the principles propounded by Helmuth von Moltke almost a century before. Beck advocated the meticulous, logical and objective approach that should be adopted by a good general staff officer – considering all possibilities and justifying the most probable course or recommending the most suitable course of action, but most importantly avoiding any temptation to rush to act without proper analysis and planning. However, by not only omitting to politicize his speech and praise the Führer, but also by lauding staff operating principles that were directly contrary to the intuitive and 'instant decision' approach advocated and relied upon by Hitler, Beck's speech drew sharp criticism from several of those attending the ceremony, as well as aggravating Hitler's relationship with his chief of the general staff. The Führer – a corporal in World War I – had long mistrusted the general staff ('just a club of intellectuals', he had confided to his close associates) and the army's officer corps, so for him this event served to confirm that such views were not misplaced. Remarkably, it appears that Hitler had only one short conversation with Beck between 1934 and 1938, apart from several meetings in 1938 specifically in connection with the Blomberg–Fritsch crisis that year.[47]

While establishing the conceptual foundation and operational doctrine upon which the general staff was to base its activities, Beck directed a study by the department of military science into whether or not the traditional and long-standing concept of military co-responsibility for the actions of the army and the good of the nation that had obtained in former times was still sustainable in the sort of authoritarian 'leader state' that Germany had become. Certainly Hitler chose not to involve his military advisers in many decisions of strategic and diplomatic policy, while even his announcement in 1935 of the introduction of conscription was made without prior consultation with those military leaders who would be most affected by it. In any event, the conclusion of the study was that co-responsibility was no longer viable in post-1933 Germany. Despite this, Beck directed that the principle should be re-established – thus reintroducing what was now a controversial concept that not only conflicted with Nazi thinking on command and control responsibilities but which would also be used increasingly by those who opposed Hitler to justify their actions in the years ahead.

A fundamental review of operational doctrine was also carried out, with a return to the primacy of the offensive being enshrined in a new *Battle Instructions* publication, the development of which was initiated by Generaloberst von Fritsch, who at that stage was still head of the army. During the Reichswehr era, the Truppenamt had based its doctrine upon a concept of mobile defence – something von Fritsch had disparaged as 'organized flight'.[48] The work was co-authored by Beck and Oberst Karl-Heinrich Graf von Stülpnagel – a rising star within the general staff, as indeed were two of his fellow deputy chiefs of staff, Generalleutnant Franz Halder (who in due course would succeed Beck) and Generalmajor Erich von Manstein. Despite this change of operational emphasis, however, the general staff's revised deployment plans produced in 1935 and 1936 still envisaged a primarily defensive posture in both east and west, including the development of fixed lines of fortifications to protect Germany against incursions by France or Poland. In 1936 this reflected Beck's own view that any proposed move towards involvement in a new war should be resisted. Such thinking reflected the general staff's assessment that the army lacked sufficient trained reserves and that the potential threat to German cities and industries from strategic bombing was considerable. However, such reservations were totally at odds with Hitler's as yet undeclared strategic intentions, as well as with the ideas of officers such as Guderian, who already saw the battle-winning potential of large mobile armoured forces closely supported by air power. Also, at that stage, Beck could not have anticipated and taken into account Hitler's imminent actions to extend Germany's borders outwards in the Rhineland, in Austria and into Czechoslovakia.

Even though there there were uncertain times ahead for the resurrected general staff, and a return to its former power and prestige was already somewhat problematical, the Truppenamt quickly became a distant memory. Beck continued to believe in the traditional primacy of the army – and by implication that of its general staff – and argued that the operational planning of the Luftwaffe and the Kriegsmarine should always be shaped to support the needs and plans of the army. In the years that followed, Beck, von Fritsch and von Blomberg engaged in successive rounds of internal politics and power-plays set against the inescapable impact of the OKW and the Wehrmachtsamt, and the pressing need to develop an effective army general staff in anticipation of a future war. Beck's own view in 1935 was that the army as a whole could not be made ready to fight a war in less than seven or eight years. A further consideration was Hitler's well-known reservations about the general staff, with his desire to curtail its authority. None the less, Beck eventually secured formal agreement to the chief of the general staff having responsibility for all matters relating to the preparation, planning and conduct of warfare, but – in a compromise measure – he would have no command authority. Thus the intellectual role and authority of the general staff were officially acknowledged, but the price was the loss of its traditional power of command. Although the heads of the army and navy were accorded 'ministerial status' on 20 April 1936 (a status Germany's minister for air, Göring, the head of the Luftwaffe, already enjoyed) these 'promotions' were largely irrelevant and also diminished von Blomberg's authority as war minister.

In due course, a standard career pattern emerged for those officers destined to serve as members of the general staff in the army of the Third Reich. This pattern largely reflected many aspects of the well-proven system that had been applied in the old imperial army from the mid-nineteenth century, although it was now progressively and pragmatically modified in various ways, once the war was under way, to speed up the output of suitably qualified general staff officers. Maintaining the professional standards of the general staff remained paramount, and the young officers who qualified as members of the general staff corps continued to be an elite group within the wider officer corps: as ever, these officers were the most talented and professionally competent in the army. Subject to gaining the usual recommendation from their commander, general staff candidates were eligible for selection up to the age of 28, by which stage they would typically be serving in the rank of captain. With the onset of active hostilities in 1939, an added dimension was injected into the pre-selection process. Thereafter, the would-be general staff officer was required to have proved his leadership and tactical abilities on the battlefield, with a mandatory requirement for his performance in combat to have been graded by his commander as exceptional, based on at least six months of front-line service.

The formal period of general staff training lasted twelve months, during which the officer was nominally assigned to the Kriegsakademie (the war school, restored to its former status as the principal focus of general staff training in 1935), the first month usually being spent at the appropriate special service school. This was to ensure that the candidate was entirely up to date concerning the organization, doctrine and technological aspects of his own arm or branch of the service. Thereafter, the candidate completed six months of intensive centralized training at the Kriegsakademie before being attached to the general staff on probation for a further five months. At the end of the year, if he had successfully completed all the mandatory training and passed the various qualifying exercises, tests and examinations during the course and his final Generalstab attachment, the candidate was formally accepted into the general staff corps and adopted the Karmesin (carmine-red) coloured Waffenfarbe shoulder strap, collar and trouser stripe distinctions that indicated his membership of that elite body. However, for the general staff officer, the process of training, rigorous assessment and the constant broadening of his experience continued in the months and years that followed, as he progressed through a succession of general staff appointments while also completing periods of service with troops in various types of field unit. In precisely the same way that the system had operated in the old imperial German army, for the general staff officer in the army of the Third Reich, a performance failure or serious personal indiscretion at any stage during this process could still result in an officer's removal from that corps and his return to mainstream military duties, notwithstanding his earlier selection, training, qualification and acceptance as a member of the general staff corps.

During the pre-war years from 1935, the general staff focused upon the practical problems of rearmament and the dramatic expansion of the army, with its conversion from the primarily 'framework' or 'instructional' organization it had been as the Reichwehr into that of a comprehensive war machine, the principal combat arm of the Wehrmacht. Within its own organization, the problem of selecting and training suitable general staff officers in the required numbers mirrored the army's wider difficulties in recruiting sufficient officers. This in turn meant that there were wide variations in social background, academic qualifications, political views, leadership qualities and military experience among the newly commissioned (the German term is 'promoted' rather than 'commissioned') officers of the post-1935 army. During these formative years, the workload of the general staff officer was so great that the desirable practice applied in former times of these officers serving periods of time at regimental duty and with various support units was temporarily abandoned. Their day-to-day work focused upon the great issues of the time: these included matters such as Germany's strategic posture, external threats and the responses to them, the army's organization and balance of capabilities, and the implications of technological advances in areas such as aviation, rocketry, mobility, armoured protection and the tank. Every issue had its supporters and opponents, and the general staff was required to consider objectively a very diverse range of issues. Typical examples included whether or not the cavalry arm still had a place on the future battlefield; the precise role of armoured vehicles – tanks, artillery and troop carriers – in the the the sort of mobile offensive operations upon which the army's doctrine was based by 1939; and the introduction of a host of new weapons, both in the German army and in the armies of other nations.

The cavalry versus armoured forces debate attracted a great deal of attention and study, especially after the inclusion of mobile motorized units on the Reichswehr manoeuvres of 1932 indicated the future potential of armoured and motorized forces. In a portent of future developments, during a visit by Hitler to Kummersdorf in 1933, Guderian (who was by then chief of staff to the inspector of motorized troops, General Lutz) had briefed the newly-appointed chancellor on mobile operations and then demonstrated a motorcycle platoon, an anti-tank platoon, a platoon of experimental Pz.Kpfw.I tanks, and one platoon each of light and heavy armoured reconnaissance cars. Significantly, Guderian recalled that Hitler 'was much impressed by the speed and precision of movement of our units, and said repeatedly: "That's what I need! That's what I want to have!".' [49]

Dealing with inter-arm rivalries and internal Wehrmacht politics was an unwelcome but inevitable feature of the general staff's work. One such ongoing issue was the regular need to counter the Luftwaffe lobby for air force operational primacy within the Wehrmacht in a future war. (Göring had already, most inappropriately in operational terms, gained control of the ground forces' air defence artillery, and this was later followed by all of the Wehrmacht's airborne (paratroop) forces coming under Luftwaffe command).[50] Throughout, however, the overriding responsibility of the general staff was the need to direct and oversee virtually every aspect of the expansion and rearmament of the army between 1935 and 1939, and the sheer scale of that undertaking was quite unprecedented.

Germany's New War Machine

In March 1935, Hitler had revealed to the nation and to the world the rearmament programme upon which Germany had embarked; however, the process had actually begun as soon as the Nazis came to power in

January 1933. It then continued apace until it was more or less complete at the end of 1938. From 1 October 1935, all of Germany's paramilitary police units were incorporated into the army, which in practice produced an army of about 480,000 men in 10 corps, comprising 24 infantry divisions and 3 panzer divisions. Following the German reoccupation of the Rhineland in 1936, the Landespolizei battalions from that area were incorporated into the army without delay. On 1 October 1936, the last two of the 12 army corps Hitler had declared as the new army's target size on 16 March 1935 were formed, some fifteen months earlier than had originally been anticipated. The fully mobilized army now fielded 36 divisions, including 3 panzer divisions as well as a mountain brigade and a cavalry brigade. There were also 4 reserve divisions and 21 Landwehr divisions. Just a year later, on 19 October 1937, XIII and XIV Corps were formed, both of which were in addition to the 12 original corps declared in 1935. During 1938, XV, XVI, XVII and XVIII Corps joined the army's order of battle, the creation of these additional formations being made possible by the Austrian Anschluß of March 1938 and the Munich settlement signed that September (which ceded control of the Sudetenland in Czechoslovakia to Germany). These two events enabled the immediate incorporation into the German army of 5 existing divisions from the former Austrian army, together with the conscription of numbers of individual Austrians and Sudeten Germans for military service in the Wehrmacht.

By 1938, the army numbered no fewer than two million men, with intakes of 500,000 newly conscripted recruits joining for training each year. This produced an army of some 51 divisions, which included 5 panzer divisions, 2 independent panzer brigades, 4 light armoured (cavalry) divisions and 3 mountain divisions. These numbers masked capability shortfalls in several important areas, however, including the development of an armoured force large enough to ensure the success of Hitler's strategic aims. Also, between 1933 and 1939, the army experienced considerable difficulties with officer and non-commissioned officer (NCO) recruitment and training, as the burgeoning numbers of new battalions, regiments, divisions and corps outstripped the availability of men qualified to train and command them.

The fully mobilized strength of the army in theory further increased to 103 divisions by mid-1939, but in practice the real strength of the Feldheer remained at about 51 divisions, as the larger total included many framework formations and units for which the necessary manpower was still largely untrained or part-trained. Also, there were only 7 panzer divisions and 4 fully motorized infantry divisions in the army, while the larger part of the army (some 86 divisions) still relied upon horses to tow its artillery and supply wagons, and upon requisitioned civilian motor vehicles to carry out a wide range of transport tasks. Most infantry units had no integral transport, routinely deploying on foot and using requisitioned and captured vehicles when available. Rail movement was utilized whenever possible. Such practical considerations and limitations would affect the general staff's operational planning throughout the war. At the same time, Hitler and other members of his inner circle (and even some senior officers) would choose to rely more and more upon the theoretical and largely irrelevant figures for the number of divisions available without taking any account of their actual strength, capability and real combat effectiveness.

Ever since the Nazis gained power in 1933, the party's own paramilitary security force, the Schutzstaffel (SS), had been expanding in size and extending its influence in parallel with developments in the Wehrmacht. Since its first formation as the SS-Stabswache in Berlin in 1923, the SS had grown apace, and by 1936 an SS-VT (SS-Verfügungstruppe) inspectorate had been established to oversee the administration and development of what by late 1939 had become the Waffen-SS. Prior to and throughout the coming war, all elements of the SS – together with the Gestapo – were headed by Reichsführer-SS (RF-SS) Heinrich Himmler, whose ultimate ambition was for the SS to displace the army as Germany's principal military force. By early 1937, the SS fielded some 11 battalion-size units (the core of the future Waffen-SS), and about 5,000 SS personnel were employed as concentration camp guards. The burgeoning size and influence of the SS would eventually prove to be one of the greatest handicaps and distractions for the general staff; as well as a wider tragedy for the nation and for the populations of the territories occupied by German forces in the years ahead. Although neither a part of the army nor of the Wehrmacht, the members of the Waffen-SS were generally ideologically motivated, loyal Nazis and were therefore considered politically reliable by the Nazi leadership. Consequently, this military organization enjoyed a uniquely privileged position in Hitler's Germany, while its operational activities increasingly overlapped those of the army from 1939, Waffen-SS units increasingly serving alongside those of the army in several theatres as the war progressed. However, the discrete command, control and support arrangements of the SS sometimes resulted in Waffen-SS units competing with army units for often scarce resources within the same operational area.

Generally speaking, the army was always able to obtain the necessary numbers of soldiers to fill its lowest ranks, both through conscription and from the numbers of young men seeking a career and a generally better and more exciting lifestyle than many of them could have aspired to in civilian life as labourers or unskilled workers. However, as with the general staff corps, the problem of increasing the size of the officer corps as a whole posed a particular and daunting challenge. At the time that its expansion was ordered, there were only 4,000 serving army officers, of whom about 450 were in the medical and veterinary branches. The army's difficulties were exacerbated by the re-assignment of some 500 officers and a number of NCOs to the newly formed Luftwaffe. Meanwhile, only one war college existed, its training intake limited to 180 officers each year. As a result of all this, there was an overall shortfall of no fewer than 30,000 officers in 1933. In the short term, this deficiency was addressed by recalling recently retired Reichswehr officers, by transferring paramilitary police officers into the army, and by promoting several hundred NCOs to officer rank. However, the last of these measures depleted numbers of those NCOs whose experience was also of critical importance to the successful development of the army in the future. In October 1934, officers who had been forced by the provisions of the Versailles treaty to retire in 1919 were recalled to duty, and on 1 April that year the first large-scale enlistment of volunteers for one year of military service was announced. About 18,000 officers were in post by March 1937, but this still represented a significant shortfall against the 30,000 that the army required, with a particular problem affecting the general staff, which needed staff officers to fill key posts in the headquarters of the many new corps and divisions.

Meeting this requirement led to much cross-posting and curtailing of many officers' planned tours of duty, which was disruptive and affected unit cohesion. A year later, the government announced that all officers (including retired officers) would henceforth be liable for indefinite military service. This edict also applied to former officers living outside Germany and to over-age former officers, although where appropriate the latter would be required to serve as instructors if they were assessed unfit for active service. Although less than ideal, these measures together increased the number of serving army officers to about 25,000 by the end of 1938, and, despite continuing difficulties in a few areas, the deficiencies of the mid-1930s had been more or less resolved by early 1939. By then, five military academies were conducting training, with a total output of 3,000 officers per year based upon a training course that had pragmatically been reduced from two years to between eleven and fourteen months. Officer recruitment was buoyant, some 60 per cent of German boys leaving high school in 1938 declaring their wish to become army officers. However, at the same time some of the more traditional aspects of the country's education system had stagnated due to the need to accommodate National Socialist ideology, with its narrow approach to academic and cultural matters in the standard curriculum. As a result, many boys lacked the necessary academic skills or intellectual aptitude to qualify for entry to the military academies. Inevitably perhaps, once the war commenced, and with officer casualties mounting, formal educational qualification requirements for officer candidates would eventually be abandoned altogether in November 1942.

As the size and capability of the army increased, a new Kriegsheer or 'war army' concept and organization was now developed by the general staff. This involved a professional standing or peacetime Feldheer (field army) designed to meet Germany's immediate strategic and security needs on a day-to-day basis and (ideally) to fight a short war without recourse to further military manpower. To back up the Feldheer there would be an Ersatzheer (replacement army) to provide reinforcements and a sustained depth of military capability in the post-mobilization period and during a protracted conflict. The viability of the Kriegsheer concept was considerably strengthened by the period of obligatory military service being increased from one to two years from 24 August 1936: within a few months of its implementation, this measure effectively doubled the overall size of the Feldheer.

For the general staff, manpower was only part of the equation – the development, manufacture, testing and acquisition of equipment of all sorts also occupied much staff time. The army required ever greater quantities of weapons, transport and supplies to support it on a day-to-day basis as well as in anticipation of future operational needs. The sheer scope and scale of the army equipment programme, and the various ways in which it was carried through both within Germany and also in countries overseas, including Spain, Sweden and even Soviet Russia, is a story in its own right. In the case of Russia, a secret military agreement signed at the same time as the Rapallo agreement of 1922 placed huge areas within Russia at the disposal of the German army. There, troops could develop their operational techniques and tactics, as well as training with the full range of offensive warfare weapons – tanks, aircraft, chemical weapons and heavy artillery – prohibited by the Versailles treaty. In the meantime, senior German army officers frequently visited Russia to view the various projects then in progress as well as to observe Red Army manoeuvres.[51] Indeed, the process of German rearmament actually began well before Hitler achieved power, being carried through largely by von Seeckt and the Truppenamt during the Reichswehr years, all the time circumventing the constraints imposed by the Versailles treaty and concealing these activities from the Allied Control Commission inspectors. Whereas turning men into passable soldiers can be achieved within months, the procurement and production of major items of military equipment and reliable weapon systems usually takes years, especially – such as the tank – where the equipment and the concepts it supports are innovative in nature. Consequently, without the earlier staff work by von Seeckt and the Truppenamt during the 1920s the spectacular escalation of German rearmament from 1933 would have been virtually impossible, and it is unlikely that the German army could have been adequately equipped for war in 1939. The success of German rearmament in the 1930s was stated succinctly in a US government intelligence assessment of the state of the German army in March 1945, which noted that, 'the German army of [September] 1939 was a model of efficiency, the best product of the concentrated military genius of the most scientifically military of nations'.[52]

A particular training and weapons-proving opportunity was presented to the Wehrmacht in 1936 when General Franco of Spain asked Hitler for tanks, aircraft and three German divisions to assist his military campaign against the Spanish Republican government. Although Hitler was inclined to acquiesce, von Blomberg and von Fritsch speedily dissuaded him from sending the three divisions of troops. Nevertheless, the Spanish Civil War did enable the army to try out quantities of its weaponry and equipment in live combat conditions. The experience gained using tanks, other motor vehicles, motorcycles, aircraft, machine-guns and other small-arms in combat was of considerable benefit to the development of the army, particularly for those officers who would command the panzer forces just a few years later. Despite the useful experience it provided, however, the war in Spain also produced some misleading over-estimates of the efficacy of the armour protection and weapons of the early types of German tank, which were usually employed against the predominantly infantry Republican forces or against armoured vehicles of inferior quality. And while the army avoided any large-scale involvement, Göring seized the opportunity to test the new Luftwaffe in action. With no fewer than eleven squadrons of fighters, fighter-bombers, seaplanes and reconnaissance aircraft, the 'Condor Legion' was formed, and this developed many of the techniques that would be used to support the army during the coming campaigns in 1939 and 1940.

During the final years of the decade, the differences between the general staff and Hitler became ever more evident. They had always existed, but the last few years of peace before 1939 highlighted an irreconcilable gap that was fast becoming a metaphorical chasm. Indeed, in light of the pre-war differences between Hitler and the army general staff, it is perhaps remarkable that it was not until 1944 that matters would finally come to a desperate and violent head. At the same time, Hitler's continued mistrust of the general staff and what he perceived to be its questionable loyalty is perhaps understandable: time and again, the aims and ideology of National

Socialism proved diametrically opposed to the concepts and culture of German military duty and honour that had for so long lain at the heart of the Prussian and German army, especially that of the officer corps and the general staff. That an unsatisfactory situation was allowed to persist once Hitler achieved power is testimony to the fact that the general staff was still crucial to Hitler's strategic objectives. But the general staff misjudged its ability to influence, modify or forestall those objectives until it was simply too late. By then the burgeoning power of the SS not only competed with that of the army but also provided Hitler with various options that did not exist before the war. And serving as a backdrop to all of these matters were several international events that – perversely – favoured Hitler and strengthened his position while also requiring the general staff to analyse and advise on national defence and the military options regarding them and conducting the necessary planning for them.

Reoccupation of the Rhineland, March 1936

In mid-1935 the general staff had studied the implications of reoccupying the demilitarized zone in the Rhineland. It concluded that, quite apart from being a violation of the 1925 Locarno Pact (which had not only secured German admission to the League of Nations but was also designed to reduce the possibility of a future war in Europe), the army was inadequately prepared for this task at that time, especially as such action would risk a military counter-move by France. Beck supported the simple logic of this line, while von Fritsch and von Blomberg were keen to regain the Rhineland but agreed that it was not yet appropriate to do so with the army's restructuring at such an early stage. However, Hitler needed to reoccupy the Rhineland for political and military purposes, and early in 1936 a treaty signed between France and Russia provided the necessary excuse, the rationale being that this treaty had violated the Locarno Pact. Von Blomberg knew of Hitler's intentions in January, and von Fritsch knew them in February, when the latter argued strongly against the risk of war. However, Hitler had ascertained that the Western powers were unlikely to intervene – the League of Nations had already demonstrated its impotence over Italy's invasion of Abyssinia the previous year – and on 6 March Beck and the general staff were informed that German forces would reoccupy the Rhineland 24 hours later. In practice, just one division was needed to carry out the operation. The remarkably late notice given to the general staff illustrates Hitler's dismissive attitude of General Beck as chief of the general staff, and of that body as a whole. In the event, France mobilized some thirteen major units and fully activated the Maginot line defences, but neither France nor Britain were inclined to go to war over this matter. Hitler had been proved right, while the general staff appeared to many as having been over-cautious or too negative in its assessment of the possible consequences of this action. Later that summer, the Spanish conflict saw German forces in action supporting General Franco's Nationalist forces, but the combined weight of advice from von Blomberg and von Fritsch kept the army's involvement in Spain at practicable and beneficial levels. Meanwhile, despite an historical reluctance by Germany to enter wholeheartedly into coalition warfare other than as the dominant power, Hitler set about consolidating his position internationally with the 'Rome–Berlin Axis',[53] first referred to as such by the Italian leader Mussolini on 1 November 1936 in connection with the support provided by both countries to Franco during the Spanish Civil War.

The Hossbach Conference, November 1937

However, Hitler was already looking even further ahead, and on 5 November 1937 he propounded his philosophy for future military aggressive action at the so-called 'Hossbach Conference'[54] in Berlin, which was attended by the heads of the army, navy and air force, together with von Blomberg and other senior military and diplomatic staff members. The Führer's words at this conference would underscore and shape the general staff's war planning thereafter, as well as forcing those present to declare their position on these matters. It was also the moment at which Hitler's aggressive intentions were thrown into stark relief against what might now be seen quite clearly as the general staff's reluctance to engage Germany in a new war in Europe, especially against the principal victors of 1918, France and Britain. Arguably, the general staff might reasonably have anticipated this new strategic policy, having been ordered in June 1937 to maintain the army in a state of permanent preparedness for mobilization and for offensive operations at short notice. Ostensibly that order was designed to counter a surprise attack against Germany, but only the most naïve general staff officer would have failed to recognize its more likely applications.

In summary, although Hitler had already indicated informally on several occasions that a clash with Russia would eventually become unavoidable, the 5 November conference focused primarily upon Germany's western border and the conditions in which military action would be taken against France. A definite intention to do so once German rearmament had been completed was now stated, but it was not expected that this could be before 1943, which more or less matched Beck's own assessment of future military readiness (although Beck had based his assessment primarily upon self-defence). However, if France were to be weakened through internal disruption or by involvement in a separate war, then Germany should be prepared to seize the opportunity to attack and defeat France at any stage, even before the completion of Germany's rearmament. A prerequisite for such action was to secure the country's eastern and south-eastern flanks, this being achieved by bringing Austria into a 'Greater Germany' and through the neutralization and occupation of Czechoslovakia. At the same time, Japan would be cultivated for the part it could play in posing a valuable distraction and threat to Russia in the Far East, until Germany was in a position to deal with Russia directly. This conference set out the broad strategy that the general staff would now be required to take as its baseline for planning, while Hitler's words that November day in 1937 generally reflected the operations subsequently carried out by the Wehrmacht between 1938 and 1941.

Predictably, both von Blomberg and von Fritsch immediately stated their opposition to a war against France (and by implication against Britain), doubting that France would ever be sufficiently weakened for an opportunistic attack to succeed. Furthermore, the strength of the fortifications on the eastern flank in northern Bohemia put the success of any operation against Czechoslovakia in question. Nevertheless, von Fritsch directed the general staff to review its existing assessment of the likely outcome of *Fall Grün* (literally 'Case' or 'Situation' Green, but possibly more accurately described as 'Operation' Green in English military terminology), a surprise attack against Czechoslovakia. He was confident that the result of this would show such an attack to be ill-advised and that he could then present this to Hitler and dissuade him from such action.

However, such confidence was misplaced and, as we have already seen, within a couple of months both von Blomberg and von Fritsch had been falsely accused of various offences and forced to retire as war minister and head of the army respectively. By the end of 1939, von Blomberg would be living in exile on the Isle of Capri and von Fritsch would be dead, killed in action on a Polish battlefield near Warsaw. Meanwhile, Beck for the time being continued as chief of staff, although his own position was becoming increasingly tenuous. His status as the most senior member of the general staff also further diminished the stature of that organization in Hitler's eyes, much to the delight of those Nazi leaders who despised the general staff and those senior army officers who supported or sought to succeed him.

5

Distrust and Dissent

The Czech Crisis and the Halder Plot

1938

In March 1938, Germany annexed Austria and made it part of 'Greater Germany' by the Anschluß (or 'Union'). Although many Austrians had long supported unification with Germany, this had been specifically forbidden by the Versailles treaty. Despite this, troops of the German Eighth Army were mobilized on the evening of 10 March, and on 12 March executed Operation *Otto,* entering Vienna the next day to 'quell disorder and re-establish the rule of law'. This was in response to a request contrived by Hitler and initiated by Seyss-Inquart, a prominent Austrian Nazi. Within days Austria had been absorbed into Germany, and on 10 April the Austrian population sanctioned the country's new status with a plebiscite. Once again Hitler's policy and the army's actions in direct contravention of Versailles had been successfully carried through without counter-action by France or Britain. Despite the patriotic enthusiasm with which the Anschluß was viewed by much of the population of Germany and Austria, many members of the general staff viewed the precedent set by this action with unease. Certainly some aspects of the mobilization process and deployment into Austria had revealed weaknesses in the army's organization and equipment – especially that of some of its motorized transport. Nevertheless, the general staff now embarked upon the planning for a future reoccupation of Memel (held by Lithuania since World War I), while Beck, now fully apprised of Hitler's strategic aims following the Hossbach Conference, produced a general staff study assessing the likelihood of Germany being able to defeat Czechoslovakia by a surprise attack before France could strike Germany from the west. Most importantly, the study assumed that an attack against the Czechs would result in French, British and possibly US counter-action, an eventuality that would logically make a German attack against Czechoslovakia a 'non-starter'. Beck briefed Hitler accordingly; Hitler dismissed the study conclusions as generally irrelevant.

However, for Beck and the general staff this was in many ways a defining moment, as Hitler informed the chief of the general staff quite clearly that the army (and therefore the general staff) was 'the instrument of the statesman' and that its duty was 'to find a way of carrying out the tasks with which the statesman charged it – not to discuss them.'[55] This was the moment at which the new position and reduced status of the general staff in Nazi Germany became abundantly clear. However, at that stage the fear of Hitler and the SS that would emerge in later years was not yet evident, either in Beck's belief that he could disagree with Hitler with impunity or in the idea that the general staff would be allowed to continue to criticize or oppose Hitler's plans. Beck's meeting with Hitler ended with the general stating that he would take no responsibility for any orders of which he did not approve – by implication those issued by Hitler and the Nazi government. After this meeting, Beck's effectiveness as chief of the general staff was severely diminished, but he still resolved to pursue his objective of stopping, or at least postponing, what he viewed as Hitler's preparations for war.

With the benefit of hindsight and knowledge of how the Third Reich and the SS state developed within Germany in just a few years, the action now taken by Beck, the general staff and various senior army officers appears at the very least to be reckless. Direct opposition to the wishes of the Führer could be deemed treasonable, potentially risking disgrace, imprisonment or execution. However, in mid-1938 (and irrespective of Hitler's so recent statement on the relative positions of the army and the statesman) Beck still believed that the power and influence of the army were sufficient to carry the day by reasoned argument and – if necessary – by force of arms. Accordingly, he used the earlier study as the basis of a staff paper showing the risks of German military intervention against Czechoslovakia. In parallel, he also solicited support from numbers of generals for the use of force against the Nazi regime if logic and reason should fail. Beck asked the head of the general staff's operations department (Oberquartiermeister I), Karl-Heinrich Graf von Stülpnagel (now a Generalmajor), to carry out this highly sensitive and potentially treasonable work. The close association between these two officers and their ongoing opposition to Hitler were to have tragic consequences for both of them some six years later. Beck tried to secure von Brauchitsch's support and prevailed upon him to sway the other generals. However, although a meeting did take place with von Brauchitsch at the Bendlerstraße headquarters[56] on 4 August, the army commander's address to the assembled generals – all the army group, army and corps commanders – was lukewarm. It also fell well short of the sentiments expressed in Beck's memorandum to von Brauchitsch, which had included the words, 'In order to safeguard our position before history and to keep the repute of the Supreme Command of the Army unstained, I hereby place on record that I have refused to approve any warlike adventures of the National Socialists.'[57] Neither did von Brauchitsch mention Beck's suggestion that the generals should threaten their mass resignation if Hitler proceeded with his war plans. Nothing of consequence emerged from this meeting, but once the fact that it had taken place became known to Hitler, Beck's position finally became untenable, his early dismissal or resignation now inevitable. As an indication of his displeasure, Hitler ordered the chiefs of the general staff of the army groups and corps and of the air force to attend a meeting with him at the Obersalzberg in Bavaria on 10 August – but deliberately excluded von Brauchitsch and Beck from attending. Presentationally, Hitler intended this meeting as a snub to the generals who opposed his plans but with the subsidiary aim of creating a rift between these younger or less senior staff officers and their older, possibly more traditional, commanders. More significantly, the Führer chose this occasion to announce his decision to invade Czechoslovakia.

Meanwhile, Hitler's lack of any action against Beck to secure his immediate dismissal, even with his knowledge of the full extent of Beck's active opposition, was intriguing. It surely indicated how little real influence the chief of the general staff now enjoyed, and therefore the relative ease with which his well-nigh treasonable – or mutinous – action could be dismissed or safely overlooked. This also underlined the fact that in 1938

Hitler's popularity with the German public was considerable, while the German civilian population was barely aware of the existence of Beck and the general staff. Neither was the population generally aware of Hitler's expansionist plans then afoot. However, Hitler's apparent reluctance to deal with Beck and the others may also be taken as evidence of the fact that Hitler none the less understood that the general staff was still an essential part of the command and control arrangements of the army, despite its reduced status within Germany compared with that during the old imperial era. This meant that it was also an indispensable element of his future plans and of the Wehrmacht's part in the realization of his strategic ambitions.

Once Beck understood that his bid to gain the active support of the other generals to oppose Hitler's plans had failed, and that Hitler was no longer prepared to retain him in post as chief of the general staff, he had no option but to resign: in truth, he was dismissed. Furthermore, the rejection of his study showing that offensive action against Czechoslovakia was ill-advised meant that his credibility as the principal military adviser to the Führer had been invalidated. Beck formally resigned on 18 August, but the resignation was not finally accepted by Hitler until the 21st, when it was also stipulated that no public announcement of Beck's departure as chief of the general staff should be made. Von Brauchitsch invited General Franz Halder, a close associate of his who was by then serving as Oberquartiermeister I within the general staff, to succeed Beck. Von Brauchitsch and Halder now held two of the army's key posts, and both still had significant reservations about Hitler's plans. However, they were minded to try to influence these plans from within the high command rather than mounting them from beyond that inner circle – the lesson of Beck's progressive isolation and eventual departure was not lost upon either of them. Halder became the new chief of the general staff on 1 September 1938 and was destined to occupy that post until September 1942.[58]

Although he was sometimes described as professorial, pedantic and cynical – a planner and organizer rather than a leader – Franz Halder's intellect, intelligence, staff experience and considerable ability in many ways suited him very well for his new role as chief of the general staff. Born into a traditional military and strongly Christian family at Würzburg on 30 June

1884, Halder's military career began with service as a regimental officer in the 3rd Bavarian Regiment of Field Artillery two years after having joined the army in 1902. His specialist artillery officer training took place in 1906–7. In 1911–14 he attended the Kriegsakademie in Munich, subsequently filling various general staff posts during World War I. He was promoted captain in August 1915, serving on the general staff of the Crown Prince of Bavaria's 6th Infantry Division. In 1917, he served in the headquarters of Second Army and later that of Fourth Army. Halder first met Hitler in the 1920s and maintained contact with him in the aftermath of the 'Beer-hall putsch' of 1923; Hitler rather derided Halder's intellect and depth of political and military knowledge. He had also worked with Röhm while serving with the Bavarian general staff. During his post-war service with the Reichswehr, by then a major, he was appointed as the senior quartermaster and director of operations in Wehrkreis VII in Munich 1926. In February 1929, Halder was promoted lieutenant colonel and served on the training staff of the Reichswehr ministry from October 1929 to 1931. He was promoted colonel in 1931, major general in 1934 and lieutenant general in 1936. Halder commanded the 7th Infantry Division in Munich from October 1934 through 1935, while subsequently, as director of the training department of the army general staff in Berlin, he was responsible for planning and overseeing the large-scale army manoeuvres that were staged by the Wehrmacht in 1936. Later that year, in November, he was once again appointed as a director of operations, but this time it was of the Wehrmacht, a post that he held until his appointment as chief of the general staff in September 1938. In the meantime, Halder was promoted General der Artillerie on 1 February 1938.

In the story of the general staff, Halder's appointment was particularly significant – he was destined, with von Brauchitsch, to plan and oversee some of the army's greatest successes during the first three years of the war. But his formidable intellect and professional abilities would not prevent Halder finding himself presiding over a continuing erosion of the general staff's responsibilities and authority, as events on the Eastern Front battlefields and the power-playing ambitions of the OKW together conspired to weaken the position of the army general staff. Whereas Beck's approach to matters was generally philosophical or academic, Halder's was direct, pragmatic and forthright, while maintaining the niceties and courtesies typical of his generation of army officers. Certainly Halder was by nature more decisive and inclined to act than Beck, and his pragmatic view of the situation in Germany enabled him to reconcile satisfactorily in his own mind the conflicting issue of loyalty to Hitler, enshrined in the soldier's oath, and that of his duty as a soldier and to the Fatherland. However, as was the case with many senior army officers, the arts of subterfuge and the role of conspirator did not come easily to him. In the wider history of the general staff, it was of note that Halder was both the first Bavarian and first Roman Catholic to be appointed chief of the general staff. Bizarrely, within a matter of months he was also the first chief of the general staff to be actively involved with others in planning a coup d'état against the head of the state that he served! This conspiracy was subsequently known as 'the Halder plot' or 'the September plot', the first of these titles implicitly linking the plot directly to the general staff.

The trigger for this action was a growing unease in some parts of the German population over the matter of Czechoslovakia and a requirement placed upon the general staff to prepare *Fall Grün*: a plan to accomplish the invasion and defeat of Czechoslovakia within four days, followed by a redeployment of forces to Germany's western frontier in anticipation of a campaign against France. In light of Generaloberst Beck's earlier work, the general staff was convinced that an attack on Czechoslovakia would invite war with France, Britain and possibly Russia. However, these officers were unaware that Hitler had already ascertained from German diplomatic representatives in Moscow, London, Paris and elsewhere that the Russians, British and French were most unlikely to resort to armed action in support of the Czechs, irrespective of any public pronouncements or military posturing by the governments of these powers.[59] Consequently, at the same time that *Fall Grün* was being developed, a parallel plan was set in train. This plan had the displacement of Hitler as its objective, thus avoiding what the general staff and many other senior officers and prominent civilians viewed as a potentially disastrous war for which Germany was unprepared. In addition to members of the general staff, together with other staff and regimental officers serving in military intelligence and various headquarters and army units, those who opposed Hitler and his policies by now included prominent civilian officials in some of the key ministries of state, such as the ministry of the interior, the foreign office and some government financial departments. By mid-1938 even the head of the Berlin civil police force, Wolf-Heinrich Graf von Helldorf, had indicated his support for the movement against Hitler.[60]

This alternative plan was remarkable both for its scope and level of detail, as well as the fact that it was being developed by German officers and others against the country's duly elected head of state. It was to be implemented as soon as deployment for *Fall Grün* was ordered, with troops under the command of General Erwin von Witzleben, commanding Military District III (which included Berlin), occupying the part of the capital in which most of the government ministries were located. Von Witzleben's commitment to the task in hand was absolute; earlier that summer he had said to Oberstleutnant Hans Oster: 'I don't know anything about politics, but I don't need to in order to know what has to be done here.'[61] With the principal government buildings secured, the Reich Chancellery guards at the main entrance at 78 Wilhelmstrasse were to be overcome, followed immediately by any guards barring the way to Hitler's offices. Hitler was to be arrested by a force under von Witzleben, then quickly removed by car to a secret destination and there held in readiness to stand public trial.[62] Simultaneously, troops of the 1st Light Division, commanded by Generalmajor Erich Höpner, would be directed to prevent any move into Berlin and intervention by the Leibstandarte SS 'Adolf Hitler' (the 'LAH') motorized regiment, always one of Hitler's most loyal Waffen-SS units. Fortuitously, Höpner's division would already be conducting manoeuvres in the area between Thuringia and Saxony prior to deploying eastwards to the Czech border in readiness for *Fall Grün*. Hitler's removal was to be followed by temporary military control of the government pending an early transition to some sort of constitutional administration. Both in the army and in the country there was a feeling that Hitler was moving Germany into an unsought and ill-advised conflict. The popularity of the Führer that had been engendered by the successful reoccupation of the Rhineland and the Austrian Anschluß was now visibly waning as the prospect of another war loomed. The German historian Walter Görlitz caught the mood of the time:

> Never before had the general mood been so favourable to the success of a *coup d'état*, as it was in the close and thunderous atmosphere of that autumn [of 1938], nor was it ever to be so favourable again. Hitler's frantic speeches, his wild threats against Czechoslovakia, the sinister propaganda on behalf of the Sudeten Germans, with whose problems the German public had hitherto only the most negligible acquaintance – all these things produced among the masses nothing but the vague foreboding of war. The ordinary German could not understand how the imperfectly apprehended problems of Northern Bohemia could justify the horrors of another conflict. For the first time – and it was to be the last – the General Staff had the chance of striking a blow, and discontent with Hitler was so widespread as to promise such a venture an excellent chance of success. The masses had cheered Hitler rapturously when he brought them peace and bread [Author's comment: together with full employment and a restoration of national pride]. The masses were now wavering, for he was bringing them peace no longer.[63]

Although Hitler was well aware that foreign military opposition to German intervention in Czechoslovakia was unlikely, the arrangements for *Fall Grün* proceeded apace through September, with the 28th set as the date on which to execute the plan. The general staff was occupied day and night with work to coordinate and carry out construction of defensive positions in the west facing France. These were for occupation while the action against the Czechs was completed. At the same time, prioritization of resources for the 'West Wall' meant that transportation of matériel to the Czech border was disrupted, especially that which was moved by rail. In the meantime, motor transport and the fuel for it were both in short supply. Early indications of future problems between the army and Nazi paramilitary organizations emerged when SA units refused to cooperate with army requests for local support. While all this was going on, Neville Chamberlain, the British prime minister, conducted a series of visits to Hitler with a view to negotiating a peaceful outcome to the accelerating crisis. The general staff had ascertained that it needed five days' notice to put its alternative plan to displace Hitler into effect, and on 8 September arrangements were put in place for von Brauchitsch's headquarters to be notified in writing five days before any date on which Hitler intended to order *Fall Grün* to proceed. Ostensibly this was in order that the necessary action to support *Fall Grün* could be completed; in practice it was to trigger the sequence of actions that would result in the 'Halder plot' coming to fruition.

As September drew on, Hitler became ever more convinced by his two face-to-face meetings with Chamberlain that the British prime minister lacked the resolve to use force to counter German action against Czechoslovakia. This confirmed the reports already received from Hitler's other diplomatic sources. Meanwhile he continued to believe that any French military action could be contained while he dealt with Czechoslovakia. Consequently, the general staff were now directed also to consider unopposed options for intervention as well as continuing the work on *Fall Grün*. Between 22 and 24 September, war again appeared to become more likely when German air defences were put on alert at Berlin and on the Czech border, while in the west Germany's border with France was closed. Then, at 13.30 hours on 27 September, General Halder received the order to move the army's assault units into their forward assembly areas close to the Czech frontier. That telephone call also signalled the start of the preparatory action for the coup in Berlin. Elsewhere in the capital that day, a morale-raising parade by infantry and artillery troops of the 2nd Infantry Division (Motorized) in full battle array was ordered by Hitler – but this backfired when, from the crowds lining the streets, 'there was no cheering, only an uneasy and sullen silence'.[64] Most of the spectators believed that the troops were en route to entrain for the front line, that the outbreak of a new war was imminent, and indeed these units were earmarked for deployment to the Czech border. Hitler and Goebbels, who were watching the troops march past from the Chancellery building, noted the crowd's reaction with some concern, the former angrily declaiming that, 'With people like that you could never carry on a war.'[65] The commander of the parading troops, General Erwin von Witzleben (already an active member of the coup conspirators), 'later confessed that he was tempted to unlimber his guns right there before the Chancellery, and then go in and lock "that fellow" up'.[66] What the plotters – certainly the general staff – were apparently unaware of was that on 20 September Britain and France had in effect already abandoned the Czechs and had told the Prague government that it should deliver the areas inhabited by the Sudeten Germans (part of Bohemia and Moravia) to Germany in order to prevent a new war in Europe. Once again, this illustrated the extent of the disconnection between the general staff and military intelligence, and political and diplomatic developments and decision-making in Hitler's Germany by 1938.

War loomed, and the sense of crisis grew both within the general staff and in various political and other civilian organizations in Berlin and elsewhere. Halder prepared to issue the necessary final instructions for the coup on the following day, the 28th. Realistically, the conspiracy now actually needed Germany to be brought to the very brink of war for the coup to succeed. Although torn between his duty to his Führer and that due to his country and the army he commanded, von Brauchitsch was fully aware of these developments and – despite considerable personal reservations about taking such action – was generally favourable to them, or at least to allowing them to take place unopposed by him.[67] None the less (with the possibility of an attack against Czechoslovakia still in mind), he also liaised with Keitel at the OKW to emphasize that whatever might transpire in the coming days, German forces should not in any circumstances move beyond the Sudeten area of Czechoslovakia, and that this deployment constraint needed to be impressed upon Hitler. As the morning drew on, some of the panzer units commanded by Generalmajor Erich Höpner prepared to drive to Berlin, while the other army units under his command stood ready for an imminent clash with the Leibstandarte SS 'Adolf Hitler' if and when that Waffen-SS unit should be called upon to drive northwards into Berlin to save the Führer. Meanwhile, General von Witzleben's infantrymen stood ready to secure key points in the city. At this point, no irrevocable action had yet been taken either by Halder or any of these troops. Then, with the coup on the point of taking place and with the whole course of history about to be altered, the whole situation suddenly changed.

Mindful of Halder's imminent intentions, just before noon on the 28th von Brauchitsch visited the Chancellery to gain a further update on the overall situation. There, he learnt that, consequent upon a new proposal that had just been made by the Italian leader, Mussolini, another meeting between Hitler, Chamberlain and Daladier (of France) would now take place the next day at Munich. At that meeting it was already clear that Mussolini would mediate a solution to the Czech crisis by which the Sudetenland would be ceded to Germany without resort to armed intervention. This dramatic development entirely undercut the principal rationale for the coup as it would have been presented to the German population – the prevention of a war – for Mussolini's intervention enabled Hitler to achieve all that he planned for Germany and the Sudeten Germans without the need for any direct military action against Czechoslovakia. Immediately, von Brauchitsch contacted Halder to ensure that orders were issued forestalling any further troop deployments or action against Hitler, and the intended coup simply withered away.

With the benefit of hindsight, one can see that the Halder plot had offered the best chance of dealing with Hitler and forestalling what became World War II. However, despite the application of much analysis, intellectual debate and practical planning by the general staff conspirators and others, they had quite bizarrely developed a plan that depended for its success upon two actions or events, both of which were always beyond their control. The first of these was Hitler ordering an invasion of Czechoslovakia; the second was the British and French governments declaring war or indicating unequivocally their intention to do so. Such a major flaw in its planning process hardly reflected the legendary professionalism of the general staff and undoubtedly indicated the extent to which these matters had moved its activities and thought processes far beyond its more traditional competences. A few days after 28 September, Oberstleutnant Oster and Hans Bernd Gisevius (a former assistant secretary in the ministry of the interior) met with von Witzleben, and together, in what was both a practical and a symbolic act, they burned all of the plans, discussion notes and correspondence relating to the coup, using the general's fireplace to do so.

In fact, as Britain and France had already secured a Czech surrender on the Sudetenland issue, Hitler was able to secure even more extensive concessions at Munich than those he had originally intended. The Munich agreement was drawn up on 29 September 1938 and signed the next day. This agreement was subsequently presented by Chamberlain to the British people as having secured 'peace in our time' – but it actually indicated and confirmed to Hitler the parlous state of British and French preparedness for war compared with that of Germany, and thus made the coming war even more likely. Meanwhile, Hitler's international status and popularity in Germany were enhanced, and his position as a successful statesman and national leader was reinforced. Even within the general staff, Hitler's achievement could not be denied.

However, during the months and weeks of the Czech crisis very many officers had been placed in the position of disclosing to varying degrees their opposition to Hitler. Also, the general staff's warnings of war and pessimism regarding German intervention in Czechoslovakia (albeit without access to, or knowledge of, important matters on the international stage that would certainly have informed their work and assessments) had been shown to be over-cautious, pedantic and obstructive, thus confirming Hitler's long-standing lack of confidence in the general staff and setting the stage for its relations with the Führer when the army commenced all-out hostilities just a year later. Meanwhile, German troops began their occupation of the Sudetenland on 1 October. Then, following further political intriguing and coercion by Hitler during early 1939, the Czech president, Emil Hácha, was forced to invite the Wehrmacht to occupy the rest of his country, and on 15 March the German army completed its occupation of the remainder of Czechoslovakia. In a remarkably short period of time, the principal objectives set out by Hitler at the Hossbach Conference had been achieved and the way prepared for further successes in the future.

The 1938 crisis over Czechoslovakia is rightly perceived by historians to have been one of the defining moments of world history. The consequences of it in due course precipitated and provided yet another step towards the world war in 1939. Nevertheless, in terms of German history and the story of the general staff and the army, historian Walter Görlitz's view that Hitler's position was not yet entirely secure in the late summer and early autumn of 1938 is significant and to some extent balances the Nazi propaganda produced by Goebbels at the time. For the general staff, this was a missed opportunity of historic significance. Görlitz observes that the wider unease over Hitler's publicly declared policies and intentions regarding the Czech issue and the Sudeten Germans had indeed provided the first and last chance that the general staff had of taking effective action against Hitler. Despite several subsequent attempts made during the war, culminating in the 20 July 1944 bomb plot, Hitler's position by autumn 1938 was generally unassailable, while the power of the Gestapo and the SS would ensure that it continued to be so. That power had been further increased in August 1938 when Hitler formalized the special position of the police and various SS units and formations (including the Leibstandarte SS 'Adolf Hitler'), removing them from military control and providing the Waffen-SS with a status that placed it alongside the army, navy and air force, but maintaining (via Himmler) his personal control of these forces rather than incorporating them into the Wehrmacht. Once it became plain to all that Hitler had brought the Sudeten Germans into the Fatherland and that his policies regarding Czechoslovakia would not result in war, the general staff had lost what would arguably prove to have been its best and only chance to mobilize the mass of the German population, in common cause with the army, against Hitler and the Nazis.

Meanwhile, having initially built up the power of the OKW, Hitler's adoption of a system of personal adjutants (the principal of whom was Oberstleutnant Rudolf Schmundt) in 1937 resulted in a gradual reduction of the OKW's influence as Hitler increasingly 'short-circuited' the formal chain of command via these powerful and influential Wehrmachtadjutanten, all of whom were particularly loyal to the Führer. Just two weeks after the occupation of the Sudetenland, Hitler directed the OKW that as a matter of policy the general staff would no longer have any role in political decision-making; neither would any dissenting or critical views submitted in writing by members of the general staff be accepted in the future. This directive ended working practices and traditions that had been followed by the general staff for at least a century.

It also ended the concept of joint responsibility, whereby a commander and his chief of staff shared responsibility for decision-making, but with the chief of staff entitled to submit a critical report through the general staff chain of command if he disagreed with his commander's decision. Now the considerable power that this arrangement had conferred upon chiefs of staff at all levels ever since the days of the Prussian army was removed by Hitler, the commander henceforth bearing absolute responsibility for his decisions and the actions taken by his command. The introduction of these changes by Hitler was intended to prevent in the future any more of the sort of cautionary and negative papers that the general staff and individual senior officers such as Beck had provided in connection with the Czech crisis. However, the policy was also intended further to weaken the general staff as well as to create a rift between the OKW and OKH.

Although the army general staff had already suffered its own loss of power and influence in the wake of the the creation of the OKW, both organizations now experienced similar effects as Hitler drew his personal authority over the Wehrmacht ever closer, while at the same time the Nazi leadership continued to centralize and extend its direct control over all of the significant institutions of state. Such policies and agendas meant that the revival of the general staff since 1935 had been conducted in the febrile, often unsettling and frequently unpredictable political environment of National Socialist Germany, as well as against a backdrop of accelerating German foreign policy decisions and European events. Nevertheless, despite the growing sense of crisis and the risk of armed conflict that this invited (as perceived and regularly highlighted by the general staff), for most of the German population 1933 to early 1939 had been years of peace, renewal and increasing prosperity and stability (notwithstanding the Wehrmacht's relatively small involvement in Spain's civil war from 1936 and internal incidents such as the Nazi party's action against Ernst Röhm and the SA in 1934). However, in 1939 the general staff and the Wehrmacht would fulfil the role that was their principal raison d'être as Hitler at last pursued his expansionist policies by committing Germany to military action, and Europe to a conflict that would rapidly escalate into a world war.

Soon after his retirement as chief of the general staff in 1938, Generaloberst Beck wrote a paper setting out his personal analysis and assessment of *Germany in a Future War*. Prophetically, he concluded that:

'A war begun by Germany will immediately call into the field other states than the one she has attacked, and in a war against a world coalition she will succumb and for good or evil be put at that coalition's mercy.' However, by 1939 Beck was no longer in a position to influence either Hitler or the high command. Certainly the general staff was made aware of the well-argued but predictable conclusions set out by its former chief, but by 1939 such timely and accurate warnings were of little real consequence to the decision-makers of the Third Reich, already convinced of the intuitive leadership of their Führer by the evidence of Hitler's successful policies in the Rhineland, with the Austrian Anschluß and against Czechoslovakia. Neither could such dissenting or negative views be allowed to distract or divert the high command of an army about to go to war and which was now extensively populated by officers generally supportive of Hitler's strategic policies, many of whom perceived the benefits and opportunities that a war might provide for the rearmed and reinvigorated German army, as well as for their own professional careers. During the late summer of 1939, just two decades after the end of the 'Kaiser's War' in 1918, German soldiers were again on the march. Europe was once more about to become the focus of armed conflict on a grand scale, and World War II was about to begin.

6

At War Again

The Polish Campaign

1939

On 28 April 1939, Hitler addressed the assembled members of the Reichstag at some length, denouncing Britain, the United States and Poland for their joint condemnation of his lack of respect for the rights and liberties of small nations in the aftermath of the Czech affair. His inclusion of Poland in this diatribe was significant, as the German territory lost to the Poles at Versailles – notably that affecting Danzig and East Prussia – was a particularly emotive and long-running issue in Germany. However, Poland's strategic position also provided Hitler with an excuse to act against the country, for, as he had propounded to a meeting of senior officers in April, if Germany went to war against France and Britain the neutrality of Poland could not be guaranteed, posing a threat on Germany's eastern border. This assertion raised the spectre of a war on two fronts, which meant that Poland had to be removed from the strategic equation before France or Britain could intervene on its behalf. In the course of this address, Hitler accepted that a Munich-style negotiated resolution of the Polish problem was not practicable, but that (in his view) a German subjugation of Poland would not result in another world war. In fact, Hitler needed a war against Poland in order to achieve his expansionist and ideological aims, including the acquisition of 'living space' (Lebensraum) for Germany in the east. On 23 May, Hitler disclosed these wider aims to the heads of the Wehrmacht and other senior officials at the chancellery, emphasizing the inevitability of a clash with Britain and France, both of which countries posed significant obstacles to his declared intention of entirely re-ordering the balance of power in Europe. Although Keitel, von

Brauchitsch and the general staff had already received on 3 April Hitler's initial instructions to prepare plans for an attack against Poland, all were unaware of the secret negotiations then in train between Berlin and Moscow and so had seriously doubted the wisdom or strategic feasibility of such a venture unless Russian acquiescence was assured. However, secure in the secret knowledge that a non-aggression pact with Stalin was well and truly in prospect by late May, Hitler confidently directed the general staff's planning for a campaign against Poland to move forward apace.

Preparations for the coming attack against Poland – *Fall Weiß* – continued throughout August 1939, with an accelerated call-up of reservists obscuring what was in all but name a general mobilization within Germany and the deployment of forces towards the Polish border. There was a much greater public awareness of the issues and concerns surrounding the matter of the return of the Free City of Danzig to German control and the arrangements regarding the 'Polish (or 'Danzig) Corridor' than had perhaps been the case with the Sudeten Germans a year earlier. But the apparent imminence of war was again viewed with a degree of trepidation in many parts of the civilian population – despite Nazi propaganda. Fabricated stories about 'Polish atrocities' against German citizens were circulated, and the Nazi leadership developed secret plans to stage a series of contrived border incidents and incursions along the German-Polish border in Upper Silesia. These incidents were to be carried out almost exclusively by SS and Gestapo personnel or their agents, including the Sicherheitsdienst (security service) the 'SD'. This organization was headed by SS-Gruppenführer Reinhard Heydrich, a man who would in due course attract notoriety for his pivotal role in developing the 'Final Solution' for the resolution of the 'Jewish Question' by the Nazis.[68] On 11 August, Hitler declared to Professor Carl Burckhardt, the League of Nations high commissioner in Danzig: 'If there is the slightest provocation, I shall shatter Poland without warning into so many pieces that there will be nothing left to pick up.'[69] Also in August, von Ribbentrop discussed Danzig and Poland with Italian foreign minister Count Ciano, Mussolini's son-in-law, at the von Ribbentrop estate near Salzburg. During that meeting the German foreign minister reportedly stated that in reality Germany wanted neither Danzig nor the Corridor, but that, 'What we want is war.'[70]

Contrary to Hitler's assertion to Burckhardt on 11 August that his generals were enthusiastic for a campaign against Poland, many members of the general staff were somewhat less sanguine about it. They included its head, General Halder, who had even taken steps in June and July to alert the French and British ambassadors to his personal belief that Hitler was convinced that neither France nor Britain would be prepared to go to war to support Poland. Of course, at that stage Halder had not known about the impending German-Soviet non-aggression pact, ratified on 23–4 August. Confident of the lack of Franco-British resolve, and with foreknowledge of Russian neutrality and Moscow's future complicity in the partition of Poland, Hitler announced his plans to implement *Fall Weiß* at a meeting of all Wehrmacht senior commanders at the Obersalzberg on 22 August, setting 26 August as the day on which the invasion would be launched. Meanwhile, on 23 August Jodl was appointed head of the Wehrmachtführungsstab at OKW in Berlin, a move that pre-empted and prevented Halder's aspiration to place General Georg von Sodenstern (an officer whose views were in line with his own) into that key post. Remarkably, the day after Hitler's declaration on 22 August, the Führer ordered a halt to the army's deployment into the Polish border area: this was in light of renewed uncertainty over Britain's intentions and his hope that Britain might yet remain neutral. In separate negotiations, the Polish government had suggested that it was prepared to discuss major concessions, but by late August it had also taken the precaution of mobilizing some two and a half million men for military service (which Hitler represented as proof of Poland's aggressive intentions). However, while Halder and others viewed the order to halt the army's deployment as an indication that war was still not inevitable (evidence also of the general staff's dislocation from and ignorance of the wider international machinations then in progress), Hitler was by then irrevocably committed to carry out *Fall Weiß*. Troop deployments and preparations for the invasion quickly resumed, the initial attack now being set for 30 August; this was finally postponed to 1 September. By the night of 31 August 1939, as many as one and a half million German troops, 2,500 tanks and 10,000 guns were concealed in assembly areas in the villages and woods of East Prussia and elsewhere along

Germany's eastern border. Even now, within the general staff and at some army group headquarters, commanders still chose to believe that *Fall Weiß* was no more than a grand strategic bluff, anticipating until the very last minute that they would receive an order to stand down their troops.

With the German onslaught now imminent, the SD escalated its campaign of border incidents or 'provocations' during the night 31 August / 1 September. Three such incidents were staged by the SD that night, using SS men and a number of coerced concentration camp inmates (selected political prisoners and criminals) in Polish uniforms. These incidents included the seizing by 'Polish rebels' of the radio station in the German border town of Gleiwitz, some 100 kilometres south-east of Breslau, an attack by 'Polish terrorists' on a forestry station at Pitschen, about 75 kilometres to the east of Breslau, and an assault by 'Polish soldiers and rebels' against the German custom post at Hochlinden, about 20 kilometres south of Gleiwitz. Although these 'attacks' lacked finesse and displayed a certain amount of disorder, they generally achieved the aim of providing 'evidence' of Polish warlike intentions and a final excuse for Germany to launch its invasion. Any fall-out from exposure of the fabricated nature of these incidents on the night 31 August / 1 September was quickly overtaken by the onset of general hostilities.[71]

Fall Weiß: The Invasion

At dawn on 1 September, two German army groups crossed the border, supported by the concentrated fire of 10,000 artillery guns and an overwhelming amount of close air support provided by the Luftwaffe. The armoured units with their 2,500 tanks quickly lanced through the Polish border defences and roared on into Poland and towards Warsaw. Infantry divisions provided the follow-on forces, moving behind the panzer and motorized units, albeit and unavoidably at a much slower rate of advance. The panzer spearhead was crucial to the army's success. Its four light divisions, seven panzer divisions and four motorized divisions caused havoc as they speedily broke through the thinly-spread Polish defence forces – even though these forces comprised some thirty infantry divisions, one understrength tank division, one cavalry division and eleven cavalry brigades, supported by 475 tanks and 2,800 artillery pieces, manning well-established fixed fortifications and sheltered by several major river obstacles.[72] Behind the leading German armoured divisions came no fewer than forty infantry divisions and one cavalry brigade. Fourth and Third Armies of Army Group North struck from Pomerania and East Prussia, while Eighth, Tenth and Fourteenth Armies of Army Group South surged north-east from Slovakia and Silesia towards Warsaw and eastwards towards Lvov (Lemberg). In the meantime, on Germany's western border, the West Wall defences were occupied by reserve, second-line and Landwehr units to counter any armed response to the invasion by France or Britain. On 3 September both countries formally declared war on Germany. These events demonstrated all too clearly the dominance of Hitler's political and strategic ambitions over the assessments and consequent warnings that had been developed and propounded by the general staff and a succession of senior army officers during the 1930s. None the less, the plan of attack for *Fall Weiß* had of course been produced by that same general staff.

As the battle in Poland progressed, XIX Army Corps, now commanded by General Heinz Guderian, was in the van of Fourth Army's assault against the heavily fortified zone to the south of Danzig. This army was commanded by General Hans Günther von Kluge. The tanks advanced echeloned in waves, attacking on a frontage no greater than 5,000 metres, while Stuka dive-bombers and artillery bombarded the Polish positions ahead of the panzer units and to their flanks. In many places the panzers rolled through close terrain that the Poles had believed impassable for armoured forces. In more open country, the run of dry weather had produced ideal ground conditions for the German vehicles. Motorized infantry moved behind the tanks, ready to deal with any well-defended anti-tank positions or strongpoints blocking the way ahead that could not be by-passed. During these early engagements, Guderian directed his corps from a command tank at the forefront of the action, frequently coming under direct Polish fire and, on at least one occasion, fire from his own artillery as well. Initially the panzer forces suffered significant losses at the hands of the Polish anti-tank gunners. This was due largely to the relative inexperience of the German commanders now dealing with the unprecedented speed, scale and all-arms nature (including close air support) of this new sort of combat. However, the attacking forces learned fast, and by 5 September the Danzig Corridor was in German hands. Polish resistance was crumbling everywhere, and Fourth and Third Armies (the latter commanded by General Georg von Küchler) had linked up in East Prussia.

Meanwhile, in the south, the armoured divisions of the three armies of Army Group South, commanded by General Gerd von Rundstedt and his chief of staff Generalleutnant Erich von Manstein, thrust rapidly past Lodz and on in the direction of Warsaw, and farther south passing Krakow (Crakow) and then on towards the River Vistula, beyond which lay Lvov and the River Bug. The Polish forces were split, those in Warsaw cut off by the advance of Generaloberst Walther von Reichenau's Tenth Army while the Polish forces in the south had little option but to capitulate to Fourteenth Army, commanded by Generaloberst Siegmund Wilhelm List. Everywhere the Polish defences were breaking down, large numbers of shocked troops surrendering as their defences simply collapsed when faced by the sheer speed, concentrated force and overwhelming firepower of the German invaders. In the meantime, with its initial objectives achieved, Third Army advanced on Warsaw from the north while Guderian's XIX Corps of Fourth Army now struck south towards Brest-Litovsk to the east of the River Bug, and even more deeply into Polish territory.

Only to the west of Warsaw were the Poles able to launch a counterstroke. There, on 9 September, the Poznan Army, supported by the residue of the Pomorz Army to its north, struck the flank guard of General Johannes Blaskowitz's Eighth Army. This attack came just as the Germans were focused primarily upon the bombardment and capture of Warsaw, where the 4th Panzer Division had already that day experienced the limitations of armour in built-up areas, losing 57 of 120 tanks engaged during three hours of hard fighting. At the same time, von Reichenau's Tenth Army had outrun its supply lines and was short of fuel. In this area, the Poles initially achieved some successes against the German infantry divisions. However, the timely redeployment of 1st and 4th Panzer Divisions from the Vistula and Warsaw, together with German forces from the north-west, quickly enveloped and routed the Poznan Army. By the evening of 15

September the Polish counterstroke had been effectively neutralized by a combination of German air attacks, artillery fire and the attacking panzer divisions. It was during the fighting for Warsaw on 22 September that Generaloberst von Fritsch, the former commander-in-chief of the army forced to resign in 1938 but who had subsequently been recalled to active duty a year later, fell on the battlefield. Elsewhere, on 14 September, Guderian's two panzer divisions and one motorized infantry division had successfully encircled the strategically important communications hub of Brest-Litovsk. That city capitulated on 17 September, while Warsaw fell on 27 September, with the last Polish resistance ending at Kock on 6 October. By then, although France and Great Britain had declared war on Germany, there was no sign of an imminent threat from the west, France already having failed to make good a promise to support Poland with an attack into western Germany on 17 September. At the same time, large numbers of Red Army troops had occupied much of eastern Poland.

The precise timing and extent of the Russian intervention came as something of a surprise to the general staff as well as to Halder and von Brauchitsch, both of whom had advised Hitler that the bombardment of Warsaw he had ordered was an unnecessary distraction, as the Polish capital would soon be forced to surrender in any case. However, having made secret arrangements with the Russians, Hitler needed to bring about the city's fall as soon as practicable in order to avoid it falling to the Russian forces then advancing into Poland from the east. Given the potential impact of the Russian intervention upon German ground operations and the need to prevent conflict between the Russian and German forces, the fact that neither the German army commander nor the chief of the general staff had been forewarned of this was remarkable – although unsurprising in the light of Hitler's relationship with his generals.

For these generals, and indeed most general staff officers, the fact that a full-scale war was now in progress accentuated the dilemma and growing crisis of conscience concerning their honour, duty and loyalty to the Führer as head of state at a time when that which Hitler required of them ran contrary to their perception of the best interests of Germany. Certainly the true implications of the soldier's oath introduced in 1934, demanding absolute loyalty and unquestioning obedience to Adolf Hitler personally, were now all too evident. While Germany was still at peace, the doubts or dissent of many army officers could more or less be accommodated and alleviated by offering constructive professional advice – including the several attempts by the general staff to dissuade Hitler from embarking upon a war (at least, not before 1943). However, on 1 September 1939 it was abundantly clear that all such persuasive action had failed. Consequently, a great deal of soul-searching took place, necessarily leavened by a considerable amount of pragmatism. For many of the younger and more junior officers, Hitler already represented the very embodiment of the Fatherland of which he was the leader; indeed, this was a concept that he had time and again stated in his speeches since becoming Führer. For such officers, loyalty to Hitler and the rightness of the war against Poland to regain Danzig, together with the other territories to the east lost after World War I and the acquisition of what was seen as the necessary 'Lebensraum' ('living space') now required by Germany, posed little or no problem of conscience. Their obligation of obedience to Hitler was now perceived to be indivisible from their duty to Germany. Their loyalty was based upon an unquestioning assumption that Hitler invariably knew what was best for Germany and would always place the interests of the Fatherland before any less altruistic agenda or priorities.

For those officers who in former times had sworn an oath, not to an elected politician, but to an hereditary monarch, the Fatherland and its people, the new situation that obtained from September 1939 raised some difficult questions. Now it might be argued that the emerging policies and orders of the head of state were at odds with the best interests and security of the state. The wording of the soldier's oath was unequivocal; the obligations that it conferred were sacrosanct; and for men whose military service had always been governed by a strict culture of duty, honour, loyalty and obedience, there was really little alternative but to carry out the orders and directives issued by the Führer and the Nazi government, however unpalatable or perverse these might be. Neither was resignation an option. Even if that had been permissible, for a German officer to resign on a matter of conscience was unthinkable in wartime: it would have been an abrogation of his duty and therefore contrary to the oath he had sworn.

The significance and power of the soldier's oath of 1934 for all those who served in the Wehrmacht (but for the officer corps especially) might be questioned by a modern reader in an age where patriotism and duty to one's country and the use of armed force by states are increasingly and widely scrutinized and questioned by all sorts of groups and individuals. But in 1930s Germany the practical effect of the oath stemmed from a military heritage developed over almost three centuries, based first upon that of the army of Brandenburg-Prussia, then of Prussia and finally of imperial Germany. For the good German soldier, when all about him was chaos, the overriding thought that might guide and sustain him was his duty of loyalty and obedience, as set out in the oath. Irrespective of whether he lived or died, if he carried out his orders to the best of his ability then his duty was done and his honour secured. Humanitarian, legalistic or other extraneous considerations were largely irrelevant. No matter how technologically advanced or modernized the army of the Third Reich might have been, this concept remained fundamental to the way in which its officers and soldiers had conducted themselves in peace and were now required to do in war. Little wonder, then, that many of the German officers charged with war crimes and eventually arraigned at Nuremberg after the war based their defence upon the fact that they were simply carrying out orders. If such a defence had been accepted, this would have meant that the only indictable and truly culpable German war criminal would have been Adolf Hitler himself. This goes some way towards explaining the genuine surprise of these officers when a concept and safeguard that lay at the very heart of their understanding of military service was rejected by the Allied prosecutors and judges at Nuremberg. In 1939 such considerations were, of course, still very much matters for the future.

In September 1939 the army's officer corps fell very broadly into three groups. There were those who accepted Hitler's leadership and policies without question. Then there were those who were already convinced that a war begun at that time could not be won, but who would none the less do their duty as loyal German officers irrespective of the inevitability of defeat. Former chief of the general staff Generaloberst Beck was one such officer. Finally, there were those who would continue to do their duty but who would become increasingly concerned and disillusioned by the Nazis' ideologically based policies and actions as these impinged more and more upon the army's operations. For these men the dilemma and their agonizing over how to deal with it was perhaps the greatest, eventually prompting some to adopt dangerous and extreme courses of action during the years ahead. In any event, soon after the army had occupied its part of Poland in strength, this first campaign of the war provided the first indications of such concerns and a foretaste of more troubling events yet to come. It also highlighted and fuelled the growing rift between the army and the SS, and therefore between the general staff and the head of the SS, Heinrich Himmler.

Fall Weiß: The Aftermath

As soon as the Polish campaign was concluded, an organization was put in place to administer the territory now under German control. This included the areas that had been German before World War I, which were incorporated directly into 'Greater Germany' as sovereign territory, while the remaining land was designated as the Generalgouvernement (General Government [of Poland]), under the control of Hans Frank and the Austrian Artur Seyss-Inquart, who were charged with imposing Nazi ethnic and ideological policies and agendas upon the defeated Poles. The Russian forces continued to occupy their part of Poland, a demarcation line being established between these troops and the German occupiers. The army established a military authority, headed by Generaloberst Blaskowitz, to control the Polish territories as soon as the campaign ended, but this body's authority was quickly supplanted by the Generalgouvernement. Certainly the army had been wary of the presence and activities of the very few Waffen-SS units that had participated in the Polish campaign. The three Waffen-SS infantry regiments (Leibstandarte, Germania and Deutschland), an artillery regiment and an armoured reconnaissance battalion that were involved had all been incorporated within, and under the command of, army formations. These Waffen-SS units achieved little of military consequence in Poland. Their casualties were quite high, a fact that army officers attributed to their poor leadership and training – Himmler's response was to blame the army for failing to support his Waffen-SS units adequately. However, if the army was critical of the professional performance of the Waffen-SS in combat, it viewed the activities and excesses of the SS and SS-controlled police units in Poland, and against its Jewish population, with extreme distaste. General Blaskowitz – still the military commander but now subordinated to the head of the Generalgouvernement – prepared a detailed report on these excesses, including the deliberate persecution of the Polish Jews, the country's intelligentsia and governing class. This report followed a period during which a number of SS men in Poland had been arraigned by army courts and condemned to death for carrying out acts of murder, rape and arson. At the same time, various senior army officers in the occupied territories clashed with Gauleiters and other civilian officials and local police commanders over the oppressive policies that these Nazi officials were now implementing or condoning. Blaskowitz's report was apparently never forwarded for action, but both Hitler and Jodl were aware of its existence and general content. They viewed it as little more than an irritation and an irrelevance, typical of what Hitler opined to von Brauchitsch was the army's 'outmoded conception of chivalry'.[73] None the less, in the aftermath of the Polish campaign Himmler managed to turn army criticism of the SS to his advantage by citing any perceived failings of the Waffen-SS in combat as the justification for significantly improving its training and resources, as well as progressively increasing its size. Predictably, Hitler supported this expansion of what was in practice the Nazi party's private army. The growing power of the Waffen-SS dissipated the finite amounts of military manpower and resources available to the armed forces – inevitably to the detriment of the Wehrmacht (but primarily the army) in the years ahead, thus creating considerable practical difficulties for the OKH and the general staff.

One example of the very different perceptions by the army and the SS, and consequently of the sort of friction that was already arising between these two organizations, occurred some time after the Polish campaign, when Himmler reportedly published a decree to the effect that it was the duty of married women whose husbands were away serving in the field 'not to deny themselves to members of the SS'. Accordingly to the SS leader, this bizarre suggestion was to compensate for the 'blood-letting' and 'dissipation of the best blood' in the course of hostilities. When this policy proposal was made known at least one army divisional commander protested by immediately refusing to serve any longer. For this he was imprisoned and condemned to death, but – following the vigorous intervention of his army group commander, Generaloberst von Leeb – this senior officer was later released, and the SS decree was withdrawn.[74]

For the army and the general staff basking in the success of the Wehrmacht's resounding victory in Poland, the validity of the 'lightning war' or Blitzkrieg concept had generally been proved, while those who had counselled against *Fall Weiß* had been shown to be over-cautious and lacking in imagination. Overall, the panzer forces had performed well, with no more than 25 per cent of their tanks out of action due to mechanical problems at any one time. Of the 217 tanks destroyed by enemy action, these were mainly the light tanks that had been successfully engaged by Polish anti-tank guns. Few significant tank-versus-tank actions had taken place during the campaign. The general staff was very aware that the panzer units had relied extensively upon their holdings of Czech and light tanks, underlining the need to speed up the production of the more capable Pz.Kpfw.III and IV models. The campaign had confirmed that the best mix of divisions in a panzer corps was two panzer divisions and one motorized infantry division, all with integral supporting arms and tank and infantry sub-groupings. The role of the Luftwaffe had also been critical. Air-to-ground cooperation and support had worked well, but it could be improved further, especially the techniques employed for the close support of ground formations directly engaged with the enemy. Meanwhile, the Wehrmacht's victory reinforced a growing international perception of German military invincibility and the view within the country that Hitler's judgement and strategic acumen were indeed infallible. However, the general staff also acknowledged that this new form of war-fighting carried with it its own difficulties and new challenges, and that it was now necessary to analyse and rectify faults as a matter of urgency; command and control, logistic resources and training all needed attention. In anticipation of the strategic and operational focus now switching to the Western Front, the general staff embarked upon the work required to ready the army for its next campaign.

e murder of General Kurt von Schleicher, former minister for the Reichswehr, by the SS
ortly after 30 June 1934 was noteworthy for the lack of condemnation it attracted from the
rmy high command and general staff officers. Von Schleicher is pictured (left) with
neralfeldmarschall Gerd von Rundstedt in November 1932.

Despite the increasing mechanization of the Wehrmacht, the use of horses was widesprea throughout the army both before and during the war. Here general staff officers under training at the Berlin Kriegsakademie in 1935 are engaged in a lesson at the academy's riding school. Prior to the war, every general staff officer would routinely be expected to k able to ride a horse.

General staff officers under training at the Berlin Kriegsakademie, 4 November 1935. Classroom instruction was inevitably a significant part of the general staff training course.

ne gateway to a potentially glittering military career: the old Berlin Kriegsakademie located
Wilhelmstraße/Dorotheen-straße/Unter den Linden, 1935. This building hosted general
aff training courses for generations of Prussian and German officers from the beginning of
e nineteenth century until 1919, when this was prohibited by the Treaty of Versailles. The
ew Kriegsakademie in the Moabit district eventually fulfilled this role when unconstrained
eneral staff training resumed after 1935.

Map studies and the development of operational plans based both on these studies and on actual ground reconnaissance were core elements of the general staff training course at the Berlin Kriegsakademie. These general staff officers are shown carrying out such training on 4 November 1935.

The Berlin Kriegsakademie in Kruppstraße, Moabit district, 19 March 1938. Within this new building the wartime general staff training courses were conducted until the intensity of the Allied bombing of Berlin necessitated their relocation to Hirschberg, in the Sudetenland mountains of Silesia, during 1944.

eraloberst Walther von
chenau, then commanding
th Army, and General-
tnant Friedrich Paulus
iew the plans for the
asion of Poland, September
39. Von Reichenau was a
npetent commander and a
ong supporter of Hitler's
gressive strategy. Paulus
uld later be a principal
neral staff planner of
eration *Barbarossa* but
sequently commanded the
ated Sixth Army when it
s defeated at Stalingrad in
43.

ler with the principal Wehrmacht, SS and NSDAP staff of Führerhauptquartier
fschanze, June 1940. The members of this powerful core of political, military and
amilitary personnel pursued numerous agendas and personal rivalries, which frequently
strated the work of the general staff and the army high command. Shown (left to right)
: SA-Obergruppenführer Helmut Brückner; OKH-Adjutant Major Engel; Reich Press Chief
Otto Dietrich; Hitler's personal doctor and Führerhauptquartier doctor, Dr. Karl Brandt;
ad of the OKW, Generaloberst Wilhelm Keitel; Luftwaffe Adjutant Generalmajor
lenschatz; Adolf Hitler; Wehrmacht Adjutant Oberst Rudolf Schmundt; SS-Adjutant SS-
ppenführer Julius Schaub; Head of Wehrmacht Operations Branch of the OKW, General
red Jodl; Adjutant to Himmler and SS liaison officer to the Führerhauptquartier SS-
ppenführer Karl Wolff; NSDAP Leader Reichsleiter Martin Bormann; Hitler's personal
sician, Prof. Dr. Theo Morell; OKW-Adjutant Hauptmann von Below; and the official
otographer to Hitler and the NSDAP, Heinrich Hoffmann.

The general staff relied upon the 'Enigma' encoding system to transmit top-secret orders and directives, unaware that the Allies were able to intercept and read these messages. Here General Guderian's field headquarters staff are using an 'Enigma' machine mounted in the General's Sd.Kfz.251/3 armoured command and communications vehicle in France, June 1940.

order to support their commanders effectively, general staff officers in Panzer formations
 itinely operated from armoured vehicles and forward command posts. Here, General
derian (in his Sd.Kfz.251/3 command vehicle) is in discussion with General Adolf Kuntzen,
mmander of the 8th Panzer Division, in France, May/June 1940.

neralmajor Ferdinand Neuling (second right), commanding the 239th Infantry Division,
h members of his staff at Mulhouse, Alsace-Lorraine, 19 June 1940. Note the (carmine-
oured) general staff distinguishing stripes just visible on the riding breeches of the staff
icer standing to the left of General Neuling.

During a visit to the OKH in late 1940 or early 1941, Hitler discusses future operations with (left to right) Generalfeldmarschall Keitel, Generalfeldmarschall von Brauchitsch and Generaloberst Halder. At that time, Hitler had not yet assumed direct command of the army from von Brauchitsch.

During the early days of *Barbarossa* in Russia, summer 1941, Generalfeldmarschall Fedor v Bock, Generaloberst Hermann Hoth and Luftwaffe General Wolfram Freiherr von Richthofe consider the future tasks for Army Group Centre and Panzer Group 3, and the necessary air support. The original OKH aspiration for this army group to drive on to seize Moscow was frustrated by Hitler's conflicting strategic priorities.

During the four-week Polish campaign it had quickly become clear that the high command, always geographically well separated from the fighting army groups, had failed fully to appreciate the speed with which the new armoured formations now moved and the scale of technical support and resources these forces required to maintain their momentum. Also, the disconnect that frequently occurred between the well-armoured tanks and their supporting, but largely unprotected, motorized infantry had to be resolved. Any physical separation of the infantry from the tanks could at best slow down the advance and at worst leave either arm isolated and vulnerable to enemy action. Meanwhile, logistics – especially the provision of sufficient fuel – was correctly identified as another major issue. These matters were speedily addressed and largely resolved as training was modified and as organizational, equipment and technological changes were made. Even so, the problem of ensuring adequate resupply would continue to hamper the general staff's aspirations and limit the true potential of the German armoured forces in the coming campaigns as, time and again, they exhausted or outran their logistic support. This persisting problem also tended to support the pre-war contention of Generaloberst Beck and others that Germany was inadequately prepared for war in 1939 – certainly the Wehrmacht was ill-prepared for what would eventually become a war of attrition.

The army's many non-motorized infantry divisions – moving on foot and with horse-drawn artillery and other transport – were unable to match the tempo of the armoured divisions, and this was also reflected in the sometimes pedestrian and unimaginative style of command displayed by a number of infantry commanders. Indeed, the high level of casualties amongst regular infantry officers reflected the extent to which the troops in some of these units had needed to be motivated by the personal example of these officers on the battlefield. One of the principal lessons of the Polish campaign was that the army would need considerably more armoured divisions in the future. In the rush to create these in later years, the pursuit of quantity would eventually be at the expense of quality. Indeed, in light of Germany's inability to achieve a full, motorized capability for the army, large numbers of horses would of necessity continue to be widely used for support and transportation tasks throughout the war. Meanwhile the rapid and bloody demise of the Polish cavalry units early in the campaign demonstrated all too clearly that the use of mounted cavalry for offensive action in a modern war was no longer a serious option.

With the end of the campaign in Poland, all eyes now turned westwards. France was in the process of deploying no fewer than 92 divisions along the Maginot Line and in reserve in northern France, while a British Expeditionary Force (BEF) totalling ten divisions had arrived in France and moved east to take its place in the Anglo-French defensive line by 12 October. At first, these substantial forces faced no more than some 33 relatively weak German divisions, constituting First, Fifth and Seventh Armies, under the overall command of Generaloberst Wilhelm Ritter von Leeb. With an apparent stalemate in prospect in the west, cautionary voices once again began to be heard from the general staff and the army high command. These officers were especially concerned about the physical strength of the Maginot Line fortifications and the sheer size and capability of the French army (its combat effectiveness, morale and motivation would in due course prove to have been considerably overestimated). On this matter the general staff and the OKW's Wehrmachtführungsstab were broadly in agreement.

In fact, abundant evidence of the French high command's lack of resolve had already been provided by its failure to order any meaningful attack to relieve pressure on Poland. Limited forays into the Saar and Moselle areas during September and October hardly qualified, and in any case all of these forces had withdrawn into the Maginot Line by the end of October. This so-called 'Saar offensive' cost the French no more than 27 dead, 22 wounded and 28 men missing, and left the Germans free to follow-up and reoccupy all of the ground so briefly vacated by them. Despite the French reticence to engage in offensive operations, the scale of the Anglo-French defensive deployment was significant. Consequently, as one of the army's foremost defensive strategists and intellectual thinkers, von Leeb was firmly of the opinion that a new German offensive in the west defied military logic, while he also predicted in October 1939 that the adoption of any plan that violated Belgian or Dutch neutrality would invite worldwide condemnation and armed action against Germany. Prophetically, in a report provided to von Brauchitsch advocating adoption of a defensive posture, von Leeb also suggested that any widening of the war would inevitably precipitate American involvement at some stage – which by implication would be directed against Germany. Halder and von Brauchitsch, although now of the view that the onset of war meant their obligation to Hitler more or less coincided with their duty to Germany and the army (and that therefore their consciences were clear), both held similar views to those of von Leeb. Consequently they resolved to promote a defensive rather than an offensive strategy in the coming months, this providing a backdrop to what they considered would be a period of diplomatic negotiations with the French and British. Von Leeb's report coincided with one produced by the general staff under the auspices of Generalmajor Karl-Heinrich Graf von Stülpnagel, who at that time was Oberquartiermeister I. A gifted officer, von Stülpnagel was a confidante of both Halder and Beck and, as early as the end of 1939 (the success of the Polish campaign notwithstanding) he stated to another officer, 'The people in the Reich government are all criminals. It's high time to put an end to their activities.'[75] Yet again, the apparent extent and level of opposition to Hitler within the general staff and the high command at such an early stage of the war is striking. The bizarre situation of officers openly critical of Hitler continuing to hold key command positions is illustrated by the case of General Erwin von Witzleben, who in autumn 1939 commanded First Army as part of von Leeb's army group. This was the very same officer whose designated task had been to take control of the government sector of Berlin and arrest Hitler in September 1938 had von Brauchitsch and Halder not been forced to abandon the army's intended coup in light of the last-minute Munich agreement on the 28th of that month. There was thus a general consensus within the army's high command and principal army group commanders favouring the von Brauchitsch and Halder approach.

On 9 October, Hitler issued *Directive No. 6*. This document was the first version of his orders for a campaign against Belgium and Holland, pursuant to defeating the French army and BEF and seizing an area of the Channel coast from which to launch air and maritime operations against Britain. Accordingly, the general staff found itself actively preparing plans for a new offensive in the west, all too aware that this strategy was opposed by, and contrary to the advice of, the army high command that it served; indeed, many of its own staff believed it to be ill-conceived. In preparation for the offensive, units were deployed from the East to join those facing the Anglo-French forces and to the Belgian and Dutch frontiers. Three army groups were created by the end of November. In due course, Generaloberst Karl Rudolf Gerd von Rundstedt was appointed to command Army Group A, with Generalleutnant von Manstein as chief of staff. Army Group B was commanded by Generaloberst Fedor von Bock with Generalleutnant Hans von Salmuth as chief of staff. Finally, the commander of Army Group C was Generaloberst Wilhelm Ritter von Leeb, who had until then been in overall command of the German defensive forces on the Western Front.

Somewhat unimaginatively, the first plan that the general staff produced in response to *Directive No. 6* broadly adhered to the old Schlieffen Plan that the imperial army had adopted in 1914. It might be argued that this rather traditional approach reflected the general staff's lack of enthusiasm for the enterprise, especially as the French commander-in-chief had already placed much of his army's strength on the Belgian frontier in anticipation of a re-run of the August 1914 campaign. A view that France's Maginot defensive line was all but impregnable was widely held within the general staff – a position further strengthened by assessments that had grossly overstated the quality and fighting spirit of the French army. In any event, in the general staff's first plan for the *Fall Gelb* ('Case Yellow') offensive, Army Groups A and B were together to conduct a major thrust into northern France through neutral Belgium, destroying the Anglo-French forces north of the Somme and then advancing speedily to the Channel coast. Other forces would screen and secure the right flank, carrying out limited incursions across the border into the Netherlands if necessary. In the north, Army Group B consisted of three armies that included eight panzer and four motorized divisions, while in the centre Army Group A had two armies under its command but with only a single panzer division. In the meantime, in the south, Army Group C was to maintain a primarily defensive posture with two armies along a line from the Ardennes to the Swiss border, thus forcing the French to maintain large numbers of troops in the Maginot Line fortifications. The OKH operational reserve constituted some nine divisions, including one panzer division.[76] Dutch neutrality was to be respected if practicable, with the likely passage of German troops through Dutch territory achieved through negotiation if possible, although the possible need to launch a subsidiary offensive against the Netherlands was also well recognized. All units were to be in position by 5 November, and the attack was to be launched on the 12th.

The onset of particularly bad weather that autumn soon indicated that Hitler's original intention to strike in the west straight after the success in Poland was no longer achievable. Consequently, and with winter fast approaching, the senior commanders who would be required to carry out *Fall Gelb* had time to consider the general staff's plan in detail and to modify and refine it. At the same time, those army officers and prominent civilians within Germany who still had considerable reservations about Hitler's strategy against France and Britain viewed this enforced delay as a welcome opportunity both to avoid widening the war and to revive the debate about ways in which Hitler and the Nazis might be displaced, thus avoiding what they firmly believed would be a disastrous conflict while simultaneously safeguarding the honour and political integrity of the Fatherland.

However, the months between the victory in Poland and an offensive in the west would also provide Hitler with an opportunity to increase his personal control of the army through the progressive marginalization of Halder and von Brauchitsch. This further reduction of the authority of the OKH and the general staff was offset by the growing influence of the OKW, and therefore that of Generals Keitel and Jodl, both of whom had by now placed their own fortunes irrevocably into Hitler's hands. As a result, during the months between October 1939 and spring 1940, the strategic direction of German operations would be brought even more closely under the control of Hitler and his favoured generals at OKW. In just a few years the system of military command and control that had existed in Germany since the mid-nineteenth century and up to 1918, with the army's direction firmly in the hands of the general staff, was changing irrevocably, as operational authority over both that force and the whole of the Wehrmacht became more and more centralized and focused directly upon the Führer.

7

Blitzkrieg

The Defeat of France

1940

In practice, the three army group commanders were right to express reservations about the general staff's first version of the *Fall Gelb* plan when it was produced in October 1939. Quite apart from any concerns over the wider international implications of the offensive and the breaching of Belgian neutrality, the presence of some of the strongest Anglo-French forces – specifically Seventh, First and Ninth French Armies and the BEF – along the Belgian frontier between the Channel coast and the Ardennes would have forced the German Army Groups A and B into a major battle that they might well not have won. The predictability of this approach would also have denied the Germans the advantage of surprise, while the ground in that area was also less than ideal for the army's new panzer forces to be employed to best effect. Although a purely quantitative analysis of relative strengths indicated that the OKH plan was at best somewhat risky, the much better training, morale and operational concepts of the Germans might yet have won the day against the more numerous Anglo-French armies, despite the relatively large numbers of tanks (including the new Somua and 'B' types) available to these forces. At the same time it hardly played to two of the army's particular strengths – the armoured mobility of its panzer forces and their ability to conduct Blitzkrieg operations. As the intended date for launching *Fall Gelb* – 12 November – drew closer, other plans were advanced and debated. Foremost amongst these was a proposal by Generalleutnant von Manstein that the main armoured thrust – a sweeping 'Sichelschnitt' (sickle cut) attack launched in response to an assumed pre-emptive French offensive – should be through the Ardennes towards Sedan. This could achieve a considerable degree of surprise while also striking the French at a weak point in their defensive line and avoiding the need to violate Belgian neutrality. Once Sedan was reached, the open country beyond would enable the sort of enveloping and breakout operations for which the panzer divisions had been created. Anything that avoided an incursion into Belgium was widely viewed as preferable to the original plan, not only within the OKH but even by some officers within the OKW. One such was Generalmajor Walter Warlimont, a senior staff officer and close colleague of Jodl in the Wehrmachtführungsstab who in 1937 had been instrumental in proposing the concept of a Wehrmacht reorganized under one staff organization and a single supreme commander. Ever loyal to his Führer, Warlimont retained Hitler's trust throughout the war, but on this particular matter even this senior staff officer had misgivings. Despite (or possibly because of) its innovative nature, the general staff's initial response to von Manstein's proposals was lukewarm.

Elsewhere, as the 12 November deadline drew closer, some officers in the general staff resurrected the idea of an army coup against the Nazi government. Once again plans were discussed for infantry and armoured forces to move against Berlin, and Halder even moved the conspiracy forward to the extent of creating a planning staff for such action, headed by military intelligence staff officer Oberstleutnant Helmuth Grosscurth. It was intended that Generaloberst Beck should assume overall command of the Wehrmacht once the coup had taken place. In parallel with this plotting within the general staff, prominent diplomatic, political and other influential civilian figures who had been aware of the earlier conspiracies were briefed on the new plan, and a shadow government-in-waiting was once again formed. However, by late October 1939 not all senior army officers were convinced of the wisdom or viability of such action. One such was Generaloberst Friedrich Fromm, commander of the Ersatzheer. Although sympathetic to the aims of the conspiracy, Fromm advised that events had moved on significantly and that the army was now more likely to follow Hitler than to support a coup led by their generals. Despite this, Halder judged that a demonstration of opposition to Hitler by the army would at the very least add weight to the strategic arguments against a new offensive in the west, irrespective of the actual outcome of a coup. In hindsight, Halder's continued misunderstanding of the true nature and obsessive determination of the Führer was quite remarkable, as was his naïve lack of awareness of the real and growing peril to all involved in any such conspiracy within Nazi-controlled Germany. For his part, von Brauchitsch, once again aware of the plans being laid for this new move against Hitler, indicated that he was content to let matters take their course.

On 5 November, with all preparations for *Fall Gelb* virtually complete, von Brauchitsch, as army commander-in-chief, took a final opportunity to brief Hitler on his continuing concerns about the offensive, the potential success of which had by then been further prejudiced by the rapidly deteriorating weather. Hitler lost his temper, and in the course of accusing the generals of resisting his plans he implied or gave the impression to von Brauchitsch that he knew of the conspiracy. Before storming out of the meeting, Hitler referred to the 'spirit of Zossen' (i.e., the general staff and the OKH headquarters at Zossen-Wünsdorf) of which he was well aware and would soon destroy.[77] Hitler's 'spirit of Zossen' reference struck a significant chord with von Brauchitsch, just as it did later that afternoon when he recounted the story of the briefing to Halder. Understandably, both officers feared that the coup itself had been discovered, and on Halder's return to the OKH he ordered all documents and correspondence relating to the coup destroyed immediately. This was premature: there is no evidence that Hitler was in fact aware of the planned coup, but he was all too aware of the ongoing resistance to the offensive. Von Brauchitsch, not unreasonably, assumed the worst and alerted all those involved. As a result, all further preparations for the coup were abandoned forthwith.

In practice, this was probably fortuitous, for the victory in Poland, closely following Hitler's successes in Austria and Czechoslovakia in 1938, undoubtedly reinforced the validity of Generaloberst Fromm's cautionary advice concerning the levels of popular support for Hitler that by then existed within the wider army and the country as a whole. Whatever the outcome of a coup might have been, it was now becoming ever more difficult for the army high command and the general staff, having failed to act decisively before the war, to rectify a situation that they had in large part enabled by their acquiescence in the rise of Hitler and the Nazis in the pre-war years. In the meantime, von Brauchitsch judged that an offensive in the west was now inevitable: although he was no longer prepared to try to prevent it, he indicated, he would not oppose anyone else who wished to try and do so. Later on 5 November in the afternoon, the anticipated order to commence the offensive in the west on 12 November was received by the OKH. Where the general staff's arguments had failed, however, the weather finally succeeded, and on 7 November the attack scheduled for the 12th was postponed by Hitler, first to the 15th, then to the 19th and finally to 22 November. These postponements further reduced (albeit temporarily) the impetus for any action against Hitler, as several senior officers within the general staff, including Halder, von Leeb, von Stülpnagel and Georg Thomas, acknowledged the new realities of the situation produced by an impending war against France and Britain in the west. Mid-November 1939 was the point at which the uncomfortable truth – that the general staff had all but lost its traditional ability to influence the course of strategic events in Germany – at last began to be understood by these and other officers. At the same time there was a belated but increasing awareness of the true nature of the politically volatile, unpredictable and populist form of Nazi government that was now systematically widening its power base and imposing its perverse ideology throughout the country.

Meanwhile some individuals within and beyond the military resistance movement remained determined to deal more directly with Hitler, and, while the issues about the new offensive were under discussion, the Führer avoided one actual attempt on his life and a second that was aborted. On the evening of 8 November, Hitler delivered a speech at the Bürgerbräukeller in Munich to mark the anniversary of the Nazi 'Beer Hall putsch' launched there in 1923. Hitler began speaking at 8.00 p.m. and was scheduled to do so for at least one-and-a-half to two hours. However, due to a subsequent commitment in Berlin, he concluded speaking at 9.08 p.m. and left the hall together with a number of senior Nazis. No more than ten minutes later, a violent explosion blasted apart the swastika-bedecked column immediately behind the podium from which Hitler had just spoken, destroying much of the hall and collapsing its roof, killing 8 and seriously injuring another 60 of those present. Had Hitler's speech been of its usual length, there is little doubt that this powerful time-bomb would have killed him. The well-planned but ill-fated assassination attempt was carried out by a 36-year-old cabinet maker, Johann Georg Elser, who was arrested that same night while trying to cross the border into Switzerland.[78] It was unrelated to the wider resistance movement, but it did impact upon the more extreme plans of officers such as Oberstleutnant Hans Oster and his co-conspirators within the military intelligence staff, who were forced to abandon their own plan to assassinate Hitler with a bomb in the wake of the much-increased security restrictions in place after the Bürgerbräukeller bombing. The possibility of blaming the bombing on Himmler and the SS was also considered by Oster and others, using this as an excuse for a coup, but the idea was soon rejected.

Although he would much later be recognized as a hero of the anti-Nazi resistance movement, Oster's virtually unbounded passion and commitment to opposing Hitler were potentially dangerous to all those with whom he had close contact. Earlier, on 8 November, he had visited von Leeb at Frankfurt am Main to explore the possibility of the three army group commanders – von Leeb, von Rundstedt and von Bock – refusing to carry out the order to launch the offensive in the west when it was received. At the meeting in von Leeb's office, Oster not only discussed the main purpose of his visit but also recklessly produced copies of two documents drafted by Beck which were to be used in the event of a military coup. He also enthusiastically mentioned the names of many of the other dissenters and conspirators, both within the general staff and those civilians with whom he had established links. Von Leeb's chief of staff, Oberst Vincenz Müller, was present at this meeting and – absolutely appalled by Oster's indiscretion – persuaded him to burn the two Beck documents immediately, while also emphasizing the need for greater circumspection and security awareness. Word of Oster's stormy meeting with von Leeb and Oberst Müller later reached Generalfeldmarschall von Witzleben, who had viewed a refusal by the army commanders to launch the offensive as the only remaining option for those who opposed the new campaign and had therefore suggested that

Oster should meet von Leeb. The field marshal judged that Oster had now become a liability and declared that he was no longer prepared to deal with him. In any event, von Leeb did subsequently raise the suggestion with von Rundstedt and von Bock at von Rundstedt's army group headquarters in Koblenz on 9 November. Both army group commanders indicated that a refusal by them to carry out the attack order would constitute nothing less than mutiny and could not be entertained in any circumstances. Meanwhile, by that stage von Leeb had begun to attract the interest of the Gestapo and was routinely a target of that organization's surveillance.

Just as November 1939 marked a growing awareness of the enormity and potential implications of trying to gainsay Hitler's strategic aspirations, it was also the month in which attitudes to this matter became more polarized within the army. Many of those more senior officers who had challenged Hitler relatively openly during the late 1930s now tended to set aside such activities in order to confront the unavoidable task of an all-out war against the Anglo-French allies in the west. At the same time, within the army a number of younger and more impatient officers – men such as Hans Oster – were beginning to emerge as the core and main impetus of the military resistance movement against Hitler in the years ahead. Remarkable though it seems in the context of German military efficiency and planning capabilities, the hallmarks of the military resistance movement would continue to be its fragmented, often naïve and introspective approach to the relatively straightforward matter of devising an effective means of killing Hitler – as well as an instinctive reluctance to allow the army to be 'used' by any one of the various civilian opposition groups. It may be argued that the standard approach to operational planning and problem-solving imbued in every general staff officer had actually resulted in the excessively prolonged and over-exhaustive analysis of this matter, one that was uniquely different from the usual military challenges with which these officers had been trained to deal. What cannot be denied was Hitler's charisma and popularity within Germany by 1940: no suitably charismatic military or civilian opposition leader and man of action emerged to head a populist resistance movement capable of sweeping aside both Hitler and the Nazi regime. Certainly the 'old guard' – officers such as Beck, von Witzleben and so on –

could not fulfil this role. The opposition activities would continue both within and beyond the general staff in the coming years, but the overriding professional responsibility of these officers was now to support and direct the new campaign in the west.

On 23 November, Hitler capitalized upon the evidence of his growing popularity in the country as a whole and seized the moment to strengthen military resolve and support for his plans. He did so by staging a major briefing – the event has also been described as a spectacle – for a large number of senior army, navy and air force commanders and general staff officers in the impressive Marble Hall of the Berlin Chancellery building. Goebbels and Göring both spoke, then Hitler entered the room. After providing an historical perspective, in which he asserted that the coming conflict was in reality nothing less than a continuation of the unfinished business of 1918, his address focused upon two main themes. First, he left none of those present in any doubt of his determination to crush any doubters or opponents of his vision and plans for German primacy both in Europe and in the wider world. This vision included the need to gain 'Lebensraum' ('living space') into which the National Socialist German state could expand and prosper. Second, he addressed the strategic rationale for the attack in the west, emphasizing the need to safeguard the industrial Ruhr by maximizing the amount of territory occupied by German forces west of that region and seizing this ground in the west while the non-aggression pact with Stalin still safeguarded Germany's eastern flank. Despite Hitler's thinly veiled criticism of, and implied warning to, the army high command and general staff, a number of those senior army officers who had earlier sought to delay or baulk a campaign in the west conceded that Hitler's speech and his strategic arguments had impressed them. Certainly, with the outbreak of a much wider conflict now apparently imminent, this carefully orchestrated military event further weakened the resolve of many of those already less than wholehearted in their opposition to Hitler. However distasteful, by early 1940 there was also a reluctant acceptance by the Western powers that Hitler did now indeed speak for the German people. This view was reinforced by the Under Secretary of State of the United States, Benjamin Sumner Welles, who visited Germany at that time in an unsuccessful attempt to mediate a solution to the growing crisis in Europe. His visit also underlined the extent to which the potential significance of the commanders, general staff officers and German diplomats who opposed Hitler was hardly recognized or taken into account by the US, British or French governments, the Wehrmacht's officers simply being categorized en masse as the collective military leadership of an aggressively hostile power.

In practice, however, the start of the campaign in the west proved to be rather less imminent than had originally been anticipated. Offensives based upon the original *Fall Gelb* plan were ordered and subsequently postponed no fewer than sixteen times between mid-November 1939 and 20 January the following year, by which stage other operational priorities had emerged to force a final postponement of the offensive to the spring of 1940. In the course of all this, the plan had been extensively reviewed, further refined and modified. This process was especially affected by an entirely unforeseen event that occurred on 10 January, which forced a major change in the *Fall Gelb* concept and brought about the general staff's return to serious consideration of von Manstein's earlier proposals for this offensive. Rather than providing a template for a counterstroke against a pre-emptive French attack, von Manstein's ideas would eventually provide the basis of an aggressive strategy initiated by the Germans and employing the Blitzkrieg concept to best effect.

On 10 January 1940, a Fieseler Storch liaison aircraft was flying from Münster to Köln (Cologne) with several staff officers on board. In rapidly deteriorating weather, the pilot lost his way, subsequently being forced to land on Belgian territory with his aircraft about to run out of fuel. One of the passengers was a Major Reinberger of the 7th Fallschirm Division who, contrary to orders, had a copy of the 1st Luftflotte (1st Air Fleet) operation order for *Fall Gelb* in his briefcase. The pilot and passengers were detained temporarily by the Belgian authorities while the documents they were carrying were examined. Reiberger did attempt to burn the operation order, but was unable to destroy the bulk of it before the party's detention. Consequently, the Belgians found themselves in possession of a major part of the plan developed by Halder and the general staff for the German offensive in the west, which was largely based upon the old Schlieffen Plan of former times. Although Belgian military intelligence accepted the veracity of the captured plan, and their border defences were immediately reinforced in an attempt to safeguard the country's neutrality, this vital information was not passed to the British or French governments. The Germans did not know this: Hitler and the general staff believed that their intentions in the west had been fatally compromised and now needed to be changed significantly; it would also be necessary for the Germans to conduct a positive campaign of disinformation and deception directed primarily at the French in order to convince them that the Wehrmacht did indeed propose a re-run of the Schleiffen Plan. Fortunately for the general staff, this also fitted the French commander's somewhat unimaginative assessment of Germany's military intentions, and the bulk of his armoured and other mobile forces had been deployed along the frontier with Belgium.

In the meantime, von Brauchitsch and Halder had deliberately sidelined von Manstein's innovative proposals for an attack through the Ardennes towards Sedan. Weary of his enthusiasm for what they feared might result in a premature offensive, they arranged his posting to command XXXVIII Corps (a second-line or follow-on army corps comprised predominantly of infantry units and based at Stettin) in an attempt to distance him from direct involvement with one of the main operational headquarters of the coming campaign. Unknown to von Brauchitsch and Halder, however, Hitler was already aware of von Manstein's ideas. This had come about from a routine visit to von Rundstedt's headquarters by Oberst Rudolf Schmundt, Hitler's principal army adjutant.[79] During his visit to the headquarters where von Manstein served as chief of staff until February 1940, Schmundt had sight of a note on his concept for the western offensive and duly passed a copy to Hitler. The Führer expressed his wish to discuss the matter with von Manstein, and so Schmundt scheduled a meeting at the Reichskanzlei (Reich Chancellery) for 17 February. In order not to alert the OKH to Hitler's particular interest in von Manstein's ideas at that stage, this meeting was presented simply as a working breakfast, being primarily an opportunity for Hitler to meet a number of newly appointed army corps commanders; four other corps commanders duly joined von Manstein at the Chancellery in Berlin that morning but after breakfast they left, at which point von Manstein was asked to remain for a further hour in order to brief Hitler in detail on his concept for the western offensive. Subsequently, Hitler apprised Halder and von Brauchitsch of his enthusiasm for what he viewed as a bold and speedy way to win the war in the west, which took full account of the capabilities of the army's panzer forces. Thereafter, Hitler's clear support for the von Manstein plan, together with the loss of the Halder document to the Belgians that January, provided an irresistible impetus for its detailed consideration and eventual adoption, with Halder – now fully supportive of the von Manstein plan – bringing his own energy and considerable ability to bear upon the matter.[80]

While the general staff at OKH developed, refined and updated their plans for the attack against the Low Countries and France, the staff officers of the Wehrmachtführungsstab at OKW were working on the plans for an entirely separate offensive, not in the west but on Germany's northern flank, against Denmark and Norway. This new venture, designated *Weserübung*, finally forced the postponement of any action against France until the campaign in Scandinavia had been successfully concluded. It involved a collaborative army-navy operation as well as the violation of Germany's non-aggression pact with Denmark. It was also one of a very few joint army-navy or amphibious landing operations conducted by the Wehrmacht during the war.

Weserübung: The Invasion of Denmark and Norway, April to June 1940

The operation against Norway was mounted in response to Hitler's concerns that Anglo-French support for the Finns (by then under Soviet attack) would prejudice the security of the routes through which Germany received its vital supplies of Swedish iron ore. Strategically, German control of the Norwegian air bases and harbours made further sense in anticipation of Hitler's future intentions and a need to dominate the North Sea and Atlantic sea lanes. When this action was first proposed it received a very lukewarm response from the general staff, who believed that transportation of the required invasion forces by sea was impracticable. Von Brauchitsch in particular was of the opinion that the British Royal Navy would destroy any seaborne invasion force long before it could carry out landings in Denmark or Norway. However, Hitler wasted no time in pursuing the matter with OKH and simply ordered the OKW with Admiral Raeder to plan and direct the invasion of Denmark and Norway. The army was instructed to make six divisions available for the operation, and overall command of the offensive was given to Generaloberst von Falkenhorst. The Kriegsmarine would provide virtually all of its forces in the region to support and protect the invasion. *Weserübung* would also provide the Luftwaffe with an opportunity to use its parachute or air-landed troops for the first time in a major operation. Thus Hitler removed the army general staff from direct involvement in this major military enterprise and set a precedent for delegating the responsibility for specific campaigns or theatres of operations separately to the OKW or OKH. In practice, this established a parallel or 'alternative general staff', which weakened the army general staff by allowing it to be displaced by Hitler if and whenever it chose to oppose the Führer's ideas in the future. As the authority of the OKW was enhanced, so also was that of its principal military officer, Generalmajor Alfred Jodl. The *Weserübung* planning, command and control staff formed up in Berlin on 5 February. Although responsibility for it had been removed from the OKH, the planning process for the Danish-Norwegian campaign was inevitably conducted by many officers who were products of the general staff system.

This planning required a fair amount of improvisation and innovation – a thrust such as this, northwards into Scandinavia, had hardly been contemplated. Maps were surreptitiously acquired from a number of Berlin bookshops, various merchant vessels were hastily requisitioned and joined a growing fleet of transports and other ships at Stettin, while every effort was made not to alert the Norwegian and Danish military attachés of the impending attack. In fact, neither of these attachés believed that the German activity was anything more than some sort of strategic deception – both were of the same opinion as the general staff, certain that the Wehrmacht lacked the capability to carry out such a venture. Ironically, only the Swedish government became at all alarmed by this, fearing that Germany might in fact be contemplating an invasion to gain absolute control of Sweden's iron ore deposits. As well as developing the detailed plan for the invasion, some staff officers also considered linking the impending attack in Scandinavia to one conducted simultaneously against the Netherlands. The idea was eventually rejected on the grounds that any offensive into the Low Countries was already an integral part of the *Fall Gelb* plan for the attack against France, and simultaneous implementation of *Fall Gelb* and *Weserübung* had never been a viable option. By mid-March, the preparations were more or less complete, and on 2 April Hitler issued the order to commence the occupation of Denmark and Norway. The first landings of German troops in the harbour of Copenhagen took place seven days later and were unopposed, the Danish government formally capitulating the following day.

The British, French and Norwegians were all taken by surprise when the Germans launched *Weserübung* early on 9 April, with paratroop and air-landed infantry assaults on the air bases at Oslo and Stavanger and seaborne troops attacking the most important coastal towns and cities from Oslo in the south to Narvik in the north. By midday, Stavanger, Bergen, Narvik, Kristiansand and Trondheim were under German control. The subsequent consolidation and occupation of Norway proved to be somewhat less easy. As von Brauchitsch and others had anticipated, the presence of British warships in the North Sea and Norwegian coastal area meant that the number of sunk and damaged Kriegsmarine ships and the merchant vessels used as transports was relatively high – the cruiser *Blücher* was sunk in Oslo fjord on 9 April by the guns and torpedoes of Norwegian shore batteries; the cruiser *Karlsruhe* was torpedoed and sank the same day; the light cruiser *Königsberg* was bombed and sank a day later; and the heavy cruiser *Lützow* was damaged by torpedoes on 11April. The Royal Navy had also, somewhat belatedly, laid mines at key points along the Norwegian coast on the morning of 8 April.

Once landed, the Wehrmacht ground troops quickly overwhelmed the Norwegian forces. Within four weeks most of the serious fighting had ended, despite the deployment of British, French and Polish troops to support the Norwegian units still fighting in the north of the country. By 3 May the non-Norwegian forces in southern Norway had been evacuated, and on the same day the remaining Norwegian units in that part of the country capitulated. Only at Narvik was there any significant continuing resistance by the Norwegians and Allied troops. There, the port had been recaptured by these troops, the Germans forced to withdraw temporarily from the immediate area. This reverse prompted Hitler to consider sending a relief force to Narvik overland through Sweden, but he was quickly dissuaded from such action when the Swedish authorities made it clear that they would resist any such incursion by German forces. In any event, the potential threat to the success of *Weserübung* posed by Narvik was resolved in early June, when all of the non-Norwegian Allied troops were evacuated in order to join the Anglo-French armies by then involved in countering the Wehrmacht's offensive against the Low Countries and France. As a result, Norway fell completely under German control by 7 June.

Operation *Weserübung* cost the Wehrmacht some 5,500 men, more than 200 aircraft and Kriegsmarine losses that impaired its surface fleet's capability for the rest of the war. It provided a significant strategic victory, however, as well as allowing the Luftwaffe's paratroopers to carry out their first major airborne operation and thus prove the effectiveness of this relatively new capability as a part of the Blitzkrieg concept. Just as importantly, various tank units (but not panzer divisions) had taken part in the ground assaults, which enabled them to build upon the experience gained by the panzer troops during the previous autumn in Poland. For the general staff, *Weserübung* demonstrated that a successful operation could be developed and mounted by the OKW without direct OKH oversight or involvement – indeed, the OKW could be used as an alternative to the OKH and army general staff if circumstances called for it in the future. The success of *Weserübung* also strengthened Hitler's reputation as a strategist.

Fall Gelb: The Plan

For more than 200 years, France had been Germany's foremost continental rival. In more recent times, in the aftermath of the devastation of eastern France from 1914 to 1918, it had been one of the most intransigent and unforgiving signatories of the Versailles treaty. For two decades the German officer corps and much of the German population had known that an eventual reckoning with France was virtually inevitable. Accordingly, while *Weserübung* was in progress, the general staff had remained almost exclusively focused upon *Fall Gelb*. In 1939, Hitler had intended to attack westwards via Belgium as soon as the Polish campaign was concluded, with a view to subduing France as early as practicable, safeguarding the future security of the Ruhr, seizing control of the Channel coast and then establishing the forward air bases necessary to commence a bombing campaign against Britain. Despite the various attempts by the general staff to delay or prevent this offensive, it was finally the particularly bad weather through the winter of 1939/40, together with the need to conduct operation *Weserübung* to secure the northern flank in Scandinavia, that had forced the delay until the spring of 1940. Now Hitler was adamant that the offensive should proceed as planned, and any lingering doubts were put aside. On 27 April, he decided that the offensive in the west should begin between 1 and 7 May, this date being subsequently postponed to 10 May in light of a concern that the attack plan had been compromised (a fear reinforced on 8 May by evidence that the Dutch forces were being mobilized).[81]

As at 10 May 1940, the army consisted of 156 divisions (including 10 panzer and 6 motorized infantry), of which no fewer than 136 were available for operations in the west. Of the remainder, 8 divisions were deployed in Norway and Denmark, 3 in Germany and 9 in eastern Germany, Poland and Czechoslovakia. In addition, 3 Waffen-SS divisions were available for operations alongside those of the army.

Originally, OKH had planned for two army groups – the predominantly armoured Army Group B in the north (with three armies[82]) and Army Group A (two armies) in the centre – to strike into France through Belgium and the Ardennes respectively, while a third, Army Group C (two armies), secured the southern border area and flank and was then retained in reserve. By May 1940 the whole emphasis had changed from the fairly conservative OKH plan, based upon the old Schlieffen concept, to that of von Manstein. Now the main thrust of the panzer spearhead would be not in the north but in the centre, through the densely forested Ardennes and towards Sedan. In addition to being attracted by the plan's daring nature, Hitler was very aware that Sedan had particular historical significance for both Germany and France – this was the fortress town at which Wilhelm I, Bismarck and von Moltke had completed the comprehensive and humiliating defeat of Napoleon III and the French Second Empire in September 1870. In addition to such intangible and subjective considerations, it was undeniable that von Manstein's plan had several substantial military factors in its favour. Not least of these was the likelihood of achieving surprise with an armoured attack through the densely wooded hills and valleys of the Ardennes, building upon the proven success of the panzers that in 1939 had successfully traversed parts of Poland originally judged unsuitable for tanks. Despite months of resistance within the high command to any change from Halder's original plan, a number of officers who had fought in Poland supported the new approach enthusiastically. Foremost among these were, of course, von Manstein himself and General Heinz Guderian. Setting Sedan as the initial objective had, perhaps, a particular significance for Guderian, as he had completed his formal general staff training on the general staff course conducted at Sedan in 1918. The final deciding factor in the long-running debate about *Fall Gelb* had been the loss of the copy of the Halder plan to the Belgians on 10 January, which had occurred at about the same time that Schmundt first apprised Hitler of von Manstein's innovative ideas for the western offensive. At the time, it had not unreasonably been assumed by the German high command that the Belgians would automatically pass on the intelligence gained from this captured document to France and Britain. In any case, the document confirmed that the Germans' preferred option was that which the French and British commanders had always expected the Germans to adopt. This was based upon their own analysis of the ground, the perceived defensive strength of the French Maginot Line and their own perceptions of the correct use of armour on a modern battlefield and of the type of war that the German army was about to unleash against them. Now, however, with the decision taken to adopt von Manstein's plan, the OKH and supporting general staff had revised its plans and preparations accordingly. In its speedy and practical modification of the plan for *Fall Gelb* and the growing enthusiasm for the development and implementation of what was increasingly being acknowledged as an innovative operational concept, the general staff once again showed many of the abilities for which it had justly been acclaimed in the past. Arguably, these officers had been forced by circumstances to concentrate upon that which they did best, and – temporarily at least – in most cases to suspend their active opposition to the

Führer's strategic aspirations. After all, not only the campaign against Poland but also the invasion and occupation of Denmark and Norway had been concluded successfully, confounding the pessimistic predictions of men such as von Brauchitsch, Halder and many other senior army officers.

The much-modified *Fall Gelb* plan still called for a diversionary attack against the Netherlands, Belgium and Luxembourg in line with the original concept, and this part of the offensive would initially be spearheaded by two panzer corps, supported by airborne and infantry units. It was designed to convince the Anglo-French forces that the long-anticipated 'hook' through Belgium and then south-west to seize Paris was indeed still the German intention, and it was expected to provoke an Anglo-French counter-move into Belgium, thus extending their lines of communication and support. But in reality the main attack would now emanate from the depths of the heavily forested Ardennes, with 44 divisions assigned, of which 7 were panzer divisions. There, the armoured spearhead of Army Group A comprised a panzer group based on two panzer corps, but equivalent in overall size to almost three corps, with the whole group under the command of a cavalry officer, General Paul Ludwig Ewald Baron von Kleist. This force would be deployed in two echelons of predominantly tank units, with a third echelon comprised mainly of motorized infantry following closely behind. The principal blow of this concentration of mobile armoured might would fall upon Sedan, where the breakthrough and consequent dislocation of the Anglo-French forces would be achieved. Thereafter the panzer divisions would not race for Paris. They would instead seize crossings over the Meuse river and outflank the Maginot Line, cutting through the Anglo-French armies and separating them. Finally, they would complete their sweeping 'Sichelschnitt' campaign by striking west and north-west to trap the British and the residue of the Belgian and French armies against the Channel coast and complete their destruction. The ground attacks were to be preceded by a number of daring coup de main operations carried out by parachute troops. Some 1,000 combat aircraft were allotted to support the panzer spearhead's advance.

These plans reflected the Blitzkrieg[83] concept, a framework of seven overlapping phases that, where practicable, would begin before hostilities commenced and were designed to maintain the momentum of the offensive and carry the ground forces and their supporting air power through to victory. Throughout, the destruction of the opposing forces was a higher priority than the capture of ground. Both in its planning for the offensive and in the subsequent conduct of *Fall Gelb*, the general staff's application of these phases was evident. In the form that this doctrine was finally applied in 1940 and 1941, the seven phases of the Blitzkrieg may be summarized as follows:

• The preparatory disruption of the enemy's rear areas and command, control and fixed communication facilities by fifth columnists, saboteurs and small groups of infiltrated special troops. This weakened his overall military capability and prejudiced his mobilization plans, as well as creating fear and uncertainty and lowering his morale. Such operations were regarded as long-term, being conducted over as much as ten to twelve months prior to overt offensive action.

• The destruction of the enemy air power on the ground by a surprise bombing attack in overwhelming strength. The enemy air force always posed the single greatest threat to the ground forces of an attacker moving in the open.

• The interdiction of enemy troop movement and command facilities by bombers and fighter ground attack aircraft. This prevented the movement of reserves and logistic resupply to counter the attack and sustain the defence.

• The neutralization (by preventing their re-deployment or movement out of protected cover) or destruction of enemy units and formations by air attack, usually by dive-bombers such as the Ju-87 Stuka.

• Infiltration and exploitation of gaps in the defence lines by light armoured and motorized all-arms forces to carry out reconnaissance in depth, identify undefended routes and exploit opportunities as they presented themselves. These operations signalled the start of the envelopment of the enemy forces.

• The armoured assault by panzer units and their supporting arms, to achieve deep penetrations, seize key objectives, and to shock, overrun

and destroy enemy forces, while bypassing major urban areas and well-defended strongpoints. These operations continued and reinforced the envelopment of the enemy forces, thus enabling their subsequent annihilation by panzer units and follow-on ground forces.
• The follow-up assault by non-motorized infantry divisions and their supporting arms, to destroy the enemy in detail, establish secure rear areas including the suppression of any irregular resistance forces, impose military administration upon occupied areas, and deal in detail with any locations bypassed earlier by the mobile forces. Finally, these less mobile forces linked up with the panzer formations to complete the operation or campaign.

At the outset of the *Fall Gelb* offensive the opposing forces were fairly evenly matched in quantitative terms – the total number of Anglo-French divisions slightly exceeded the German total, although the difference was more marked if the Dutch-Belgian divisions were also taken into account. Qualitatively, however, the Germans possessed a significant edge. The Dutch and Belgian armies consisted of no more than eight and eighteen divisions respectively, in addition to which they had their various reserve forces; the British Expeditionary Force had nine divisions under its command in northern France, with a further division grouped with the French 2nd Army Group in the south. The main strength of the Allies lay in the three French army groups. These were the 1st Army Group with 22 divisions, including 2 light armoured and 3 motorized, the 2nd Army Group with 36 divisions (including its single British division), the 3rd Army Group with 14 divisions, and the Seventh Army with 7 divisions, including 1 light armoured and 2 motorized. The French reserves comprised 22 divisions, 3 of which were armoured. Within these army groups the French had about 3,000 modern, well-armed and well-armoured tanks, with 1,292 of these grouped separately into light and heavy tank divisions. The British had 210 light and 100 heavy tanks, but all of these were allocated to support the infantry. Significantly, the relative paucity of French anti-tank guns – no more than about 8,000 in May 1940 – fell well short of the numbers needed to counter the armoured threat that was even then massing just across the frontier.

On the German side, the final plan for *Fall Gelb* had been produced on 24 February 1940. Army Group B (Sixth and Eighteenth Armies) in the north would comprise 28 divisions (including 3 panzer and 2 motorized) to carry out its deception mission. The southern Army Group C (First and Seventh Armies) had 17 divisions assigned for its security tasks in the south opposite the Maginot Line defences, while in the centre was Generaloberst von Rundstedt's Army Group A with 44 divisions (including 7 panzer and 3 motorized).[84] The divisions of Army Group A were further sub-allocated within Fourth, Twelfth and Sixteenth Armies. The key to the success of *Fall Gelb* would always be the armoured forces, now grouped into Panzer Group Hoth (2 panzer divisions, one of which was commanded by Generalmajor Erwin Rommel, later to become one of the best-known German commanders of the war) and Panzer Group Kleist (5 panzer divisions). These were the formations that would bring about the defeat of France – the forthcoming offensive would be very much centred upon their actions. Within Panzer Group Kleist were XLI Panzer Corps and XIX Panzer Corps, commanded respectively by Generalleutnant Georg-Hans Reinhardt and General Guderian. Von Kleist's chief of staff was Oberst Kurt Zeitzler, a future chief of the general staff, whose mastery of the business of supplying armoured forces during long-range advances and fluid mobile battles stood von Kleist's panzer group in particularly good stead during the coming campaign. A sizeable OKH reserve of almost 45 divisions was also formed: this follow-on force did not include any panzer divisions, all of these being needed to spearhead the initial Blitzkrieg.

In terms of equipment, the German armoured forces deployed with no more than 627 Pz.Kpfw.III and Pz.Kpfw.IV tanks, 1,679 Pz.Kpfw.I and Pz.Kpfw.II tanks, and 381 Czech 38(t) tanks seized in 1939, a grand total of just 2,687 tanks. But by May 1940 Germany also possessed more than 3,000 combat aircraft, including 400 of the Ju-87 Stuka dive-bombers so vital for the support of the panzer formations, while the French opposed them with a total of no more than some 1,200 aircraft and no dive-bombers. The relative strengths of other aircraft categories indicated that the French and British deployed about 800 fighters, compared with 1,000 German aircraft of this type (virtually all of which enjoyed a technological superiority), while

France had just 150 medium and heavy bombers, compared with Germany's 1,470. In artillery, France had less than 3,000 anti-aircraft guns while the Germans had 9,300. Although the German field artillery, with some 7,700 guns, possessed many fewer than the 11,000 of the French, the latter's almost total reliance on horse-drawn guns meant that France was ill-prepared to conduct – or to counter – motorized and mobile operations by armoured forces.[85]

Fall Gelb: The Invasion of France and the Low Countries, May to June 1940

During the first week of May, Hitler asserted that an Anglo-French attack upon the Ruhr via the Netherlands and Belgium was imminent: plainly no more than a pretext for war, this became the justification for launching *Fall Gelb*. The ground attack against the Low Countries began on the night of 10 May. In the meantime, a glider-borne assault by specially trained airborne troops of Sturmabteilung (assault unit) Koch had already that morning launched a daring and most successful assault directly on to the massive complex of Belgian fortifications at Eben Emael – the key to the defence of the Meuse bridges. It achieved complete surprise and linked up with the advancing ground forces during the night 10/11 May. Throughout the attack against the Low Countries, Luftwaffe Generalmajor Kurt Student's airborne forces were used to particularly good effect, including at Rotterdam, Dordrecht and Moerdijk. These paratroopers and glider-borne troops seized strategically vital ground and important installations ahead of General Georg von Küchler's advancing Eighteenth Army (an army consisting mainly of infantry divisions).

Within four days, the armed forces of the Netherlands had collapsed, and as anticipated the Allies moved troops forward into Belgium, engaging Army Group B along the River Dyle. Then, on the morning of 13 May, the first real tank battles took place between Huy and Tirlemont, where XVI Panzer Corps, supported by the ever-present Stukas, infiltrated through the French armoured screen. By 5.45 that afternoon the Germans had forced a general French withdrawal, which continued during the following two days. However, this action was no more than a continuation of the wider deception, and in the face of more resolute opposition from the French First Army, XVI Panzer Corps soon extricated itself from this battle prior to joining the fighting that was by then developing farther to the south. In the meantime, the main blow had already smashed into France from the woods and defiles of the Ardennes as XV Panzer Corps struck at Dinant, XLI Panzer Corps at Monthermé, and XIX Panzer Corps at Sedan. On a frontage of no more than 80 kilometres the three panzer corps raced to secure the crossings over the River Meuse, and by the night of 12 May they were on the east bank of the river, preparing to cross the next morning.

Despite heavy resistance, by mid-afternoon on 13 May all three corps had secured infantry bridgeheads on the far bank, and the engineers had begun to construct the ferries and bridges necessary for the tanks to cross. By midnight, XV and XIX Panzer Corps had these in place, using them to reinforce their bridgeheads with armour as quickly as possible. The French failed to exploit the temporary vulnerability of the German bridgeheads (especially that of XLI Panzer Corps) and, as the panzers prepared to break out to the west and north, General Corap, commanding the French Ninth Army, ordered a general withdrawal on the night of 14 May. The tactical focus of this army had already been upset by an earlier directive for it to look north rather than east, with a view to it preparing to counter the German thrust into Belgium. By the following evening, elements of 1st and 7th Panzer Divisions – the former from Guderian's XIX Panzer Corps and the latter from Hoth's XV Panzer Corps – were respectively 24 and 42 kilometres west of the Meuse. In scenes reminiscent of the Polish campaign, the opposition collapsed wherever the German tanks appeared – prisoners surrendered in huge numbers, and French morale was shattered as the Blitzkrieg struck fear into the consciousness of the French commanders and their soldiers.

The tanks rolled on, protected and supported by the virtually unchallenged air power of the Luftwaffe. But then, with total victory well within the grasp of their enthusiastic commanders, the panzer units became victims of their own success as the high command – specifically Hitler and von Rundstedt – began to fear for the vulnerability of the armoured divisions that had advanced so far ahead of the rest of the invading ground forces. Admittedly, these divisions were both indispensable and irreplaceable, but with the French and British defences crumbling it would none the less have been worthwhile allowing the advance to continue, and the only proper decision for the German high command at that stage should have been whether to strike at Paris or for the Channel. However, caution prevailed and a halt was ordered to enable the non-panzer formations to catch up. Despite this, Guderian did persuade his panzer group commander, von Kleist, to allow him a further 24 hours of activity, during which he advanced more than 60 kilometres farther to the River Oise. Rommel also pushed his 7th Panzer Division on another 80 kilometres, reaching Le Cateau by the morning of 17 May. However, Halder observed that Hitler had become increasingly nervous of the remarkable progress of the offensive and was now concerned that the extent of the advance had left the southern flank of the operation exposed. Consequently, at that point a complete halt was ordered. The growing evidence of the rapidly escalating French collapse (apart from a few local counterattacks, which were soon dealt with), and of the westwards retreat of the BEF with the remaining Belgian and French forces in northern France, later prompted the high command to order a resumption of the advance. This also reflected Hitler's mercurial changes of mind. Just two days after calling a halt to the advance, Jodl noted that the 'Führer [was] beside himself with joy. Concerning himself with peace conditions. Restoration of territory of which [the] German people [had been] robbed for 400 years. Preliminary negotiations [with the French] in Forest of Compiègne as [in] 1918. British can have separate peace any time they like after handing over colonies.'[86]

By mid-morning on 20 May the three leading panzer corps occupied a line from Arleux, close to the River Scarpe, running generally south to Péronne on the River Somme. During that evening the tank crewmen of the 2nd Panzer Division had their first view of the English Channel from their positions in Abbeville. The 1st Panzer Division was well established in Amiens, while the two panzer divisions of XLI Corps, 6th and 8th, were in positions centred upon Le Boisle and Hesdin respectively. Meanwhile in XV Panzer Corps, the 7th Panzer Division had reached Arras, with 5th Panzer Division in the Cambrai area. Apparently, the way now lay wide open for the panzer corps to seize the Channel ports from Dunkirk to Boulogne and so envelop the remaining undefeated Allied troops in northern France. But then the Germans suffered their first significant reverse, when the motorized infantry of Rommel's 25th Panzer Regiment – the 7th Division's spearhead – was surprised by a group of 70 British heavy tanks near Arras, just when the German tanks were moving well ahead of, and separated from, their supporting infantry. The British tanks wrought havoc among the unprotected infantry, and only when they were engaged by the divisional artillery and by a number of 88mm anti-aircraft Flak guns (used most effectively in the anti-tank role) did the slaughter of the Panzergrenadiere (armoured infantrymen) abate. Some 36 Matilda Mark I and II tanks were destroyed by the devastating fire of these 88mm guns. Nevertheless, even the speedy return of the 25th Panzer Regiment's tanks made little difference to the outcome of the engagement, for they were then met in their turn by a storm of fire from a number of well-concealed British anti-tank guns, which quickly reduced twenty German tanks to burning hulks. Eventually the 5th Panzer Division, urgently summoned from Cambrai, arrived on the scene, but by then the battle was more or less over.

This short, sharp and relatively insignificant tactical encounter near Arras had much wider implications at the operational and strategic levels of command, for the German losses served to reinforce the high command's fears about over-extending the lines of advance of the panzer divisions, while also underlining the vulnerabilities inherent in these particular divisions as then structured and equipped. As well as confirming the ineffectiveness of the German 37mm PAK anti-tank gun against the armour of the latest Allied tanks, it had also shown those who witnessed this battle the enormous potential of the 88mm anti-aircraft gun utilized as an anti-armour weapon – a potential that Rommel would later employ very effectively during his campaign in North Africa. It also highlighted to the general staff the importance of routinely deploying, controlling and using the 88mm as an anti-tank weapon in the future. But, as the Wehrmacht's anti-aircraft weapons were routinely manned by Luftwaffe personnel, the 88mm guns were all under Luftwaffe control – a situation that generated a degree of inter-service rivalry and operational inefficiency, which would blight relations between the army and the Luftwaffe on a number of occasions during the war.

In any event, fearful of losing its most important war-winning fighting formations, the high command now ordered a general halt to the spectacular, if somewhat helter-skelter, advance that had taken place during the first three weeks of May 1940. A general consolidation was to take place, with flanks and lines of communication properly secured, while the remaining ground forces caught up. This decision followed a visit by Hitler, Jodl and Schmundt to the forward headquarters at Charleville on 24 May, when Hitler once again justified the order, citing the risk of over-extending the German forces. Other, non-military, considerations were also in play, not the least of which was the suggestion (reported by Halder) that Göring had made to Hitler that it might now be politically advisable to deny the army and general staff the prestige that would result from the capture or destruction of the BEF. While Göring's own agenda for the Luftwaffe was all too clear – he had confidently asserted that the Luftwaffe would deal with this residual rump of the Allied armies in northern France – he also knew that anything that might curtail the power of the general staff would undoubtedly find favour with Hitler. However, the decision to postpone a direct attack against the Dunkirk salient was also strongly influenced by Hitler's continued belief that Britain could still be persuaded to sue for peace and that the wholesale destruction of the BEF or its humiliating surrender might prejudice this aspiration. Despite their personal reservations about going to war against Britain, von Brauchitsch and von Rundstedt argued for the army to be allowed to complete the task. They did so in vain. In the meantime, with a ground attack against the rapidly filling Dunkirk salient in abeyance, the panzer corps prepared deliberate attacks to take Boulogne and Calais.

In the event, air power alone proved unable to defeat the Allied forces at Dunkirk: although Calais fell on 26 May, thus releasing XIX Panzer Corps for operations against the salient, it was by then defended strongly and in such depth that only a major operation could overcome it by that stage. Consequently, time was now needed to prepare for this operation, as well as to develop the additional forces necessary to guarantee its success. Between 26 May and 4 June, before this attack could be mounted, a mixed fleet of British, French and Belgian naval vessels, together with a disparate armada of privately owned craft of every type, embarked a total of 338,226 soldiers (of which 198,315 were British and 139,911 were Allied, but predominantly French) and conveyed them to safety in England. Then, while this evacuation was still in progress, on 28 May the panzer divisions were withdrawn from their positions close to the Channel coast to prepare for the task of defeating the remaining French forces to the south. So it was that the opportunity for the German armoured units to annihilate the Anglo-French forces at Dunkirk had been denied them by their own high command, a decision that probably reflected wider strategic considerations and internal Nazi party politics, but which also underlined – and arguably had been precipitated by – the overall paucity of panzer forces then available to the army.

With most of the Anglo-French troops successfully evacuated from the beaches, Dunkirk finally fell on 4 June. This provided the general staff logistics officers and their commanders with an early opportunity to exploit the spoils of war and offset some of the army's matériel deficiencies, especially in transport. Within the former salient and the Dunkirk area the Germans found a massive haul of abandoned weapons and equipment, including some 600 tanks of various types, no fewer than 75,000 motor vehicles, 1,200 field guns and heavy artillery guns, 1,350 anti-aircraft and anti-tank guns, 6,400 anti-tank rifles, 11,000 machine-guns and many tens of thousands of rifles, together with 7,000 tons of ammunition.[87] Although various attempts had been made by the Allies to disable or destroy this matériel before it was abandoned, the sheer scale and nature of the evacuation meant that great quantities remained entirely serviceable, were readily capable of being restored or were suitable for cannibalizing. There was a 'down side' to this: while the capture and re-use of enemy weapons and vehicles was actively pursued as a well-established general staff policy, every new item thus adopted also had the effect of complicating the Wehrmacht's supply and maintenance arrangements, which in turn increased the complexity of the general staff's logistical planning.

With the northern coastline secured, on 5 June the panzers struck south and west supported by the bulk of the Fall Gelb non-motorized follow-on forces, all of which were by then well-established on French territory.

Generaloberst Fedor von Bock's Army Group B struck in the Somme area while von Rundstedt's Army Group A attacked at the Aisne. Although some stiff French resistance was encountered, with what were often spirited attacks carried out by a number of French armoured units, such action was generally isolated and unsustainable. Undeniably, the heart had gone from the French army, and both its high command and its government lacked the resolve to fight on.

An unfortunate aspect of the campaign that had emerged especially during the post-5 June operations against the remaining French army units to the south, was the ill-treatment and summary execution of some prisoners-of-war by army units. Instances of similar actions against the civilian population were also recorded. While such incidents are virtually inevitable in any war and rarely the prerogative of one side only, of particular note was the preponderance of black soldiers among those French soldiers who were the victims of such atrocities. In these cases, the frustration of some units at having their advance delayed, together with the often significant casualties they had sustained at the hands of black African and North African soldiers deemed 'racially inferior' by the Nazis undoubtedly provoked extreme reactions and excesses on the part of some German officers and soldiers. And the army had increasingly found itself operating alongside SS units whose agenda and battlefield behaviour were wholeheartedly approved by the Nazi government and driven by an ideology and policies that openly encouraged them to eliminate Jews and other racially and ethnically 'undesirable' groups, and with no regard for the civilian population. As the war progressed, the excesses of some Waffen-SS and other SS special units would be condemned by several army commanders, roundly criticised by many general staff officers and eventually prompt some to join the clandestine resistance movement against Hitler and the Nazi regime. However, the army itself was neither blameless nor unaware of these matters during its campaign against the Low Countries and France in 1940. Indeed, clear evidence of this was established as early as 25 October 1939 during the latter stages of the Polish campaign, when von Brauchitsch issued a directive that specifically forbade 'all criticism of the measures of the state leadership' (referring to the actions of the SS in the occupied territories) and called for 'strict silence' and the 'avoidance of all gossip and the spreading of rumours' concerning those matters.[88]

The several high-profile atrocities committed by Waffen-SS units during the 1940 campaign are well documented. Three particularly notorious examples were the killing of 23 civilians by troops of the SS-Totenkopf Division at Arras on 23 May and of British prisoners-of-war by the same unit at Le Paradis on 27 May, together with the massacre of British prisoners by the Leibstandarte-SS 'Adolf Hitler' at Wormhout on 28 May.[89] Where similar atrocities were perpetrated by army units, they are possibly less well known, although these were in any case neither widespread nor on a scale comparable with what would soon become a growing litany of crimes carried out by the Allgemeine-SS (the 'general SS') and the Waffen-SS. At Vinkt in Belgium, soldiers of the army's 225th Infantry Division summarily shot 86 civilians after the capture of the town on 27 May. Then, on 7 June, a number of soldiers of the 53ème Régiment d'Infanterie Coloniale were shot, probably by troops of the 5th Panzer Division, following their surrender after a resolute defence in the area of Airaines, near Le Quesnoy. Similar acts had also been perpetrated by soldiers of Rommel's 7th Panzer Division on 5 June against the defenders of Le Quesnoy. Indeed, Rommel noted in his own account of the action that 'any enemy troops were either wiped out or forced to withdraw'. At the same time he also provided the disparaging (but possibly somewhat contradictory in light of his original note) observation that 'many of the prisoners taken were hopelessly drunk'.[90] Most of the French colonial soldiers involved in these particular engagements and their unfortunate aftermath were black. Soon afterwards, on 17 June, the 1st Panzer Division summarily executed 7 surrendered soldiers of the 61ème Régiment Régional at Sainte-Suzanne, near Montbéliard, while on 19 June 10 members of the 55ème Bataillon de Mitrailleurs were shot by 6th Panzer Division troops at Dounoux, north of Epinal. Also in the Epinal area, soldiers of the 198th Infantry Division were responsible for shooting many members of the 146ème Régiment de'Infanterie de Forteresse at Domptail on 20 June as soon as they surrendered. In some cases the army sought to justify or legitimize such summary executions by alleging that the French troops had used illegal ammunition (such as 'dum-dum' bullets).[91] Whether premeditated, punitive or carried out in the immediate aftermath of battle, incidents such as these not only tarnished the reputation of the army but also weighed heavily upon the consciences of many of its officers while generating a degree of unease on the part of the general staff and some senior commanders. A minor portent of future friction between the army and the Waffen-SS was an incident between Generalleutnant Erich Höpner, commanding XVI Panzer Corps, and the commander of the Leibstandarte-SS 'Adolf Hitler', SS-Gruppenführer und Generalleutnant der Waffen-SS Josef 'Sepp' Dietrich, during the advance into France. In response to Dietrich's remark prior to an attack that 'he would complete his task and that human life mattered little to the SS', an enraged Höpner responded that this 'was not the language of a decent-minded officer. Only a butcher could think like that.'[92] Tellingly perhaps, it was also Höpner who subsequently ordered an inquiry into the massacre of the captured soldiers of the Royal Norfolk Regiment by the SS-Totenkopf Division at Le Paradis on 27 May. By mid-1940, the army was beginning to experience some of the wider implications of the unholy alliance forged between it and the Nazis – largely through the tacit acquiescence of much of the officer corps in the mid-1930s.

From 10 June the French government was actively seeking ways in which to end the conflict, and on 13 June Paris became an open city, being entered by the Germans the next day. Elsewhere, Guderian's panzers reached the Swiss frontier on 16 June, enveloping a huge number of French units between his corps and the French border. Cherbourg fell to Rommel's division on 19 June, where the British 1st Armoured Division belatedly and ill-advisedly had been sent from England to fight alongside the French defenders – 174 light tanks and 156 medium tanks were lost by the British at Cherbourg. Lyons fell on 20 June, and by 25 June the German line ran across southern France from Angoulême in the west, north of Limoges, through Clermont-Ferrand and St-Etienne, and then along the south side of the River Rhône to the Swiss border close to Geneva. The newly installed French president, Marshal Pétain, had already ordered an end to further resistance on 17 June, and by 25 June the battle for France was over. The formal surrender of France was finally signed at Rethondes in the Compiègne forest at 5.50 p.m. on June 22, the list of non-negotiable terms having been presented to the French by Hitler and the German delegation the previous day. The Germans now controlled the Low Countries and all of northern France, and a compliant French government had assumed power in the as-yet unoccupied south of the country. The general staff established the army of occupation's main headquarters in France at Fontainbleau and reflected upon the remarkable victory that had been achieved, including the significant part played by the panzers in that victory, and the many operational, tactical and organizational lessons that now needed to be learnt and applied in order to build upon the successes of 1939 and 1940.[93]

In 1942, Guderian provided a personal view of the development and nature of all-arms combat and the role of of the panzer forces in the defeat of France in 1940. He wrote:

> 'The tank crews did not fight alone. From the inception of the new [panzer] weapon, its creators' thinking about modern tank warfare led to the close involvement of support units that were fully motorized and to some extent armoured. The German Army created tank divisions that formed large self-contained units which included all arms of the service. After reconnaissance, in combat the tanks and the supporting riflemen and motorcycle troops, artillery, engineers and signal corps, could exploit their joint successes instantly, thanks to the mechanization common to all these arms. Further backing was given to the tank divisions by motorized infantry. The tank divisions became the natural partners of the air force, with whom they soon formed the closest bonds of comradeship. The enforced [strategic] delay imposed upon the forces by the winter conditions of 1939–40 was utilized to build up the tank formations. In May 1940, they advanced with renewed vigour in the west. Their achievements exceeded all expectations.'[94]

Two years later, Guderian would be appointed chief of the general staff, but by then the Wehrmacht would no longer be capable of mounting the sort of Blitzkrieg operations that it had carried out in 1940.

The army's victory against the Anglo-French forces had been comprehensive (apart from Hitler's failure to allow a ground assault into the Dunkirk salient). The Blitzkrieg concept had been well and truly validated, with the role of the Luftwaffe in that form of warfare also confirmed. At the same time, the Luftwaffe's inability to contain or destroy the Dunkirk salient also showed that air power had significant limitations. More widely, for those unaware of the mood swings that had resulted in prevarications and poorly judged operational interventions by Hitler during the short campaign, the Führer's apparently brilliant strategic acumen was now acclaimed enthusiastically throughout Germany. By that stage, those who were now prepared to give their unqualified support to Hitler included a growing number of general staff and other army officers who had previously doubted the perilous course upon which Nazi Germany had embarked. These officers might earlier have been unsettled by the excesses perpetrated by SS units serving alongside those of the army, but they were now prepared to accept that such matters were probably unimportant when set against achieving victory for the Fatherland and the restoration of the army's traditional primacy and status within the nation.

8

Strategic Options and Operational Sideshows

1940–1941

Despite Hitler's disdain for the army high command and his distrust of the general staff in particular, traditional views are sometimes hard to dispel, and for most of the war those officers who qualified as members of the general staff corps continued to be regarded as an elite group within the wider officer corps. During the pre- and early-war years, the gradual erosion of the general staff's traditional power and influence under the Nazi regime was undoubtedly more evident at the higher (and therefore more political) levels of command than at the operational and tactical levels, while it was at these lower levels of command that many of the younger and newly qualified general staff officers were to be found.

Although some aspects of the general staff selection and training process were necessarily modified during the war years to reflect the prevailing circumstances, the core elements remained largely unchanged from those of the pre-war era, with the successful candidate undergoing an intensive period of training that subsequently opened the way to a fast-tracked career and potential employment in the highest staff and command positions of the army and the armed forces. Although by no means a typical general staff officer, Guderian had a clear vision of the ideal qualities that should be found in a general staff officer of the 1939–45 war. According to Guderian, these officers should demonstrate:

> sincerity of conviction, cleverness, modesty, self-effacement in favour of the common cause, and strong personal convictions combined with

the ability tactfully to present these convictions to his commanding general. If his opinions were not accepted he must be sufficiently master of himself loyally to carry out his commander's decisions and to act at all times in accordance with his wishes. He must fully understand and feel for the needs of the troops and he must be inexhaustible in his efforts to help them. He must have operational, tactical, and technical understanding; in technical matters he must not allow himself to become swamped in details, but yet must know enough to be able to correlate technical innovations with the command of troops in war.[95]

As we saw earlier, the formal period of general staff training at the Kriegsakademie, which was preceded by that at the appropriate special service school and culminated in a probationary attachment to the Generalstab, lasted for about a year. However, Guderian emphasized the vital importance of every general staff officer completing the 'regular tours of duty with troops, both [with those] of his original arm of the Service and of other arms, in all sorts of conditions, so that he may collect practical knowledge of various types of fighting and of actual command'.[96] This was fine in principle, but reality and practicality inevitably impacted upon accomplishment of the ideal. Referring to the period between the two world wars, Guderian highlighted the problem of providing this vital experience to general staff officers within the constraints imposed during the Reichswehr period (when the general staff did not officially exist). Of course, such officers, who would also demonstrate qualities of 'courage, determination, willingness to accept responsibility, a gift for improvisation, physical endurance, as well as considerable industriousness', were very much in demand, and Guderian highlighted the understandable reluctance of the 'higher staffs' and headquarters to suffer the inconvenience of sending high-quality general staff officers to the front for periods of time just so that they could gain this experience. Writing after the war, Guderian was particularly scathing about the OKW and OKH, where 'there were members of those staffs who, during a war of almost six years duration, never once saw the front'. [97]

The process of creating a general staff officer actually began some years before he embarked upon that special career path. This was because every army general staff officer had first of all been selected and trained as an officer of his own branch, arm or regiment of the army and would have already demonstrated his aptitude and suitability for advancement, and for possible general staff employment in the future, while serving with these units. In many cases the social backgrounds of these officers were diverse and very different from those of the generations of army officers that preceded them. This reflected the post-1935 emphasis upon merit rather than precedent, patronage or privilege, which meant that any man who was academically qualified might now reasonably aspire to officer rank in the army of the Third Reich, irrespective of his parentage and economic or social background.

Although the onset of hostilities necessitated various modifications to the process, the selection and training cycle for most officers generally followed a standard pattern, although this was adapted slightly to take account of whether the officer was a candidate for a regular commission or for a reserve officer commission.[98] Regular officer candidates – those who would eventually provide the members of the general staff corps – were selected as untrained volunteers at age sixteen or seventeen, or from serving conscripts aged less than 28 years, or by application from regular NCOs with at least two months' field service. Once selected, regular officer candidates were generally first trained as NCOs, then as officer candidates or junior officers, and finally as specialist officers for their own branch or service. The whole process was conducted within a multi-faceted but always closely coordinated training regime, with the potential officers or officer candidates classified and grouped as such throughout their training. In addition to the Ersatzheer and the Feldheer, a host of individual training units, field units, military schools and other agencies were involved in the three phases of training that a regular officer candidate was required to undergo.

During the pre-war years, Phase I of regular officer training comprised four months of basic infantry training followed by six months of NCO training, at the end of which the potential officer was promoted to NCO rank. During Phase II the potential officer first spent three months with a field unit, and if this was completed successfully he was then promoted to 'officer candidate' (Fahnenjunker). Next, he attended a course at an officer training school or at the special-to-arm infantry, panzer or artillery officer training schools for up to four months. Finally, Phase III of his training was an advanced or special-to-arm course, at the end of which the successful officer candidate was promoted second lieutenant (Leutnant). Once the war began, the training of potential officers and officer candidates was adjusted to take account of the time many had already spent on active service, as well as the pressing need to produce additional leaders as quickly as practicable, with army officers always suffering a disproportionately high rate of battle casualties within the Wehrmacht.[99] Although the standard three-phase training course was still planned to take place over a period of between sixteen and twenty months, provision also existed for soldiers with extensive combat experience, proven leadership qualities, and who were aged 30 and above, to be promoted to second lieutenant after just a few months as an officer candidate with a field unit. Undoubtedly, the way to officer rank in the new Wehrmacht had been eased for many. Nevertheless, eventual acceptance into the general staff corps remained a distant aspiration for the majority of army officers. This elitist approach maintained the general staff's tradition of professional excellence, but at the same time it also served to perpetuate and exacerbate the gulf between members of that organization and the Nazi leadership, as well as engendering a degree of envy on the part of some members of the wider officer corps.

Seelöwe: Planning the Invasion of England, July to December 1940

By July 1940, with France subdued and Britain beleaguered, general staff planning was directed towards a combined airborne and seaborne operation against England in the west and contingency planning for an eastern deployment should it prove necessary to secure the Romanian oilfields against a possible Russian threat at some time in the future. At the same time, the apparent lack of any imminent requirement for further large-scale fighting also prompted the general staff to consider options for returning the army to its peacetime state, although concurrently forces were earmarked and began preparing for *Seelöwe* ('Sea Lion'), the codename for the cross-Channel invasion of southern England.[100] On 16 July, Hitler confirmed his intention to launch Operation *Seelöwe* in the event that London still refused to submit and accept his peace terms, albeit that a British capitulation appeared increasingly unlikely despite the country's isolation. He stated, 'as England, in spite of her hopeless military situation, still shows no sign of willingness to come to terms, I have decided to prepare, and if necessary to carry out, a landing operation against her. The aim of this operation is to eliminate Great Britain as a base from which the war against Germany can be continued, and if it should be necessary, to occupy the country completely.'[101] And yet, on 19 July, a passing comment by the Führer made during an address to senior Wehrmacht officers at the Kroll opera house in Berlin indicated his continuing desire to conclude an armistice with the British rather than precipitating the destruction of the British Empire through further hostilities. He said: 'In this hour I feel it my duty before my conscience to launch once again an appeal for reason on England's part. I believe I am qualified to do this, not because I ask for something as the defeated party, but rather as the victor I speak for common sense. I see no grounds for the continuation of this conflict.'[102] At that stage most general staff officers undoubtedly agreed that continued resistance by Britain alone was militarily illogical. However, Hitler's desire to conclude matters in the west as soon as possible also reflected his future intentions concerning Russia. In any event, the ongoing strategic assumption upon which the general staff now based their activities was that an invasion of England was probably unavoidable, or that, at the very least, their development of a viable invasion plan and the evidence of those preparations might yet persuade London to seek a peace settlement.

The OKW and OKH planning for Operation *Seelöwe* involved all branches of the Wehrmacht. The army would play the main part in the venture, but the Luftwaffe and Kriegsmarine roles would be absolutely critical, as local air superiority and maritime security were essential prerequisites for success in this as in any amphibious landing operation. Some 13 army and airborne divisions were assigned to the initial assault, with at least 26 more providing the reserve and follow-on divisions. An airborne assault was to be followed by large-scale amphibious landings, with two armies (Ninth and Sixteenth) of Army Group A embarking at French ports from Dunkirk to Étaples, and Le Havre, as well as at Rotterdam, Ostend and Antwerp in the Netherlands, before crossing the Channel to carry out landings from Brighton in the west to Hythe in the east. The first plan called for two separate landings – one between Hastings and Margate and the other between Portsmouth and Brighton. If successful, landings on this massive scale would secure a line running from Tilbury in the east, through Aldershot and down to Southampton. This would occupy the British defenders to such an extent that a subsequent landing in the area from Bournemouth to Weymouth could then have been carried out, thereby consolidating the Wehrmacht's hold on the south coast and south-east England. However, this ambitious plan was discounted when Admiral Raeder, commander-in-chief of the Kriegsmarine, indicated on 11 July that, due to its recent losses in the campaign against Norway, the navy now lacked the capability either to support such widespread initial landings or to protect the follow-on troops crossing the Channel. The Kriegsmarine's high command (the OKM) advocated smaller-scale landings on a narrower front, with a slower build-up of the follow-on divisions. This proposal contravened several of the basic principles of warfare – certainly of land warfare – and was rejected out of hand by the general staff, including the recently promoted Generaloberst Halder. At that stage it should have been clear to all that an invasion of England was not practical, while the longer *Seelöwe* was postponed the stronger the British defences would become. In any event, Hitler finally ordered a compromise solution that significantly reduced the frontage of the seaborne landings, with none now taking place to the north of Dover.

As the months passed, the invasion units assembled in northern France and the Netherlands, while large numbers of invasion barges were constructed or acquired, along with other vessels, and concentrated at or close to the Channel and North Sea ports and harbours. It was estimated that the operation would require in excess of 1,700 barges, 1,000 lighters and other light craft of various types, 150 large transport vessels and 500 tugboats.[103] Many of the barges brought from the Netherlands and Germany had to be modified extensively so that vehicles – including tanks – could be driven out through doors in their bows. In the meantime, thousands of soldiers and Luftwaffe parachute troops continued to train for the great amphibious and airborne invasion that they believed would finally defeat Britain and end the war in the west. Some 250,000 troops were earmarked for the operation. The specialist nature of an amphibious assault, together with the uniqueness and multiple types of vessels and much of the equipment involved, imposed a considerable burden of training time upon the invasion force. A number of officers in the general staff still doubted that the plan was really viable, with particular concerns about the achievable tempo of cross-Channel reinforcement and the risk of the first assault armies to land becoming cut off. Arguably, the Kriegsmarine would never have been capable of providing the required levels of troop transportation or naval power in the Channel area in 1940. Nevertheless, Reichsmarschall Göring confidently stated that the Luftwaffe would sweep the British RAF from the skies and thus guarantee the security of the landings as well as preventing any serious intervention by the Royal Navy. On that basis, on 31 July Hitler directed the planning to continue, with *Seelöwe* to take place no later than 15 September, that being the date by which Admiral Raeder had declared that the Kriegsmarine could conclude the maritime preparations for the invasion. And so, despite its reservations, the general staff proceeded to prepare for *Seelöwe* in accordance with Hitler's directive.

In the final *Seelöwe* plan that was produced, the 7th Fallschirmjäger Division was due to support the seaborne invasion with an advance airborne assault on to the Lyminge, Lympne and Hythe area. The assault armies would be Ninth (Generaloberst Adolf Strauss) and Sixteenth (Generaloberst Ernst Busch), with Sixth Army (Generaloberst Walther von Reichenau) providing the follow-on force. It was anticipated that von Rundstedt would have overall command of the invasion force, although he was one of many who seriously doubted its viability. The army group's objective was then to seize a line running north-east from north of Brighton to Ashford and Faversham, while the follow-on forces were to advance to a line from Portsmouth to Guildford and across to Gravesend – thus directly threatening London. In the meantime, the Luftwaffe fought in the skies above Britain and the Channel area to deliver Göring's promise of air superiority, and in practice events and the future of *Seelöwe* were now driven by the air campaign. On 14 September, Hitler acknowledged that the air situation was still unfavourable and postponed the invasion to 27 September, with a confirmatory decision to be made on 17 September. In fact, the Luftwaffe had already lost the 'Battle of Britain' on 15 September, although its campaign against the RAF was not finally concluded until about 31 October, by which stage the Luftwaffe had lost almost 1,300 aircraft since 10 July.[104] On 19 September, the OKW ordered the dispersal of barges and other vessels due to the growing losses resulting from RAF attacks against them, while Raeder had already acknowledged that *Seelöwe* could not now be launched before 8 October, if at all. Almost by default, the impetus behind the invasion gradually slipped away. Further staff planning largely ceased, and specialist invasion training was drastically curtailed. On 2 October, Hitler acknowledged the strategic reality of the situation and ordered that all measures taken in conjunction with *Seelöwe* were to be dismantled, although this was followed by a directive issued on 21 November indicating the possibility of reviving the operation in 1941. On 5 December, Halder noted with some relief that '*Seelöwe* can be left out of account', by which time Hitler's strategic priorities already lay elsewhere, on what would soon become the Wehrmacht's Eastern Front.

The Luftwaffe's failure to defeat the RAF during the Battle of Britain had finally resulted in the abandonment of *Seelöwe* in October, and later the bombing of British cities and strategic targets from August 1940 to May 1941 during the 'Blitz' would also fail to force a British capitulation. However, Hitler's assessment as at June 1940 was that for all practical purposes Great Britain had already been defeated militarily and was therefore neutralized strategically. He continued to believe that it was only a matter of time until London accepted the inevitable and sued for peace, at which time he anticipated that its armed forces would eventually join Nazi Germany's great crusade against the menace of Bolshevism. Many general staff officers were less sanguine and well knew from the lessons of history how easily unforeseen external events could change the situation.

Many reasons for Hitler's apparent lack of enthusiasm for, and final abandonment of, *Seelöwe* have been suggested. Von Rundstedt later opined,

'I have a feeling that the Führer never really wanted to invade England. He never had sufficient courage. He used to say, "On land I am a hero, but on water I am a coward". Hitler definitely hoped that the English would make peace overtures to him.'[105] Hitler and Mussolini discussed a whole range of other options for striking against Britain or British overseas interests indirectly. These included an attack on Gibraltar, possibly using the French fleet under Admiral Darlan, who had stated his readiness to lead it against Britain if required to do so; or a campaign launched from Syria (where the French governor had declared for Pétain); or possibly by persuading Russia to launch a campaign in the Middle East, the Persian Gulf or against northern India. However, such options were in reality little more than intellectual exercises. Above all else, the decisive factor that sealed the fate of *Seelöwe* was the inability of the Luftwaffe and Kriegsmarine to achieve the required level of air and naval superiority. This inability supported the general staff's own assessment that, while the army's ground forces could probably have achieved success against a weakened and ill-prepared British army in mid-1940 once across the Channel in strength, the Wehrmacht was simply not capable of conducting an amphibious operation on that scale. Therefore, what might or might not happen once on British soil was always largely academic. Halder was also very aware that Germany's industrial base in 1940 was not capable of providing the necessary matériel support for such a venture – something that Beck had foreseen in the pre-war years.[106]

But for the general staff, particularly the OKW, a significant and indirect consequence of the planning for *Seelöwe* was the German conclusion that a cross-Channel invasion was only viable using the shortest sea route between France and England, at the Pas de Calais. Consequently, almost four years later, there is little doubt that this coloured the unshakeable belief of Hitler and senior officers within the OKW that the main Allied seaborne invasion in mid-1944 would be there, at the Pas de Calais, with any other landing merely a diversion. Anything else ran contrary to the cross-Channel invasion option the high command had studied so exhaustively in 1940, having finally assessed it to be the only one both feasible and likely to succeed given the necessary resources and local air and naval superiority to support it.

Felix and Isabella: Iberian Options, October to December 1940

In the wake of the *Seelöwe* saga, the possibility of striking against Gibraltar was pursued further, with Hitler meeting the Spanish nationalist leader, General Francisco Franco, in late October to discuss a joint or collaborative operation to seize Gibraltar and enable an occupation of Portugal, which would provide the Kriegsmarine with submarine bases on the Atlantic coastline. The general staff indicated that the army would need two months to prepare for this action, and on 12 November Hitler ordered the necessary planning to proceed. The operation in collaboration with Spain against Gibraltar was named *Felix*, while that against Portugal was *Isabella*. The commander of this venture was to be Generalfeldmarschall Walther von Reichenau (promoted from Generaloberst on 19 July 1940), the commander of Sixth Army – which would have had an important role within the follow-on and breakout forces for *Seelöwe* if it had taken place (although in August 1940 von Reichenau had already voiced his personal misgivings about the viability of *Seelöwe*). Despite the production of the necessary plans by the general staff, *Felix* and *Isabella* proved to be short-lived: although the attraction for the Spanish leader of wresting Gibraltar away from Britain was very considerable, Franco declined to commit Spain as a member of the Axis. With no Spanish military support for Germany forthcoming, *Felix* was finally abandoned in December, which also made *Isabella* non-viable. Although Franco declared himself generally supportive of Germany, and had benefited considerably from German military support during the Spanish civil war from 1936, Spain thereafter remained officially neutral, while at the same time it pragmatically strengthened its defences along the border with German-occupied and Vichy France – just in case.[107]

At about this time, in late 1940, it became increasingly clear to the general staff that Hitler was minded to embark upon a new offensive in the east, against Russia. For those officers who were familiar with *Mein Kampf* and who had paid close attention to Hitler's speeches about his aspirations to acquire Lebensraum in the east, this significant change of course should have provoked little surprise. The willing acceptance by Germany of what would now potentially be a war waged on two active fronts flew in the face of all military logic and ran contrary to virtually every general staff assessment of the nation's strategic capability. However, developing events in early 1941 resulted not only in the general staff having to consider a major new front in the east, they also precipitated a spate of unsought and unwelcome subsidiary campaigns or new fronts in Greece, the Balkans and North Africa. Primarily, the strategic misjudgement and military ineptitude of Germany's Italian allies were now responsible for destabilizing and reshaping several aspects of German strategic policy. Although the circumstances surrounding Hitler's fatal decision to invade Russia and the general staff's preparation for that campaign were conducted in parallel with these lesser operations, the importance and complexities of what became Operation *Barbarossa* are best understood if dealt with separately. Furthermore, there was a separation of command and control by mid-1941 that saw the OKH assuming total responsibility for the Eastern Front, while the OKW took on responsibilities for all other fronts, which in turn produced a division of command and control. Consequently, the preliminary action that produced *Barbarossa* is considered in detail and as a whole in a later chapter. It is important to remember, however, that everything that occurred between the late summer of 1940 and June 1941 was unavoidably conducted against the backdrop of the general staff's preparations to launch the Wehrmacht's greatest and most significant campaign of the war, the invasion of Russia, and that these sideshows were largely unwelcome distractions that also drew scarce resources away from the great new enterprise in the east.

Somewhat precipitately, despite Italy's ongoing campaign against the British in Libya, Mussolini had decided to invade Greece, but by the spring of 1941 the Italian forces were proving woefully incapable of making any progress against the Greek and British forces in Greece, North Africa and the Mediterranean. Indeed, in Albania the Greek forces had not only halted the Italians but had launched a counteroffensive. The rapidly deteriorating military situation of Germany's Axis ally, together with the need to safeguard the Romanian oil supplies for German use, brought about the campaign in the Balkans and Aegean region from April 1941. In fact, general staff contingency planning for this eventuality had actually begun on 18 November the previous year. This work for what was designated Operation

Marita had been prompted by Hitler's long-standing intention to secure Germany's southern flank by drawing Romania, Bulgaria, Hungary and Yugoslavia into the Axis fold before embarking upon the campaign against Russia. However, the British intervention in Greece had contributed to a military coup in Yugoslavia, which deposed the pro-Axis regent, Prince Paul, and placed King Peter on the throne. This had in turn positioned that country on the side of the Allies, and at the beginning of April an extended version of the *Marita* plan was implemented as German and Hungarian forces were launched into Yugoslavia.

On 6 April, German forces, consisting mainly of Generalfeldmarschall Siegmund Wilhelm List's Twelfth Army and Generaloberst Maximilian Freiherr von Weichs' Second Army, struck simultaneously into Yugoslavia from Bulgaria, Austria, Romania and Hungary. List's Twelfth Army comprised no fewer than fifteen divisions, of which four were panzer divisions. Faced with weak Yugoslav resistance, a failure to exploit Yugoslavia's rugged terrain for defence, and Greek animosity towards the British within the Anglo-Greek command structure, the onslaught moved swiftly to outflank the Anglo-Greek forces and cut off the Greek army in Albania. Tank units of Twelfth Army entered Athens on 27 April. Everywhere the Allies had been forced to withdraw, while already on 20 April the British had recognized the inevitable and ordered the evacuation of its expeditionary force, thus consigning Greece to German occupation. Sensibly, von Brauchitsch and Halder had ignored Hitler's initial directive to deploy strong German forces to assist directly the beleaguered Italian forces in Albania at the outset of the campaign, as the general staff had assessed quite correctly that success in Albania was contingent upon the prior defeat of Greece. Belgrade fell on 13 April; the Yugoslav army surrendered at Sarajevo on 17 April, and this was followed by the Greek capitulation on 23 April.

Some 27,000 of the troops evacuated were transported to the island of Crete, where they joined an Anglo-Greek garrison of about 3,000 British and British Commonwealth soldiers (predominantly the 6th Australian and 2nd New Zealand Divisions) and several thousand Greek troops. However, in an evacuation reminiscent of that at Dunkirk a year earlier, most of the Allies' heavy weapons, support equipment and artillery used in Greece had to be abandoned during the evacuation, and so it was not available for the defence of Crete. In the meantime, while the Balkan campaign undoubtedly detracted from German preparations for the forthcoming invasion of Russia, the large quantities of matériel captured from the Allies once again provided a welcome boost for the army's logistics staff officers, who were by then trying to match the available resources to general staff projections of the army's anticipated requirements in Russia. Arguably (and apart from the opening stages of the forthcoming campaign against Russia), the campaign in the Balkans in 1941 was the last of the true Blitzkrieg operations, with exemplary air-ground cooperation, devastating air strikes ahead of the advancing ground forces, and a speed and shock effect achieved by the effective use of panzer units and motorized infantry, all of which were in line with the principles of Blitzkrieg. Luftwaffe ace Generalleutnant Adolf Galland, writing about this campaign in 1954, observed that, 'This was the last time that motorized German army units, perfectly coordinated with the air force, decisively defeated in the shortest possible time a courageous and well-mobilized adversary.'[108] The Balkan campaign also demonstrated the sort of success that could still be achieved when a general staff operational plan was properly resourced and subsequently implemented largely without political or other non-military interference. It was the sort of short, high-tempo campaign to which the German army had always aspired, and which also provided the principal operational commanders with opportunities to operate in the best traditions of the doctrine of Auftragstaktik, largely unconstrained by the oversight and intervention of any superior head-quarters or senior commanders.

Merkur: The Invasion of Crete, May 1941

The German victory in the Balkans in April precipitated a major airborne assault against Crete the following month. Although this assault was primarily an OKW and Luftwaffe operation, its uniqueness and strategic importance warrant its inclusion in any account dealing with the general staff and the wider aspects of the command and control of the Wehrmacht. This operation, designated *Merkur* ('Mercury'), was the first airborne assault of the war conducted on a large scale, and although it was a strategic success the high numbers of casualties incurred meant that it was also the last such operation carried out by the Germans. As this was clearly an airborne operation, most of the staff planners and the vast majority of the fighting troops involved in Operation *Merkur* were members of the Luftwaffe rather than the army, although there was necessarily some OKH participation, as the assault against Crete also involved a sea-borne army element. In any event, the fact that the staff planning for *Merkur* was conducted predominantly by officers all of whom were serving within the same arm or branch of the Wehrmacht undoubtedly simplified the preparation for *Merkur*. Despite this, the planning for the operation inevitably bore the stamp of general staff competence and thoroughness. This was hardly surprising, as many of the officers involved in this process at OKW and within the Luftwaffe general staff were former army general staff officers who later found themselves in the newly formed German air force when it was created during the pre-war period. Indeed, the Fallschirmjäger (paratroopers or parachute infantry) had been under army control until 1935, when they had been transferred to the Luftwaffe as a result of lobbying by Göring; once landed, whether by parachute or glider, the Fallschirmjäger served as normal soldiers under army command.

Operation *Merkur* also highlighted a command and control matter that would significantly affect the course of the war to the detriment of the German high command, as this was one of many occasions on which the Allies had successfully intercepted the high command's 'Enigma' coded communications system and thus knew about *Merkur* in advance – but chose not to take extensive new measures to defend Crete in order to avoid revealing that the 'Enigma' system had been compromised. The Allied intelligence (known as 'Ultra') derived from breaking the 'Enigma' code messages had revealed that the Germans intended to seize the island in order both to prevent the bombing of the Romanian oilfields and to forestall a British offensive being launched into the region from North Africa. However, although General Freyberg, the British commander on Crete, was fully aware of the impending attack, he was not permitted to enhance the airfield defences to the extent he deemed necessary. At the same time he was directed or encouraged to promote the line that the main attack against Crete would be amphibious, not airborne.[109] Although these ploys maintained the security of 'Ultra' and the continued belief of the German high command that 'Enigma' remained secure, it nevertheless proved to be a major contributor to the impending Allied defeat on the island.

The plan for Operation *Merkur* called for the airfields at Maleme (close to the town of Canea), Heraklion and Retimo to be seized in an assault by the paratroopers of Generalleutnant Kurt Student's Fliegerkorps 11, supported by Fliegerkorps 8 (the air strike component), the two formations making up Generaloberst Alexander Löhr's Luftflotte 4. The capture of the three airfields was designed to enable one regiment of the army's 5th Mountain Division to be landed by transport aircraft shortly thereafter. The German airborne and air-landed forces together numbered about 15,750 men, while the balance of the 5th Mountain Division of up to 7,000 men was a follow-on force transported to Crete by sea. The airborne assault was supported by 500 transports (mainly Ju-52s), about 80 gliders, 280 bombers, 180 fighters, and 40 reconnaissance aircraft.

Soon after dawn on 20 May, the airborne assault against Crete began, initially suffering very heavy casualties at the hands of the lightly armed and thinly spread, but determined and well-trained British Commonwealth troops. Meanwhile, at sea the Royal Navy destroyed the 5th Mountain Division's sea-landing component in their transports en route to their intended landing beaches on the island. On 21 May, however, the precipitate abandonment by its New Zealand defenders of Hill 107, which overlooked Maleme airfield, allowed Student to call in the Ju-52 transports, despite Allied artillery fire still falling on the runway. The tide turned, as the German main effort switched from Heraklion to Maleme, where the build-up of the 5th Mountain Division continued apace, and the island's defence swiftly crumbled from the west. With the battle lost, the Royal Navy managed to evacuate about 7,000 British Commonwealth troops from Heraklion and Sphakia harbours to Egypt between 27 and 30 May, nine warships being sunk and a further seventeen badly damaged at the hands of the fighters and bombers of Fliegerkorps 8 during the battle. By 1 June the fighting for Crete had ended. The garrison's British and Commonwealth casualties amounted to 1,742 killed and missing, 2,225 wounded and 11,370 captured. Of the almost 17,530 German troops who actually landed on Crete between 20 and 23 May, no fewer than 8,000 had been killed, including about 6,500 of the Fallschirmjäger. Although the strategic mission had been accomplished, with the Balkan and Aegean flank and Romania secured against any possible British interference in the Wehrmacht's impending attack on Russia, such losses to the German airborne forces were unsustainable – some 56 per cent overall.

The OKW had anticipated a similar airborne assault being launched against Cyprus once Crete had been secured, but the high toll of German casualties during *Merkur* resulted in Hitler never again sanctioning the large-scale use of airborne units, and thereafter the Fallschirmjäger were used only for conventional ground combat and certain small-scale commando operations. While the Fallschirmjäger losses on Crete had undeniably been heavy, Hitler's decision to abrogate the German airborne assault capability (development of which was already well ahead of that of the Allies) was nevertheless short-sighted. It denied the Wehrmacht a capability that (with the lessons learnt in Crete taken fully into account) could have been used for similar operations against Gibraltar or Malta as well as Cyprus, or possibly for launching airborne assaults ahead of the advancing panzer forces in Russia. Although they remained members of the Luftwaffe, the subsequent use of the Fallschirmjäger as conventional ground troops meant that these troops increasingly served within army formations rather than under Luftwaffe command. From time to time this situation inevitably produced friction between the the army's general staff and operational commanders, and a Luftwaffe headquarters that jealously sought to protect Göring's power-base and breadth of military command within the Wehrmacht, although such clashes were usually at the more rarefied and politicized levels of command rather than at the practical or tactical level. Variations in the basic equipment, personal weapons and uniforms of the Fallschirmjäger also complicated general staff management of the logistic supply arrangements where airborne units operated alongside army units. At the same time, these Luftwaffe units acting as conventional ground forces demanded heavy weapons, armoured vehicles and other equipment that had to be found by general staff officers from army sources – a situation exemplified by the transformation of the parachute infantry troops of the Regiment 'General Göring' of 1935–1942 into a panzer division by May 1943, which subsequently became the Fallschirmpanzerkorps (literally, 'airborne armoured corps') 'Hermann Göring' by October 1944!

Sonnenblume: The Campaign in North Africa, 1941–1943

While the Balkan and Aegean campaigns had been in progress, another largely unanticipated campaign was already underway against the British and Commonwealth forces in North Africa. Although the need for German involvement in this theatre was both unwelcome and something of a surprise when it arose early in 1941, the concept of a North African deployment had been considered as early as July the previous year, when von Brauchitsch had proposed an expansion of operations in the Mediterranean theatre as a means of breaking the strategic stalemate that he anticipated would develop if and when the *Seelöwe* operation became unachievable. (At that time von Brauchitsch was unaware that just twelve months later a whole new Eastern Front would have opened up in Russia.) The army commander-in-chief's proposal had some merit, and the general staff believed that a new campaign could build on the Italian operations then in progress (which had enjoyed some early successes) and strike at Britain's presence in the area, including the North African littoral, Egypt and the Suez Canal, thereby displacing British control of the Mediterranean and persuading additional non-aligned states to join the Axis. The concept was taken under consideration alongside Hitler's deliberations about Spain, Gibraltar and other possible options for action against British interests overseas in the wake of *Seelöwe*. Although much discussed and accepted in principle, von Brauchitsch's proposal was subsequently scaled-down by Hitler, who feared that at that stage it would detract from his plans for the invasion of Russia. Accordingly, further work on the general staff's embryo plans for a North African campaign was accorded a low priority and all but ceased.

By early 1941, however, German optimism about the capabilities of their Italian allies in Libya proved to be seriously misplaced, when a series of significant Italian defeats at the hands of the British Western Desert Force prompted the urgent deployment of German military units to redress the rapidly deteriorating Axis situation in North Africa. Suddenly, the general staff was faced with the need to prepare and deploy at short notice a strong force to fight a potentially protracted campaign in an environment very different from the European theatre in which the Wehrmacht had operated thus far. The OKH was taken largely by surprise, so that preparations for this campaign were somewhat limited, and the short notice deployment meant that the troops involved only had time to concentrate upon the essentials. Despite this, and a widely held belief that effective Axis control of the North African coast was ultimately untenable due to the problems of supporting and reinforcing a theatre in which the British generally had few such problems, the general staff set about creating, preparing and deploying to North Africa what would soon be known as the Deutsches Afrikakorps (DAK).

The officer nominated as the DAK's commander was Generalleutnant Erwin Rommel, the officer who had commanded the 7th Panzer Division so successfully during the campaign in France. An accomplished tactician, staff officer and commander, Rommel was to become probably the best-known German general of the war, although he was never formally a member of the general staff. In 1935 he had served as an instructor at the Kriegsakademie at Potsdam; in 1937 he had been given responsibility for overseeing the military training of the Hitler Youth (Hitler Jugend); and in 1938 he had been appointed commandant of the Kriegsakademie at Wiener Neustadt. Having favourably attracted Hitler's attention, in October 1938 Rommel was appointed commander of Hitler's headquarters bodyguard, serving in that capacity in Austria, Czechoslovakia and Poland before being promoted to command the 7th Panzer Division in February 1940. While Rommel's lack of a formal general staff background was certainly not to the detriment of his performance as commander of the DAK, it could be argued that the relatively small size and semi-independent nature of the German forces deployed to North Africa in 1941 made this deficiency less important. However, it might also be argued that Rommel was less well prepared for the later high-level command appointments and politicized events with which he eventually became involved than if he had been a fully qualified member of the general staff – and therefore more alert to the often perverse imperatives, influences and agendas that increasingly affected this organization as the war progressed.[110]

Despite the deployment to North Africa, Operation *Sonnenblume* ('Sunflower'), being mounted at short notice, the planning work already completed enabled the general staff to implement some critical measures immediately. Among the preparations that could be carried out speedily was ensuring that the troops earmarked for North Africa were medically fit for tropical service, with particularly rigorous standards being applied, and training them on those aspects of health and hygiene peculiar to desert regions. The normal training programme was also adapted where practicable to reflect the anticipated nature of desert warfare, especially the command and control of armour and mobile operations in the open desert. To that end, all personnel were briefed extensively on the various types of desert terrain and their advantages and limitations, as well as about the Italian allies alongside whom they would fight and the British and Commonwealth forces that would oppose them. However, any practical training for desert warfare was largely limited to attending a series of lectures about tropical medicine and talks about their personal experiences by officers who had by chance travelled in various desert regions before the war. This information was then supplemented by individual research carried out in military libraries. The unique conditions imposed by the desert environment also called for an innovative approach to logistic support. Arrangements were made to ensure the provision of water supplies, with special units created specifically to source, purify and transport drinking water, as well as specialist engineer units to drill new wells. Suitable desert uniforms were available from the outset, while programmes to provide other specialized equipment, rations, suitable combustible fuel for field kitchens, vehicles and vehicle modifications for desert use were set in train; in most cases these items did not appear until well after the initial deployment. Some problems and requirements – such as those involved with using equipment and rations designed for Europe to provide meals in the desert – were only fully revealed after the DAK took the field. Even Rommel had little time to prepare. He was briefed by von Brauchitsch on 6 February, arrived in Rome on 11 February and flew to Tripoli on 12 February, while the principal headquarters staff for this generally unexpected mission had only formed up in late 1940, on a contingency basis, finally deploying to North Africa on 24 February 1941.[111]

All in all, the general staff's deployment plan worked remarkably well, and on 14 February the first German combat troops of the DAK arrived at Tripoli, where they were reviewed by Rommel. In due course the DAK would consist of the 15th and 21st Panzer Divisions, 90th Light Division, 164th Infantry Division and an airborne brigade (Fallschirmjäger-Brigade Ramke). Later, as 'Panzerarmee Afrika' (from 30 January 1942), it operated with X, XX and XXI Corps of the Italian First Army. Although the build-up of the DAK to its full strength was not achieved for a number of months, Rommel was able to launch a limited offensive with one armoured division as early as 3 April. This force first captured Bardia, then effectively neutralized the predominantly Australian garrison at Tobruk, laying siege to the port and finally forcing a British withdrawal into Egypt. In just two weeks the DAK regained Libya for the Axis and reversed the course of the North African campaign. If the general staff had been fairly unprepared for *Sonnenblume*, Hitler and the OKW were equally unprepared for the early success of Rommel's first offensive. They urged caution and directed him to adopt a primarily defensive posture: the Wehrmacht's principal strategic priorities were by then the campaign in Greece and the impending invasion of the Soviet Union. Indeed, Hitler continued to regard the North African campaign as little more than a side-show and a distraction from the offensive against Russia. He therefore denied the DAK the combat strength – some four or five panzer divisions instead of just two – with which Rommel might well have completed the defeat of the British and Commonwealth forces in North Africa and Egypt during 1941.

Despite an ongoing lack of resources and always being outnumbered in men and tanks, the DAK continued to out-fight the British from March 1941 to the late summer of 1942. The tide began to turn again in December 1941 when a well-planned British offensive forced the DAK back to El Agheila and enabled the relief of Tobruk, the DAK withdrawing from Cyrenaica in good order to the border of Tripolitania. Early in 1942 the arrival of some 50 new tanks by sea allowed Rommel to resume the offensive in February, and by the end of May he had reached Gazala. There, despite being temporarily trapped between a complex of strongly held British and Free French positions and his own minefields, he extricated the DAK successfully and forced a British withdrawal back to Egypt and El Alamein. In the meantime, Tobruk capitulated to the Germans, where about 2,000 much-needed vehicles fell into their hands. Hitler promoted Rommel to Generalfeldmarschall.

However, the DAK was always handicapped by a lack of resources, both as a consequence of the lower priority allocated to it by the high command and as a result of the failure of the Luftwaffe and Kriegsmarine to neutralize Malta and thereby secure the lines of supply between North Africa and continental Europe. Rommel consistently criticized the German high command and the Italians concerning Malta. He viewed the British-owned island as the strategic key to his operations in North Africa and berated Berlin for having attacked Crete rather than Malta in mid-1941 and the Italians for their inability to subdue Malta. The DAK had advanced to within 100 kilometres of Alexandria by July 1942, but Rommel was there confronted by the rested, reinforced and well-resourced British Eighth Army. This army was now commanded by General Bernard Montgomery, who benefited from access to the 'Ultra' intelligence derived from the interception of 'Enigma' transmissions and was thus able to exploit his prior knowledge of Rommel's intentions. By forcing the DAK to engage in a battle of attrition, and denying it the sort of free-flowing mobile battle that had enabled its earlier successes, the Eighth Army inflicted a major defeat on Panzerarmee Afrika at El Alamein on 23 October. Thereafter, despite the belated arrival of reinforcements, the Germans retreated westwards during the following six months, eluding every Allied attempt to outflank it. All the while, the Allied naval blockade in the Mediterranean continued to deny Panzerarmee Afrika the reinforcements and matériel that it needed to sustain its operations while simultaneously enabling a largely unrestricted flow of men and resources to the Allies – by that stage of the campaign, Rommel's forces were receiving little more than a third of the supplies that they actually required. During the autumn of 1942, only the 164th Light Division and Parachute Brigade

Ramcke had been added to the German strength, while the British and Commonwealth forces had continued to receive a steady flow of new divisions arriving from India, Syria and Iraq. Meanwhile to the west, soon after El Alamein, Anglo-US forces landed in strength at Casablanca, Algiers and Oran on 8 November 1942, and with the Eighth Army pressing hard from the east the eventual outcome was inevitable. The remaining German and Italian forces in North Africa finally surrendered in Tunisia on 12–13 May 1943 at the end of a campaign characterized by their resolute fighting withdrawal conducted over a period of several months. The defeat of the US II Corps at Kasserine Pass in February was the only significant victory during the German withdrawal more than 3,000 kilometres. Shortly thereafter, Rommel was invalided back to Germany, leaving his successor General von Arnim to make the final surrender.

By that time, significant changes had taken place in the high-level command arrangements for the Wehrmacht and the division of operational responsibility between the OKW and the OKH. While the OKH had led on the initial deployment for *Sonnenblume*, by its end in the spring of 1943 the OKW had assumed primary responsibility for the direction of these operations in North Africa and the Mediterranean, while the OKH focused almost exclusively upon the much greater conflict that was raging on the Eastern Front.

9

The Path to Barbarossa

1940–1941

Following the abandonment of *Seelöwe*, Hitler ordered the general staff to make planning for an invasion of Russia its highest priority. The strategic rationale for this was Germany's need to secure the oil, food supplies and other raw materials necessary for the Wehrmacht to conduct a protracted conflict, and to neutralize the potential ally of an undefeated Britain. More subjective considerations – such as Hitler's desire to acquire 'Lebensraum' in the east and his distrust of Stalin's possible expansionist intentions in Finland and on Germany's eastern border – also played a significant part in this.[112] Nazi ideology also influenced the matter: Hitler was obsessed by a belief that the greatest threat to Germany was a Bolshevik-Jewish conspiracy, intent upon the annihilation of the German state and its culture, and its replacement with a Soviet-style communist system.

Although the staff planning process was then still at a relatively early stage, some signs of Germany's changing strategic focus were evident as early as the late summer of 1940. Following the Wehrmacht's 1939 campaign, most of Poland was firmly in German hands, and in August 1940 work began to establish the infrastructure in that country necessary to support a new campaign in the east against Russia. German-occupied Poland lacked many of the facilities found in Germany, so new roads, railways, air bases and all sorts of accommodation and storage facilities for personnel and equipment had to be constructed. Meanwhile, a rapid reduction of German forces in occupied France and elsewhere on the western front allowed some twelve divisions to begin moving to bases and assembly areas in Poland that

August. These troops were merely an advance guard, preparing the way for what would eventually be a mighty invasion force of no fewer than 120 German divisions, plus various military contingents provided by some of Germany's Axis allies.

Hitler's direction to prepare for a campaign against Russia prompted diverging reactions within the general staff. On the one hand, the Wehrmacht's continued successes on the battlefield – in Scandinavia, the Low Countries and France, then in the Balkans in 1941 – had significantly enhanced Hitler's reputation as a leader and strategist. The pre-war assessments and predictions of men such as Generaloberst Beck had been shown to be operationally flawed and overly pessimistic. Consequently, more and more members of the army and the general staff – amongst them, of course, many officers who had experienced the army's stunning Blitzkrieg victories at first-hand – were now disinclined to gainsay the Führer's strategic aspirations. Indeed, the earlier scepticism of many had been largely overtaken by enthusiasm and an increasing belief in the invincibility of the Wehrmacht. On the other hand, these successes revived some of the misgivings and fears that had almost resulted in a military-led coup in late 1939. In the wake of Hitler's direction to begin planning the invasion of Russia – *Fall Otto*, later renamed Operation *Barbarossa* – a resurrected conspiracy against Hitler began to coalesce. Among those who were most prominent or deeply involved in this conspiracy were men such as the former mayor of Leipzig, Carl Goerdeler, the diplomat and financier Ulrich von Hassell, the retired Generaloberst Beck and serving officers such as General Georg Thomas, Oberst Henning von Tresckow, the ubiquitous Oberst Hans Oster, Generalfeldmarschall Erwin von Witzleben, Leutnant Fabian von Schlabrendorff and General von Falkenhausen. For some, an end of Hitler and the Nazi regime continued to be the primary aim, while for others the belief that a new war against Russia would be disastrous for Germany provided the impetus for their commitment. However, while the general staff's criticism of Hitler's early strategic decisions had often been widespread and forthright, the Wehrmacht's successes during 1940 had led many such officers to revise their views to varying degrees.

Accordingly, the general staff now set about developing the detailed assessments and operational plans for *Fall Otto* with a fair degree of enthusiasm. The projected timetable called for plans to be ready for the campaign to begin in the spring of 1941, probably during May, with the subsequent military action being concluded speedily and certainly well before the end of that year. In July 1940, Generaloberst Halder noted that the military aim of *Fall Otto* would be, 'To defeat the Russian army or at least to occupy as much Russian soil as is necessary to protect Berlin and the Silesian industrial area from air attack. It is desired to establish our positions so far to the east that our own air force can destroy the most important areas of Russia.'[113] Broadly, this fairly conservative and (at that stage) achievable aim shaped the OKH planning process thereafter, but, as we shall see, it would eventually fall well short of what Hitler actually intended for his Russian campaign.

As with any such staff planning process, the general staff's work on *Fall Otto* was intelligence-led. In 1940, the estimated combat strength of the Russian forces in the western part of the Soviet Union amounted to between 50 and 75 divisions, although the veracity of this estimate was by no means certain. The questionable accuracy of this intelligence was perhaps surprising in light of the Russian-German pact and of the extensive German-Russian military cooperation that had taken place between the two countries during the pre-war years, as well as in Poland during the Red Army's occupation of part of that country in 1939. It also raised questions about the practical effectiveness of the OKH intelligence staff who analysed and assessed the Russian capability on a day-to-day basis. The branch dealing with foreign armies in the east (the Fremde Heere Ost, or 'FHO'), was at that time headed by Oberst Kienzel. One officer particularly well placed to advise on this matter was the German military attaché in Moscow, Generalmajor Ernst Köstring, who cautioned against underestimating Russian strength, citing the Red Army's lacklustre performance in Finland as unrepresentative of its true potential. But Köstring's reports may have been accorded less weight than they deserved, as he was well known to be opposed to a war against Russia. In any event, based upon the OKH's assessment of the relatively benign threat posed by the Russians,

Generalmajor Erich Marcks, at that time chief of staff at the headquarters of Eighteenth Army, produced the first detailed operational plan for *Fall Otto* and presented it to Halder on 5 August.

Fall Otto: The First Plan

This plan indicated a need for 147 divisions, including 24 panzer and 12 motorized. Generalmajor Marcks assumed the use of Finnish and Romanian territory from which to launch flanking forces, a major thrust in the centre, and an operational concept that would result in the encirclement and destruction of the Soviet forces in western Russia. The need to prevent either a Russian withdrawal into the interior or a reinforcement of the Red Army in the west was crucial to achieving a quick victory, while also pre-empting the threat of air strikes against Germany launched from bases in western Russia. Even at this early stage it was evident to the general staff that only a Blitzkrieg-type operation would do, as the Wehrmacht lacked the logistical support, transport, communications, supply and other resources – including the necessary winter warfare capability – to conduct and sustain a campaign of more than four to six months in such a vast country with limited and often non-existent road and rail systems. It was also significant that, although *Fall Otto* rapidly assumed a high priority, in parallel with planning the attack on Russia the general staff were also required to consider and deal with a range of other scenarios. These included *Seelöwe*[114] as well as various options for Spain and Portugal (*Felix* and *Isabella*), the impending operations in Greece and Albania (*Marita*), the *Sonnenblume* expedition to assist the Italians in North Africa, and the airborne invasion of Crete (*Merkur*). With so many competing priorities and commitments it was small wonder, therefore, that just as Marcks was completing the work on his plan for *Fall Otto* on 26 July the senior signals officer, General Fellgiebel, stated that it would not be possible for the Wehrmacht to provide communications to support *Seelöwe* and *Fall Otto* simultaneously. The same situation undoubtedly also obtained to varying extents in a range of other support areas.

The operational plan produced by Marcks was developed primarily for the OKH, and so General Alfred Jodl, the chief of operations at the OKW, also commissioned a study of the projected eastern campaign by his own headquarters staff. This work took proper account of the OKH plan and was carried out by Oberstleutnant (later Generalmajor) Bernhard von Lossberg, whose general comments included two important observations. The first of these was whether or not it really was practicable to pursue the planning for an attack against Russia before the defeat of Great Britain had been achieved. The second was the need to ensure that the Russians remained entirely ignorant of German intentions until the defeat of Britain had been accomplished. The OKW and OKH were both conscious of the implications of a breakdown of German-Soviet relations – it would, at best, cut off the flow of important resources to Germany and, at worst, could lead to Stalin pre-empting *Fall Otto* by initiating a Russian offensive against Germany. At the OKH, the OKW and elsewhere, the abiding fear within the general staff of becoming engaged in a two-front war was in evidence. The study by Oberstleutnant von Lossberg was presented to Jodl on 15 September.

That same month, an officer whose eventual role during the forthcoming campaign would prove especially prominent, became involved with the development of *Fall Otto*. Generalleutnant Friedrich Paulus, was appointed Oberquartiermeister I and deputy chief of the general staff. A former chief of staff to General von Reichenau, he was at that time chief of staff of XVI Panzer Corps. The appointment came at the direction of Hitler, who overrode Halder's wishes for an older officer (Oberst von Greiffenberg) with wider experience and a more traditional approach to fill such an important position overseeing the activities of the OKH operations branch. Soon after assuming his new post, Paulus directed that a series of interlinked war games should be conducted during late November and early December to test the Marcks plan and identify any aspects requiring further review or modification. The general staff officers anticipated to head the command staff and occupy other key staff posts within the invading army groups conducted these war games, fulfilling roles on both the German and the Russian sides. For the war games, the overall Russian force level was set at 150 divisions (including 15 motorized), 32 cavalry divisions and 36 motorized or mechanized brigades. Of these formations, some 116 divisions were assessed available to oppose the invasion directly. The officers who played the part of Russian commanders were required to operate in accordance with comprehensive directives developed by the intelligence staff, based upon German knowledge of the Russian forces. They then represented the Red Army's strategic and operational decision-making at levels of command down to army level, as well as the plans and activities of the Russian air force. These war games produced an indication of a practicable limit of exploitation, together with the deployment and scale of forces necessary to achieve this.

As a result of the war games, Paulus concluded that the offensive could reasonably achieve a line from Leningrad to Smolensk and to the Dnieper river; at which stage a new or complementary plan would be required, depending upon the operational situation and updated strategic goal. To do this, the Germans would need no more than 120 divisions, rather than the 147 identified by Marcks, this reduction being made primarily in the follow-on or reserve formations. Beyond the Dnieper the main assault would be carried out by three army groups, with objectives that included Leningrad, Smolensk, Moscow, Kiev and Kharkov. Paulus proposed that Moscow should be the key objective, the city to be taken by the central army group's main thrust by the sixth or seventh week of the campaign. General staff consensus was achieved, although the OKH logistics staff sounded a note of caution with estimates indicating that the advance risked outrunning its lines of supply about two-thirds of the way to Leningrad and Smolensk and halfway to the River Don beyond Kharkov. Overall, however, the general staff's conclusions provided a sound planning basis for producing what Paulus, von Brauchitsch and Halder believed would be the final version of the OKH plan for *Fall Otto*.

In November the Führer's long-held suspicions about Stalin's future territorial intentions in Finland, the Balkans, South-East Europe and the Black Sea had been reinforced during a visit to Berlin by Soviet foreign minister Molotov. This visit was meant to be placatory and an opportunity for Germany and Russia to resolve any areas of difficulty between the two governments, but Hitler chose to interpret Molotov's requests and proposals quite differently. Irrespective of what had actually been said, it now directly served his purposes and intentions by adding weight to his existing mindset concerning the strategic priorities for the invasion. Together, these factors were about to have a significant impact upon the general staff's plan.

The strategic plan for *Fall Otto* was briefed to Hitler by Halder during a four-hour seminar on 5 December. By then it had been further modified to take proper account of the Pripet Marshes, a major obstacle that would unavoidably separate the three army groups, with two now advancing north and east towards Leningrad and Minsk and the third striking south-east towards Kiev and the Ukraine. This deployment also reflected the general staff's view on the strategic importance of Moscow as a key communications hub. Once these armies had achieved their objectives, with the Russian forces in the west destroyed, it was anticipated that only about one fifth of the invasion force would need to remain in place to occupy the territory gained and secure the line.[115] In total, Halder now envisaged 105 infantry divisions and 32 panzer and motorized divisions being needed to carry out the plan. The deployment of the *Fall Otto* forces would take eight weeks, and it was unlikely that the security of the intended invasion could now be maintained much beyond mid-April.

During the discussions that followed this presentation, Hitler declared himself in agreement with the overall concept but then went on to add a few potentially most significant observations of his own. First, he emphasized the need for a rapid advance that would put Russian centres of industry within the range of the Luftwaffe's bombers while denying the Russian air force a similar opportunity to attack German industry. In order to ensure the destruction of the Red Army where the main blow would first fall, at the centre, Hitler directed that strong armoured forces should be deployed on the inner flanks of the northern and central army groups – ready to envelop the Russian forces trapped close to the border as early as possible. Developing this theme further, Hitler indicated the need for the northern army group to encircle the Russian forces in the Baltic area, and in order to enable this the central army group would have to be sufficiently strong for part of it to be detached to reinforce the northern army group. Meanwhile, the southern army group would need to sweep southwards in concert with those formations advancing eastwards from Romania, in order to encircle the Russian forces in the Ukraine. Hitler's next point was highly significant: no decision on whether or not to advance on Moscow could be made at that time, and even though the northern and southern encirclements might have been successfully accomplished, the advance on Moscow that lay at the heart of the general staff's plan should not be assumed.

Remarkably, Halder failed to attach sufficient importance to Hitler's observation that the Russian capital should not be attacked until Leningrad and the nearby port of Kronstadt had been taken and the Russian forces in the Baltic region destroyed. The Führer's acknowledgement of the need for the main effort and consequent strength of the invasion to be placed in the centre (as already planned by the general staff) may have led all concerned to dismiss the true implications of Hitler's subsequent intention to reallocate forces from the central to the northern army group at an early stage of the offensive. These observations had undoubtedly been made with Molotov's recent visit in mind and reflected Hitler's desire to support Finland in the north, while also deploying sufficient strength into southern Russia and the Ukraine to seize its industrial facilities, oilfields and natural resources. Hitler's observations were not translated into changes of operational priority as a result of this briefing, and so the general staff's subsequent planning proceeded based upon the results of the war games and with Moscow still the main objective. It is unclear why Hitler did not persist with his views or specifically direct their adoption at this stage; perhaps in his own mind he judged that an expression of his views was sufficient to prompt these changes. In any event, Halder – certain of the strength of the general staff's case for adopting the plan as briefed that day – apparently failed to anticipate that Hitler's desire to prioritize the thrust against Leningrad might yet affect the enterprise. Certainly, by the end of the briefing, Halder and the OKH presenters were left with the impression that Hitler was content with the plan and operational priorities as briefed. Arguably, the dislocation of the general staff from the wider political and diplomatic scene had unsighted many of these officers on various peripheral but nevertheless important matters and agendas that should have been taken fully into account throughout the *Fall Otto* planning process.

Although the general staff had remained largely excluded from the political deliberations concerning the follow-on action and future of the captured Russian territory once victory had been achieved, Halder also envisaged that, rather than maintaining large numbers of German occupation troops in western Russia, the conquered territories would be subdivided into a number of non-Bolshevik states. This would capitalize upon the pre-existence of various anti-Stalin groups in parts of Russia, with the areas they populated comprising a wide protective buffer zone between Russia and Germany. Just three months later, in March 1941, Halder, the army commanders and the general staff would be disabused of this idea when Hitler revealed his own, ideologically driven and much more far-reaching requirements for the way in which the invasion of Russia was to be carried out. That occasion would be a defining moment of the war, setting the tenor of the forthcoming campaign and thereafter leaving only the most naïve commander or staff officer in any doubt as to the true nature of the Wehrmacht's offensive in Russia. Meanwhile, considerably earlier than March, the general staff was about to have its finely-honed plan for *Fall Otto* thrown into disarray.

Fall Otto: Hitler's Intervention

Despite the Führer's apparent acceptance of Halder's proposals on 5 December, just a couple of weeks later the general staff were advised of what the OKW war diary described as 'a substantial alteration' to the OKH operational plan. This significant change came about following Halder's briefing, when Jodl decided that Hitler's direction that full planning of *Fall Otto* should proceed implicitly required the OKW to produce its own over-arching directive for the offensive. This work was duly carried out by the OKW staff, with the resultant draft *Directive No. 21* for what the OKW now called Operation *Fritz* being completed on 16 December. The draft directive was in large part simply a re-statement of the OKH plan – but now with the OKW stamp upon it – and was passed to Hitler on 17 December for his approval. Now, without further reference to the OKH, Hitler seized the opportunity to change the operational balance of the forthcoming offensive by returning to the ideas he had discussed with Halder on 5 December, which he noted had not been incorporated into the final plan. Now, with several strokes of his pen, Hitler replaced Moscow with Leningrad as the principal objective and formalized the reduction of the strength of the central army group early in the invasion in order to reinforce the northern army group for its advance against Leningrad. These amendments fundamentally changed the whole operational concept, while ignoring months of meticulous work by the general staff, the Führer's apparent endorsement of the Halder briefing on 5 December and the lessons of history regarding the disastrous invasions of Russia by Charles XII of Sweden and Napoleon I of France in earlier times. If Hitler's decision to invade Russia in 1941 was his greatest single error of judgement, then his subsequent decision not to strike hard and fast against Moscow was surely a close second. On Wednesday 18 December 1940, Hitler signed the amended OKW directive for Operation *Fritz*. Only nine copies of the new *Directive No. 21* were made, and these now bore the title *Barbarossa*.

Barbarossa: The Final Plan

Although well aware of Hitler's earlier preoccupation with Finland and the Leningrad option, Jodl had certainly not expected that any significant changes to the Halder plan would be made, and he was well aware of the operational implications of these changes. However, he judged it inappropriate for the OKW to criticize Hitler's decision or lobby on behalf of the OKH. In any case, the OKW could now derive some kudos from this turn of events, as the updated directive would be viewed as an OKW plan rather than one developed exclusively by the army general staff. When the new directive reached the OKH, Halder and the staff were stunned and frustrated by the major change of emphasis and operational balance; but they accepted the inevitable while resolving to restore the original balance and objectives of the Halder plan as and whenever the situation might permit.

In the meantime, based upon Hitler's official approval of this plan, the OKH was now able to allocate its divisions to the various theatres of operations, with 120 for *Barbarossa*, 50 in the west (mainly in France), 7 in Norway, 3 in the Netherlands and 1 in Romania. But all too soon other operations and priorities would impinge upon the preparations for *Barbarossa* from early 1941, fatally delaying the start of the campaign beyond its original May 1941 date and also diverting some resources from it to other theatres. Examples of this were the invasion of Greece and Yugoslavia, which inflicted a four-to six-week delay; the loss of almost one-third of the southern army group's tanks to the Balkans until after *Barbarossa* was well under way; and the withholding of air support from *Barbarossa* to support Operation *Merkur* in Crete. *Merkur* also resulted in no airborne forces being available for parachute assaults in support of *Barbarossa*, due to the policy banning such operations following the large-scale losses incurred by the airborne troops on Crete.

Much-needed equipment and potential army manpower was also being diverted to the other services, the Waffen-SS and civilian, paramilitary and other Nazi-inspired organizations within Germany. Having accepted that only a Blitzkrieg offensive could deliver a victory within the necessary timeframe, the army's lack of large-scale panzer forces – tanks and self-propelled guns – and motorized infantry was a continuing cause of particular concern within the general staff. Meanwhile, the questionable assessments of Russian strengths and capabilities remained largely unresolved. Notwithstanding the general mood of optimism about the coming campaign, worrying new reports were beginning to circulate by early 1941 – these possibly indicating much greater Russian tank strengths than had been assessed during the previous summer and autumn. Similarly, the old 1940 assessments of no more than 50 to 75 Red Army divisions being based in western Russia were increasingly questioned, as reports of the deployment of at least 200 such divisions now began to reach the OKH intelligence staff, although to some extent this had already been recognized in the size of opposing Russian forces prudently set by Paulus for the war games in November and early December. Nevertheless, Hitler remained buoyant, rejecting such reports as incorrect and all the time convinced that (as he told Jodl), 'We have only to kick in the door and the whole rotten structure will come crashing down!'[116] Such statements accorded with Hitler's belief that the Soviet state was fundamentally so flawed and its armed forces so weakened (36,671 of its best military personnel having been executed, exiled or dismissed during Stalin's widespread purges of the officer corps since 1937) that the mere fact of the German offensive would precipitate its rapid demise. The Führer also placed considerable weight upon the disquiet provoked by Stalin's repressive totalitarian regime among the population in western and southern Russia. Such assessments would in due course prove to be flawed, over-simplistic and wildly optimistic. In the meantime, the general staff had already been forbidden from criticizing any policies or directives emanating from the Führer. Consequently, it was within this rarefied and most unsatisfactory form of planning 'vacuum' that the general staff was constrained to carry out its further work to bring *Barbarossa* to fruition.

In fact, the Red Army forces defending Western Russia in spring 1941 amounted to almost three million men, supported by 9,000 aircraft and no fewer than 15,000 of the army's 24,000 tanks (although some 60 per cent of the tank fleet was non-operational in spring 1941, while the formidable T-34 and KV tanks had only just entered service with front-line units). By the time that Germany launched *Barbarossa*, these forces would comprise some 132 divisions (of the army's overall total of about 240 divisions, some of which were not fully manned), of which 77 were infantry, 34 armoured or tank, 13 motorized and 8 cavalry. These divisions were organized into nine armies deployed close to the border with a further two armies deployed in depth farther east. All of these armies were grouped within four military districts. While the overall strength of these forces was considerable, the Germans enjoyed the advantage of being able to concentrate their forces against an opponent that was necessarily stretched out all along the whole length of Russia's western border from the Baltic to the Black Sea. Although well-trained, the Red Army lacked expertise and experience in warfare of the Blitzkrieg type, and its armoured forces were in any case in the midst of an extensive reorganization in spring 1941, Stalin having judged incorrectly that a German attack on Russia could not take place for at least two years, by which time the restructured and modernized Red Army would be capable of countering such an attack.

In several significant respects, the revised plan for *Barbarossa* issued by the OKW on 18 December represented a considerable compromise for the general staff. Halder's original concept for the campaign had envisaged that the main effort should be by Army Group Centre towards Moscow, where any enemy forces not destroyed during the initial offensive could be forced to fight a final decisive battle for what was not only the Russian capital but also the main hub of the country's rail network, while the panzer forces would secure the flanks and prevent the Russian forces escaping or being reinforced. However, Hitler's modification of this plan in order to satisfy the higher priority he had accorded Leningrad – with the consequent relegation of Moscow as a main objective – now meant that the invasion would be launched on a broad front, and initially with much less ambitious objectives set for the three army groups. Hitler and all three army group commanders were of the same mind concerning the need to destroy the Red Army as early and as close to the border as possible, in order to prevent its forces withdrawing into the interior on a steadily expanding front – a situation that they well knew would progressively over-extend the German resources. In the meantime, if the overall combat effectiveness of the Red Army could indeed be destroyed during the first month, then capturing Moscow could possibly prove less important than the general staff had originally suggested. On the other hand, the Führer's direction to pause on the general line of the Dvina–Dnieper watershed might prematurely curtail the depth of German penetration necessary to prevent the Russian withdrawal, thus allowing these forces to reconstitute and consolidate the subsequent defence of Moscow. Also, the strategic significance of Leningrad was always somewhat problematical, especially as the assault on the city would now automatically (as directed by Hitler) involve weakening Army Group Centre by the redeployment of much of its armour to reinforce Army Group North, despite the central army group until then being the one best placed to strike strongly against the Russian capital. In the spring of 1941 all this was in the minds of the army group commanders and of the general staff at OKH. However, having considerably overestimated the combat potential of the French in 1940 – and suffered a significant loss of credibility in consequence – many were now keen to take a less pessimistic view of the anticipated effectiveness and strength of the Red Army, especially when that assessment was set against the proven quality of the Wehrmacht, based upon its almost two years at war.

In March 1941, Hitler called the army group and army commanders and their senior staff officers – more than 200 officers in all – to a meeting at which he set out his vision for the attack on Russia. Of course, those attending were already fully aware of the contents of the *Barbarossa* directive that had been amended and approved by Hitler on 18 December and issued through the auspices of the OKW that same day. This gathering and the directive upon which Hitler based his address together constituted a defining moment in the story of the Third Reich, but especially that of the general staff and the Wehrmacht. Hitler's address on that day in early March was concerned less with operational matters than with the overall nature and conduct of the campaign and occupation, including the approach and attitude to be adopted when dealing with the Russian population – whether soldier or civilian. This would be 'a battle of annihilation' against 'Bolshevik commissars and the communist intelligentsia' and 'a battle between two opposing world views'.[117] Particular attention was to be paid to various ethnic and political groups and individuals – such as the Red Army's political commissars. Hitler emphasized that the offensive would be very different from those waged thus far, assuming the nature of an ideological crusade against communism, the Jewish-Bolshevik conspiracy against Germany and the Slav people and Slavic culture. Much of what Hitler said at the meeting reflected the ideas expressed directly or indirectly in *Mein Kampf*, and the Führer undoubtedly regarded *Barbarossa* as the means of realizing many of the ideas and beliefs that he had set out in his book in the late 1920s.

Far from establishing a protective cordon of neutral or submissive non-Stalinist states on Germany's eastern border in the manner that had been envisaged by Halder and the general staff, the occupied territories in Russia were to become 'protectorates' of the Third Reich, administered by Nazi political appointees, their security the responsibility of the SS and Gestapo, not the army. Where industrial plants and quantities of war matériel, raw materials and other resources were overrun, these would be assessed and appropriated by a special economic staff organization established specifically for the purpose and led by a general staff senior officer. In fact, as soon as the probability of a German invasion of Russia became known in late 1940, the forerunner of this economic exploitation organization had been established on 10 December, under the codename *Oldenburg*. Later, a directive issued on 24 May would call for at least seven million tons of grain to be sent annually from Russia to Germany, irrespective of the food needs of the civilian population. The ordinary Russian people were to be regarded as nothing more than a source of forced labour and utilized accordingly. In the occupied territories, any evidence of the Slav culture was to be obliterated, as would a whole range of ethnic and political groups and individuals prominent within the Soviet communist system and Russian society. The 'commissar decree' (Kommissarerlaß) issued in March 1941 was subsequently promulgated throughout the army as the Kommissarbefehl (commissar order) and dealt specifically with the way in which the Red Army political commissars were to be dealt if captured. The preamble to this decree or directive also encapsulated the essence of the March meeting and the much-changed nature of the conflict upon which the Wehrmacht was about to embark. The words used by Hitler in the Kommissarerlaß were chillingly clear:

> The war against Russia cannot be fought in knightly fashion. The struggle is one of ideologies and racial differences and will have to be waged with unprecedented, unmerciful, and unrelenting hardness. All officers will have to get rid of any old-fashioned ideas they may have. I realize that the necessity for conducting such warfare is beyond the comprehension of you generals, but I must insist that my orders be followed without complaint. The commissars hold views directly opposite to those of National Socialism. Hence these commissars must be eliminated. Any German soldier who breaks international law will be pardoned. Russia did not take part in the Hague Convention and, therefore, has no rights under it.[118]

The Kommissarerlaß sat uneasily with many of the older army officers, and for some it was the point at which their conscience, traditional understanding of honour, and sense of right and wrong at last out-balanced the stringent requirements that had been imposed by their oath of loyalty and obedience to the Führer. Anticipating the instinctive reaction and ible reservations of some of the senior army officers present at the ng, Hitler directed that, in order to carry through the particular es he required both during and after *Barbarossa*, special detachments (Sonderkommandos) and task forces (Einsatzgruppen) of SS and SD troops would be attached to each army group for that purpose. So it was that the Führer presented the general staff and the army with a preview of the much-changed environment in which it would be required to conduct its forthcoming offensive. The die was cast. Hitler had made his will abundantly clear, and all that remained was for the general staff to confirm and promulgate the final plan and then complete the necessary troop movements in time for the Wehrmacht to launch *Barbarossa* in early May, in accordance with the current timetable. In practice, however, Mussolini's ill-judged invasion of Greece and the German response there in April and then in the Balkans meant that the start of *Barbarossa* would unavoidably be delayed to late June – raising the possibility that the campaign might not be concluded before the onset of the Russian winter.

The general staff's final plan for *Barbarossa* still maintained wherever possible those key aspects of the overall concept that Halder had presented to Hitler on 5 December the previous year, but now with Leningrad rather than Moscow as the priority objective, in accordance with Hitler's direction on 18 December. In the north, Army Group North (commanded by General-feldmarschall Ritter von Leeb), consisted of 3 panzer divisions, 2 motorized divisions and 24 infantry divisions. These divisions comprised Sixteenth Army (Generaloberst Ernst Busch), Eighteenth Army (Generaloberst Georg von Küchler) and Panzer Group 4 (Generaloberst Erich Höpner). This army group would launch its attack from East Prussia, through Lithuania, Latvia and Estonia, with Leningrad as its principal objective. It was also anticipated that Army Group North would link up with Finnish forces when that army group reached the Leningrad area. Meanwhile, Generalfeldmarschall von Bock's Army Group Centre, with 9 panzer divisions, 6 motorized divisions, 33 infantry divisions and 1 cavalry division would advance eastwards from occupied Poland towards Minsk, with Smolensk as its primary objective. The headquarters of Army Group Centre was at Warsaw, and its divisions were distributed within the group's three armies and two panzer groups. These were Second Army (General von Weichs), Fourth Army (General von Kluge), Ninth Army (General Adolf Strauss), Panzer Group 2 (Generaloberst Heinz Guderian) and Panzer Group 3 (Generaloberst Hermann Hoth). Once

Smolensk had been taken, Army Group Centre would send half of its panzer forces to reinforce Army Group North for its advance on Leningrad, in accordance with Hitler's wishes. The remainder of Army Group Centre would then be held in readiness either to redeploy south towards the Ukraine or to continue its advance on Moscow, although adoption of the latter option would depend upon the prior capture of Leningrad. These two army groups would both operate to the north of the Pripet Marshes. Finally, Army Group South, under the command of Generalfeldmarschall Gerd von Rundstedt, with 5 panzer divisions, 3 motorized divisions and 34 infantry divisions, as well as a number of Romanian (and later Hungarian) units, would strike south-east into the Donets basin, towards Kiev, Kharkov and Odessa. This army group was deployed in Galicia and comprised 3 armies and 1 panzer group. They were Sixth Army (Generalfeldmarschall Walther von Reichenau), Eleventh Army (Generaloberst Ritter von Schobert), Seventeenth Army (General Karl-Heinrich von Stülpnagel), and Panzer Group 1 (Generaloberst Paul Ludwig Ewald Baron von Kleist). The main offensive would be supported by a number of special forces or commando units, such as the 'Brandenburg' Regiment, whose soldiers were trained to carry out demolition, sabotage and similar tasks ahead of the advancing armoured forces.[119] For planning purposes, it was anticipated that the ultimate objective of *Barbarossa* would be a line along the River Volga that then branched away to Archangel in the north, and along the Don river in the south-east running down to the Crimea. However, confirmation of this would not be issued by Hitler until the army groups had taken Smolensk and reached the line of the Dvina and Dnieper rivers.

During August 1940, Hitler – mindful of his future intentions for Russia – had directed that the army should increase its strength to 180 active divisions, and in fact no less than 205 divisions were in the order of battle by mid-1941. Even so, since late 1940 the OKH, increasingly aware of the rapidly escalating number of operational commitments with which it would have to deal and the army's lack of adequate reserves, had submitted numerous requests for the creation of additional forces for use on *Barbarossa* and elsewhere. During the winter of 1940/1, this lobbying did result in the reactivation of 35 divisions that Hitler had somewhat precipitately ordered disbanded shortly after the fall of France, together with the creation of 11 new panzer divisions and 10 new motorized divisions. However, the new panzer divisions were created by halving the tank strength of the existing panzer divisions, and so the real effect of this action fell well short of that which was required. Between January and June 1941, monthly tank production in Germany averaged only 212 vehicles, so that by June 1941 no more than 5,262 tanks were available for all theatres of operations, with only about 4,198 fully available for operations. Of these, only 1,404 were the better-armed Pz.Kpfw.III and IV medium tanks.[120] Thus by the spring of 1941 the forces available for *Barbarossa* amounted to four million men, comprising some 120 divisions plus various other contingents, 3,648 tanks, 600,000 other vehicles, 7,184 artillery guns, most of the Wehrmacht's 600,000 horses and with some 2,000 aircraft in support.[121] Only time would reveal whether or not this combat power would be sufficient to defeat the Russians on the battlefield.

Barbarossa: Command, Control and Other Issues

An important matter of command and control had occurred during the period shortly before *Barbarossa*, which directly affected the general staff and the forthcoming operation. Hitler ordered that henceforth the high-level control of the Wehrmacht's several campaigns and operational theatres was to be divided between the OKW and the OKH. This meant an end to any continuing pretence that OKW was a supreme headquarters controlling the army, navy and air force, at a level of command above that of the OKH, OKM and OKL. This change created a situation in which OKW – while still being regarded by many as a higher-level headquarters – now competed with the OKH for the resources needed to control the operational theatres within its new remit. That remit was extensive, for Hitler decreed that the OKH was to assume responsibility exclusively for the conduct of *Barbarossa* and the subsequent operations on what was about to become the Eastern Front, while the OKW would take on the responsibility for all of Germany's other operational theatres worldwide. However, overall administrative responsibility for the army was necessarily retained by the OKH, and some operational functions still overlapped to varying degrees. This compartmentalization and separation of the high-level command and control of Germany's war had important and unwelcome implications for both headquarters. Within this arrangement, single-service command and control issues persisted within the OKW, while occasionally impinging upon the OKH, such as the matter of the operational control of Luftwaffe 88mm flak gun units used in the anti-tank role and of the Luftwaffe's airborne troops operating as infantry. In another example, the OKW ordered an army division from the forces in Norway to deploy into Finland, which had the effect of creating a new theatre of operations – and thus an increase in the power of the OKW – albeit that operations in Finland should more properly have been the business of OKH and the forces engaged in *Barbarossa*, specifically Army Group North. Meanwhile, Heinrich Himmler and the Waffen-SS continued to guard jealously that organization's separate status and discrete chain of administrative command, irrespective of the impact this had upon operations and the wider needs of the Wehrmacht.

From 1934 to 1938 Hitler had been Führer, chancellor and supreme commander – but with supreme command exerted through the commander-in-chief, who was also the minister of war. From 4 February 1938, following the demise of the former war ministry, with the departure of Generalfeldmarschall von Blomberg and Generaloberst von Fritsch and the subsequent removal of many other senior officers, Hitler had exercised supreme command of the German armed forces as Führer und Oberster Befehlshaber (leader and supreme commander). This had provided him with an opportunity to meddle in military matters at virtually any level of command to satisfy his own beliefs, prejudices and agenda, and this latest, major change to the existing structure of military power was a significant example of this. It accorded with Hitler's well-known policy of creating division, suspicion and rivalry between various organizations, thereby limiting the opportunity for alternative power-bases or coordinated opposition to emerge, as well as further side-lining the OKH and reducing the influence of the general staff. However, this change also reduced the ability of the general staff to perform its core functions, by increasing its strategic isolation and in due course creating duplication and inefficiency as the OKH and OKW competed for a diminishing amount of war matériel and manpower to sustain separately, but in parallel, a multiplicity of operational commitments. At about this time, Hitler also limited the OKH general staff's access to the newly constructed Führerhauptquartier (Führer headquarters) – where key operational decisions would be made daily – at the Wolfschanze[122] in East Prussia. Instead of being co-located with the OKH forward command element, the Wolfschanze was sited about 35 kilometres south-west of the OKH Mauerwald command complex and was therefore at least half-an-hour away by motor vehicle.[123] At the lower levels of command, some tactical commanders no doubt relished the prospect of dealing only with a 'single-service' OKH during the forthcoming campaign, but in practice this would not insulate them from interference by Hitler or from difficulties attributable to the OKW. Neither would the physical distance between the Wolfschanze and the OKH reduce Hitler's unwarranted and unwelcome involvement in the latter's day-to-day work once *Barbarossa* was under way.

Irrespective of any advantages that Hitler may have perceived in dividing the responsibilities of the OKW and the OKH in this way, that he was prompted to do so at all was evidence both of the number of commitments by then in train and of the sheer scale of the impending offensive. Despite an overall mood of optimism about the outcome of the new campaign, the general staff was well aware that the Wehrmacht was already over extended – especially in terms of resources, logistics and communications – and that the invasion of Russia would further exacerbate the situation. The OKH well understood that a victory in the east had to be achieved as expeditiously as possible, with the army neither equipped nor prepared to fight on through the Russian winter. A campaign of five or possibly six months would probably be feasible if *Barbarossa* were to be launched in early May, but every subsequent week of delay made its success increasingly problematical. Originally 15 May had been the intended start date. However, the need to conclude operations in the Balkans and factors such as delays in preparing the Luftwaffe's forward airfields, together with the time taken to procure and allocate the required amounts and types of motor vehicles to divisions, all imposed delays upon the general staff's planning targets. Meanwhile, in an unwelcome foretaste of difficulties that would re-emerge some months later, the unusually heavy rainfall during spring 1941 severely hampered vehicle movement and access, along with a host of other key activities within the deployment areas.

Eventually, it was determined that operation *Barbarossa* would definitely be able to commence at the end of the third week of June. Accordingly, the extensive troop deployments and huge concentrations of matériel, ammunition, vehicles and all manner of equipment on what was about to become the Wehrmacht's Eastern Front were complemented during the early weeks of June by a range of diplomatic, propaganda and deception actions and activities, all of which were designed to allay Russian fears and lull Stalin into a false sense of security. These included an article produced by Goebbels highlighting the significance of the 1941 invasion of Crete (Operation *Merkur*) and implying that a similar airborne invasion of England was still Hitler's principal intention. Indeed, until the final hours before *Barbarossa* was launched, very many of the soldiers directly involved in the deployment still believed that they were actually engaged in a gigantic diversionary operation to conceal an invasion of England. Ultimately, however, the German preparations over the preceding months and weeks were on a scale that could not be disguised.

During 'a perfect summer's morning' on Saturday, 21 June, a flurry of ever more urgent messages passed between Moscow and the Russian embassy on the Unter den Linden in Berlin. These added to more than 80 warnings of Hitler's intentions that had been passed to Moscow during the previous eight months, ever since the first drafts of plans for the invasion had been produced by the general staff. Stubbornly, Stalin and his ambassador in Berlin continued to maintain the view that these activities were designed merely to strengthen Hitler's bargaining position in his future territorial negotiations with Stalin, rather than being evidence of Germany's intention to take military action against Russia. Furthermore, Stalin believed that the events unfolding that June were actually part of a deliberate plot by British prime minister Winston Churchill to precipitate a war between Germany and Russia, and this conspiracy theory had been reinforced by Rudolf Hess's bizarre solo flight to Britain just a few weeks earlier on 10 May.[124] Throughout 21 June, German foreign minister Joachim von Ribbentrop made himself unavailable to respond to the Russian ambassador's attempts to contact him, his staff declaring that he was not in Berlin that day. In fact, Ribbentrop was in the foreign ministry, where he was busy finalizing instructions to the German ambassador in Moscow concerning a list of contrived grievances that would constitute the justification for Germany's action and which was to be presented to the Russian government shortly after the invasion had begun.

By the evening of 21 June, the OKH preparations were virtually complete. Early the next morning the Wehrmacht would unleash a whirlwind of death and destruction upon Russia unprecedented in the history of modern warfare. As night fell, hundreds of guns were moved from heavily camouflaged positions and towed by tractors with masked headlights, or by teams of horses or mules and in some cases by the gunners themselves, to be placed into carefully reconnoitred and well-prepared firing positions. Overall, a mood of optimism prevailed throughout the OKH immediately before the attack, and there was a widely held view both in the high command and throughout much of the army that the offensive would be another Blitzkrieg, similar to those of 1939 and 1940, but on a much larger scale. In many command posts, officers enthusiastically toasted the forthcoming venture with fine wine, vintage champagne and cognac that had been 'liberated' from occupied France. Their talk was of the victories to come, the final defeat of the Bolshevik threat, and the impending opportunities for distinction in combat together with the promotions to follow. Only the clouds of mosquitoes that buzzed incessantly and aggressively all about the soldiers sought to dampen the spirits of the hundreds of thousands of men who were now at maximum readiness and impatient to begin this great new Blitzkrieg – one that had been presented to them as a crusade against a dehumanized Bolshevik communist enemy rather than a campaign against a valorous Russian opponent.

Little did the general staff officers in the headquarters or the commanders and troops concealed in their camouflaged bunkers and forward positions know that the Fatherland they served would ultimately pay a catastrophic price for what would prove to have been an historic miscalculation by their Führer. Even the most pessimistic officer or soldier could hardly have anticipated that by the end of the war in May 1945 no fewer than 80 per cent of the army's total casualties from 1939 to 1945 would have been sustained during four years of continuous fighting on the Eastern Front, while the Wehrmacht as a whole would eventually incur a staggering 1,015,000 fatal casualties on that front alone between June 1941 and May 1945.

10

Unleashing the Whirlwind

June to December 1941

Throughout much of Saturday 21 June, Stalin remained in denial, despite a torrent of reports of German activities on Russia's western frontier that clearly indicated offensive action was imminent. Bridges were being constructed over rivers, frontier obstacles such as barbed wire and vehicle barriers were being removed by army engineers, light reconnaissance aircraft flew low along the border, and all the time clouds of blue smoke and dust rose above the German-occupied forests, accompanied by the noise of vehicle engines and tank movement. Finally, at midnight on what was the shortest night of the year, Stalin accepted the possibility – but not yet the inevitability – of a German attack and issued the order to mobilize the Russian forces in the Western military districts. Many Red Army units in the forward area did not receive this alert message until well after events had rendered it irrelevant. Despite his reluctant and last-minute acknowledgement of the German threat, in the face of all the evidence to the contrary and notwithstanding the sheer scale of the Wehrmacht onslaught that would shortly be unleashed upon Russia, Stalin maintained his state of 'semi-denial' for some time after the start of the offensive. He was still unable to accept or rationalize the fact that Hitler had both reneged on the German-Soviet non-aggression pact and embarked upon a course of action which seemed to confound all military commonsense and strategic logic.

As dawn broke at 4.00 a.m. on Sunday 22 June 1941, ending a hot and sultry night, thousands of guns were unmasked and began their bombardment of the Russian border defences. Overhead, waves of

Luftwaffe ground-attack aircraft screamed eastwards to strike Red Army positions and headquarters in depth and destroy the Russian air force on the ground. Meanwhile, the engines of thousands of tanks, armoured infantry carriers, trucks and motorcycles started up, radio silence was broken, and the huge troop concentrations at last moved out of their concealed hide areas. The panzer and motorized infantry units quickly forged ahead, while many of the infantry formations now on the move were not vehicle-borne and would therefore march into Russia on foot. These infantry units – which considerably outnumbered those that were motorized – did have some motor transport vehicles but had nevertheless to rely in the main upon horses and mules to draw their guns and supply wagons, much as their predecessors had during the 1914–18 war. The great mass of men, machines and animals gradually gained momentum. As the columns of vehicles and marching troops moved on to and along their designated routes eastwards to overwhelm the Russian forward defences, choking clouds of dust rose ever higher into the summer sky, mingling with the fire and smoke of the battle ahead. Well to the south of the main part of Army Group South, the Romanian Third and Fourth Armies, together with the German Eleventh Army (Generaloberst Ritter von Schobert), advanced north-eastwards towards Kiev, with the task of securing the southern flank of *Barbarossa* and the line of the river Dnieper as their eventual objective.

At its outset, and during the first three or four months of Operation *Barbarossa*, the general staff was delighted with the impressive progress made by the invading forces. Although it could not have escaped the attention of every officer that Russia was now firmly allied with Great Britain against Germany, and that the two-front war had therefore become a self-inflicted reality, the early success of this new Blitzkrieg augured well for its speedy conclusion – any future threat to the Third Reich from Russia would be effectively neutralized. The Wehrmacht's battlefield successes, its rate of advance and the apparent weakness of the opposing Russian forces together allayed any residual reservations at OKH about the advisability of the venture, while many within the army high command revelled in the army's return to what it did best, with the opportunity for the OKH to command a theatre of war on a front that was almost 1,600 kilometres long and ran from the Baltic in the north to the Black Sea in the south. While the significant progress made by the Wehrmacht and its Romanian allies during the first days and weeks of the invasion was undeniable, it is noteworthy that this was due primarily to concentration of force, surprise and superior tactics, rather than to the application of overwhelming strength on a strategic scale. Neither was the qualitative imbalance as great (other than in aircraft) as has sometimes been suggested, the Russian T-34 and KV heavy tanks – both of which were superior to the Pz.Kpfw.IV, the main German tank in June 1941 – providing a most unpleasant surprise for the invaders when first encountered.

While the coloured symbols on the operations maps at OKH showed the territory gained in a fairly sterile and dispassionate form, the evidence of the progress made was somewhat more immediate for the combat troops. Twenty-year-old infantryman Harald Henry, advancing with the second echelon units, recorded that, 'We've been marching for twenty-five kilometres past images of terrible destruction. About 200 smashed-up, burnt-out [Russian] tanks turned upside down, guns, lorries, field kitchens, motor-cycles, anti-tank guns, a sea of weapons, helmets, items of equipment of all kinds, pianos and radios, filming vehicles, medical equipment, boxes of munitions and books, grenades, blankets, coats, knapsacks. In among them, [there are] corpses already turning black … A stench of putrefaction [from dead horses] hangs numbingly over our columns.' Some six weeks later, he wrote of, 'endless hours of marching ahead … The strange smell everywhere, a mixture of fire, sweat and horse corpses that will probably remain with me forever as part of this campaign. [And meanwhile] the dust shrouds us all. This unending eastern land is so vast, it's quite impossible to try to gauge its extent … the featureless spaces flow endlessly as far as the horizon.'[125] Certainly Harald Henry's first-hand experience tended to confirm the OKH view of the initial success of *Barbarossa*, although his observations on the sheer scale of the rapidly expanding campaign highlight what would soon become an increasing concern for those general staff officers charged with providing the necessary logistical and communications support for the invasion, as the German armies advanced ever deeper into Russia during the late summer of 1941.

During the first few months of *Barbarossa*, the Wehrmacht's progress had generally been most satisfactory and sometimes quite spectacular. Some Russian counterattacks in the north had been spirited, while the rate of German advance in the south had been somewhat slower than anticipated. The overall Russian strength proved significantly greater than the OKH had originally anticipated, while at the same time the Russian ability to fight delaying operations and exploit the inherent lack of mobility of the German reserve or second-echelon divisions improved noticeably as the weeks passed. In late August, Generaloberst Halder conceded in a diary note that: 'The whole situation shows more and more clearly that we have underestimated the colossus of Russia ... We have already identified 360 [Russian divisions]. The divisions are admittedly not armed and equipped in our sense, and tactically they are badly led. But there they are, and when we destroy a dozen, the Russians simply establish another dozen.'[126] Nevertheless, the three German army groups quickly overcame the Russian border defences, taking hundreds of thousands of prisoners, with the panzers advancing rapidly onwards into western Russia.

In the north, Generalfeldmarschall Ritter von Leeb's army group had attacked from East Prussia, striking through Lithuania, Latvia and Estonia and capturing Riga on 1 July before finally reaching positions from which it could cooperate with Finnish forces about Leningrad from 19 August. (It would be mid-September before the siege of that important city was fully in place.) However, von Leeb's advance northwards to Leningrad had hardly been a speedy affair. This was partly due to the difficult coastal terrain that had to be negotiated, but also to differences of opinion on the use of Panzer Group 4 – against Generaloberst Höpner's advice, von Leeb had split his panzer group, one panzer corps moving directly towards Leningrad while the other carried out a flank-protection task in the area of Lake Ilmen, to the east. Furthermore, Hitler's direct interference in the operation to capture what he had always viewed as the most important objective also affected the army group's timetable. One such interference involved his modification of von Leeb's orders to the two panzer corps to move ahead of the advance. In that case (which was very reminiscent of Hitler's similar worries about risking the armour during the campaign in France a year before) Hitler ordered the panzer corps to halt and thereafter to conform to the much slower movement of the main body of the army group as it advanced northwards, necessarily clearing the Baltic ports as it did so. Similarly, Hitler's insistence that Army Group North should, as a matter of priority, capture the bauxite-mining town of Tikhvin to the east of Leningrad resulted in ten weeks of heavy fighting in the area's closely wooded terrain before the place fell on 8 November. This prolonged operation absorbed and diverted disproportionate amounts of logistic resources and resulted in high casualties, all of which depleted the strength of the forces necessary to capture Leningrad. Such interference was merely a foretaste of much worse yet to come. In any event, all this resulted in delays that afforded the defenders of Leningrad time to consolidate and strengthen the city's defences to such an extent that it was no longer vulnerable to a direct assault, leaving the Germans with no alternative but to besiege the city.

In the centre, von Bock's army group advanced rapidly from its concentration areas in occupied Poland to capture Smolensk on 15 July. In the meantime, by 29 June, Army Group Centre's Panzer Group 2 and Panzer Group 3 had also cut off some 300,000 soldiers at Minsk. By 5 August the army group had advanced more than 800 kilometres, taken some 600,000 prisoners-of-war and seized or destroyed some 5,000 Russian tanks. While von Leeb and von Bock had experienced varying degrees of success, Generalfeldmarschall Gerd von Rundstedt's southern army group (which included the two Romanian armies) had driven on towards the Ukraine, into Bessarabia, and onwards to Odessa and Kharkov, the latter city falling on 24 October. Initially, Army Group South had encountered strong Russian forces, and its progress had therefore been slower than that of the other two army groups. However, by 8 August this army group had also achieved a notable success, with the capture of 103,000 men, 300 tanks and 800 guns in the Uman pocket (to the east of the southern River Bug). In early October, some 106,000 Russians were also taken in the Zaporozhe–Osipenko pocket. Although Army Group South also managed to capture Rostov, on the Don, in early November, it was unable to retain control of the town in the face of strong Russian counterattacks launched from the 29th of that month.

By mid-July, von Bock's Army Group Centre had achieved all that the general staff had envisaged it would in the original planning for *Fall Otto*. That force now stood ready to strike out and capture Moscow before the Russians could recover from the initial onslaught and consolidate their forces. But on 19 July Hitler invoked his previously stated intention to re-allocate panzer forces from Army Group Centre to support the other army groups. As early as 28 July, Halder observed that Hitler's orders had 'led to a dissipation of forces and had caused the attack on Moscow to come to a standstill'.[127] Generaloberst Halder, Generalfeldmarschall von Rundstedt and Generalfeldmarschall von Bock, together with two panzer group commanders, all lobbied Hitler in an attempt to persuade him to rescind this directive and resume the advance on Moscow. In response, the Führer stated that the importance of securing access to Swedish iron ore in the Baltic and to the oil, coal and corn in southern Russia far outweighed the significance of capturing Moscow. Subsequently, Halder arranged for Generaloberst Guderian, commanding Panzer Group 2, to meet Hitler on 23 August with a view to changing his mind – and, to Halder's irritation, Hitler apparently persuaded Guderian that the depletion of Army Group Centre's armoured strength was the right solution. However, Guderian's account of the circumstances of this meeting is somewhat different. Neither von Brauchitsch nor Halder, nor any general staff representative from the OKH, were present during Guderian's discussion with Hitler, and his own account of the meeting seems to indicate that von Brauchitsch – if not Halder – had in any case already accepted that Hitler could not be moved on the issue. According to Guderian, immediately before the meeting von Brauchitsch told him: 'I forbid you to mention the question of Moscow to the Führer. The operation to the south has been ordered. The problem now is simply how it is to be carried out. Discussion is pointless.' Nevertheless, the subject of Moscow was raised – by Hitler himself – and Guderian maintains that he did set out, as originally intended, his view of the advantages of the early capture of Moscow, but that Hitler was not prepared to modify his direction on the matter.[128] At the operational level, Hitler's direction did produce another significant success, as Guderian returned to the front in time to detach his panzer group from von Bock's command and lead his tanks in a sweep southwards to meet Army Group South's Panzer Group 1 across the Dnieper at Lokhvitsa on 15 September, where a further 450,000 Russians were trapped in the Kiev pocket. Spectacular though this was, however, it was strategically ill-judged and obscured the fact that the diversion of so much combat power – notably the panzer groups – from Army Group Centre had effectively placed Moscow beyond its reach.

Taifun: Moscow and the First Winter Campaign, September to December 1941

Perversely, in spite of his earlier strategic arguments to Halder and the other senior commanders and general staff officers and the meeting with Guderian just two weeks before, Hitler did then change his mind on 6 September, when he issued a directive ordering operation *Taifun* ('Typhoon') – a major offensive against Moscow. But by then the opportunity had passed. The OKH required three weeks to concentrate the 70 divisions needed for *Taifun*, most of which were by that stage widely dispersed, carrying out tasks in accordance with the original operational plan for *Barbarossa* and the subsequent directive issued by Hitler on 19 July. Consequently, by the time that the redeployment of these divisions was under way, the onset of the autumn rains first of all severely affected preparations for the offensive and then, despite some early successes, impacted even more significantly upon the operation itself. When *Taifun* was eventually launched on 30 September, the tank holdings of the panzer divisions were at only 75 per cent, while the infantry divisions were down to 50 per cent strength due to a dearth of manpower reinforcements. (In September the army was already short of 200,000 men who should by then have been in training ready to join front-line units.) Despite this situation, just a month later an ever-confident Hitler ordered the disbandment of a number of reserve divisions and the return of parts of German industrial output to peacetime levels. Fuel and maintenance and repair facilities for the panzers were also inadequate, and movement problems meant that the start line (line of departure) for the offensive was almost 650 kilometres long. At the OKH, the frustration of the general staff with *Taifun* was palpable. First of all it had to change the whole emphasis and focus of the campaign, then redeploy the requisite forces in ever-worsening weather conditions, all of which was set against a background of inadequate resources, an unrealistic timescale and the knowledge that, while this was the right operation, now was the wrong time to carry it out. At the heart of its frustration was an awareness that the army that had been prepared and resourced for another Blitzkrieg campaign was moving inexorably into a war of attrition – a winter war, no less – for which it was woefully unprepared. Although more than 730,000 Russians were taken prisoner in the Vyazma and Bryansk pockets, with Guderian's tanks advancing to Orel – more than 200 kilometres – in the first four days of *Taifun*, the operation finally ground to a halt during the third week of October, amidst torrential autumn rain and sleet and the sea of mud that this produced.

Artillery officer Siegfried Knappe noted that, 'By late October, the mud was so bad that nothing could move in it. All movement stopped except on railroads and paved roads ... even infantry on foot could move only with the greatest difficulty. Nothing on wheels or tracks could move at all except on the [main] post road or railroads. The only way we could move vehicles was to corduroy the roads with small tree trunks laid side-by-side to provide a solid surface. We established corduroy roads between our gun positions and our source of ammunition and supplies at division headquarters. Such roads were difficult footing for the horses, and the vehicles jolted over them, but at least we could transport supplies and ammunition.'[129]

Only the real onset of winter, with sub-zero temperatures freezing the saturated ground in November, allowed the attack to be resumed on 15 November. However, there was a certain irony in this, as the increasingly severe winter weather, which in the short term enabled the resumption of the drive towards Moscow, soon mitigated against its success. As Siegfried Knappe recorded, 'A hard freeze came on November 7, which proved both an advantage and a disadvantage. We could move again, but now we were freezing because we still did not have winter clothing. We had the same field uniforms we had worn through the summer, plus a light overcoat ... We tried to spend the nights in villages so we could get out of the weather ... The fahrers [*sic:* horse handlers] would keep the horses behind houses at night, and strap blankets on them as well, to try to shelter them from the wind. The horses had [their] winter coats of fur, which helped them, although a few of them died at night from the cold. On November 12, the temperature dropped to twelve degrees below zero Fahrenheit.' Then, as the division at last approached the outer suburbs of Moscow at the end of November, 'a paralyzing blast of cold hit us, and the temperature dropped far below zero and stayed there. Our trucks and vehicles would not start, and our horses started to die from the cold in large numbers for the first time; they would just die in the bitter cold darkness of the night, and we would find them dead the next morning. The Russians knew how to cope with this weather, but we did not; their vehicles were built and conditioned for this kind of weather, but ours were not ... On December 5, the temperature plummeted to thirty degrees below zero.'[130] The situations described by Knappe were both typical and widespread, and by the first week of December Hitler was forced to accept that operation *Taifun* had run its course.

Some of Generaloberst Höpner's panzer units did eventually reach a point less than 35 kilometres from the centre of Moscow on 25 November, but it is virtually undeniable they could have arrived there some two or three months earlier, and most significantly before the onset of winter. Arguably, but much as the general staff had feared, Hitler's original decision to switch the emphasis of *Barbarossa* away from Moscow in July prejudiced the outcome of the whole campaign and committed the army to continue fighting through the Russian winter, an unplanned contingency for which it was therefore largely unprepared.

Ahead of Army Group South in the Ukraine, contacts that had been carefully cultivated by the Abwehr and other agencies with anti-Soviet nationalist groups before the war had been activated as soon as *Barbarossa* began. Consequently, as the campaign proceeded, large-scale desertions took place from numbers of Russian Ukrainian units, together with the defection of significant numbers of the Red Army's Cossack forces, who had long opposed Stalin's rule in the Ukraine and southern Russia. However, true to his perverse view of the nature of Russia and its people, Hitler did not allow the Wehrmacht to treat Russian deserters other than as prisoners-of-war, and so these men were held in often inadequately provisioned camps in the forward areas and in Poland, where large numbers eventually died of disease or starvation. By and large, only the Cossack units eventually found gainful employment with the Axis forces (primarily within the Waffen-SS), and they would later pay a heavy price for this following their enforced repatriation to the Soviet authorities after Germany's defeat in 1945. The mistreatment of Russian prisoners, specific individuals and groups, and the population as a whole – exemplified by measures such as the Kommissarerlaß – disturbed and offended many officers, including von Brauchitsch, von Leeb and Höpner. Quite apart from any humanitarian considerations, the general staff was frustrated by the squandering of much of the pre-war work to prepare the way for the invasion within Russia and by the loss of military manpower that might well have been turned against the Soviet regime. The OKH also knew that a hostile population would spawn partisan and other resistance forces that would in turn force the use of much-needed German troops to police the ever-expanding rear areas. And, as *Barbarossa* stormed on, it would prove increasingly difficult for the OKH and army commanders to maintain their traditional principles and distance themselves from the actions and nature of what had become an ideologically-dominated National Socialist crusade. Therein lay the roots of a new and more urgent resistance movement against Hitler centred upon the general staff, and the revival of the wider military opposition that had been discredited and lain dormant following the victories in the west during the previous year.

Given the presence of the SS-Einsatzgruppen and SS-Einsatzkommandos ('killer units') operating in the areas immediately behind the advancing army formations and in the occupied territories, it was virtually inevitable that army units would become drawn into their activities, and neither senior army field commanders nor the OKH could escape this unpalatable fact. The job of these SS units and special police units was to follow up the army's main advance and secure the rear areas, a task that routinely involved the extermination of any partisans, saboteurs, political commissars and others designated 'enemies of the Third Reich', as well as others categorized as 'Untermenschen' ('subhumans'), which included Jews and gypsies. These SS units were routinely placed under army group headquarters for administrative and logistic support but without the army group commander having any command authority over them.

Certainly any pretence that the army had been able to distance itself from the political dogma of the time had become illusory by mid-1941, when orders issued by senior army commanders included such statements as, 'The annihilation of those same Jews who support Bolshevism and its organization for murder, the partisans, is a measure of self-preservation' (Generaloberst Hoth), and, 'The Jewish-Bolshevik system must be rooted out once and for all.' (General von Manstein).[131] Revealingly, there was evidence of a reluctant pragmatism at the highest level, with Generaloberst Halder having already acknowledged prior to the offensive the inevitability of the army having to carry out collective reprisals against Russian civilians, and that the coming campaign would be a 'war of extermination'. Considered as a whole, such statements, together with numerous policy documents and directives, represented a watershed for the general staff. It changed the traditional German view of war and indicated that the campaign against Soviet Russia would routinely disregard the needs and rights of the Russian civilian or soldier, being generally conducted as a punitive operation to eliminate a dangerous political ideology and against a lesser race that deserved nothing less than annihilation.

After June 1941, there was little room for members of the general staff to occupy a middle course between outright abhorrence of the way in which the war in the east was to be waged and total support for Hitler and all that he stood for. An opponent of the Hitler regime, former ambassador Ulrich von Hassell, highlighted the consequences for the German army of these orders and policy directives when he noted that, 'The army must [now] assume the onus of the murders and burnings which up to now have been confined to the SS.'[132] The massacre between 18 and 20 October by an SS-Einsatzkommando of a large number of Jews at Borisov, some 80 kilometres east of Minsk in Belorussia, typified the dilemma faced by senior army commanders and staff officers. Borisov lay within the Army Group Centre area of operational responsibility, and the army group staff, appalled by the atrocity, urged Generalfeldmarschall von Bock to act decisively to bring the SS to account. But, while by no means approving of the SS action, he did no more than submit a written report to Hitler indicating his concerns over the incident. By late 1941, von Bock was just one of an increasing number of general staff officers and commanders who found themselves having to reconcile their military duty, desire for professional advancement and the obligations set out in the oath to the Führer with considerations of honour and common humanity. Another consideration was a not unnatural fear of the potentially fatal consequences of opposing or criticizing Hitler's policies at a time when it was evident that the power and influence of the SS and the Gestapo were expanding throughout the Third Reich. Symptomatic of this was the 'Nacht und Nebel Erlaß' ('Night and Fog Decree') issued by Hitler on 7 December, authorizing the arrest of any 'persons endangering German security'. These people were not to be executed immediately but were to 'vanish without a trace into the night and fog', with no information provided to their relatives or others about their alleged crime or ultimate fate. The aim of the decree was deliberately to initiate a new dimension of fear in Germany and the occupied territories. No enquiries about missing friends, colleagues or relatives would be answered, and no confirmation that they had even been arrested would be given. Although the SD had the practical responsibility for applying this decree (and a still unknown number of unrecorded Europeans did indeed subsequently 'vanish into the night'), Hitler gave Keitel, head of the OKW, the task of introducing the policy and ensuring that it was acted upon. This was a clear case of a senior army officer being directly involved in the development of what was becoming the SS state, albeit that Keitel had already largely forsaken his traditional values as a German officer and his loyalty to the army in favour of total obedience to Hitler as an individual.[133]

Despite the tactical and operational achievements of the Wehrmacht during the early months of *Barbarossa*, Operation *Taifun* showed that the Wehrmacht's ability to conduct Blitzkrieg operations had all but run its course. It also shortly preceded yet another major change in the strategic command and control of the war – but of the army in particular – that would have yet more consequences for the general staff. Between July and December, Hitler's direct involvement in operational matters in Russia yet again sidelined his two most important military advisers, von Brauchitsch and Halder, and undermined the OKH and the wider general staff, which found itself being required to prepare and launch concurrent operations despite directly conflicting force requirements. While the original aim of *Fall Otto* stated by Halder had probably been achievable, the new strategic aims and objectives set out by Hitler as *Barbarossa* developed, together with the lack of critical resources and manpower to sustain a war of attrition in a vast, largely non-industrialized and generally hostile environment (the population, terrain and climate alike), meant that the sort of German victory on the Eastern Front envisaged by Hitler was never viable.

Meanwhile, as *Taifun* gradually drew to a close in Russia, in the Pacific region Germany's Axis ally Japan attacked the US Navy base at Pearl Harbor, Hawaii, on 7 December. This precipitated a declaration of war against the United States by Germany just four days later, which allied America with Russia and Great Britain against the Axis powers. The general staff was very aware that continued British involvement in the conflict meant that the two-front war Germany had long sought to avoid was already an uncomfortable reality, but America's entry into the war meant that this situation – with the potential use of Great Britain as a base from which to invade mainland Europe – now assumed much greater significance. In practice, had Hitler chosen not to declare war on the United States at that juncture, US President Roosevelt would undoubtedly have had considerable difficulty persuading the US Joint Chiefs of Staff and Congress of any need to prioritize the defeat of Germany over that of Japan, or indeed to commit American forces to the landings in North Africa the following year.

By late November 1941 the succession of advances by the three army groups had slowed as they experienced various tactical reverses and other setbacks. While the impact of the territorial gains of the summer together with the annihilation of much of the Red Army in western Russia and the thousands of prisoners taken could not be denied, by the end of the summer the length of the Wehrmacht's lines of communication and resupply was unprecedented. Meanwhile, Russian resistance was stiffening all the time, with fresh divisions being rushed from Russia's eastern provinces and prepared for a major winter counter-offensive. While this was happening, the Wehrmacht was beginning to face up to the unpalatable and unanticipated prospect of having to fight on through the Russian winter, just as it was starting to experience real difficulties due to critical shortages of the spares, fuel and other resources so essential to its offensive capability – a capability that was dependent upon the combat effectiveness of the army's panzer and motorized divisions, of which there were still too few. On 27 November, the quartermaster-general, General Eduard Wagner, observed to Halder that 'Germany was at the end both of her human and material resources', although many within the OKH still believed that Moscow might yet be captured before the full onset of winter.[134]

During November the German offensive gradually ground to a halt along a generally north-south line that ran so close to Moscow that some German soldiers could see the 'onion-dome' towers of the Kremlin from their forward positions. The campaign had reached its high-watermark. Tellingly, just a month later, on 26 December 1941, an item published in *Militär-Wochenblatt* (a weekly summary of the operational situation on the Wehrmacht's various fronts) was headed 'Stellungskrieg (positional war) in the East'.[135] 'Stellungskrieg' was the term that had eventually described the situation on the Western Front in 1914–18 and was the absolute antithesis of the Blitzkrieg as well as being a form of warfare in which the general staff had vowed the army would never again become engaged. In the south, von Rundstedt's army group had been forced to relinquish Rostov. General-feldmarschall von Rundstedt had requested permission to withdraw to consolidate and adopt a strong defensive posture in anticipation of the arrival of winter, but Hitler refused to authorize this, and during a stormy visit to the headquarters of Army Group South at Poltava on 10 November, accompanied by Halder and von Brauchitsch, he blamed von Rundstedt personally for the loss of Rostov. The Field Marshal responded that any blame lay with those who had devised the campaign, which provoked Hitler's fury and also triggered a mild heart attack in von Brauchitsch (who had been suffering from heart disease and stress-induced ill health for much of the year). Subsequently, several senior commanders in Army Group South were relieved of their commands, including General von Stülpnagel of Seventeenth Army. A request by von Rundstedt to be permitted to retire was refused: Hitler stated that he would not entertain any such requests by generals in the future, as retirement and the abandonment of his duties and obligations was an option not open to him as Germany's Führer.

On 1 December, Hitler did replace von Rundstedt with Generalfeldmarschall von Reichenau (then commanding Sixth Army). The catalyst for von Rundstedt's final removal from Army Group South once again involved the field marshal's wish to withdraw some of the forces under his command, in this case the panzer force that had become over-extended and now needed to pull back to the area of the River Mius. Von Rundstedt believed that Hitler had authorized a 'slow withdrawal, fighting all the way,' but then, 'Suddenly an order came to me from the Führer: "Remain where you are, and retreat no further," it said. I immediately wired back, "It is madness to attempt to hold. In the first place the troops cannot do it and in the second place if they do not retreat they will be destroyed. I repeat that this order be rescinded or that you find someone else." That same night the Führer's reply arrived: "I am acceding to your request," it read; "please give up your command." I then went home.'[136] However, as we shall see, von Rundstedt was destined to return to high command once again later on during the war. The final irony of his dismissal was that his successor, von Reichenau, almost immediately found that he had no alternative but to carry out the plan that von Rundstedt had originally intended, with a withdrawal to the line of the Mius.

In early December, the Red Army – by then reinforced by the arrival of more than 30 divisions of Mongolian troops from Siberia – launched a series of concerted attacks to save Moscow. This first major Russian counteroffensive involved 500,000 troops attacking on a frontage of almost 1,000 kilometres from Leningrad to Kursk in an onslaught that forced parts of Army Group Centre to withdraw into defensive positions as much as 350 kilometres to the west of the front line they had held a few days before. Remarkably, the Germans had little or no warning of this offensive, which was a significant indictment of the intelligence staff at the OKH and the Abwehr. Coincidentally, on 6 December, just before the first blow fell upon Army Group Centre, Halder had sought Hitler's approval of a planned major withdrawal of that army group to a defensive line based on Ostashkov and Rzhev and then as far west as Smolensk, with the other two army groups withdrawing to the Baltic states in the north and to the western Ukraine in the south. Once there, they would consolidate, reinforce and prepare to resume offensive action in the spring of 1942. Predictably, the Führer refused even to consider this plan, while the Russian offensive had in any case already rendered Halder's request somewhat academic. After two days of furious combat, conducted in snow storms and bitterly cold temperatures, the Russians broke through at Kalinin and followed this with another major breakthrough on 10 December. On 8 December, von Bock had recorded in his war diary: 'My troops have given all that they have; they can do no more. Their supreme efforts are reflected in the shockingly high losses among both commanders and men ... All along I demanded of army high command the authority to strike down the enemy when he was wobbling. We could have finished the enemy last summer. We could have destroyed him completely. Last August, the road to Moscow was open; we could have entered the Bolshevik capital in triumph and in summery weather. The high military leadership of the Fatherland made a terrible mistake when it forced my army group to adopt a position of defence last August [when the panzer groups were redeployed to the other two army groups]. Now all of us are paying for that mistake.'[137] Hitler's response to the Russian offensive was to issue a general Haltebefehl (order to stand fast), ordering all units to hold in place and defend to the last man and last round, even if cut off or surrounded. This Haltebefehl order exemplified the dominance of political, ideological and propaganda perceptions over logical military decision-making. On the battlefield, such simplistic and inflexible direction denied the Wehrmacht manoeuvre options, including that of withdrawing, regrouping and counterattacking, something at which the German army was particularly adept.

In a bitter indictment of the general staff and the high command, von Bock also highlighted the failing supply system, the underestimations of enemy strength and the lack of preparedness of the army to cope with the mud and the primitive road and rail systems in Russia. All this was true, although von Bock was also guilty of maintaining his offensive for too long when it should already have been abundantly clear at the operational level that Moscow could neither be taken nor enveloped in time. However, in

In order to advise their commanders, general staff officers regularly visited the forward positions to observe the fighting at first hand, as here in Russia, summer 1941.

Hitler reviews the Wehrmacht's progress on the Russian front with (right to left) Keitel, von Brauchitsch and Paulus, at the OKW, October 1941. Just two months later the Führer would dismiss von Brauchitsch and assume direct command of the army himself.

Konrad Hommel's 1941 painting of Hitler with Reichsmarschall Hermann Göring and senior officers (predominantly army) of the OKH and OKW exemplified the Führer's position as supreme commander of the German armed forces. It also emphasized his assumption of direct command of the army from December 1941, a move that subsequently proved to the significant disadvantage of the OKH and army general staff.

Senior commanders and general staff officers within army groups and armies frequently use front-line positions from which to observe, plan and control operations in progress. Here, Generaloberst Erich von Manstein observes an attack at Kerch in Russia, May 1942, togethe with Luftwaffe Generaloberst Wolfram Freiherr von Richthofen and these generals' army an Luftwaffe staff officers.

General staff officers and other military staff officers of the Foreign Armies East (FHO) intelligence branch of the OKH Mauerwald HQ, 1943. Of the staff officers pictured, only seve – all of them ranked major to colonel – have the 'i.G.' suffix after their rank on the original photo caption, identifying them as members of the general staff.

enior staff officer using a field telephone to make a report or receive orders in a forward
nmand post, southern Ukraine, Eastern Front, January 1944. Despite being vulnerable to
ysical attacks such as shellfire and bombing, telephone systems were still widely used by
e Wehrmacht for command and control at all levels.

Despite occasional disputes over the command and control of Luftwaffe anti-aircraft and paratroop units, Luftwaffe close air support for the army was generally good until combat attrition, over-commitment and the superior industrial capacity of the Allies progressively degraded Luftwaffe air support from 1943. Here an army staff colonel and major plan a futu air support operation with a Luftwaffe lieutenant colonel at Luftwaffe Headquarters West, St. Lô, France, July 1944.

photo of Hitler and Keitel (shown right) greeting an unnamed visitor at the Wolfschanze on July 1944, together with Oberst Claus Schenk Graf von Stauffenberg (on the left). Just five s later von Stauffenberg carried out his abortive assassination attempt against Hitler at headquarters.

The devastated conference room in the Lagebaracke at the Wolfschanze following the bomb explosion on 20 July 1944.

The scene in the courtyard of the Bendlerblock in Berlin on the morning of 21 July 1944. The vehicle entrance from Bendlerstraße is shown, as is the pile of builders' sand to the left of the picture, in front of which von Stauffenberg and his co-conspirators had been shot the previous night.

Hitler's mind, any and all blame for the adverse consequences of the Russian offensive lay primarily with von Brauchitsch. On 19 December, von Bock relinquished his command, ostensibly because of ill health (he did suffer from a digestive disorder), and was replaced by General von Kluge (then commanding Fourth Army), who still shared the OKH belief that Moscow might yet fall and planned accordingly. Despite his criticism of the conduct of the campaign and the less than ideal circumstances of his departure, von Bock was destined to return to Russia just one month later, when he would be given command of Army Group South following the unexpected death of Generalfeldmarschall von Reichenau on 17 January, two days after he suffered a heart attack. This would be the second change of command of Army Group South in less than two months.

The Russian winter offensive in early December had implications that extended far beyond the battlefield. Shortly thereafter, Hitler's impatience and lack of trust in the general staff manifested itself in an action that further reduced the army's ability to shape and control its operational affairs, while also effectively placing the OKH under his direct command. On 19 December 1941, at the end of a year in which the whole course of the war had changed dramatically, Hitler replaced von Brauchitsch as commander-in-chief of the army, assuming direct command himself.[138] In doing so, the Führer remarked to Halder that, 'This little affair of operational command is something that anyone can do. The task of the commander-in-chief is to educate the army in the idea of National Socialism, and I know of no general who could do this in the way I want it done. That is why I have decided to assume command of the army myself.'[139] This comment to Halder encapsulated the essence of the fundamental problems that had for so long existed between Hitler and the army. In a single statement it demonstrated the Führer's lack of understanding of the art of warfare, and therefore his unsuitability to exert operational command, while at the same time it illustrated his deep desire for the army to be politically or ideologically driven and motivated – arguably, in a way similar to that of the Waffen-SS. This was something that had been anathema for the general staff ever since the days of von Seeckt and the Reichswehr, although in large measure the Wehrmacht's campaign in Russia was already ideologically and politically based, being underscored by policies designed to further the tenets and objectives of National Socialism by annihilating Bolshevism and Russian Jewry.

With von Brauchitsch's departure, Halder might well have decided that it was time for him to resign. However, he decided that – with the general staff coming under ever-greater criticism and pressure from Hitler and a deteriorating situation on the Eastern Front – it was his duty to remain in post and continue to attempt to advise Hitler, in the hope of preventing even greater disasters in the future. He was supported in this decision by several other senior army officers, including Generalfeldmarschall von Leeb. Meanwhile, in Russia, various army and army group commanders continued to advocate or request – or were obliged to undertake – tactical withdrawals and consolidations, despite Hitler not only refusing all such requests but also directing the removal of those commanders who had been forced to take such action. Eventually, even such talented panzer commanders as Guderian and Höpner would suffer such summary dismissal. At the highest level, the disparity between the OKW and the OKH grew,[140] as did the perceived gap between the high command in Berlin and East Prussia and the front-line soldiers now fighting in deepening Russian snows. Many soldiers believed that the general staff officers based far away in their headquarters bunkers no longer understood the circumstances and needs of the fighting units. The vastness of Russia and now open-ended nature of *Barbarossa* contributed directly to this view within the army, reinforced by the self-evident failings of the general staff to provide adequate clothing, vehicles and equipment for a winter war or sufficient reinforcements and armoured vehicles to sustain a protracted non-Blitzkrieg campaign. Concerning this criticism, the general staff felt justifiably aggrieved, being all too aware that Hitler himself had categorically dismissed any need for the OKH to provide for the continuance of *Barbarossa* into, or indeed through, the Russian winter. He had also underestimated the Russian ability to fight on after the initial German onslaught, although in the two matters of underestimating the enemy and of overstating the Wehrmacht's capability, the general staff was by no means blameless. With such matters very much in mind, in the closing weeks of 1941 the OKH looked towards a somewhat unpredictable future. The army's professional commander-in-chief had been replaced by its political leader and head of state, and its chief of staff had been further isolated, just as the army was suffering significant reverses on the Eastern Front. Strategically, an active two-front conflict was now very much in prospect following America's entry into the war, with Germany facing a war of attrition in the east for which the general staff, the Wehrmacht, the nation and its industrial capability and resources were all woefully unprepared.

11

A War of Attrition

1942–1944

In the wake of the final departure of Generalfeldmarschall von Brauchitsch on 19 December 1941, various changes were made so that Hitler could exert his newly acquired direct command of the army and also adopt a more 'hands on' approach to his dealings with the OKW. A new liaison staff was formed within the OKW specifically to conduct liaison between Hitler and the OKH, comprising one general supported by two staff officers. Furthermore, two general staff officers now reported directly to Hitler: the quartermaster-general and a general with a non-specific or 'special purposes' portfolio (General zur besonderen Verwendung). Apart from these changes, the OKH and general staff continued much as before but with the addition of several senior posts dealing with weapons development and technical matters. The disappearance of the last professional head of the army meant that the general staff had been further isolated from the centre of power and strategic decision-making, while nominally retaining responsibility for its core functions, including operations, training, logistics and intelligence. The centralization of several of the army's other powers and responsibilities within the OKW rather than the OKH, including the army's long-standing and traditional right to select and promote its own officers, was an ongoing process, so that by late 1942 the general staff would have all but lost the ability to control its own destiny, both operationally and administratively. Another important change early in 1942 was a series of directives to army group and army commanders from Generaloberst Halder. In these directives the chief of the general staff indicated on 6 January that the army's long-standing system of command and control based upon the concept of Auftragstaktik should henceforth be replaced by a much closer adherence to the letter rather than the spirit of operational directives – thereby avoiding 'serious disadvantages for the overall situation' as 'the duty of soldierly obedience leaves no room for the sensibilities of lower headquarters', while, 'On the contrary it demands the best and most rapid execution of orders in the sense that the one issuing them intended.'[141] While undoubtedly intended to support Hitler's idea of centralized command by him as supreme commander, this pronouncement by Halder was particularly significant, as it not only challenged a core element of the army's doctrine but also recognized that Auftragstaktik as originally conceived and applied in former times had almost run its course, if indeed it had not already done so. Arguably, Halder's directives on this matter were both pragmatic and insightful.

The OKH was still the headquarters by and through which the practicalities of the campaign on the Eastern Front were directed and dealt with, but it was undeniable that operational direction of the army was now focused ultimately upon the Führerhauptquartier Wolfschanze – Hitler's field headquarters at Rastenburg, deep in the dark forests of East Prussia.[142] There, a formidable array of military and political officers, staff members and others, together with a succession of visitors, experienced an increasingly unreal existence driven largely by the eccentricities of Hitler's own daily routine. This invariably began with a solitary walk with his dog between about 9.00 and 10.00 a.m., after which the Führer would deal with any pressing matters arising from the morning courier delivery of mail. Next came the main event of the day, the operational situation briefing session at midday, which often lasted for up to two hours. A leisurely lunch began at about 2.00 p.m. and frequently ran on well into the afternoon. Any non-operational matters were then dealt with until afternoon tea and coffee were served at 5.00 p.m. A further operational update would be provided by Jodl at 6.00 p.m. followed by dinner at 7.30 p.m. This meal frequently went on until 9.30 or 10.00 p.m. and was usually followed by Hitler and the closest members of his entourage watching a film show or (less often) listening to gramophone records of German folk songs, Beethoven symphonies or

Wagnerian operas. In separate accounts of everyday life at the Wolfschanze provided after the war by Jodl and by Warlimont, who was at that time serving as Jodl's deputy in the Wehmachtführungsstab, the headquarters was described as 'a mixture of a monastery and a concentration camp', its complement of military officers being 'for the most part only tolerated guests'. Hitler regularly presided over 'long tea parties which lasted far into the night ... [suffering from] insufficient sleep in the early hours of the morning ... failing to get any fresh air or take any exercise whatsoever. Officers only met Hitler at meals and at the daily reviews of the situation. No officers were admitted to the circle of intimates except his adjutants.'[143]

The extensive self-contained complex of buildings and reinforced concrete bunkers that comprised the Wolfschanze had been constructed in anticipation of *Barbarossa*. During its construction, the site had been given the cover name 'Chemical Works Askania' in order to conceal its true purpose. The buildings of the complex were grouped within three security zones. Of these, the outer two were populated by the OKW military personnel and other support staff, while the inner zone housed Hitler's close political associates and his SS and other National Socialist advisers and staff members. Patrolling guard units and various lines of defence and obstacles safeguarded the whole complex. Access to the outer perimeter was strictly controlled, with further checkpoints limiting and controlling access to the inner zones and to the individual buildings and bunkers. The Reichs-sicherheitshauptamt (RSHA, Reich central security office) was ultimately responsible for security within the complex, the SD dealing with the practicalities within the Wolfschanze. The Führer-Begleit-Bataillon (FBB), a regiment-sized military unit equipped with tanks, anti-aircraft guns and heavy weapons, was responsible for the external security of the Wolfschanze, with a secondary response force based about 75 kilometres away. To the south-west lay a small landing field at Wilhelmsdorf, near the village of Weischnuren, almost ten kilometres away by road. This provided ready access to the headquarters by air, the road journey taking about twenty minutes. A specially built railway station within the security perimeter enabled Hitler to travel securely right into the Wolfschanze in his armoured mobile headquarters train 'Amerika'.[144] From 1941 to late 1944 a steady stream of visitors travelled to and from the Wolfschanze, including all of the most senior Nazis, the generals, admirals, specialist staff officers and advisers, scientists, political figures and Hitler's prominent allies, such as the Italian leader, Mussolini. As time passed, despite the flow of information provided by these people, the decision-making process at Rastenburg became ever further removed from reality and increasingly reflected Hitler's primarily map-based and often out-of-date, false perceptions of the way in which the war was proceeding. The OKH had no alternative but to carry out its work in spite of the often ill-informed and flawed operational directives being issued from the Wolfschanze, where the Führerhaupt-quartier staff now enjoyed unprecedented power and influence over the conduct of the war.

The fundamentally different and diverging perceptions of the general staff and Hitler concerning the conduct of the campaign in Russia at the operational level were now very clear. As a matter of policy, Hitler would permit no withdrawals and directed that where a breakthrough by the Russians might occur the response by any units thus isolated should be to form defensive 'hedgehog' positions that could support a future counterattack. In a theatre of operations as huge as Russia, this static and inflexible concept was both inappropriate and unrealistic, militating directly against the possibility of the army to regain the initiative at either the operational or the strategic level. On the other hand, true to the traditional German war-fighting principles of concentration of force and manoeuvre, the general staff and the commanders on the ground continued to advocate planned withdrawals, to enable effective short-term defensive operations on ground of their own choosing, preparatory to launching counteroffensives employing the maximum amount of force, including the concentrated mobility and firepower of the limited numbers of panzer units available. These unreconcilable differences between the thinking of the man who was now commander-in-chief of the army and the thinking of virtually all of those he now commanded would blight the conduct of the campaign on the Eastern Front until the end of the war and contribute very directly to its ultimate failure. For the general staff – where all this was so obvious to the professional soldier – doubt and frustration increased in equal measure as the winter crisis of 1941/2 ran its course and the OKH began to come to terms with the new command and control arrangements that now existed. In the meantime, the army's toll of casualties and equipment losses on the Eastern Front mounted steadily as the Russian winter gradually gave way to spring.

By the spring of 1942 the army in Russia had sustained about 900,000 casualties and lost more than 2,300 armoured vehicles, as well as 50 per cent of its original complement of horses. Although no fewer than 29 new divisions had been created and dispatched to the Eastern Front since June 1941, this had generally been achieved by omitting to replace the casualties sustained by the original divisions. This meant that the impressive number of divisions shown on the maps at the OKW, OKH and in the operations rooms of the Wolfschanze portrayed a somewhat false picture of the army's order of battle, very many of these divisions being seriously below their established levels of men and equipment, especially the former. By the end of the winter of 1941/2, at least two and a half million men were needed to return the army to its original fighting strength and enable it to resume large-scale offensive operations with a realistic chance of success. The Ersatzheer was still capable of providing about a million men through the in-place system of call-up and training, while a further half million men who had been wounded or fallen ill would over time return to active duty. However, the general staff identified a shortfall of one million that would have to be found from manpower already employed in occupations previously exempted from full military service or from the other (generally over-manned) branches of the Wehrmacht and the Waffen-SS. Not surprisingly, this situation quickly brought the army into conflict with the Luftwaffe, the Kriegsmarine and the Waffen-SS, all of which jealously guarded the manpower already within their organizations, and their own bids for reinforcements in the future. In the case of the Luftwaffe, rather than allowing any of its manpower to be diverted into the army, Luftwaffe field divisions (Luftwaffenfelddivisionen) were formed in late 1942, being manned primarily by non-flying Luftwaffe personnel and anti-aircraft gunners, personnel who were considered to be less needed in that role by that stage of the war. Several of these divisions subsequently suffered particularly heavy losses on the Eastern Front, and during 1943 the remaining

Luftwaffe field divisions (but never the Luftwaffe's airborne infantry units) were finally absorbed into the army.[145] Generalfeldmarschall von Manstein spoke for many army commanders when, during the presentation to him of his field marshal's baton by Hitler at Vinnitsa on 26 October 1942, he exposed the 'sheer nonsense' and adverse practical consequences of the development of these Luftwaffe field divisions. In a response that once again highlighted the gulf between political imperatives and military pragmatism in Nazi Germany, the Führer supported Reichsmarschall Göring's argument that he should not 'hand over "his" [Luftwaffe] soldiers, reared in the spirit of National Socialism, to an army which still had chaplains and was led by officers steeped in the traditions of the Kaiser'.[146]

Arguably, the existence of a Wehrmacht general staff that truly embraced all branches of the Wehrmacht might have been in a position to deal with the problems of the equitable and logical distribution and acquisition of manpower, but no such staff existed and so the army general staff found itself competing for a diminishing amount of manpower with the equivalent staff organizations at the headquarters of the Luftwaffe, Kriegsmarine and Waffen-SS, all of which were more favoured by Hitler and the Nazi leadership than was the OKH.[147] Within the Wehrmacht, this policy of preferment was exerted through directives issued by the Wehrmachtführungsstab, which acted as the final arbiter in the matter of military manpower. Accordingly, just as Germany embarked upon a war of attrition that would require major increases in industrial output and natural resources, manpower was conscripted or brought from reserve to active status from strategically important employment in the industrial and agricultural sectors. The jobs left vacant by these men in the armaments factories, other industrial plants and the fields and farmland of Germany would in due course be filled by impressed and volunteer foreign workers from the occupied territories. While some of these were suitably qualified specialists, many were simply unskilled workers, and this labour force was eventually supplemented with large numbers of slave labourers – and even by employing prisoners-of-war – as the Wehrmacht's demands for ever-increasing quantities of war material became insatiable.[148]

Remarkably, however, despite the often critical shortages and the hardships suffered during its first winter in Russia, in the early spring of 1942 the field army's morale generally remained high as it received the initial warning orders from OKH to prepare for a new summer offensive ordered by Hitler. At that stage, the Führer was convinced that the adverse impact of *Barbarossa* and the winter campaign upon the Russian forces had been so great that one further offensive would swiftly result in the total collapse of the Russians. However, the mood at the OKH was somewhat less sanguine. There, the general staff viewed the coming of spring as a much-needed opportunity to carry out essential redeployments, and to consolidate and strengthen those divisions that had been worst depleted by the Russian offensive and ravaged by months of fighting in severe winter weather. The general staff was also very aware of the hard lessons learnt from its under-estimation of the Russian capability in 1941, although a general perception of Russian military inferiority still pervaded much of the headquarters, reinforced by an incessant flow of ideology-based propaganda about the National Socialist view of Russia and its people. Halder's assessment was that the Wehrmacht might yet be able to develop defences strong enough to hold a summer onslaught by the Red Army, but that any attempt to resume the German offensive on a wide scale in 1941 would be extremely ill-advised. He was strongly supported in this view by General Wagner, the quartermaster-general, whose duties meant that he, even more than some other senior officers, was very conscious of the parlous state of the army's logistic support and the critical deficiencies in its communications and transport arrangements on the Eastern Front. Nevertheless, the cautionary words and advice of the general staff were once again over-ridden by Hitler, and in late June 1942, twelve months after the commencement of *Barbarossa*, the Wehrmacht resumed large-scale offensive operations on the Eastern Front.

Fall Blau: The Ukraine and Caucasus Offensive, May to November 1942

Instead of resuming the assault to capture Moscow, this new attack – *Fall Blau* (Case Blue) – was to be carried out by Army Group South in the Ukraine, with a subsequent advance into the Caucasus to seize its strategically vital oilfields. Army Group South launched its offensive to regain control of the Kerch peninsula and the Crimea on 8 May, making rapid progress and laying siege to Sevastopol from 3 June. Then, on 28 June, while Army Group North and Army Group Centre held firm, 68 German divisions supported by a further 50 Italian, Romanian and Hungarian formations struck north towards Voronezh on the River Don. After a week of heavy fighting, Voronezh fell on 5 July, just a couple of days after the capture of Sevastopol. At that stage, on 9 July, Army Group South was divided into Army Groups A and B, the mission of gaining control of the oilfields by first of all securing the Donets Basin north of Rostov and then moving south into the Caucasus to a line from Baku to Batumi being given to Army Group A. Simultaneously, Army Group B advanced towards the military-industrial complex on the River Volga at Stalingrad, with the objective of capturing the city before driving north to deal with the growing concentration of Russian forces to the east of Moscow. The offensive progressed well at first, with Army Group B making particularly rapid progress, and by early July German forces had closed up to the Don river on a broad front. Thus began a series of events and decisions that would result in one of the defining moments of the war.

At that stage, convinced that the Russians were a spent force and that a complete victory on the Eastern Front was imminent, Hitler decided to transfer his command functions as army commander-in-chief from the Wolfschanze to the Führerhauptquartier 'Werwolf' ('Werewolf'), which had been established at Vinnitsa in the Ukraine. He remained at Werwolf through most of July before returning to the Wolfschanze, which was the field headquarters he favoured from mid-1941 until late 1944. Once at Werwolf, Hitler announced his intention to assume direct control of the southern part of the front. On 16 July, he ordered Fourth Panzer Army (from Army Group B) to re-deploy to assist Army Group A, just as Army Group B was approaching Stalingrad. Then, belatedly, he realized that this city might provide a base from which Army Group A could be threatened and countermanded his earlier order, returning Fourth Panzer Army to Army Group B. This succession of 'order, counter-order, and disorder' meant ultimately that neither the Caucasus oilfields nor Stalingrad had been accorded the higher priority. As a result, neither army group had sufficient combat power to achieve its objectives, and so the offensive gradually lost its momentum. The capture of Stavropol on 5 August and Krasnodar on 9 August marked the limit of Army Group A's progress. Meanwhile, well to the north-east in the western suburbs of the great city of Stalingrad, which stood astride the Volga, the infantrymen of Sixth Army, commanded by Generalleutnant Friedrich Paulus, had been fighting on the city outskirts since 7 August and began to encounter steadily growing resistance as they fought their way into the city on the 23rd and 24th. As both army groups slowed and faltered, the stage was being set for what would prove to be the historic battle of Stalingrad. At the same time, the general staff had been dealing with other problems somewhat closer to home.

Despite the early success of *Fall Blau*, the first half of 1942 had been difficult for the general staff, with no prospect of any improvement in the months ahead. Throughout the period preparing and launching *Fall Blau*, the OKH had been coming to terms with the new high-level command and control arrangements following the disappearance of von Brauchitsch the previous December and Hitler's assumption of the role of army commander-in-chief. By June, the general staff had already incurred the loss of several competent senior commanders and other officers due to ill-health, retirement or dismissal by Hitler in the wake of the withdrawals forced by the Russian winter offensive and the winter and early spring battles thereafter.

Von Rundstedt, commander of Army Group South, had already gone on 1 December, being succeeded by von Reichenau, who had in turn been replaced, following his heart attack, by von Bock, who had been recalled to active duty on 19 January. Undeniably, von Bock's army group achieved some noteworthy successes in April, May and June, with about 200,000 prisoners taken during the operation by Generalfeldmarschall von Kleist's panzer group – Group Kleist[149] – to clear a large area west of the Don in April. This was followed by the army group attack to regain the Kerch peninsula, which resulted in a further 170,000 prisoners being taken and 1,133 guns and 258 tanks captured between 8 and 18 May. Then, when Sevastopol fell to Generaloberst von Manstein's Eleventh Army[150] at the beginning of July, another 90,000 prisoners, 467 artillery guns, 155 anti-aircraft and anti-tank guns and 758 mortars were taken. Nevertheless, von

Bock's relations with Hitler became increasingly strained, the Führer openly criticizing his conduct of operations and even redeploying Army Group South units and headquarters – such as that of Generaloberst Hoth's Fourth Panzer Army – without consulting von Bock. Matters finally came to a head, when, on 9 July, Army Groups A (commanded by Generalfeldmarschall List) and B (commanded by von Bock) were created from von Bock's Army Group South, with Hoth's panzer army allocated to Army Group A on 13 July. On the day that Hoth's army moved to join List's army group, Keitel telephoned von Bock and directed him to hand over command of his own army group to Generaloberst von Weichs, citing von Bock's ill-health as the justification for this – which was, of course, officially the reason he had relinquished command of Army Group Centre the previous December. Von Bock's outrage and protests at what he regarded as his totally unjustified dismissal were in vain, and on 15 July he handed over his command to von Weichs and returned to Berlin. Such dismissals, appointments and reappointments were hardly helpful to the high command or the general staff. However, they also created uncertainty and risked a loss of confidence among ordinary soldiers and junior officers, who saw such events either as an indication of professional incompetence on the part of those commanders who were dismissed, or (where they knew and still trusted the ability of these officers) of illogical decision-making and incompetence on the part of a high command located far from the front-line and which had evidently lost touch with the realities of the battlefield.

Such potentially disruptive command and control changes were less evident in the other two original army groups. In Army Group North, Generalfeldmarschall von Leeb remained in command until his replacement by Generalfeldmarschall Georg von Küchler on 18 January 1942. Von Leeb's departure followed a relatively amicable dispute with Hitler over the withdrawal of one of his corps, which afforded the field marshal a long-sought opportunity to be relieved of his command on what could readily be construed as a matter of principle. Meanwhile, at Army Group Centre, Generalfeldmarschall von Kluge remained in command and would do so until January 1944. Changes and uncertainties such as these also exacerbated the serious logistical problems encountered by the Wehrmacht during the winter fighting and the differences of opinion between various commanders, the OKH and the Führerhauptquartier over the conduct of the campaign in Russia. Inevitably, with Hitler now directly overseeing the army's operations, this unsatisfactory situation deteriorated even more as the new offensive proceeded.

At the OKH another significant change had been developing during the summer of 1942, as Halder consistently counselled against Hitler's direction that simultaneous operations were to be conducted at the same tempo on the River Volga – including against Stalingrad – and into the Caucasus to secure the oilfields. The vast distances between them meant that these concurrent offensives really needed to be regarded almost as separate and discrete fronts for operational and command and control purposes, something that was beyond the Wehrmacht's capability. At the same time, Halder warned of the existence of ever-increasing numbers of fresh Russian formations concentrating to the east of the Volga, with others already in place in the Caucasus. Although now almost a lone dissenter at the very highest levels of command (but of course still supported within the OKH by the general staff officers upon whose assessments he based his advice to Hitler), the chief of the general staff's misgivings were also supported by the quartermaster-general, General Wagner, who reinforced his cautionary advice of the previous year and now stated that it was simply impracticable for the Wehrmacht to provide the required levels of logistical support for two such major offensives at the same time. As August 1942 drew on, with the lines of communication on the Eastern Front lengthening, the distance between the various army groups growing, the outcome of the intense fighting for Stalingrad becoming ever more uncertain, and the strained relations between the OKH and Hitler's Führerhauptquartier increasingly evident, Generaloberst Franz Halder's four-year period as chief of the general staff was nearing its end.

Halder's dismissal on 24 September was finally triggered by events surrounding the dismissal of Generalfeldmarschall von List from command of Army Group A just over a week earlier. List's army group had accomplished much during its hard-fought advance towards the Black Sea ports of Tuapse, Novorossiysk, Batum, Sochi and Sukhumi, with Baku and the oilfields as its subsequent objective. But, by 30 August, although Novorossiysk had been captured, as the panzer units reached Mozdok on the Terek river and the infantry broke out of the close country some 50 kilometres from the port of Sukhumi, Army Group A simply ran out of the combat resources necessary to complete its mission of seizing the strategically vital Black Sea ports. Simultaneously, strengthening Russian resistance forced von Kleist's panzers to halt, while a lack of ammunition, mule transport, motor vehicles and air support made an enforced halt by the less mobile infantry divisions unavoidable. This was unacceptable to Hitler, for whom the capture of the oilfields was now the highest priority, and on 7 September Generaloberst Jodl was duly dispatched from OKW to List's army group headquarters at Stalino to report on the reason for the unsanctioned delay. In his briefing to Jodl, List stated that it was essential to carry out a re-balancing of the forces right across the front in order to concentrate the necessary combat power to resume the advance and, possibly, achieve the *Fall Blau* objectives. Jodl concurred with List's assessment and reported back accordingly to Hitler. Predictably, the Führer did not accept Jodl's report and ordered the advance to be resumed. During this extremely acrimonious briefing meeting, both Jodl and Keitel came close to being dismissed for supporting List. In any event, Hitler ordered List's dismissal, and when he left Russia on 10 September Hitler himself assumed temporary responsibility for the operational direction of Army Group A.

Halder had also supported List, not only in the matter of the operational pause at the end of August, but also on the frequent occasions on which Hitler had – quite unjustifiably – criticized List for poor judgement and tactical decisions and for ignoring Hitler's direction. Over time, Halder's strong support for Generalfeldmarschall List had come to mean that by the time List was dismissed Halder's own position had finally become untenable, especially as Hitler had long sought a suitable opportunity to replace him with a chief of the general staff more amenable to his National Socialist agenda. Consequently, on 24 September, Generaloberst Franz Halder was finally dismissed by Hitler, at the end of what had become an increasingly difficult and often stormy relationship. From the beginning of

1942, Halder's eventual removal had probably been inevitable. In June that year he had attempted to alert Hitler to the latest strategic intelligence on Russian industrial output, manpower reserves and force development. However, as he related after the war,

> When I presented [Hitler] with the figures of Russian tank production he went off the deep end. He was no longer a rational human being. I don't know whether he didn't want to understand or whether he really didn't believe it. In any event it was quite impossible to discuss such matters with him. He would foam at the mouth, threaten me with his fists and scream at the top of his lungs. Any logical discussion was out of the question.[151]

Halder's final dispute with Hitler came on 24 September, when Halder persisted with his assessment of the threat posed by the Russian reserve armies to the extended flank that had been created by the decision to commit Sixth Army into Stalingrad. The line taken by Halder on this occasion prompted Hitler to recount all the other times that Halder had disputed his own views, direction or decisions in the past, saying that, 'The problem which the army had still to solve was not a matter which required technical proficiency. What was needed was the "glow of National Socialist conviction", and that was something he could never expect from officers of the old school.'[152] On the same day, Halder relinquished his appointment as chief of the general staff.

Clearly such a flawed relationship between a commander-in-chief and his chief of the general staff was unsustainable. Indeed, it is remarkable that Halder – a man who had actively planned Hitler's removal some years earlier – had managed to remain in post for a full four years. While his dismissal in September 1942 at once denied the Wehrmacht the services and wisdom of an experienced and professionally very competent chief of the general staff, so the whole general staff organization and the OKH lost at a stroke the means to influence future events at the highest level by channelling its assessments via an officer who had rightly been viewed as 'one of its own' – however much that influence might already have diminished during the previous two years.

In a move designed further to reduce the status and authority of the general staff, Hitler appointed Generalleutnant Kurt Zeitzler, a relatively junior officer despite his rank,[153] to succeed Halder as chief of the general staff. The son of a Protestant minister, Zeitzler was born in Goßmar, Brandenburg, on 9 June 1895, joining the army in March 1914, subsequently achieving officer rank in recognition of his bravery in combat and eventually command of an infantry battalion. He served as a staff officer in the Reichswehr, and later the Wehrmacht, from 1919 to 1937, being appointed to the OKH in 1937. In 1934 he transferred from the infantry to the panzer arm.

In choosing Zeitzler, Hitler believed that he had at last found a reliable, professionally competent and committed National Socialist who would be entirely compliant in implementing the Führer's directives and policies. Certainly Zeitzler was energetic, practical and capable, with a particular flair for organization – including the support of fast-moving panzer forces. His record both as a regimental commander and as a general staff officer serving in several posts during the takeover of Czechoslovakia and the Blitzkrieg campaigns between 1938 and 1941 had been noteworthy. In September 1939, Zeitzler was chief of staff to General List in XXII Corps of Fourteenth Army during the invasion of Poland. He had also served as a staff officer within the Wehrmachtführungsstab. Although one historian has described him as 'an obedient optimist'[154] who routinely acquiesced to Hitler's wishes, Liddell Hart's assessment of his abilities while chief of staff to von Kleist's panzer group in the campaign of 1940 was much more positive: 'It was he who found a way of supplying armoured forces during long-range advances and rapid switches [of axes and objectives] ... Zeitzler was an outstandingly resourceful organizer of strategic moves, with an exceptional grasp of what could be done with mechanized forces.'[155] He surpassed this while serving in the same capacity with Kleist's group. Immediately prior to his appointment as chief of the general staff, from early 1942 he was chief of staff of Army Group D on the Western Front, which had responsibility for the defence of the Low Countries and the Channel coast in France. Zeitzler was promoted General on assuming his new appointment.

Clearly the new chief of the general staff was a thoroughly competent, thinking soldier and general staff officer: as such it was almost inevitable that his views and advice would eventually bring him into conflict with Hitler. Now required to work in the volatile, intrigue-ridden and politicized atmosphere of the Führer's headquarters, it was undeniable that Zeitzler lacked the wider depth of experience, and the intellectual skills and political acumen, that men such as Beck and Halder had brought to the post. Although an understandable degree of circumspection on Zeitler's part delayed a clash with Hitler for some weeks, his first on a matter of policy resulted from the developing and potentially dangerous situation regarding Sixth Army at Stalingrad in November 1942.

By November, Generalleutnant Paulus's army was already immersed in high-intensity urban fighting for the city. Responsibility for the security of Sixth Army's flanks had been allocated by Army Group B to the disparate Italian, Hungarian and Romanian units that had accompanied their German allies into Russia the previous year. On 19 November the Red Army launched a major counterstroke, the unexpected onslaught cutting through the Romanians and isolating 250,000 men of Sixth Army, two Romanian divisions and part of Fourth Panzer Army within the city itself. By 22 November these forces were effectively cut off from the rest of the German forces and became dependent upon air resupply, something the Luftwaffe patently lacked the capability to achieve despite Göring's assurances to the contrary. At the outset of the Russian attack, Zeitzler advised Hitler that Sixth Army should immediately be withdrawn. Predictably, Hitler disagreed. Then, two days later, when Göring stated to Hitler at a planning meeting that the Luftwaffe could provide the 700 tons of supplies required each day to maintain Sixth Army at Stalingrad, Zeitzler – who had already opined that the Luftwaffe simply did not have the capacity to do this – lost control and shouted out, 'It's a lie!' Hitler placated Göring and said that he was obliged to believe the Reichsmarschall rather than the chief of the general staff.[156] Hitler directed Sixth Army to stand and fight on until relieved.

These incidents marked the beginning of strains in Zeitzler's relationship with Hitler, who began to regard him more guardedly and increasingly distanced him from the operational planning process thereafter – particularly so when his warning about Stalingrad proved correct. For all practical purposes, Hitler now limited Zeitzler's span of responsibility to being little more than what Generalleutnant Dr. Hans Speidel termed 'the C-in-C East',[157] acting merely as a conduit for Hitler's command decisions. Logically, Zeitzler should have been directly involved in the operational planning, policy-making and command decisions affecting the Wehrmacht not only in Russia but also elsewhere, especially as the OKW and Wehrmachtführungsstab lacked the professional expertise and organizational capacity to exert effective control over those theatres for which it was now responsible. However, logic rarely featured prominently in Hitler's decision-making where the army high command and the general staff were concerned. That this return to the deliberate policy of side-lining the chief of the general staff – and therefore the wider general staff also – should have been prompted by a dispute with Göring was rather ironic, as the Reichsmarschall had been one of Zeitzler's strongest supporters in his selection to replace Halder.

To his credit, despite the unwelcome situation in which he now found himself, Zeitzler channelled his energy and organizational abilities during the succeeding weeks and months into streamlining the general staff organization, with the removal of the post of Oberquartiermeister I (in effect, the deputy chief of the general staff), which he deemed unnecessary, and by proposing a fundamental change in the relationship between the OKH and the OKW. Generalleutnant Walter Warlimont of the Wehrmachtführungsstab (despite being well-trusted by Hitler and a close colleague of Jodl and Keitel) had acknowledged to Zeitzler that the OKW was simply too small to fulfil the operational responsibilities placed upon it. With this potential source of support within the Wehermachtführungsstab in mind, Zeitzler subsequently developed a proposal that the OKH and OKW should be merged into a single armed forces command headquarters, with overarching control not only of the army, Kriegsmarine and Luftwaffe but also of the Waffen-SS. It was by no means the first time that this sort of idea had been mooted. As a colonel serving in the war ministry in 1937, Warlimont had submitted a memorandum calling for the establishment of a single general staff to command and direct all branches of the armed forces; now Zeitzler foresaw the operational benefits this could attract. Both he and the general staff knew that potentially significant numbers of troops desperately needed in Russia were being wasted through their employment on low-tempo operations and occupation duties in the theatres of operations controlled by the OKW, which was always most reluctant to allow operational command of any of these units to be transferred to the OKH. At the same time, Zeitzler sought to improve the command arrangements on the Eastern Front by proposing that a single, independent, commander should be appointed to command operations in Russia. Naïvely, he also suggested that Keitel should be replaced and that, while continuing as supreme commander, Hitler should relinquish any direct operational control. He also proposed that German armaments production should be placed under the direct control of the quartermaster-general.

As Zeitzler might have anticipated, not one of these proposals was adopted. The fact that he believed it worth putting them forward at all is a further indication of his lack of awareness of the agendas and politics that drove decision-making at Hitler's headquarters. Predictably, the heads of the Kriegsmarine and Luftwaffe and Himmler were outraged and united in their rejection of proposals that would have resulted in a dramatic curtailing of their power and influence – that of Himmler and the SS especially. The ease with which these practical and potentially constructive suggestions by the chief of the general staff were dismissed by Hitler further demonstrated Zeitzler's lack of status within the Nazi-dominated high command. Simultaneously, those who had most to lose from the implementation of these ideas now identified Zeitzler as a positive threat to their own organizations, which also served to reinforce their existing deeply-held prejudices about the army general staff and its ambitions. Symptomatic of the reduced authority of the general staff after Zeitzler's arrival was Hitler's decision in October 1942 to remove the responsibility for personnel matters from the general staff and place this directly under the control of his adjutant, Generalmajor Rudolf Schmundt,[158]who thus became the head of the army personnel office. Ironically, Schmundt was a particular friend of Zeitzler.

The Battle of Stalingrad, November 1942 to February 1943

As a consequence of Sixth Army's commitment at Stalingrad and its consequent immobility, Army Group A became vulnerable to Russian attacks, and in late December the more than a quarter of a million German troops then in the Caucasus began to withdraw northwards into the Taman peninsula, linking up with the forces in the Crimea and removing themselves from the most immediate threat that then faced them. However, Hitler would not formally approve a general withdrawal from the Caucasus until well into January 1943. In the meantime, a number of divisions with a total of about 230 tanks were formed into Army Group Don, which was placed under the command of Generalfeldmarschall Erich von Manstein.[159] To him had fallen the task of breaking through to relieve the beleaguered army in Stalingrad. Despite their unavoidably slow advance against the combined rigours of a second Russian winter, and in the face of growing Soviet resistance, this force did manage to come within 50 kilometres of Sixth Army's defensive perimeter by mid-December. But the deteriorating situation on Army Group Don's flanks due to the collapse of the Italian Eighth Army, together with Paulus' refusal to attempt a breakout to link up with the relieving force, compelled von Manstein to withdraw his army group, and by the end of December the distance between the beleaguered Sixth Army and the nearest units of the main German force exceeded 160 kilometres. This relief attempt had always been something of a forlorn hope – both von Manstein and Paulus were well aware that by mid-December Sixth Army lacked the resources, manpower and determination to conduct a successful breakout.

Commenting upon the general situation at Stalingrad in late 1942, and relating it to the wider campaign in Russia, one senior officer, Generalmajor Hans Doerr, observed tellingly that, 'the time for conducting large-scale operations was gone forever. From the wide expanses of steppe-land the war [had] moved to the jagged gullies of the Volga hills with their copses and ravines, into the factory area of Stalingrad, spread out over uneven, pitted, rugged country, covered with iron, concrete and stone buildings. The mile as a measure of distance was replaced by the yard. Headquarters' map was the map of the city.'[160]

The Battle of Stalingrad was undoubtedly a defining moment of the campaign in Russia and is rightly cited as one of the turning-points of the war. It also exemplified the extent to which military commonsense and professionalism had been supplanted by ideologically based operational decisions by the German high command, driven always by Hitler, as supreme commander of the Wehrmacht and undisputed commander-in-chief of the army. The developing catastrophe at Stalingrad exemplified the dire consequences for the soldier when the tried and tested principles of war and military planning that had stood Germany in good stead for so long were set aside by a political leadership that had chosen to ignore its professional military advisers – the general staff – in favour of pursuing unachievable aims and objectives based primarily upon intuition, flawed judgements, unsubstantiated hopes and assessments and unsustainable aspirations.

Within the embattled city of Stalingrad, the conditions endured by the soldiers were appalling, so that even the smallest successes were viewed as victories. Following one minor territorial gain in late autumn 1942, an infantryman wrote that, 'The Reich [battle] flag has been flying over the centre since yesterday. The centre and area around the railway station [at the city centre, west of the Volga] are in German hands.' This was indeed a welcome morale-booster for the soldiers as they 'lay in the earth holes wrapped in our blankets. The cold north-east wind came whistling through the canvas strips of our tent. It was pouring with rain. By way of celebration [of Christmas] we cobbled together a mixture of flour, water and some grease [intended for lubricating guns] and fried up some pancakes. We rounded off this delicious meal with tea and the last cigarettes.'[161] But a few weeks later, with the city by then firmly in the grip of the Russian winter, another infantryman recorded that, 'From a quarter to six until two in the morning, with only a short pause, we were out in a blizzard. It penetrated our coats, our clothing gradually got soaked through, freezing stiff against our bodies. We were feeling unbelievably ill in the stomach and bowel. The cold soon exceeded all bounds. Lice! Frost gripped my pus-infected fingers … My gloves were so wet that I couldn't bear them any longer [and] I wrapped a towel round my ravaged hands … [When we] stood, wet and frozen … [our] boots froze solidly to the ground.'[162] The Christmas of 1942 brought no respite for the beleaguered troops in Stalingrad. Soldier Wilhelm Raimund Beyer wrote that, 'by Christmas Day there was almost no food left. What was being distributed can hardly be described as rations: tiny amounts of tinned bread, tinned sausage, occasionally meat from a horse that had met its end somehow or other ... Everyone had long since furtively eaten up his 'iron ration' [officially issued and kept for emergency use only]. When just before Christmas the order reached us that iron rations could now be broken into, everyone laughed.'[163] Another soldier, an infantryman, observed: 'Our rations are very poor at the moment. In the morning we get 200 grams of bread, five grams of butter, twenty grams of sausage and a bowl of soup, that's all ... Half of us are even too weak to get up in the morning, let alone do any work.'[164]

Such accounts contrasted with the somewhat better conditions enjoyed by at least one group of headquarters staff officers in their command bunker on Christmas Eve 1942, where they 'sang Christmas carols and presents were distributed. Each man [all of whom were presumably officers] received three bars of chocolate, three tubes of sweets, fifty cigarettes, half a loaf of bread, 130 grams of meat and some sandwich spread ... We had conjured up a Christmas tree from a few pine branches, decorated it with silver paper from cigarette boxes, cut one of the last candles into pieces, and used the lids from empty food tins and a nail to make holders ... Thirteen of us gentlemen were there when the general arrived with a gift for everyone: a bottle of alcohol for the senior officers, and something to smoke for the others.'[165] The apparent differences between the living conditions of these officers and those of the troops in the front line are striking. However, in practice this simply reflected the different nature of the duties and place of work of the headquarters staff officers and soldiers, compared with those of the front-line infantrymen. What was remarkable was that Sixth Army was able to fight on in such adverse circumstances. The high command had failed it, the Luftwaffe had failed it, and the eventual outcome at Stalingrad was virtually inevitable. Nevertheless, in a battle that was increasingly fought against the odds, with Russian reinforcements arriving and being committed to the fighting on an almost daily basis, Paulus and Sixth Army would still hold on for a further month beyond that Christmas Eve.

While unable to alleviate it, the senior officers at OKH in Germany were by no means unaware of Sixth Army's predicament, but Hitler's order that it should stand and fight was simply not open to negotiation. In late December, Zeitzler himself made a symbolic gesture of solidarity with these unfortunate troops by voluntarily adopting a 'Stalingrad diet' and stating that he would not eat more than that which was issued to the soldiers at Stalingrad. Consequently, for many days he was to be seen in the general staff officers' mess refusing to eat the normal food that was served, thus highlighting the failure of the Luftwaffe to supply Stalingrad as Göring had promised and at the same time providing a telling reminder of his own prediction. Quite quickly, the general visibly lost weight, and on 5 January Hitler ordered him to eat properly again and not 'to use up his strength on such gestures'.[166]

As the battle of Stalingrad raged on, the group of officers headed by retired chief of the general staff Generaloberst Beck who were opposed to Hitler was growing. They were convinced that only a more direct course of action might yet save Germany from the abyss. Beck floated a plan whereby Paulus would attempt to break out from Stalingrad, and this sortie would be the signal for all the army field marshals to confront Hitler and demand that he should resign. However, while several of the field marshals who were approached by Beck or others of the core resistance group (notably Oberstleutnant Claus Schenk Graf von Stauffenberg) sympathized with Beck's aims, the soldier's oath of duty, loyalty and obedience once again proved an insurmountable obstacle to the active participation of these very senior, and generally very traditionally minded, officers. Perhaps even more significantly, many of these same field marshals still believed that Hitler might yet be persuaded to authorize the withdrawals and consolidation necessary to shorten and hold the line on the Eastern Front. They remained convinced that such action could still provide the Wehrmacht with the opportunity to employ manoeuvre with defensive operations, thereby regaining the initiative and ultimately bringing about a German victory on the Eastern Front. Consequently, Beck's plan came to naught. Meanwhile the final tragedy of Sixth Army was drawing ever nearer, amidst the shattered factories, destroyed houses and rubble-strewn streets within the devastated city of Stalingrad.

By January 1943, Sixth Army was facing the prospect of eventual annihilation as the Russian attackers – constantly reinforced by the arrival of fresh troops ferried across the River Volga – began to consolidate their positions within the city, day-by-day gaining ground. As Zeitzler had forecast, the level of air support promised by Göring never materialized, although a number of Luftwaffe pilots regularly braved the Russian fighters and anti-aircraft guns to maintain Sixth Army's links with the outside world. These flights delivered mail and combat supplies, as well as individual officers and soldiers and small numbers of reinforcements, while also evacuating some of the more badly wounded personnel. There was a steady inflow and outflow of individual personnel – mainly officers – to deliver orders and directives, make assessments or carry out or advise on various specialist tasks. When the Russians captured the airfield in January, they finally severed Sixth Army's last link with the outside world. From that time on, increasing numbers of individual German troops began to surrender, despite the summary fate that befell these prisoners-of-war in very many cases. On 26 January, the two main parts of the attacking Russian forces linked up at the centre of the city, shattering the remaining cohesion of the German defence. The final act in the drama came on 31 January, when Hitler – mindful of the fact that no German field marshal had ever been taken alive in battle – announced that Paulus had been promoted Generalfeldmarschall. But Paulus and his army had already endured enough. On the same day, the newly promoted field marshal attempted to negotiate suitable terms of surrender, and on 2 February the last of the 91,000 German and other Axis soldiers in Stalingrad who were still more or less alive were taken into Russian captivity. In all, more than 200,000 men were killed or captured during the battles for Stalingrad; of those captured, less than 5,000 eventually returned to Germany following their release from the prison camps in Russia some ten years later.[167] Inevitably, by early 1943, Russian attitudes to their Axis prisoners had been shaped not only by the fact that the Germans were the aggressors and invaders but also by the many atrocities and reprisals carried out by the SS and some Wehrmacht units against a population that Hitler and National Socialist ideology had actively portrayed through its propaganda as 'Untermenschen' ('subhuman').

It is well-nigh impossible to represent Stalingrad as anything other than a monumental catastrophe for the Wehrmacht and the German nation. Nevertheless, von Manstein did concede that by fighting on until the beginning of February Sixth Army had safeguarded and enabled the withdrawal of Army Group A and Army Group Don by forcing the Russians to commit no fewer than seven armies (comprising some 60 corps and division-size formations) to overcoming the German forces and their Axis allies in Stalingrad. Hitler later declared that Sixth Army's protracted battle at Stalingrad had 'stabilized the Eastern Front'. Nevertheless, the outcome of the battle at Stalingrad prompted propaganda minister Goebbels to proclaim that Germany was now engaged in a 'total war'. Arguably, had Hitler understood that this had been the case from the time that he decided to attack Russia, thus invoking a two-front war, the German nation might have been better prepared industrially, militarily and mentally for the sort of conflict in which it had become engaged from 1941.

'Unconditional Surrender': The Casablanca Conference, January 1943

Meanwhile, in North Africa the fortunes of the Afrikakorps had already turned after its defeat by British and Commonwealth forces at El Alamein in October 1942, followed shortly afterwards by US landings in French Morocco and Algeria in November, which opened up another front within the North African theatre of operations. Then, at Casablanca on 24 January 1943, at a meeting of the 'Big Three' Allied leaders, President Roosevelt declared that, 'The elimination of German, Japanese and Italian war power means the unconditional surrender by Germany, Italy and Japan.' He went on to say that this did 'not mean the destruction of the population of Germany, Italy or Japan, but it does mean the destruction of the philosophies in those countries which are based upon conquest and the subjugation of other people'. The intention (in the case of Germany) was to divide the Nazis from the non-Nazis, creating dissent and calls for an end to the war. However, while Roosevelt's statement focused quite precisely upon the followers of National Socialism in Germany, fascism in Italy and imperialism in Japan, such subtlety was largely lost upon the population of the Axis states – who in any case received most of their news and information through official government broadcasts and pro-government newspapers and other media. In Germany, Goebbels seized upon the call for 'unconditional surrender' as a welcome propaganda tool, as a motivator and clear reason for Germany to fight on. In his broadcasts, he was now in a position to say that surrender to the Allies was not an option in any circumstances, since this would inevitably involve the destruction of Germany (and the destruction of Germany was certainly Stalin's own interpretation of 'unconditional surrender', even if it was not that of Churchill or Roosevelt).[168] In any event, for the general staff and others opposed to Hitler, the Allied call for unconditional surrender seriously undermined their future options and would henceforth constrain any moves to negotiate a peace other than with all of the major Allied powers simultaneously, as well as denying those who opposed Hitler any real opportunity to present to the German people a positive alternative to continuing the war. The following year this situation was further exacerbated by the disclosure of Allied discussions concerning the controversial Morgenthau Plan, which had been developed in the United States with the intention of reducing post-war Germany to a primarily pastoral and agriculture-based economy with no industrial capability, its people entirely demilitarized and little more than a peasant population conducting a form of subsistence farming on a national scale. Although US Treasury Secretary Henry Morgenthau's proposals were not adopted by the Allied leaders, the revelation that such matters were under serious consideration provided yet more valuable propaganda material to Goebbels and further weakened the case for any sort of negotiated capitulation by Germany.

Zitadelle: The Battle for the Kursk Salient, February to July 1943

As 1942 drew on, the already severe measures directed by Hitler against partisans, Red Army commissars and others in Russia were supplemented by increasingly draconian directives concerning the treatment of specific military personnel captured in any theatre of operations. On 18 October, a secret order had been issued calling for Allied commandos captured in the West to be summarily executed. In due course, Hitler's response to the increasing tempo of Allied bombing of Germany and the occupied territories was to issue a directive that required any captured Allied aircrew to be handed over to the SD for interrogation followed by summary execution. Since the commandos and aircrew both operated in uniform, such directives directly contravened the Geneva Conventions and were illegal in terms of the laws of armed conflict. The extension of these policies into theatres of operations other than the Eastern Front troubled many in the Wehrmacht's officer corps, who viewed with considerable unease measures that were clearly contrary to the well-founded rules for the treatment of legitimate prisoners-of-war – measures that might also prompt reprisals by the Western Allies against captured German soldiers and airmen. Step by step, the sort of practices that had gradually become the norm in the bitter combat on the Eastern Front during the previous eighteen months were being applied to the other theatres of war, and this impacted upon the consciences of officers whose opposition to the National Socialist regime had until then been largely passive.

An indirect consequence of the defeat at Stalingrad, preceded by the earlier withdrawal of Army Group A in late November 1942, together with the increasing scale and success of Russian attacks, was the creation by February 1943 of a large Russian salient that projected into German-held territory. This situation was seized upon by Hitler as an opportunity to regain the initiative on the Eastern Front with an offensive that – in his view – would result in crippling and decisive losses to the Red Army. The area for which the general staff was tasked to plan the new offensive was known as the Kursk salient, the new operation being designated *Zitadelle* ('Citadel').

The sequence of events that produced the Kursk salient had begun on 8 February 1943, when a Russian attack recaptured Kursk and then drove on westwards and south towards Kharkov. The extent of this Russian advance created a salient that extended well into German-held territory and thus offered the army an opportunity to cut off and destroy much of the Soviet force. Accordingly, Hitler ordered II SS Panzer Corps to hold Kharkov, pending a major German counterattack. But after a week of bitter fighting within the largely ruined city the Waffen-SS troopers were forced to abandon Kharkov on 15 February. This withdrawal had the effect of further extending the Russian line, and on 19 February, at Krasnograd, II SS Panzer Corps and part of Fourth Panzer Army launched a surprise attack, which resulted in more than 23,000 Russian casualties and about 9,000 prisoners being taken, forcing the Russians to withdraw in some disarray. By late March, as winter turned to spring and the hard-frozen ground gradually became mud, Kharkov was again in German hands, together with Orel to the north, while well over a million Russian troops were now deployed within what had become the 250-kilometre-wide Kursk salient. This situation prompted Hitler to order a major attack upon the flanks of the salient, with the aim of isolating and then annihilating the mass of Red Army formations contained within it. At that stage, Hitler opined that these forces constituted the last of the Russian reserve forces. The consensus within the general staff remained that the Wehrmacht no longer had the capability to mount a large-scale attack such as that currently being planned and which would prove to be the last great offensive staged by the Wehrmacht on the Eastern Front. What eventually followed, though not until July, culminated in the largest tank battle in the history of warfare up to that date. It also confirmed without question that the ability of the panzer units to conduct Blitzkrieg-style operations with impunity had indeed run its course.

Necessarily, the launch of *Zitadelle* had to be delayed until the summer in order to complete other operations in the Kharkov area beforehand. The spring thaw and the need to concentrate sufficient quantities of tanks and assault guns to carry out the operation also affected the operation's start date, and, although the consequent three-month delay to July was probably unavoidable, this undoubtedly prejudiced the success of the operation. Not least, this was because the Russians were forewarned of the German plan – probably by the Western Allies exploiting the flow of intelligence they were then receiving from their 'Enigma' code intercepts.[169] In due course, the Russians were also advised of the precise date that the operation was scheduled to begin, 5 July 1943. By then, there were 1,300,000 Red Army soldiers in the salient, well-entrenched within a fortress of anti-tank obstacles, ditches and gun emplacements, minefields and well-prepared infantry strongpoints. This network of defensive positions was up to 200 kilometres deep and supported by no fewer than 20,220 guns, 3,600 tanks and 2,400 aircraft. A sizeable armoured counterstroke force was held in reserve to the east of the salient.[170] In yet another failure of German military intelligence – for which the general staff must bear considerable responsibility, even allowing for the significant constraints that Hitler had already imposed upon intelligence-gathering and processing – the Germans knew neither that the security of *Zitadelle* had been compromised nor the actual extent and strength of the Russian defences within the salient.

The general staff's plan for *Zitadelle* was relatively straightforward and called for a pincer, or enveloping, attack by two armies. Fourth Panzer Army – reinforced following the loss of a large part of the former Fourth Army during the fighting at Stalingrad in January – would strike into the salient from the south with six panzer divisions, five Panzergrenadier divisions and eleven non-armoured divisions, with a total of about 1,300 tanks, plus many self-propelled assault guns and other armoured vehicles. From the north, Ninth Army would be launched into the salient with six panzer divisions, one Panzergrenadier division, about 800 tanks and other armoured vehicles, and fourteen non-armoured divisions. With no fewer than 2,200 tanks and about 1,000 assault guns in these two armies, this meant that about 70 per cent of the German armoured capability on the Eastern Front was committed to *Zitadelle*. Some 1,800 combat aircraft supported the two armies, which was around 65 per cent of the Luftwaffe's remaining capability on the Eastern Front. In all, the two armies totalled about 900,000 men.

The attack was scheduled to begin at five o'clock on the morning of 5 July, but at 2.00 a.m. that day the Soviet artillery fired a massive bombardment against the German armour and troop concentrations, indicating very clearly that this would be no surprise attack. Meanwhile, many units had already suffered frequent harassing attacks by partisans as they moved into their starting positions for the operation. Nevertheless, the two armies crossed their respective start lines on time and began to advance towards Kursk. As they moved forward, both armies were soon inextricably enmeshed in a morass of anti-armour defences supported by a huge weight of fire from hundreds of tanks, anti-tank guns and other artillery. By nightfall the leading elements of Fourth Panzer Army had advanced no more than thirteen kilometres, the rest of that army having achieved even less. In the north, Ninth Army achieved little more than six kilometres of penetration. Luftwaffe air support could not unlock the advance, and the assault quickly degenerated into a battle of attrition, with separate deliberate attacks being required to overcome each and every strongpoint, line of defence and fortified village. Many of these positions were held tenaciously, delaying and channelling the attacking Germans into yet other killing areas. As the battle developed, the Pz.Kpfw.V 'Panther' tanks so recently introduced into service began to suffer various mechanical breakdowns, while the lumbering 'Elefant' assault guns – armed with the powerful 88mm gun, but with only one machine-gun for close protection – initially smashed through the defensive positions with relative ease, only to find themselves isolated and unsupported, so that they were then destroyed piecemeal by teams of Russian infantrymen with a variety of anti-armour weapons and explosive charges. Almost a week of bitter fighting within the salient ensued, after which the forward units of the two assaulting armies were still 225 kilometres apart.

On 11 July the attacking 1st, 2nd and 3rd SS Panzer Divisions of the Waffen-SS did at last appear to be making some progress in the area of Prokhorovka, while advancing astride the north–south rail link between Kursk and Belgorod in the vanguard of Fourth Panzer Army. However, as more than 600 Pz.Kpfw.IV, Pz.Kpfw.V 'Panther' and Pz.Kpfw.VI 'Tiger' tanks, together with numbers of assault guns, closed up and surged forward to press their advantage on the following day, the Waffen-SS panzer divisions suddenly found themselves facing most of the Russian Fifth Guards Tank Army's armoured reserve, which was equipped predominantly with the formidable T-34/76 tank. These Russian fighting vehicles were in considerably greater numbers than the German tanks. On that day, 12 July, more than 1,500 armoured vehicles manoeuvred within the southern part of the salient,[171] while at its core some 250 German tanks and 600 Soviet tanks became locked within a cauldron that fast assumed the appearance of 'a confused, dust-shrouded mass, thickened by the billowing black, oily smoke from stricken tanks and guns'.[172] This great armoured mêlée was later acknowledged to have been the greatest tank battle of the war. By nightfall, Fourth Panzer Army had lost 400 tanks and 10,000 men since the start of the offensive and could advance no more. To the north, by 12 July Ninth Army had lost about 200 tanks and as many as 25,000 men. Undoubtedly the Russians had lost more – possibly as many as 1,800 tanks and 40,000 men in the southern part of the salient alone – but they still had sufficient reserves to absorb such losses and launch further attacks at the north of the salient. The Germans had entirely exhausted their ability to advance any farther. Indeed, the Soviets claimed to have killed or captured as many as half a million German soldiers and to have destroyed 1,500 tanks since 5 July. Whatever the true figures might be, the losses to both sides and the sheer scale of the destruction that had resulted from the week-long battle were truly appalling and bore out the general staff's earlier assessment of the much-reduced capability of the Wehrmacht to mount offensive operations by that stage of the war. The overall level of destruction sustained by the defending Russian forces at Kursk at the tactical and operational levels was greater than that of the Germans; but at the strategic level the Red Army could restore such losses of men and equipment, whereas the Wehrmacht was unable to do so. At the operational level, the great tank battle of 12 July signalled the beginning of the end of *Zitadelle* and the German failure to envelop the salient. Far more significantly for the general staff at the OKH, Kursk also marked the point at which the strategic initiative on the Eastern Front passed decisively to the Russians.

Whatever Hitler chose to believe and propound at his meetings with commanders and staff, the full extent of the capability and reserves available to Moscow by 1943 could no longer be denied. Even at the OKW, the senior staff could no longer support over-optimistic estimates of relative strengths. Later that year, in an address to a gathering of Gauleiters on 7 November, Generaloberst Jodl acknowledged that the Russian armies probably numbered as many as five and a half million men, with 327 infantry divisions and 51 armoured divisions, at a time when Germany could field a total of no more than 200 infantry and panzer divisions, plus 10 divisions from Romania, 6 from Hungary and about 160 battalions of fairly unreliable so-called 'eastern troops'.[173] By the second week of July that year, even Hitler had been forced to acknowledge that the original objectives set for *Zitadelle* could no longer be achieved, and he terminated the operation. Quite apart from the obvious futility of perpetuating the offensive in the Kursk salient, this decision was also influenced by the impact of the Anglo-US landings in Sicily on 10 July, which had opened up a new front on the southern edge of the European mainland following the final demise of the Afrikakorps and its Italian allies in Tunisia during May.

The operational balance of the war on the Eastern Front had been changed irrevocably by the outcome of *Zitadelle*, and its consequences were soon all too evident. Indeed, it may reasonably be argued that the Wehrmacht's failure at Kursk was the writing on the wall for Germany. By early August, Army Group Centre and Army Group South had withdrawn from the Kursk area, abandoning Orel, Kharkov and Belgorod on 5 August. Then, on 7 September, the Germans began their evacuation of the Ukraine. Far to the north, the Red Army recaptured Smolensk on 25 September. Everywhere the Russian forces (by now organized into ten army 'fronts' stretching from the Baltic to the Caucasus) were mounting coordinated offensives as they advanced westwards against the much-weakened Wehrmacht. This was the situation so many commanders and general staff officers had predicted and forewarned both at the outset of *Barbarossa* and then again and again during the fighting of 1942 and early 1943, all to no avail. It was now simply too late for a Wehrmacht suffering seriously diminishing resources and severe manpower deficiencies to regain the initiative, while not even the undoubted competence of the ground force commanders and the officers of the general staff at the OKH could mitigate this situation. And by mid-1943, the ability of the general staff to apply its professional judgement at the operational level, unconstrained by the prejudices and agendas of the Nazi leadership, was already limited. The pleas of Zeitzler and numerous commanders to shorten the line and concentrate upon destroying the Red Army's offensive capability went largely ignored by Hitler, as did von Manstein's lobbying of the Führer to appoint a single, independent commander-in-chief for the Eastern Front. Less publicly, von Manstein had also expressed the view that the impending multi-front strategic crisis might be alleviated by negotiating a separate peace with Moscow once the Red Army's offensive capability had been neutralized, even if the restoration of some conquered territory proved necessary to achieve this. Although this was probably never a practicable course of action, that a general staff officer of the calibre of von Manstein had considered it at all is noteworthy. It indicated his belief that the terms for an unconditional and simultaneous German surrender to all of the Allies were possibly less immutable than those which Goebbels had proclaimed publicly. Similarly, there was an inference that Stalin might indeed have been prepared to negotiate with the Germans unilaterally if it had been politically advantageous for him to do so.[174]

As the Wehrmacht's third winter in Russia approached, its operations on the Eastern Front were very different from those of the Blitzkrieg years of 1939, 1940 and 1941. Now, the OKH and its armies and divisions were dealing predominantly with fighting withdrawals and hard-fought defensive battles against often overwhelming odds, and responding to events and reverses – often at very short notice – by launching counterattacks and directing limited armoured envelopments and other manoeuvres at the tactical level. At that level, the skill and leadership qualities of many commanders were remarkable, as indicated by the high casualties inflicted upon the advancing Russians and the enforced slowness of that advance despite the Red Army's superior strength and seemingly inexhaustible reserves and resources (now supplemented on an ever-increasing scale by deliveries of weapons and equipment from the United States). There was some irony in the fact that the way in which the campaign on the Eastern Front was now being fought accorded in many ways with the beliefs of the commanders and general staff ever since the end of 1941, that the front should be shortened, tactical withdrawals should be routine, and operational gains should be achieved by manoeuvre warfare. In fact, by late 1943 Germany was indisputably committed to a war of attrition fought on multiple fronts – as the general staff and army high command had forewarned both before and after 1939, this was a war Germany was neither prepared for nor, at this late stage, capable of winning. In the meantime, while the army on the Eastern Front grudgingly gave way, in Sicily and Italy a new threat was developing.

The Campaigns in Sicily and Italy, July 1943 to June 1944

On 10 July, just five days after the start of *Zitadelle* in Russia, Anglo-US forces had landed in strength on Sicily. The island was defended by an Axis garrison of 50,000 German troops in XIV Panzer Corps, commanded by General

Hans-Valentin Hube, and 315,000 troops of the Italian Sixth Army. Italian General Guzzoni was nominally in overall command, but when the invasion began he quickly handed over operational control to Hube. Despite a few instances of spirited resistance, many of the Italian defenders fled as soon as the invaders landed. Consequently, most of the short but hard-fought battles that then took place were fought by the German troops, primarily by the 15th Panzergrenadier Division and by a Luftwaffe armoured formation, Panzer Division 'Hermann Göring' or 'Panzerdivision HG'. Gradually the Germans were forced north towards Messina, and on 10 August General Hube ordered an evacuation to mainland Italy. In an operation planned and executed with the thoroughness and professionalism that had for so long characterized the work of the German general staff, the army's withdrawal was conducted with such skill that between 11 and 17 August no less than 39,569 German troops, 9,605 vehicles, 47 tanks, 94 guns and 17,000 tons of ammunition were successfully transported across the Strait of Messina to the Italian mainland. On 17 August the Allies entered Messina, and on 3 September the Italian government signed a secret armistice with the Allies. Italy's unconditional surrender was announced publicly on 8 September. Within days of the Allied invasion of Sicily, Mussolini's already weakening position had became untenable, his power base had quickly disintegrated, and he was finally ousted from power on 25 July.

The general staff had for some time anticipated Italy's collapse, and appropriate plans existed for this contingency. As a result, the German forces were able speedily to disarm the Italian forces and take over their defences. The number of German divisions in Italy was also increased from six in July to eighteen in September, with four more en route. The replacement of Italian by German units was carried out just in time, as the Italians had been responsible for the defence of the port of Salerno, and it was here that the Allies landed their main invasion force on the morning of 9 September, with other smaller landings at Taranto, Reggio and Brindisi. The unexpected presence at Salerno of the newly arrived German troops of Generaloberst von Vietinghoff's Tenth Army resulted in a hard, week-long battle for the port, and only the arrival of significant numbers of Allied reinforcements and the fire support of two additional Royal Navy battleships prevented the

Germans forcing an Allied evacuation of the beachhead. However, the sheer weight of Allied numbers and resources eventually forced a well-ordered German withdrawal, and Naples fell on 1 October, on which day the first Allied units entered the city. Thus began another campaign of attrition for the Wehrmacht, with the 'Commander-in-Chief South', the Luftwaffe Generalfeldmarschall Albert Kesselring, also using every opportunity offered him to compensate for the German army's lack of men and resources by imposing a grinding war of attrition upon the Allies, and using to best advantage Italy's rugged terrain, which generally favoured the defence. Kesselring's skilful management of the Italian campaign had important strategic implications for other theatres of operations, particularly in occupied Western Europe, for between September 1943 and May 1945 the Allies were forced to retain in Italy much of the manpower and matériel that might otherwise have been used for the invasion of France. In the meantime, they were incurring often heavy casualties during a succession of battles to overcome a series of well-sited positions and German lines of defence. One such action was the defence at Cassino between 17 January and 11 February 1944 (the fighting for Monte Cassino did not finally end until 18 May 1944), where General Frido von Senger und Etterlin's troops of XIV Panzer Corps (consisting mainly of infantry and paratroopers, with only a few tanks) forced the Allies to halt their advance in order to reinforce and replace their significant losses. The defence of Cassino prompted an Allied landing by a US-led Anglo-US force at Anzio on the west coast of Italy on 22 January 1944. This landing was designed to outflank the German defences of the Gustav Line (which incorporated the hilltop monastery of Monte Cassino) and open the way to Rome. Although the concept of the Anzio landing had been inspired and the landing itself was completely successful – it achieved almost total surprise, with the area between Anzio and Rome largely free of German combat forces – the Allies then failed to exploit their success by immediately advancing on Rome. At Anzio, the American force commander chose to consolidate the beachhead and prepare for an early German counterattack. By so doing, he entirely missed the opportunity to exploit eastwards and achieve the principal aim of the Anzio landing by outflanking the German defences and lines of communication and capturing Rome virtually unopposed. On the other hand, although the Germans had certainly been caught unawares by the landing, General Eberhard von Mackensen reacted speedily, moving units of his Fourteenth Army to contain the bridgehead. A stalemate ensued, and on 30 January a panzer-led counterattack split the Anglo-US beachheads and almost reached the sea before Allied air and naval fire forced its withdrawal.

Much has already been written about the numerous constraints imposed upon the general staff by Hitler, the Nazi leadership and the politically volatile environment in which it was required to work. On the other hand, the fighting at Anzio also highlighted the differences between the closely regulated and tight command and control doctrine of the Allies and the flexible, or intuitive, mission-orientated doctrine of Auftragstaktik applied in the German army, not only at the tactical level but also at higher levels in those conflict areas where Hitler chose not to take such a close interest in operational matters. However, the effectiveness of this doctrine was virtually negated where the Führer did choose to intervene, using modern communications to do so. Ironically, the ability of Hitler and senior commanders to speak directly to front-line commanders had the potential to constrain the application of Auftragstaktik significantly.

In the case of the Italian campaign, however, this proved to be less of a problem, and the fact that its commander was a Luftwaffe General-feldmarschall rather than an army general (although Kesselring's early service had been as an army artillery officer and he had been a member of the general staff until 1936) may have inclined Hitler to adopt a less intrusive approach to the Wehrmacht's operations in Italy. Similarly, although Hitler had always favoured the Luftwaffe and Kriegsmarine over the army, another reason for him to have adopted a relatively 'hands off' approach in Italy might have been due to that theatre of operations being nominally under OKW rather than OKH control. Finally, although he was conducting a primarily defensive campaign, Kesselring was undeniably doing so with a considerable degree of success.[175]

While Fourteenth Army continued to hold the Allies at Anzio, farther east General von Senger und Etterlin's XIV Panzer Corps, reinforced by additional Fallschirmjäger and army units, frustrated two more Allied attempts to break through the 'Gustav Line' at Cassino. During the first of these, from 15–20 February, the Monte Cassino monastery (which the Allies believed, incorrectly, to be occupied by German troops) was destroyed by bombing. The second battle began on 15 March with the Allied bombing of Cassino town, and ended on the 25th. Although the German defenders were forced to concede a few positions the fighting was exceptionally hard and frequently hand-to-hand, with very high Allied casualties. Only the committal of the full weight of Allied air and ground fire-power on 11 May, together with every ground force unit available, finally produced a German withdrawal. On 18 May, Monte Cassino fell, and the integrity of the Gustav Line was broken. This enabled the Allies at the Anzio beachhead to break out and link up with the advancing US Fifth Army on 26 May, with Rome finally captured on 4 June. Just two days later, at dawn on 6 June 1944, the Allies carried out large-scale airborne and sea-borne landings on the coast of northern France, at Normandy.

Inevitably, the nature of Germany's war of attrition and the new imperatives and priorities that this imposed upon the Wehrmacht had also necessitated various modifications to the general staff training process. Although general staff training usually occupied up to a total of two years in peacetime, by 1944 it had been condensed into less than twelve months, with up to four months training with active units, two months at the specialized arms schools, and four months at the General Staff College. This reduction had in large part been driven by the need to speed up the production of much-needed and suitably trained and qualified general staff officers. In early 1944 the young artillery officer Hauptmann Siegfried Knappe experienced these somewhat abbreviated training arrangements when he was selected for general staff training. By then he had completed almost eight years in the army. His experience of the general staff training process that applied during the final years of the war was fairly typical, and in preparation for the formal general staff training course he was first of all attached to the headquarters of the 71st Infantry Division in the area of Cassino in Italy, in order to gain practical experience of staff work and procedures at the operational level of command. Building upon that experience, he later spent time with corps and army headquarters. He learned the importance of knowing all of the division's key commanders and every detail of the division's battle plan, which at that stage of the war in Italy involved the defence of part of the Gustav Line. Time was spent observing and understudying the operations officer, the intelligence officer and the quartermaster, and then working directly with some of the regimental commanders, where he 'observed what the different people were doing, how they received reports from the regiments, and how they put them together and sent a report to the corps [headquarters]'.[176] After three weeks with the 71st Division, Knappe was attached to the headquarters of XIV Panzer Corps, where he noted in particular the importance of knowing the commanders and officers of his own corps and of the neighbouring corps personally, rather than 'from only having talked to him on the phone', as well as the value of noticing 'what military decorations those people wore, because that told me a great deal about their character and their general capability'.[177] Having gained this experience at the operational level, Knappe was attached to the army group headquarters and theatre of operations headquarters of Generalfeld-marschall Kesselring, located to the north of Rome. There he was wounded by an Allied air attack and hospitalized in Florence before being evacuated to a hospital in Leipzig in late June for further treatment and convalescence. Pronounced fit for duty again, he began the second part of his general staff preparatory training in late July 1944. At that stage this involved attending a series of short updating courses at the panzer, communications and engineering schools and other specialist establishments over a two-month period. As an artillery officer, he was not required to attend any additional specialist training at the artillery school. Once all of these preparatory activities and courses had been completed successfully he was finally ready to begin the formal period of general staff training and was ordered to attend the general staff training course scheduled to run from late 1944 into 1945.[178] Although the war was clearly going against Germany by mid-1944 – on the Eastern front, in Italy and now with the Allied landings in France – the young captains who assembled at the General Staff College at Hirschberg in Silesia in mid-1944 were still generally optimistic about the eventual outcome of the conflict and enthusiastic about their selection to become members of the general staff corps, which was still widely regarded within the army as an elite organization of outstanding officers who were destined for rapid advancement and great responsibility. However, the realities of war meant that few if any of these students would have the opportunity to realize their ambitions, and then only for a matter of weeks or months, as the general staff was by then rapidly approaching its own particular Götterdämmerung, while Germany's war in Europe had less than a year to run. As the general staff corps candidates assembled at Hirschberg, few if any of them could have anticipated the seismic event that would shortly take place at Rastenburg in East Prussia, impacting very directly upon the organization of which they aspired to become members.

For those officers who were already serving on the general staff, the worst-case scenario that they had for so long feared, anticipated and warned about – a war of attrition conducted simultaneously on multiple fronts – had finally turned into reality, and the conflict was rapidly developing into a struggle for Germany's survival and potentially its very existence. By the summer of 1944, a number of general staff officers and others – headed by retired Generaloberst Beck and firmly committed to oppose Hitler and the National Socialist regime – had already developed radical plans to take direct action to save the nation and its army from the fate that surely awaited if Hitler were to be allowed to continue unchecked to lead the Fatherland along the perverse pathway of National Socialism.

12

Duty and Honour, Plots and Conspiracies

1934–1944

The abortive attempt to assassinate Hitler on 20 July 1944 was the culmination of a conspiracy commonly referred to as the 'July plot'. It was the closest that those who resisted Hitler came to achieving their aim of removing the Führer and overthrowing the National Socialist government. Rather than being an isolated incident, it was actually the final desperate act of a movement that had existed in disparate forms ever since the mid-1930s and which then gradually coalesced in the 1940s based upon a number of prominent civilians – politicians, diplomats, government officials, intellectuals, clerics and so on – and on groups, cliques and individual officers within the Wehrmacht. Those officers who became involved were predominantly members of the army general staff, and as such they provided a usually pragmatic and proactive core for the movement and played a major part in the business of attempting to remove Hitler and return democracy to Germany. In order to understand and place in context the events of July 1944, it is necessary first of all to step back in time to the mid-1930s, to the birth and subsequent development of the organized civil-military opposition to Hitler and National Socialism during the decade that followed. (This broad overview of the wider resistance to National Socialism within Germany between 1934 and 1944 spans and overlaps much of the period that has already been covered from a primarily military standpoint. Accordingly, it necessarily revisits some aspects of some of the events and issues described earlier, in order to place these matters in their proper context.)

The movement that is today recognized as the German resistance movement (Deutscher Widerstand) against Hitler and the National Socialist state in due course provided an ever-present backdrop to Germany's conduct of the war and was a constant factor affecting the army general staff throughout the Third Reich period. Several significant examples of its activities have already been highlighted, the so-called 'Halder plot' linked to the 1938 Czech crisis being one such example during the pre-war period. Subsequently, the outbreak of war in September 1939, the reversal of Germany's fortunes on the Eastern Front from 1942, the disaster at Stalingrad in 1943, and the atrocities ordered by the Nazi regime and committed by the SS and SD against Europe's Jews and others on the Eastern Front predominated among the various reasons that an increasing number of army officers decided – despite their oath of loyalty to the Führer – to oppose Hitler and ultimately to join the resistance movement. Eventually, the involvement of these senior army officers and members of the general staff with the activities of the movement – notably its attempts to assassinate Hitler and its plans to overthrow the Nazi-led government – sealed the fate of that military organization.

The German resistance movement finally failed for a number of reasons, but foremost among these was the fact that it developed too slowly and too late, while the overall number of actively involved and totally committed members was never great enough. At the same time, the international support that the movement not unreasonably sought from countries opposed to, or threatened by, Germany was generally either very limited or simply not forthcoming at all.[179] In addition, a considerable divergence of views existed among the principal members of the resistance on aims and objectives, policy, duty, legality and the issue of whether Hitler's removal should be achieved by assassination or merely by his arrest and subsequent trial by due legal process. Crucially, the excessively idealistic or naïve views of some of the civilian members of the resistance movement were frequently at variance with those of its generally more pragmatic and decisive military members.

The Civilian Resistance Movement

In 1934 and 1935, declarations of political protest against aspects of the policies and culture of the burgeoning National Socialist state by men such as vice-chancellor Franz von Papen and the economist Dr. Hjalmar Schacht were largely ignored by the Nazis. However, the government's adoption of the policy of Gleichschaltung (grouping of all aspects of German life and activities into coordinated National Socialist entities) brought it into conflict with religious groups, particularly the Roman Catholic Church. Although a concordat had been signed with the Vatican in July 1933 guaranteeing the status and freedom of Catholics to practise their religion in Germany (in return for which the Vatican undertook not to intervene in or attempt to influence German politics), the requirements of Gleichschaltung were incompatible with the principles set out in the concordat. The Nazis actively persecuted Catholic priests and nuns, and in March 1937 a papal encyclical[180] denounced the treatment of Catholics in Germany. In the meantime, the Protestant clergy by and large accepted the inevitability of Gleichschaltung and adapted their ministry accordingly. None the less, a small protest group was established by Pastor Dietrich Bonhoeffer and Dr. Martin Niemoeller, which manifested itself in the form of the Bekenntniskirche ('Confessional Church'), dedicated to resisting what had now been identified as a dictatorship and promoting the defence of Protestantism. Church figures found common cause with groups of intellectuals such as the right-wing and fiercely patriotic Freiburg Circle, headed by historian Gerhard Ritter, at Freiburg University and the Heidelberg-based group led by Karl Jaspers. There was also the Solf Circle, originally led by Wilhelm Solf and then during the 1940s by his widow. This particular group of intellectuals was Anglophile in nature, with connections to the Kreisauer Kreis (or 'Kreisau Circle'), and also provided practical assistance to Jews persecuted by the Nazis. By the early 1940s, student protest groups also emerged, of which the Weisse Rose ('White Rose') in Munich was one of the best known and most proactive.[181] However, in the context of the story of the general staff, the creation of the Kreisauer Kreis in 1933 was particularly important.

During 1933, the year in which the Nazis finally achieved power, a small group of army officers and civilians, motivated by Christian, humanitarian and socialist ideals and a belief that Hitler would eventually destroy Germany if allowed to continue in power, came together at the family estate of the von

Moltke family at Kreisau in Silesia. The group's leaders were Helmuth James Graf von Moltke, Peter Graf Yorck von Wartenburg and Adam von Trott zu Solz. Committed to overthrowing the Nazi regime and replacing it with an ethical and socially responsible government, the Kreisauer Kreis produced a document on 9 August 1943 entitled *Basic Principles for the New Order*, setting out their plan for Germany in a post-Nazi era. By now the group numbered more than twenty army officers, academics, socialists and liberals, as well as committed Protestants and Catholics. Indeed, the need to re-establish a sound foundation of Christian belief and example in Germany was a prerequisite for implementation of the Kreisauer Kreis plan. Although relatively small, the significance of this group lay in its eventual convergence and association with those who would plan and carry out the July 1944 assassination attempt.

Several other resistance groups emerged in response to the rise of the National Socialists. One such group, formed shortly after Hitler gained power, was the MAN group at Augsburg in Bavaria. This was mainly made up of workers from the MAN heavy engineering plant and was created in the wake of the mass arrest by the Gestapo of more than 700 social democrats in Bavaria during 1934 and 1935. The MAN group was led by Bebo Wager and was prepared to confront the Nazis by force of arms if necessary. To that end it acquired quantities of weapons and conducted military training, as well as cultivating contacts with like-minded anti-Nazi and anti-fascist sympathisers in Switzerland, Austria, Hungary and Italy during the pre-war and early war years. However, in 1942 the Gestapo arrested 50 members of the MAN group, which then disintegrated. Those arrested included Bebo Wager, who was executed in August 1943. Another essentially civilian social democrat group was Neu Beginnen (New Beginning), based in the Ruhr area and in Berlin from about 1934, led by Fritz Erler and Waldemar von Knöringen, and enjoying a measure of international support from other social democrats in Spain and Switzerland. This group actively sought and passed on intelligence information about German rearmament to other nations, including breaking into military railway trains to ascertain their contents. The Neu Beginnen group regularly published an underground news sheet *Der Grüne Otto* ('Green Otto'), which condemned Nazi policies while providing uncensored news from beyond Germany. Although it almost managed to outstay the Nazi regime, Neu Beginnen finally collapsed as a result of the arrest of most of its key members by the Gestapo in 1944.

Another group promoting social democratic principles and criticizing the Nazis was the Eilbeck Kameraden (Eilbeck Comrades). It also had links to Czechoslovakia and Denmark, published a news sheet and established a conduit for passing news from and into Oranienburg concentration camp. Formed at Eilbeck, near Hamburg, in 1934, this group was somewhat short-lived, as the Gestapo arrested its leader, Walter Schmedemann, and more than 60 members in 1935–6. Schmedemann survived imprisonment and the war, but many members of his group were killed in the cells at Fuhlsbüttel concentration camp.

Although social democrats predominated, the motivation and politics of these small groups varied. The group led by Herbert Baum, which bore his name, was populated by Jewish and communist activists – providing a rare propaganda opportunity for the Nazis to make a link between the two. After these activists had carried out an arson attack on a propaganda exhibition in 1942, the Gestapo succeeded in arresting every member of the Herbert Baum group, fourteen of whom were executed, the remainder being consigned to Auschwitz concentration camp, together with their families, for eventual execution. While not strictly speaking a resistance group, the Rote Kapelle (Red Orchestra) spy network in Germany was made up of German communists and individual dissidents whose sympathies inclined towards the communist cause. This network provided much valuable intelligence to the Russians until the Abwehr (German military intelligence) and Gestapo broke the organization in August 1942, arresting 46 male and female members, all of whom were ruthlessly interrogated before being executed by hanging or guillotining at Plötzensee prison in Berlin. The most prominent members of Rote Kapelle were Harro Schulze-Boysen, a long-term opponent of the Nazi regime, and Arvid Harnack, both of whom were executed at Plötzensee, and Leopold Trepper, a Jewish communist who was arrested in France but escaped from captivity and survived the war.[182]

In addition to the Weisse Rose group in Munich, several other youth-based and student resistance groups emerged during the early years of the war. They conducted their activities from Hamburg in the north, to the Rhineland, Ruhr, Berlin, Leipzig and other towns in western, central and eastern Germany, to Munich and Bavaria in the south. Virtually all of these groups succumbed to Gestapo investigations and purges during 1942 and 1943, when they were effectively crushed by a succession of widespread arrests, imprisonments and executions. The motivating ideals and politics of these young Germans were often quite diverse, opposition to the National Socialist regime providing a common cause. The regime's concerns about the extent of disaffection among German youth were indicated by the establishment of a concentration camp at Neuwied specifically for the detention of young dissidents, as well as the creation of a special section in the RSHA (Reichssicherheitshauptamt – the Reich central security office) specifically to investigate and deal with this particular category of opposition to Hitler.

Despite the existence of so many groups opposed to Hitler and the National Socialist regime, their impact upon the Third Reich and its activities was generally negligible, which was in part a consequence of their largely discrete, disparate and uncoordinated nature. The fact that they existed at all demonstrated that by no means all Germans accepted National Socialism in the 1930s and 1940s. An awareness that they did exist also places in context the opposition to Hitler by those members of the general staff who actively participated in the resistance movement and who ultimately conspired to assassinate the Führer. Irrespective of its outcome, the July plot developed and carried out by general staff and other army officers in 1944 was assuredly the most significant (and potentially the most effective) action by the German resistance movement against Hitler and the Nazi regime.

By 1944, the principal military figures in the resistance included Generalfeldmarschall Erwin von Witzleben, Generaloberst Ludwig Beck, General Friedrich Olbricht, Generalmajor Hans Oster, Oberstleutnant Claus Schenk Graf von Stauffenberg and Admiral Wilhelm Canaris. The civilian part of the movement was headed by Dr. Carl Friedrich Goerdeler, Christian Albrecht Ulrich von Hassell, Ewald von Kleist-Schmenzin, Hans von Dohnányi and Professor Johannes Popitz, as well as Helmuth James Graf von Moltke, Julius Leber, Hans-Bernd von Haeften, Professor Adolf Reichwein and Peter

Graf Yorck von Wartenburg of the Kreisauer Kreis. Moral principles and religious imperatives continued to lie at the very heart of the philosophy of the Kreisau Circle and other groups. In 1942 von Moltke wrote secretly to the British writer, historian and diplomatic philosopher Professor Lionel Curtis, saying: 'An active part of the German people are beginning to realize, not that they have been led astray, not that bad times await them, not that the war may end in defeat, but that what is happening is sin and that they are personally responsible for each terrible deed that has been committed – naturally, not in the earthly sense, but as Christians.'[183] Two of the most prominent ecclesiastical figures were Pastor Dietrich Bonhoeffer (who, despite his vocation, was firmly of the opinion that Hitler had to be 'exterminated') and Father Alfred Delp. In May 1942, Bonhoeffer and another cleric met Bishop George Bell, the Bishop of Chichester, in Sweden, to apprise the bishop – and subsequently, therefore, the British government – of the existence and aims of the Kreisauer Kreis and associated resistance groups, in the hope of gaining a positive response and international support. However, the British foreign office declined to respond to Bell when he relayed the information from Bonhoeffer. In addition to all of these activists, very many other military men, prominent civilians and religious leaders were closely engaged in the resistance movement by the early 1940s.

While the opposition movement originated soon after the Nazis gained power in 1933, becoming more extensive each year thereafter, the military resistance gained particular impetus during Sixth Army's desperate and ultimately futile battle at Stalingrad during the winter of 1942/3. It was at that time that Beck conceived his plan for Paulus' beleaguered army to stage a breakout from the encircled city, this being the signal for every army field marshal to come together and demand Hitler's resignation. That plan had foundered when those field marshals who had been approached on Beck's behalf by Oberstleutnant von Stauffenberg were generally disinclined to commit themselves to such action, while most still believed that the operational situation on the Eastern Front could be restored. As ever, the mindset of senior officers who had lived according to a strict code of honour, loyalty and obedience throughout their military careers shaped their responses to von Stauffenberg. The disappointing lack of support for Beck's plan from senior commanders, together with the deteriorating situation at Stalingrad and an increasing awareness and unease over the atrocities and draconian security measures being conducted by the SS and SD against the Russians, Jews and others on the Eastern Front, finally persuaded more and more army officers to join or indicate (albeit with a pragmatic degree of circumspection in some cases) their support for the opposition movement. Prominent among these were a number of general staff officers, including the chief of the OKH operations department, Generalleutnant Heusinger, the head of the organization and force development section, Generalmajor Stieff,[184] the chief of the general army office, General Olbricht, the quartermaster-general, General Wagner, and General Lindemann, who was responsible for overseeing the procurement and development of artillery weapons.

With Sixth Army's battle for survival still raging amid the rubble at Stalingrad and an increasing feeling that some sort of action now had to be taken if the contagion of National Socialism were to be stopped, a potentially significant meeting took place in Berlin, which brought together the two main civilian opposition groups. The Goerdeler-led group advocated direct action to displace Hitler by any means, with a possible restoration of the Prussian monarchy thereafter. The Kreisauer Kreis members counselled a less drastic approach, based upon reform and a politically based process. The meeting eventually agreed that a moderate socialist government offered the best solution, and that those who might serve in a provisional government should be identified in anticipation of Hitler's demise. However, just 24 hours later the Allies' communiqué setting out their demand for the 'unconditional surrender' of Germany and its Axis allies was announced on 24 January 1943. This undermined the concept of a provisional government to deal with the Allies, if a negotiated peace was no longer a viable option for Germany. It also adversely affected the resistance movement within the general staff, as Goebbels could thereafter present the Wehrmacht as having nothing to lose, with any sort of surrender now inviting the inevitable destruction of the Fatherland and German culture. Despite this unwelcome setback, the final collapse of Sixth Army at Stalingrad at the beginning of February 1943 and Hitler's intrusive and ill-judged handling of that battle precipitated a change in the nature of the opposition within the general staff, as well as imbuing the resistance movement with a new impetus and urgency. It also moved the civilian part of the resistance towards much closer cooperation with like-minded officers within the general staff.

The Military Resistance Movement

Prior to 1943, any action to remove Hitler by a coup orchestrated by the general staff had been considered primarily in a legalistic or political context, ideally with the Führer being forced to resign, but with his arrest, detention and trial available as an option if he refused. However, by spring 1943, pragmatism prevailed, views had hardened, and resistance planning within the general staff now focused firmly upon an assassination of Hitler. While some officers remained reluctant to approve what they regarded as an excessively drastic, treasonable and illegal course, a preponderance of less-senior officers now dominated the active resistance, bringing with them a realistic view of the absolute need for Hitler to die in order for Germany to survive. The first assassination attempt in the post-1942 period was carried out in March 1943 by members of the general staff serving with Army Group Centre on the Eastern Front. The instigators of the plan were Oberst Henning von Tresckow, Oberst Rudolph-Christoph Baron von Gersdorff and Leutnant Fabian von Schlabrendorff. In Berlin, General Friedrich Olbricht and Generalmajor Hans Oster were co-conspirators. Retired Generaloberst Ludwig Beck was also closely involved in the development of this plan, as was Generalfeldmarschall Erwin von Witzleben. Hitler's assassination would trigger action by two panzer units, a regiment of other troops, and the 'Brandenburg' special forces division to overcome the SS and other Nazi paramilitary units in Berlin, arrest Nazi officials and seize key points throughout the capital. This action would enable a provisional government to take control, and von Witzleben would assume overall command of the Wehrmacht. Although no attempt was made to implement this plan until March 1943, it had by then been under development for at least six months and was very similar to that which would be put into action in July 1944.

The March 1943 attempt called for a time-bomb – concealed in a box ostensibly containing two bottles of Cointreau – to detonate in Hitler's aircraft during his return flight following a visit to the headquarters of Army Group Centre on 13 March. This bomb was but one of several assassination options that von Tresckow had prepared for Hitler's visit. These included a direct attack on Hitler's car by selected troops: a last-minute change of route and the presence of Generalfeldmarschall von Kluge (who supported the opposition to Hitler but was not directly involved in the assassination plot) also travelling in Hitler's car meant that this option was not viable. Similarly, a heavy SS presence by Hitler's car prevented an earlier attempt to place a time-bomb in it while it was parked. None of this should have mattered, since the bomb disguised as Cointreau bottles was duly taken on board by an unsuspecting Oberstleutnant Heinz Brandt, who believed that he was simply delivering payment of a wager to an officer in Berlin on behalf of von Tresckow. But then, with success so nearly achieved, fate intervened when – despite the success of every test detonation carried out during the preceding months – the bomb failed to explode. Subsequently, von Tresckow managed to retrieve the unopened 'bottles' from Brandt in Berlin before their true nature and purpose could be discovered, at which time he found that the acid igniter and detonation process had worked satisfactorily right up to the stage immediately prior to the detonation of the main charge, at which point it had failed.[185] Although the July 1944 plot is much better known, von Tresckow's assassination attempt of 13 March 1943 was well-planned and characterized by its simplicity and potentially non-attributable nature, and as such it had certainly deserved to succeed.

Undaunted, von Tresckow and von Gersdorff immediately planned a further attempt for Sunday 21 March, which was Heldengedenktag (Germany's national Heroes' Memorial Day), when Hitler was due to speak at the Zeughaus in Berlin and then view an exhibition of Russian weaponry captured by Army Group Centre, displayed in the Zeughaus museum. This time, von Gersdorff was to use the explosives from the abortive 13 March attempt to carry out a suicide bombing attack against Hitler at the exhibition. He managed to position himself close to Hitler and even ignited the ten-minute fuse (the only type available), but the Führer suddenly decided to divert from the intended route and to curtail his visit, with von Gersdorff only just able to excuse himself and reach a wash-room in time to pull out the fuse before the bomb could explode. This unexpected change of programme was typical of Hitler – even the details of the planned programme had only been made available shortly before the event. Indeed, Hitler had long mistrusted the professional motives and allegiance of the general staff and was already suspicious of the less-visible opposition activities of these officers, becoming ever more wary of plots against him and quite obsessive in the measures he took to minimize the possibility of any sort of pre-planned assassination attempt. While Hitler presumably had no precise knowledge of the two abortive assassination attempts that March, in the spring of 1943 he remarked to Goebbels that, 'none of the generals told him the truth. They were all dishonest and enemies of National Socialism. Hitler was absolutely ill when he even thought of them.'[186]

The relatively straightforward assassination attempt by von Gersdorff at the exhibition in the Berlin Zeughaus had once again failed largely due to ill-luck rather than bad planning or lack of imagination. Von Gersdorff's willingness to sacrifice himself for the greater good of the cause was significant – a criticism subsequently levelled at the German resistance was that its military members in particular had been afforded numerous opportunities to kill Hitler if only they had also been prepared to die in the attempt. However, the instinctive abhorrence of western European society, military and civilian alike, for what is today usually categorized as a cowardly, despicable and indiscriminate act of terrorism was probably little different from the views held by most members of the German resistance more than half a century earlier. With that in mind, it is noteworthy that at least two further suicide bombings and a close-quarter shooting attempt by various army officers were planned to take place during 1943 and early 1944, but yet again all of these were baulked either by last-minute changes to Hitler's programme or simply by bad luck.[187]

In light of the succession of ill-fated assassination attempts during 1943, it might reasonably be argued that the plot in July 1944 should certainly have relied upon a suicide bombing or close-quarters shooting attack against the Führer, thus guaranteeing the outcome of this absolutely critical matter as far as was humanly possible. However, even a close-quarters shooting attack remained problematical, as anything other than a head shot might be defeated by Hitler possibly wearing body armour (such as a bullet-proof vest) under his normal clothing. In any event, by the spring of 1943, despite ongoing discussions within the civilian groups about the precise manner of Hitler's removal, the core group of resistors within the general staff had begun to develop a comprehensive plan that would include the summary assassination of Hitler, a military coup in Berlin, the arrest of all senior SS, SD and Gestapo officials, the neutralization of Nazi paramilitary units in the capital, and the replacement of the National Socialist regime by a democratic socialist provisional government. While this planning proceeded within the general staff, together with the various planned, frustrated and aborted assassination attempts by army officers, the wider movement suffered several setbacks during the first half of 1943.

To the genuine incomprehension of its members, the resistance had received successive rebuffs to all of its attempts to establish links with the Allies. The failure of the British and later the US government even to acknowledge officially and indicate their support for the resistance movement was symptomatic of an inflexibility, a lack of imagination, and prejudices that in many cases owed much to the memories of World War I and the effectiveness of Allied propaganda that stereotyped all Germans as Nazis. While the ordinary citizens of Britain and America might possibly be excused for holding such views in this matter, their leaders and foreign ministers certainly should not. In any event, the declaration by Roosevelt during the 'Big Three' meeting at Casablanca on 24 January 1943 that the Allies would 'continue the war relentlessly' until they achieved 'unconditional surrender' was undoubtedly a serious blow to the movement. From that point onwards, Germans who opposed Hitler were forced to acknowledge that no international support or assistance would be forthcoming, and that they were generally perceived by the Western Allies to be no different from, or better than, any other German.[188]

Everyday matters of life and death also affected the movement in the early months of 1943. One member of the provisional government, Generaloberst Kurt Freiherr von Hammerstein-Equord, had died of cancer, while another, Generaloberst Beck, was incapacitated for several weeks by worsening ill-health, which culminated in surgery that proved to be less than satisfactory.

Even so, having been out of the active army since the first year of the war, Beck continued in the role of elder statesman, providing a focus for the military arm of the movement. One resistance group had been eliminated when the Weisse Rose student resistance group was broken by the Gestapo in the wake of its protest demonstration in Munich on 18 February. Then, on 5 April, a surprise investigative visit by justice ministry officials and an SS officer to the Abwehr offices at Admiral Canaris's military intelligence headquarters on Tirpitzufer in Berlin, resulted in the arrest, temporary detention and dismissal of Abwehr chief of staff Generalmajor Hans Oster from his post. This effectively removed the resistance's principal organizer and coordinator from his central and highly influential position working alongside Admiral Canaris. In the wake of this incident, the Abwehr was ordered to relocate its offices to Zossen, where it was extensively reorganized and most of its heads of department were replaced. Also on 5 April, the religious groups suffered a serious blow when Pastor Dietrich Bonhoeffer was arrested. Meanwhile, various attempts to persuade men such as Generalfeldmarschall Erich von Manstein, Generalmajor[189] Edgar Röhricht and Generalleutnant Adolf Heusinger to involve themselves actively in the conspiracy had all come to naught, despite their acknowledgement of the parlous situation by then facing Germany.

It was during 1943, in a measure designed primarily to foster National Socialism within the army but also to weaken the traditional officer corps, that Hitler introduced the Nationalsozialistische Führungsorganisation (National Socialist leadership organization, or 'NSFO') as a politically and ideologically-based body of committed Nazi officers within the army's officer corps, with a propaganda, indoctrinating and motivating role similar to that of the political commissars in the Red Army.[190] The everyday presence in virtually every unit and headquarters of these NSFO officers, drawn mainly from a pool of reserve officers who had been committed Nazi party members prior to the war, meant that the risk of discovery increased significantly for the military members of the resistance. Understandably perhaps, by the summer of 1943 some members of the resistance were beginning to lose heart, despairing that they would ever be able to achieve their objective of displacing the National Socialist regime. But then, during that autumn, the death of Hitler and overthrow of the Nazis once again appeared to be achievable as events affecting the general staff resistance group imbued the wider movement with renewed momentum.

Although many long-term dissenters and resistors within the general staff were also involved in what later became known as the 'July plot', the officer who emerged in 1943 to be at the very heart of this conspiracy, providing the impetus and enthusiasm to keep it on track, was the highly competent young general staff officer Oberstleutnant Claus Schenk Graf von Stauffenberg. This officer had already been involved in Beck's attempt to persuade the army's field marshals to demand Hitler's resignation, linked to a breakout by Sixth Army at Stalingrad. Subsequently he had been posted to North Africa and there had sustained serious wounds during an Allied air attack on 1 April 1943, losing an eye, his right hand, part of his left hand and a kneecap. Evacuated by air on 7 April to a hospital in Munich, he avoided being captured during the Axis collapse and surrender in Tunisia. Despite the severity and extent of von Stauffenberg's injuries, the renowned physician Dr. Ferdinand Sauerbruch[191] was able to restore a fairly high level of capability to him and to save the sight in his right eye, which had also suffered some damage. In a foretaste of future events, when Sauerbach informed von Stauffenberg that he would need to undergo several months of convalescence and undergo two further operations before being fit to return to any sort of active duty, he replied that he simply did not have that amount of time, as 'important things needed to be done.'[192] In any event, he was discharged from hospital soon thereafter and while still convalescing was introduced to Generalmajor Henning von Tresckow at General Friedrich Olbricht's house on 10 August. This meeting would prove to be a defining moment for the resistance. On 1 October, von Stauffenberg was appointed chief of staff at the general army office (the Allgemeines Heeresamt), assuming full responsibility for his duties on 1 November and dealing with a wide range of ordnance, organizational and other matters. Shortly after he was notified of his new appointment, although his active opposition to Hitler was already well known, he was now admitted to the inner circle of the resistance movement.

Of all those who were members of the resistance, von Stauffenberg would in due course become one of the best-known general staff officers, due largely to his very direct involvement in the final assassination attempt against Hitler and for his key role in planning the associated coup, as well as for imbuing the resistance with a revived sense of purpose, pragmatism and momentum at a time when the movement was in danger of faltering. Among the various attempts to dispose of Hitler during the war years, von Tresckow and von Stauffenberg were the two general staff officers who came closest to achieving this objective – only fate, or sheer bad luck, intervened to frustrate their separate plans at the last minute. Certainly von Stauffenberg's personal attributes well fitted him for his role: 'He seemed to send an electric charge through the lifeless resistance networks as he quickly and naturally assumed a leadership role. This effect stemmed not only from his usual combination of exuberant idealism and cool pragmatism. He was familiar with all the complex religious, historical, and traditional reasons that had repeatedly stood in the way of action, but he had not lost sight of the far more basic truth that there are limits to loyalty and obedience. He was therefore able to put aside scruples about treason and breaking of solemn oaths.'[193] Although the resistance had suffered rebuffs from the Western Allies in the past, and was now operating under the additional burden of the unconditional surrender issue, von Stauffenberg firmly believed that the Allies would nevertheless be prepared to negotiate with any democratic German government that could clearly be seen to have displaced the National Socialist regime and disposed of Hitler.

As a professional soldier, von Stauffenberg had welcomed Hitler's policies regarding the perceived injustices contained in the 1919 Treaty of Versailles and the Führer's action to achieve the Austrian Anschluß. However, by the end of 1938 he was becoming increasingly convinced of Hitler's wider incompetence as a leader, the inherent perils of his primarily ideological policies, and the threat he posed to Germany. As a German officer, once the war began von Stauffenberg applied himself to his professional duties to very good effect, which resulted in his rapid advancement; he also rationalized his personal reservations about the regime's excesses on the basis that the Nazis could be disposed of once the war had been won. But as the conflict proceeded his professional criticisms of Hitler's conduct of the war and handling of the Wehrmacht were reinforced by his moral abhorrence of the escalating atrocities and excesses being committed in Germany's name, especially on the Eastern Front, and the sheer scale of the Wehrmacht casualties that were needlessly being incurred on that front. Inevitably, the force of von Stauffenberg's personality and the certainty with which he expressed his beliefs brought him into conflict with Goerdeler and several other prominent members of the primarily civilian resistance groups. At the same time, the balance of leadership and authority within the resistance shifted inexorably from the civilian groups and resistors, who were generally against using violence to remove Hitler, to the core resistance group centred upon the general staff. By 1943, these officers had recognized not only that there was no realistic alternative to assassinating Hitler but also that the only group with the resolve, ability and resources to overthrow the Nazi regime was the army.

By that stage the main concentrations of military conspirators within the active army in Germany were in the OKH Maybach headquarters at Zossen, near Berlin; at the forward headquarters of the army general staff at Mauerwald, near Rastenburg; and at the principal headquarters and various units of the Ersatzheer in Berlin and other parts of Germany. However, a particular focus of the opposition to Hitler and later of the military resistance group was centred upon the general army office at the Bendlerblock on Bendlerstraße in Berlin. Within the Feldheer (the field army), the resistance movement was strongest in Army Group South and Army Group Centre on the Eastern Front, although various resistance approaches to the most senior commanders of these formations were generally unsuccessful, producing a qualified and somewhat ambivalent response from Generalfeldmarschall von Kluge, and outright rebuttals from Generalfeldmarschall von Manstein and Generaloberst Guderian. In the West, the resistance enjoyed the active support of General Karl-Heinrich von Stülpnagel, the commander-in-chief of the German forces in France, and of General Alexander von Falkenhausen, the German commander in Belgium and part of northern France. Many of the general staff officers within the Paris and Brussels headquarters of these two generals shared their views about Hitler and supported, or were involved in, the conspiracy and in planning the action to be taken once Hitler was dead. However, various attempts to secure the active involvement of Generalfeldmarschall Rommel in the conspiracy were unsuccessful. In addition to the serving staff officers and commanders who were involved in the conspiracy, the group of retired senior officers centred upon Generaloberst Beck, Generalfeldmarschall von Witzleben and General von Rabenau continued to fulfil the role of elder statesmen of the conspiracy, and it was intended that several appointments in the post-Nazi provisional government would be filled by these former officers. With so many military officers actively working to remove Hitler and overthrow the Nazi government, it was remarkable that the military part of the conspiracy managed to avoid the extent of penetration and consequent arrests that were increasingly undermining some of the civilian groups. However, few if any of the conspirators were under any illusions concerning the inevitability of their eventual discovery and the ever more urgent need to act as soon as practicable.

The prime movers in the development of an updated concept and plan were von Stauffenberg and von Tresckow. During September and October 1943, they worked on the plans that had been produced by General Olbricht in anticipation of a successful outcome to the March 1943 assassination attempt for the coup that would have followed this, revising and updating these plans as necessary. While the death of Hitler would be the trigger for the coup, the action taken thereafter to exploit and consolidate that success would be absolutely critical if the Nazi authorities were not to be given any chance of regaining the initiative and seizing back the reins of power. Accordingly, the plan was based upon operation *Walküre* ('Valkyrie'), an existing internal security contingency plan designed to deal with an uprising by some or all of the several million captive and otherwise pressed foreign workers within Germany.

Split into parts designated *Walküre I* and *Walküre II*, the plan covered the arrangements by which the Germany-based Ersatzheer would form cohesive combat units by speedily reorganizing its widespread and disparate training units and establishments, while simultaneously taking into these newly formed units all troops under training, together with any individual soldiers convalescing or on leave in Germany. Specifically, *Walküre I* dealt with readiness standards and the preparatory measures required to implement *Walküre II*, while *Walküre II* detailed the action to be taken to deliver these viable battle groups on the ground. A secret modification of the plan developed by von Stauffenberg and von Tresckow comprised a declaration to be issued immediately after the killing of Hitler to the effect that the crisis which had triggered *Walküre* had been precipitated by an attempted coup by disaffected Nazi leaders and officials who had tried to seize power for themselves, which also implied that Hitler had been killed by these men and that the government had therefore needed to impose martial law. This secret codicil to the main *Walküre* plan would enable the army to take direct action against Nazi party members and organizations, the SS, Gestapo and suchlike, as well as occupying the key communications and broadcasting centres that were generally closely controlled by the Nazis. The use of an existing official plan to facilitate the overthrow of the Nazi regime was a conceptual master stroke, and – although undeniably dependent upon a colossal bluff – it certainly deserved to succeed. Quite apart from those committed members of the resistance, *Walküre* would involve the use of hundreds, and potentially thousands, of troops to support the coup without them even realizing that they were doing so until it was far too late to reverse the process. However, an immutable prerequisite for the plan's successful application was Hitler's death. A further consideration was that Generaloberst Friedrich Fromm, commander of the Ersatzheer, was the only officer empowered to authorize *Walküre*, and there was an abundance of evidence to indicate that Fromm, while aware of the ongoing conspiracy and by no means a supporter of Hitler or National Socialism, had nevertheless refused to commit himself either to support the coup or to become actively involved with the resistance movement in any way.

While the general staff conspirators laid their plans, the wider resistance movement continued to suffer setbacks. Some members died in action or during the Allied bombing raids on Germany, while others were arrested. Admiral Canaris was dismissed and imprisoned on 11 February 1944. The dismantling of the Abwehr organization by the SS accelerated thereafter, which in turn reduced the effectiveness of the several resistance members serving as staff officers within the Abwehr. Others became isolated as their commitment to the cause became too widely known. Von Tresckow's attempts in late 1943 to gain direct access to Hitler through a posting to the Führerhauptquartier were ignored by colleagues in positions of influence who could no doubt have engineered this. Meanwhile, the interminable debates about policy, what to do about Hitler, and the best way to proceed continued in the civilian groups, exacerbating the growing discord between the military group of officers, who were essentially men of action, and politicians such as Goerdeler (the intended chancellor in a provisional government), who still argued for a solution to be achieved by some sort of politically based process. Remarkably, the civilian resistance even made a direct approach to Heinrich Himmler in January 1944, when Johannes Popitz (who was then minister of finance and a prominent member of the civilian resistance group) attempted to act as an intermediary to gain Himmler's support for a coup and a negotiated peace with the Western Allies. This high-risk and quite bizarre approach was unsuccessful and ultimately resulted in the arrest and execution of Popitz and his co-conspirator Carl Langbehn, who had also attended the meeting with Himmler. As the difficult weeks and months of 1943 passed by, the cohesion of the resistance – especially of its civilian groups – had weakened, and by the start of 1944 it was in danger of fragmenting.

As the year progressed, the need to deal decisively with Hitler had become ever more urgent, and on 26 December von Stauffenberg himself had attempted to kill Hitler with a bomb during a meeting with the Führer at the Wolfschanze. However, in an oft-repeated experience, the meeting had been cancelled at the last minute. For von Stauffenberg, the use of a bomb was the only practicable option, as the severe injuries to his hands sustained in North Africa would have prevented him operating a pistol with the necessary dexterity and speed. With the suicide bombing option in mind, it was noteworthy that von Stauffenberg – his work on the *Walküre* plan by then complete – had originally intended to blow himself up with Hitler but had been dissuaded from doing so by Beck and Olbricht, both of whom understood only too well that von Stauffenberg's abilities would be needed in the post-Hitler era. In any event, this abortive attempt showed that by the end of that year von Stauffenberg had clearly accepted and – mainly by default – taken upon himself the direct responsibility for killing Hitler. While various sub-plots, discussions and initiatives continued within and between resistance groups and individuals, in the story of what would prove to be the demise of the general staff in 1944 the principal focus was now on von Stauffenberg and *Walküre*. At the same time, the deteriorating operational situation provided an ominous backdrop to these events and would soon be dramatically worsened when the Western Allies at last managed to land in northern France on 6 June.

The day after the Allied invasion at Normandy, von Stauffenberg accompanied Generaloberst Fromm to a staff meeting with Hitler at the Berghof in Obersalzberg, Bavaria. His attendance at this meeting on 7 June reflected the fact that von Stauffenberg had already been informed that with effect from 1 July he would be promoted colonel and officially assume the post of chief of staff of the Ersatzheer, working directly for Fromm. Although this meant relinquishing his close day-to-day working association with General Olbricht, the new appointment would provide him with much better access to Hitler. Von Stauffenberg was replaced at the general army office by Oberst Albrecht Mertz von Quirnheim, a committed member of the resistance who was also destined to play a part in the events of that July. During his initial discussion with Fromm, von Stauffenberg had declared openly and unreservedly his views on the Nazi regime, the war situation and his intention to bring about a coup; the Ersatzheer commander simply acknowledged his frankness and then apparently let the matter pass. Perhaps von Stauffenberg interpreted this as acquiescence or even a measure of undeclared but positive support on Fromm's part. In any event, just over a week after his promotion and taking over his new job, von Stauffenberg found himself at the Berghof once again, in early July. This time he actually had a bomb with him, and a warning that Hitler's death might at last be imminent had been circulated to the other principal conspirators. However, an agreed prerequisite set by the resistance leadership was the need to kill Himmler and Göring at the same time as Hitler, neither of whom were present that day. Consequently von Stauffenberg decided against attempting the assassination on that occasion. In any case, he also anticipated that an attempt by another officer, Generalmajor Helmuth Stieff, was imminent and offered a better chance of success, but when von Stauffenberg tried to pass the explosives on to him, Stieff indicated that he was no longer prepared to carry out the task. Stieff's refusal reinforced von Stauffenberg's conviction that only he could now succeed in doing what had to be done, despite the need for him to also implement and oversee the coup after Hitler's death. Von Stauffenberg's indispensability ruled him out of a suicide bombing or suicide shooting attack, and the dismissal of this option therefore imposed an important limitation upon the resistance's plans to kill Hitler.

On 11 July, von Stauffenberg returned to the Berghof. Yet again he carried a bomb with him. However, Himmler was not present; Stieff was, and helped persuade von Stauffenberg not to make the attempt that day. Given the sheer number of times that a relatively small number of individual army officers carrying explosives had already been able to penetrate the security arrangements surrounding the Führer in Berlin, at the Wolfschanze and at the Berghof, it was truly remarkable that none of these officers had thus far been caught in possession of the bombs by the SS or the Gestapo.

At about the same time that von Stauffenberg was visiting the Berghof in early July, the resistance movement received yet another rejection of its most recent tentative approaches and proposals made to the Western Allies, when Otto John, a lawyer employed by Lufthansa, conveyed a message from the British ambassador in Madrid: this confirmed that nothing less than an unconditional surrender by Germany on all fronts would be entertained by the Allies. During the preceding months, the resistance had proposed that the Western Front could be opened, with the complicity of the German commanders in France, to allow an unconstrained and speedy advance by the Anglo-US forces into Germany, thus pre-empting the Russian advance in the East.

This contrived and thoroughly unrealistic proposal depended upon the active collaboration of the Anglo-US Allies with the German forces, all acting together directly against the interests of the Russians, and was therefore a non-starter from the outset. However, although anything less than a simultaneous capitulation on all fronts was now clearly unacceptable, the resistance still persisted with an alternative offer to surrender unconditionally the Wehrmacht forces in the West but not in the East if that was the only way to forestall the advancing Red Army. Goerdeler had particularly favoured this option, regarding it both as a way of obviating the need to kill Hitler and of assuaging his conscience on that issue. Meanwhile, arrests of members of the resistance by the Gestapo continued on a regular basis, the number of arrests increasing as some of those already in custody provided the names of others while under interrogation. Almost invariably, these arrests were followed by detention or a sentence of imprisonment but sometimes culminated in execution. This was so for several members of the Solf Circle resistance group, who had been arrested in January 1944 and were sentenced to death in late May or early June. Unfortunately, Helmuth von Moltke of the Kreisauer Kreis had also been associated with this group, and his arrest that January resulted in the dissolution of that resistance group as well.

On 15 July, von Stauffenberg and Fromm were again summoned to attend a meeting with Hitler, this time at the Wolfschanze at Rastenburg. On this occasion, the fact that General Olbricht had already taken the decision to invoke some of the initial *Walküre* measures by alerting a selection of units clearly indicated to key members of the military resistance an intention for von Stauffenberg to explode the bomb he was carrying irrespective of whether or not Himmler was present, although the requirement to kill Himmler at the same time as Hitler remained an important constraint fully endorsed by the military leadership of the resistance. However, on von Stauffenberg's arrival at Rastenburg, Generalmajor Stieff and General Erich Fellgiebel (another resistance supporter, who was the chief signals officer and had agreed to isolate the Führerhauptquartier communications for a period of time once Hitler had been assassinated) immediately sought to dissuade him from carrying out the attempt. Their argument was due to Himmler's absence from the meeting once again, which had been reinforced by the insistence of General Eduard Wagner the previous evening that Himmler also had to die in the course of any assassination of Hitler. Despite von Stauffenberg's reluctance to forgo yet another opportunity, the matter was apparently resolved when he left temporarily to discuss the matter with those at the OKH in Berlin by telephone, at which point Stieff simply removed the briefcase containing the bomb. And, by the end of a thirty-minute telephone conversation, the majority of those in Berlin had also indicated to von Stauffenberg their wish to postpone the assassination attempt. For the third time in just a week, and with *Walküre* partly initiated, von Stauffenberg had been well-placed to kill Hitler, and yet the unequivocal support of his co-conspirators was still not forthcoming when the critical moment arrived. Von Stauffenberg returned to Berlin, and the units alerted by Olbricht were stood down, their earlier action being explained away as a readiness training exercise. That evening, von Stauffenberg had a final meeting with his closest friends, when the discussion centred upon various ways in which the army acting alone might be able to bring about an accommodation with the Western Allies through various actions on the Western Front. In all these options, however, Hitler's continued existence remained a major obstacle. Soon thereafter, von Stauffenberg stated to Beck that when he was next presented with the opportunity to do so, he would go ahead with the assassination irrespective of any other constraints or considerations.

That opportunity arose just a few days later, when Oberst von Stauffenberg was ordered to report to the Wolfschanze to brief and update Hitler and the senior staff of the Führerhauptquartier on the current state of the Ersatzheer. The conference was scheduled for midday on 20 July: this time von Stauffenberg was determined that nothing would be allowed to deter him from carrying out his mission. The task became even more pressing when, on 17 July, Generalfeldmarschall Erwin Rommel was severely wounded by an Allied air attack in northern France. Although he was not a member of the resistance, the conspirators had reason to believe that he would probably support them in the aftermath of Hitler's death. Rommel was also a senior officer, whose popularity with the general public would undoubtedly have ensured him a significant role in any post-Nazi administration. Then, at about the same time, Goerdeler suddenly had to go on the run when a warning was received of his imminent arrest. And on 18 July, von Stauffenberg was warned of a new rumour circulating in Berlin, which apparently indicated that the Führerhauptquartier would be blown up that very week. With all this bad news and the likelihood that the Gestapo was now closing in, together with increasing signs that even some army officers within the resistance were possibly beginning to waver – von Stauffenberg himself was now visibly suffering from the considerable stress of his three assassination attempts having been aborted at the last minute – the die was finally cast. For all concerned, 20 July 1944 now offered what appeared to be the earliest, best and possibly last chance for the resistance to kill Hitler and finally rid Germany of the National Socialist regime that he headed.

13

The Final Gamble

20 July 1944

The events that took place at the Wolfschanze at Rastenburg in East Prussia and then in Berlin on 20 July 1944 constituted a defining moment not only for the general staff but also for Germany. Had von Stauffenberg been successful, his action that day would undoubtedly have changed the course of World War II – though not necessarily in the way the conspirators intended. If his plan had succeeded, countless lives on both sides might well have been saved, with the conflict in Europe considerably foreshortened, but it is extremely doubtful that the Allied refusal to accept anything less than an unconditional surrender would have been modified, due mainly to Stalin's determination to inflict a significant degree of retribution upon Germany and to exact huge reparations from the country to offset the death and destruction wreaked upon Russia by the Wehrmacht since June 1941. So, while the gains for Germany would still have been substantial, they might still have fallen well short of the expectations of the conspirators and the wider resistance movement. Such considerations can be no more than speculation: this last attempt to kill Hitler was yet again doomed to fail. The consequence was not only the end of the German resistance movement but also the final demise of the German general staff, which was reduced to little more than a coordinating agency dealing with the day-to-day conduct of army operations on the Eastern Front and passing on operational orders and directives issued from the various Führerhauptquartiere.

The assassination attempt and Operation *Walküre* were both based upon plans that had been conceived, developed, refined and finally implemented by members of the general staff, and as such these officers had ultimately become the architects both of their own destruction and that of the once-illustrious organization in which they served. Accordingly, the significance of 20 July 1944, the events of that day and the reasons for von Stauffenberg's failure are a key part of the story of the decline and fall of the general staff in World War II, while its aftermath – the arrests, trials and destruction of the German resistance movement by the SS, SD and Gestapo – also highlighted the extent of the involvement of the army high command, the general staff, units of the Feldheer and Ersatzheer and other parts of the army in actively resisting or otherwise opposing Hitler by that stage of the war.[194] The events of 20 July also showed the extent of residual support for Hitler despite all that had occurred since 1941, as well as demonstrating yet again the very real difficulty that a number of officers had reconciling the conflicting demands of duty, honour, conscience, obedience and the soldier's oath. Many of the army officers who later condemned the July plot conspirators as traitors, who had broken their oath and abrogated the code of the officer corps, were by no means pro-Nazi but were nevertheless unable to forsake the deep-rooted conventions and traditions that had been imbued in the army officers of Prussia and then Germany during more than two centuries.

In Berlin, the early morning of Thursday 20 July broke to reveal a familiar heat haze over the city, with another breathlessly hot and humid summer's day in prospect. At 6.00 a.m. von Stauffenberg left his home at Tristanstraße 8 in the Berlin-Nikolassee area and drove to Berlin Rangsdorf airfield, being joined there by his adjutant, Oberleutnant Werner von Haeften. The aircraft departed Rangsdorf at 7.00 a.m., and Generalmajor Helmuth Stieff subsequently joined the aircraft at Zossen.[195] The flight was uneventful, and the aircraft arrived at the airfield of Gut Wilhelmsdorf, the small military airfield that served the Führerhauptquartier at Rastenburg, just before 10.15. In von Stauffenberg's briefcase were the documents he would need to provide an updating briefing on proposals for the development of new formations and organizational changes within the Ersatzheer. Contained in the briefcase carried by von Haeften were two powerful explosive charges, each of which weighed just less than a kilogram. Once landed, the drive to the Wolfschanze took a quarter of an hour, and at 10.30 von Stauffenberg went to the officers' dining facility with Rittmeister (the rank of captain in a cavalry unit) Leonhard von Möllendorf, the adjutant of the administrative commander of the Führerhauptquartier troops, for a late breakfast. In the meantime, Stieff and von Haeften headed off to the OKH facility at the Wolfschanze, having already arranged for von Stauffenberg and von Haeften to meet up again prior to the main conference with Hitler, in time for von Stauffenberg to exchange his briefcase with that of von Haeften, fuse the explosives, activate the two timers, and then carry the two bombs into the conference room. The conference was due to begin at midday, but between 11.30 and 12.00, during a pre-conference meeting with Generalleutnant Walther Buhle, head of the army staff element at the Führerhauptquartier, and Generalfeldmarschall Keitel, von Stauffenberg was informed that due to a visit to the Wolfschanze by Italian leader Mussolini taking place that same day, the midday conference had been postponed by half an hour and would now commence at 12.30.[196] As the time to assemble for the conference drew near, von Stauffenberg asked Oberstleutnant Ernst John von Freyend, Keitel's adjutant, if he could use a room to wash and change his shirt, using the heat of the day as an excuse. He was shown to von Freyend's own room in Keitel's bunker complex, together with von Haeften, who had met him in the corridor outside as previously arranged.

With the door closed, the two officers set about fusing and activating the bombs. However, they only had time to activate one bomb, which had a ten-minute fuse, and were in the process of replacing it in the briefcase when Oberfeldwebel Werner Vogel arrived to hurry them up, as Keitel and others were already assembling ready for the conference. Apparently, a telephone call from General Fellgiebel asking to speak to von Stauffenberg had also occurred at this critical time. From the doorway, Vogel saw von Stauffenberg hastily stuffing an object into one of the two briefcases. With the meeting about to begin and no time left to complete arming both bombs, von Stauffenberg ended up with only one activated bomb in his briefcase while von Haeften quickly pushed the files and papers into the briefcase that still contained the other bomb (which would have been fitted with a thirty-minute fuse).[197] Both officers left the bunker, where von Stauffenberg joined Generalleutnant Buhle and Oberstleutnant von Freyend and walked across to the special restricted area that lay at the heart of the Wolfschanze. The briefing conference was due to take place in a wooden building known as the Lagebaracke within that secure area.[198] It is worth noting that planning for the bombing had been based on the assumption that this briefing would take place in one of the concrete Wolfschanze bunkers as usual, inside which its explosive effects would be contained and far more devastating than in a relatively lightly constructed wooden building. The particularly hot weather that day had resulted in a decision to change the venue, as well as prompting the staff to open as many windows as possible in the Lagebaracke, which was further to dissipate the effects of the explosion.[199] In the meantime, von Haeften went away to ready the car for a speedy departure.

As they walked the almost 400 metres to the briefing area, von Freyend – mindful perhaps of von Stauffenberg's disabling arm and hand injuries – twice offered to carry von Stauffenberg's brief case: both times the colonel declined. However, once within the restricted area he did accept von Freyend's offer, at the same time citing partial deafness due to his war injuries as the reason for needing to be seated as close to Hitler as possible within the conference room. In fact, Hitler was already present and the conference in progress, with Generalleutnant Heusinger providing an update on the situation on the Eastern Front, when Keitel interjected to state that von Stauffenberg would later provide a report on the Ersatzheer, at which point Hitler shook von Stauffenberg's hand (he had met him on a number of occasions previously) and turned back to the briefing. Having arrived late, and despite his request to von Freyend, von Stauffenberg could only find a seat by a corner of the heavy oak table around which they were gathered. Von Freyend meanwhile placed the briefcase by a table leg, close to Generalleutnant Heusinger and Oberst Heinz Brandt, both of whom were standing to Hitler's right. The heavy table leg was thus between the briefcase and Hitler.

A couple of minutes later, von Stauffenberg indicated to von Freyend that he needed to make a telephone call to Berlin, to obtain or verify some last-minute details for the briefing, whereupon he left the room with von Freyend, who directed the switchboard operator to deal with von

Stauffenberg's call as a matter of priority. However, before the connection was made, von Stauffenberg left the building and the restricted area, heading towards the building used by the various Wehrmacht adjutants, in search of von Haeften and the car. There he found not only von Haeften but also General Fellgiebel. The three conspirators stepped outside and walked the 250 metres to the Horch staff car that had brought the two Berlin-based officers from Gut Wilhelmsdorf airfield earlier that day. Their driver, Feldwebel (warrant officer class 2 or sergeant major) Karl Fischer, was already sitting in the car waiting for them. The time was shortly after 12.40 p.m.[200]

The Bombing and its Aftermath

Anybody who happened to be looking towards the Lagebaracke at that moment would have seen a great flash of bluish-yellow flame, accompanied by a deafening explosion, a large cloud of dust and a fast-rising plume of dark smoke. The building's windows blew out, with glass, pieces of wood, roofing material, burning papers, sections of fibreboard and insulating fabric, all thrown violently outwards and upwards – with all this debris then showering down upon much of the Wolfschanze restricted area. At least one body, possibly that of General Rudolf Schmundt or the stenographer, Dr. Heinrich Berger, was blown straight through a window. Chaos ensued, as calls for medical assistance began to ring out. When the bomb detonated, General Fellgiebel pretended innocence for the benefit of others in the area, asking von Stauffenberg what the noise might have been. Von Stauffenberg merely shook his head. Meanwhile, Oberstleutnant Ludolf Gerhard Sander, who was standing nearby, sought to reassure von Stauffenberg and von Haeften that explosions were an everyday occurrence in the Wolfschanze area, being set off by army engineers using explosives to fell trees within the secure area, and therefore not to be alarmed. At that point the two officers took their seats in the Horch and told Fischer to return them to the Gut Wilhelmsdorf airfield. As they pulled away, they saw a body covered with Hitler's uniform cloak being carried away from the ruins of the Lagebaracke on a stretcher. Pulses of flame and thick black smoke continued to emanate from the shattered building as the car passed through the inner perimeter checkpoint, where it was waved through by the duty officer who recognized von Stauffenberg, and drove on towards the guard post that controlled access to the outer perimeter of the Wolfschanze.

In the meantime, back at the Lagebaracke, it very soon became evident that, despite the violence of the explosion, von Stauffenberg had not achieved his aim. At the moment the bomb detonated, Hitler had been leaning well forward over the table to look at a position that Generalleutnant Heusinger was indicating on the map, with the heavy table top between his upper body and the bomb, while his hand may also have been on his chin, partially shielding his face. In any event, while all of the 23 people in the room were thrown down or flung against the walls by the blast – several with severe injuries, their hair on fire, and their clothing shredded and smouldering – Hitler was nevertheless able to stand up unaided, as also was Generalfeldmarschall Keitel. Although the Führer was shocked, deafened and had sustained a number of cuts and bruises, his remarkable luck had held once again. Clearly very shaken, with his clothes in tatters, but none the less still very much alive, Hitler was led away to his quarters by his aide, Julius Schaub, and his valet, Heinz Linge. One of those who saw Hitler emerge from the wreckage – and was horrified to see that the Führer had unaccountably managed to survive the blast – was General Fellgiebel, who had been about to inform those in Berlin of the success of von Stauffenberg's attack. Immediately he telephoned fellow conspirator General Fritz Thiele at the army's Bendlerstraße headquarters in Berlin and, with a degree of ambiguity, said: 'Something terrible has happened. The Führer is alive'.[201] Then, in the hope that the situation might yet be retrieved and the conspirators safeguarded, he ordered his signals staff and operators to block all communications between the Wolfschanze and the outside world.

Unaware of the actual result of the explosion, and still firmly believing that Hitler was dead at last, von Stauffenberg and von Haeften reached the outer perimeter checkpoint only to find that the road had been closed in response to the general alert that was by then in place. The checkpoint commander, Oberfeldwebel Kolbe, was not prepared to open the barrier, so von Stauffenberg took a chance and telephoned back to the office of Oberstleutnant Gustav Streve, the administrative commander of the

Führerhauptquartier troops, with whom he had originally arranged to have lunch that day. As luck would have it, Rittmeister von Möllendorf (the officer with whom von Stauffenberg had breakfasted that morning) answered the call. That officer, as yet unaware of what had actually happened, saw no reason to delay von Stauffenberg, so he ordered Kolbe to allow the Horch and its passengers to proceed to the airfield. A little later, in somewhat cavalier fashion, von Haeften threw the second bomb from the open-topped staff car into the wooded verge about half way to Gut Wilhelmsdorf, an act that was noticed by the car's driver, Feldwebel Fischer. It is unclear why the two bombs had been separated when the two officers had set about preparing the charges earlier at the Wolfshanze, although this was probably a consequence of the unfortunate interruptions and consequent lack of time left to carry out those preparations. What is very clear, however, is that if both bombs had been in the same briefcase, even with only one of them fully activated, the detonation of that one would undoubtedly have set off the explosive charge in the second, and the significantly greater explosion and blast that would have resulted would unquestionably have killed everyone in the conference room of the Lagebaracke, irrespective of that building's relatively light construction. At about 1.15 p.m. the Horch arrived at the airfield, where von Stauffenberg and von Haeften boarded the aircraft for their two-hour return flight to Berlin Rangsdorf airfield. The aircraft took off immediately, both officers still believing that they had succeeded in their mission and that Operation *Walküre* could now go ahead as planned.

While they were still travelling back, at about 3.15 p.m. General Fellgiebel had again spoken to General Thiele in Berlin, telling him that, although the assassination attempt had failed, the coup should still go ahead. This view was duly passed on to the group of officers at the Bendlerstraße waiting 'on tenterhooks' for news of Hitler's death – they were now faced suddenly with a decision of momentous importance without von Stauffenberg present to advise them. Matters were further confused by a call to General Olbricht from General Wagner at Zossen, who had apparently received some garbled information about the happenings at Rastenburg and now sought clarification on the situation. But while the conspirators debated the best way to proceed, Hitler and Himmler had already acted. By 3.00 p.m.

communications to and from the Wolfschanze had been restored. Himmler was already en route to meet Hitler at Rastenburg, as also were Ernst Kaltenbrunner, chief of the Reichssicherheitshauptamt (RSHA) (the Reich central security office), and Bernd Wehner, Berlin's superintendent of police, both of whom were to lead the investigation into the assassination attempt.

Meanwhile, at the Bendlerstraße headquarters, the conspirators – with General Olbricht now the main instigator – finally decided just before 4.00 p.m. to proceed with the coup by issuing the *Walküre* orders. However, when Olbricht approached Generaloberst Fromm to sign the orders, he refused to do so and telephoned Keitel, who confirmed to him that an assassination attempt had taken place but that Hitler was still very much alive. Keitel was lying, asserted Olbricht. But Fromm did not believe him – it was doubtful whether he would ever have risked committing himself to the conspirators – and now decisively set his face against them.

But *Walküre* had already assumed a momentum of its own. Olbricht and his chief of staff, Oberst Mertz von Quirnheim, were already issuing orders in Fromm's name – which generated much anger on Fromm's part. At 4.30 p.m., von Stauffenberg at last arrived back at the Bendlerblock building on Bendlerstraße, at which point he updated Olbricht and stated that Hitler was indeed dead, having (as he believed) seen his body being removed on a stretcher.[202] A flurry of arguments between Fromm and the conspirators culminated in Fromm's arrest and removal to an adjacent office, while Olbricht, von Stauffenberg and the others strove somewhat belatedly to convince the country that the Führer was indeed dead and that he had been the victim of a plot orchestrated by power-seeking Nazi party groups. Time passed, and the extent of confusion and disinformation increased, as the group of men at the Bendlerblock issued orders, contacted commanders and units, and all the time repeated over and over again that Hitler was dead. Everything depended upon them being able to establish a widespread acceptance that this was so. But, as the afternoon became evening, even such prominent members of the Bendlerblock group as Beck and von Witzleben began to sense that Hitler might have survived. Wherever a commander was able to contact the Wolfschanze, Keitel stated categorically that Hitler was alive, and for the conspirators it was therefore imperative that *Walküre* should be concluded well before the Führer – if he was indeed alive – was able to make any sort of live broadcast to the nation. The focus of this activity was always von Stauffenberg, whose personal energy, control and understanding of the needs of the situation seemed boundless.

Meanwhile, Hitler and Himmler had already determined that the assassination attempt was no mere isolated action, and at 4.00 p.m., in a move that struck directly against the very heart of the army and the general staff, Hitler appointed Himmler commander-in-chief of the Ersatzheer. This placed the home-based German army under SS control, making the SS responsible for the administration, training and discipline of all newly formed army units and formations and thereby greatly increasing Himmler's power (while also advancing his dream of the army eventually becoming subordinate to the Waffen-SS or of being absorbed into it). Himmler moved swiftly to begin to restore Nazi authority in Berlin. He had already deduced that von Stauffenberg was the bomber, and at 5.00 p.m. SS-Oberführer Humbert Pifrader arrived at the Bendlerblock with orders to confront him, only to be arrested by the conspirators. But the subsequent arrival of various senior officers at the conspirators' headquarters revealed a greater degree of uncertainty on the part of some of them than anticipated.

In distant France, Beck called upon Generalfeldmarschall von Kluge to instigate action in his command to support the coup, but von Kluge first of all telephoned Keitel at the Wolfschanze, to be told that Hitler had survived. Von Kluge, whose support for the resistance had always been somewhat ambivalent, decided that there was nothing more that could be done. However, in Paris, von Kluge's subordinate, General von Stülpnagel, decided, irrespective of any uncertainty over Hitler's fate, to carry through his part in the coup and ordered the arrest of all the senior SS and Gestapo members in the city. Had von Stülpnagel been in a similar position in Berlin, perhaps such timely and decisive action might have changed the course of events dramatically. By now, however, only by broadcasting the conspirators' prepared proclamation to the nation, together with a categorical and non-refutable statement confirming Hitler's death, could the balance still be tipped in their favour. And at this late stage the ability to broadcast either of these was still not in prospect.

In Berlin the early alert messages to set Walküre in motion had produced a potentially hopeful response from many of the units and commanders garrisoned in the city. The commander of the Berlin city garrison units, Generalleutnant Paul von Hase, had issued the necessary orders, and by 6.30 p.m. the propaganda ministry and other principal ministries in the government quarter had all been cordoned off, as had Goebbels' house. The Großdeutschland reserve brigade, an elite army formation, seized a number of radio broadcasting stations and transmitters, SS barracks and Nazi offices. Other army units seized similar targets, outlying ministry offices and SS facilities, and prepared to make arrests. The force involved in securing the Wilhelmstraße area in the centre of the city was the Wachbataillon (guard battalion) Großdeutschland, an elite unit of 500 troops stationed in the barracks at Döberitz, commanded by Major Otto-Ernst Remer. Despite the apparent success of these troop deployments, at least three of the radio stations they had seized were able to continue broadcasting, and from 5.42 p.m. a series of short broadcasts from the Wolfschanze provided an accurate summary of the bombing, including the fact that Hitler had not only survived but had already returned to work. Although Hitler's own voice had not been heard, these widely heard communiqués could not be rebutted, and so the seeds of doubt grew, both within and beyond the Bendlerblock. One officer who now decided to resolve in which direction his duty and future should lie was Major Remer. In the midst of mounting rumour and uncertainty, this pragmatic and generally pro-Nazi army officer was urged by the unit's NSFO officer, Leutnant Hagen,[203] to establish once and for all whether or not Hitler had died in the bomb explosion. Hagen had already contacted Goebbels at his home and was certain in his own mind that Hitler still lived. The moment at which the coup was certainly doomed to fail came at about 7.00 p.m. when Remer arrived at Goebbels' house, just as troops were in the process of trying to arrest him. Goebbels saw Remer's doubts about the situation and seized the opportunity to telephone the Wolfschanze. At Goebbels' request, Hitler himself spoke directly to Remer, whose doubts were immediately dispelled and who was then ordered by the Führer to place himself under Himmler's command and suppress the revolt and all resistance to the Nazi government with maximum energy and ruthlessness. At once, Remer issued orders countermanding those from the Bendlerblock, and as these cascaded down to the various cordons of troops, arrest squads and other army units securing key points the *Walküre* deployments began to collapse, while unit commanders already unsettled by the Wolfschanze broadcasts began turning back to the existing Nazi authorities for direction. As the evening shadows lengthened, the coup began falling apart. At 8.00 p.m. Generalfeldmarschall von Witzleben arrived at the Bendlerblock, engaged in a furious argument with Beck, von Stauffenberg and others and then, clear in his own mind that the coup had indeed failed, drove back to Zossen some forty-five minutes later. As the rumours circulated, orders and counter-orders were issued, and a steadily increasing flow of senior officers now came to see Olbricht, Beck and von Stauffenberg, all wanting to know what was happening. More and more officers distanced themselves from the conspiracy, and little if any doubt remained that Hitler was alive and that the coup was totally unsupportable.

From about 9.00 p.m. the first arrests took place as the Gestapo began to reassert its authority. Himmler was already en route back to Berlin from Rastenburg, all ready to suppress any remaining signs of resistance and to set in train the investigation and severe retribution ordered by Hitler. At the Bendlerblock, the cohesion of all but the central core of conspirators began to fragment, and a number of officers uninvolved in the coup finally assumed control of the Bendlerblock at about 11.00 p.m. They disarmed all but the six main conspirators and released Generaloberst Fromm (who had been confined in an office next to his own) to take charge of what had now become the anti-coup forces. Fromm immediately arrested Beck, von Stauffenberg and the others. Then, mindful of Himmler's imminent arrival and that these officers could provide evidence of his own earlier ambivalence over the idea of removing Hitler, he took steps to ensure their silence. Having removed all their weapons apart from Beck's pistol, he permitted the former chief of the general staff to commit suicide. Twice Beck tried to shoot himself in the head, but only managed to inflict grievous wounds upon himself. Meanwhile, Fromm declared, 'In the name of the Führer, I have convened a court-martial that has pronounced the following sentence: General Staff Oberst Mertz [von Quirnheim], General Olbricht, the Oberst whose name I will not speak [i.e., von Stauffenberg], and Leutnant Haeften are condemned to death.'[204] However, Generaloberst Höpner – the only one of the six not in a position to provide evidence against Fromm – was simply held under arrest. As the condemned men were removed, Fromm ordered an officer to dispatch the fatally wounded General Beck. However, the officer refused to do this and so a sergeant was ordered to finish Beck, dragging him into the next room and there shooting him. The other executions were to be carried out forthwith, and Fromm's adjutant, Hauptmann Bartram, was instructed to organize a firing squad. This task was delegated to Leutnant Werner Schady, who had just arrived with a detachment of Wachbataillon Großdeutschland troops and now selected ten non-commissioned officers to form the firing squad. These men lined up slightly forward of a pile of sand that had been left by builders engaged in construction work in the courtyard.

Just after midnight, the four condemned officers were taken down to the courtyard, which was by then illuminated by the headlights of a number of military vehicles. Ordered in turn to stand by the pile of sand, Olbricht died first, then von Stauffenberg was to be shot. However, von Haeften threw himself in front of him and so died second. As the firing squad aimed at him, von Stauffenberg shouted out 'Long live sacred Germany!' and died in the next volley. Finally, Mertz von Quirnheim was shot. The four bodies, together with Beck's, were thrown into a truck and taken for burial to the church of St. Matthäus at Grossgörschenstraße, less than two kilometres away from the Bendlerstraße. Following his arrival in Berlin, Himmler was to order their exhumation and cremation, the ashes being then scattered across the fields.[205] In the meantime, Fromm had moved quickly to secure his own position and ingratiate himself with the Nazi regime by sending out an immediate message to the effect that an attempted coup by disloyal generals had been suppressed, with all those leading it having already been caught and shot. Then, while the bodies of the executed conspirators still lay in the courtyard, he stood on a truck to give a rousing address to all the officers and troops who had by then congregated at the Bendlerblock, extolling Hitler and his deliverance from the attempted assassination. The other dozen or so lesser conspirators and their supporters who had been arrested at the Bendlerblock were confined in two offices. At about 00.30 a.m. on the morning of 21 July, these men were taken into custody by an SS unit led by SS-Obersturmbannführer Otto Skorzeny, but before their removal to an SS barracks, pending interrogation by the Gestapo, they were forced to listen to the living proof of their failure, as Hitler at last made a live radio broadcast to the German nation and occupied territories. During the broadcast, the Führer emphasized the actions of 'a very small clique of ambitious, wicked and stupidly criminal officers' and the providential nature of his own survival, while also providing a forecast of the merciless retribution now to come.

In the hours that followed the collapse of the conspiracy, Major Remer had continued to make arrests, enthusiastically crushing any remaining support for the coup in accordance with the direction he had received from Hitler. In recognition of his work, Hitler later promoted Remer directly to Generalmajor. Fromm's fate in the aftermath of that day's events was less happy: when he arrived at Goebbels' office early on 21 July, anticipating plaudits for having dealt with the coup, he was promptly arrested. Elsewhere, in Paris, Vienna and Prague, the widespread arrests of SS, SD, Gestapo and other Nazi officials that had been carried out in accordance with orders received from the Bendlerblock headquarters were being reversed, often in quite surreal circumstances. In Paris, where the plans to support the coup in Berlin had moved forward much more efficiently and speedily, irrespective of any doubts about the veracity of the reports of Hitler's death, it proved somewhat more difficult to restore the situation. Those who had led the action in France had by then fully shown their hand, with the fate of von Stülpnagel and (a month later) von Kluge sealed irrevocably.

Trial and Retribution, July 1944 to February 1945

Just twenty-four hours after von Stauffenberg's bomb had exploded at Rastenburg, the full wrath of Hitler, the Nazi state and its apparatus of oppression – exemplified by the SS, SD and Gestapo – fell upon the army's officer corps, as Himmler used the full force of his newly acquired power and increased authority to settle once and for all with the army high command and the general staff that served it. A special SS and Gestapo team of no fewer than 400 investigators and officials led by SS-Obersturmbannführer Georg Kiessel was quickly established to begin probing every aspect of the conspiracy and to bring to account any and all who were, or who might possibly have been, involved with it. In parallel with this, measures were introduced both to humiliate the army and to extend further the authority of the Nazi regime. During the night of 20/21 July, Hitler appointed Generaloberst Heinz Guderian chief of the general staff. He replaced Generalleutnant Heusinger, chief of the OKH operations department, who had been temporarily filling that position since 10 June following Zeitzler's withdrawal, but who had been seriously wounded in the Lagebaracke bomb blast earlier that day. Although various approaches had been made to him by individual conspirators over time, Guderian had remained uninvolved in the plot and any active opposition to Hitler, and that Thursday he was carrying out duties in East Prussia, well away from Berlin. Consequently, his selection for the chief of the general staff post was made almost by default. While his qualities as a panzer leader were well-known, Guderian was a somewhat unlikely choice for chief of staff, lacking some of the subtlety, wider intellectual skills and political awareness of many of his predecessors. However, it is likely that this was also a factor taken very much into account by Hitler when he selected him. Undoubtedly the Führer wanted to avoid having to deal with yet another army officer in the mould of Beck, Halder or Zeitzler.

Heinz Guderian was born at Kulm (Chelmno) on the Vistula in West Prussia, on 17 June 1888. Although his father, Friedrich, was an army officer, the family had no great tradition of military service, its members being mainly lawyers and landowners. After attending various military schools between 1901 and 1907, Guderian was accepted into the 10th (Hanoverian) Jäger (light infantry) Battalion as an ensign, where Friedrich Guderian was the battalion's commander. Guderian attended the Kriegsakademie in Metz and was promoted lieutenant in 1908, later being attached to the 3rd (Prussian) Telegraph Battalion in 1911. In October 1913 he married Margarete Goerne. During World War I he filled various posts as a signals officer and general staff officer, as well as being in command for a short period of the 2nd Battalion, 14th Infantry Regiment. After 1919, as a Reichwehr officer, Guderian first of all served for a time in the 10th Jäger Battalion before becoming a member of the Truppenamt staff. There he was able to develop his theories for armoured warfare, and in 1931 his special abilities in that field resulted in promotion to lieutenant colonel and his appointment as chief of staff to Generalleutnant Oswald Lutz, the army's inspector of motorized troops. In October 1935, Guderian, now a major general, was appointed commander of the 2nd Panzer Division. Promotion to lieutenant general followed in August 1936, and on 4 February 1938 he was promoted general and assumed command of XVI Army Corps. The course of Guderian's career from 1914 to 1938 could not have better prepared him for the operational challenges he faced and largely overcame between September 1939 and December 1941, when he was dismissed by Hitler following a clash with his army group commander, Generalfeld-marschall von Kluge. However, Guderian was later recalled to active duty on 1 March 1943, when he was appointed inspector-general of armoured troops.

Various aspects of Guderian's career both before and during the war as a leading exponent of armoured warfare, the Blitzkrieg concept, and as a particularly successful commander of panzer forces, have already been touched upon, while his early career had afforded him an abundance of experience in other branches of the army and of staff work, often with a technological and tactical or operational perspective. But whether Guderian was capable of taking on the increasingly frustrating and uniquely difficult duties of chief of the army general staff on 20/21 July 1944 (a career move that he surely had neither actively sought nor anticipated in light of his earlier dismissal) is open to debate; it might even be argued that his personal qualities and character, background, tactical flair and innovative acumen might have better fitted him for appointment as the army's commander-in-chief rather than as chief of the general staff. But that was never an option because Hitler had already assumed that appointment himself.

That same night, an order was promulgated to the effect that troops were only to obey the orders of officers who were personally known to them. It was also mandated that all troops in Germany were, temporarily, to be subject to the authority of the senior Luftwaffe commander within the country.[206] Next, an order issued on 23 July banned the army's traditional salute, directing that henceforth the only salute to be used was the straight-arm salute of the Nazi party (which had previously only been used by army personnel when indoors and not wearing a uniform cap). At the same time, the influence of the Nationalsozialistische Führungsoffiziere, the NSFOs, was formally strengthened.[207] Then, on 1 August, a new law further reinforced Hitler's intimidation and denigration of the army and demonstrated his obsessive mistrust of its members. Henceforth, the relatives of serving officers and soldiers became legally responsible, liable – and therefore punishable – for any perceived disloyalty, political indiscretion or significant disciplinary offence committed by family members while in military service.

On 29 July, the newly appointed chief of the general staff struck a blow against the very organization he now headed when Generaloberst Guderian directed that every general staff officer was henceforth to qualify as a Nationalsozialistische Führungsoffizier – not for subsequent employment as an NSFO but simply to demonstrate clearly political and ideological commitment and loyalty to Hitler and the Nazi regime. Any general staff officer who felt unable to comply was required to apply to transfer out of the general staff corps. This measure created huge resentment within the organization as well as a potentially unbridgeable gulf between Guderian and the general staff that he sought to lead. Guderian's motives were probably pragmatic, largely symbolic and intended merely to show Hitler that action had been taken, so that the general staff could therefore be left to focus on its principal task of managing the Eastern Front. However, his approach was over-simplistic, and this particular directive was seized upon both by those within and outside the general staff as proof of the involvement and consequent guilt of the whole organization concerning the attempted assassination and coup. Guderian had already made his own views of the matter abundantly plain just two days after his appointment as chief of the general staff, when he issued an order of the day denouncing the conspirators as cowards and weaklings who had forsaken 'the road of duty and honour', which was the only course open to the true soldier. While this pronouncement undoubtedly jarred with very many members of the general staff, it is indisputable that neither Guderian's order of the day nor the ruthlessness of the retribution set in train by Hitler and Himmler were entirely contrary to the mood of public opinion in Germany at the time.

Very many officers and soldiers, together with much of the German civilian population, condemned the conspirators as traitors, who had betrayed the army's officer corps. Irrespective of their personal opinion of Hitler and the Nazi leadership, most army officers simply could not condone the conspirators' actions or comprehend the fact that these officers had broken their oath of loyalty to the Führer. Throughout the country, people expressed genuine shock and shame that Germans could have stooped so low as to carry out such an attack against the nation's leadership in wartime. There is certainly a danger of judging the true impact of the 20 July bombing in isolation and primarily from the standpoint of senior officers and general staff officers situated well away from the front line, in Berlin, the OKH and the major operational headquarters. Undoubtedly, the reaction of the mass of soldiers to news of the assassination attempt was potentially critical, but in July 1944 the main preoccupation of most ordinary soldiers was fighting the battle in progress and surviving to fight the next one rather than worrying about political events taking place far away in Germany. The response of a battle group of the 21st Panzer Division engaged in combat near Troarn in France was typical: while news of the bombing 'spread like wildfire down the column, the front kept on fighting as though nothing had happened', allaying the initial concerns of commanders that the news might destabilize the front and even prompt a collapse. An observation by General Heinz Eberbach, commanding Fifth Panzer Army, was illuminating, as he was 'amazed' at the 'indignation and anger' that the attempted putsch had provoked 'not only among the SS divisions but also among some infantry divisions'.[208] There is little doubt that the conspirators had misjudged and been over-optimistic about the wider reactions their action might have provoked within the Wehrmacht and the nation, even if von Stauffenberg had succeeded in killing Hitler.

A full account of the retribution meted out by the Nazis in the aftermath of the 20 July falls outside the scope of this work, while the nature and workings of the Volksgericht (people's court) that convened from 7 August, presided over by Roland Freisler, to deal summarily with the conspirators and alleged plotters and satisfy Hitler's insatiable desire for revenge were outlined in the preface at the beginning of this work. However, a summary of the fate of a number of those commanders, members of the army general staff and other army officers does serve to indicate quite graphically the sheer scale and consequent impact of this action upon the army as a whole and on the general staff corps in particular. While von Stauffenberg, von Haeften, Olbricht, von Quirnheim and Beck had been lucky to suffer summary execution within hours of failing in their endeavour and before the Gestapo had an opportunity to interrogate them, very many others in the weeks and months after 20 July proved to be much less fortunate. In the case of the principal military conspirators, their arraignment before the Volksgericht was preceded by a military court of honour. This court was convened by Hitler and sat on 4 August with the express purpose of dismissing these officers from the army, thereby denying them a trial by court martial (which would otherwise have been their right) and reducing their status to that of an ordinary criminal in advance of their appearance before Roland Freisler at the Volksgericht. The court of honour was presided over by Generalfeldmarschall von Rundstedt, with Generalfeldmarschall Keitel, Generaloberst Guderian, and Generals Schroth, Kriebel, Burgdorf, Maisel, Kircheim and Specht serving as members. By the time that it had concluded its business, no fewer than 22 senior, middle-grade and relatively junior officers had been dishonoured and dismissed from the Wehrmacht in accordance with the Führer's wishes.

General von Stülpnagel, the commander in Paris, was ordered back to Berlin on 21 July; while en route he attempted to commit suicide with his pistol but only managed to wound and blind himself. He was taken to Berlin, and subsequently tried and hanged on 30 August. His superior, Generalfeldmarschall von Kluge, despite his less than wholehearted commitment to the resistance and very peripheral involvement, also chose to commit suicide, with poison, while en route to Berlin on 17 August. Generalmajor Stieff and General Fellgiebel were arrested during the night of 20/21 July at the Wolfschanze. Later they were savagely tortured; Stieff was tried on 7 August and hanged the next day, while Fellgiebel was hanged almost a month later, on 4 September. The day after the bombing, Generalmajor von Tresckow, still with his unit at Army Group Centre on the Eastern Front on 21 July, decided that suicide was now the only course left for him. He walked forward into no man's land and tried to attract Russian fire by shooting his pistol, but when there was no response he blew himself up with a hand grenade. On 22 July, Generalleutnant Heusinger was arrested, despite having been present and wounded in the bomb explosion.[209] General Wagner, the quartermaster-general, committed suicide at the OKH at Zossen shortly before the arrival of a party to arrest him. Generalfeldmarschall von Witzleben, Generaloberst Höpner, Generalleutnant von Hase, and Yorck von Wartenburg were all arraigned alongside Stieff on 7 August, being condemned and hanged at Plötzensee prison the following day.

Among the many other officers arrested was former chief of the general staff Generaloberst Halder, who was imprisoned in a series of concentration camps before being taken into special SS custody and moved south into the Tirol in an SS convoy of trucks in April 1945. At that stage his execution, together with that of almost 140 other prominent diplomatic, political and military prisoners, was imminent. However, Halder and his fellow prisoners were rescued from their SS guards by a force of German army troops on 28 April 1945, less than twenty-four hours before their probable execution.[210] Another arrestee in the aftermath of the bombing was General von Falkenhausen, the commander in Belgium, who was initially imprisoned at Dachau but eventually joined the same group of politically important prisoners as Halder. As a result, he was also freed on 28 April and lived to survive the war. General Georg Thomas, a long-standing opponent of Hitler, who had headed the OKW economic and armaments branch, was imprisoned by the Gestapo soon after 20 July but managed nevertheless to evade execution and survived the war. Most of those arrested were less fortunate. The former Generalmajor Hans Oster who had worked so closely with Canaris until Oster's dismissal from the service in April 1943, was arrested on 21 July and, having been tried, was imprisoned at Flossenburg concentration camp. He was hanged there some months later, on 9 April 1945, along with Admiral Canaris, who was also arrested after 20 July, and Pastor Dietrich Bonhoeffer. The arrest of Oberstleutnant Cäsar von Hofacker, who had served as a messenger between von Stülpnagel and von Stauffenberg and had tried unsuccessfully to persuade Rommel to join the conspiracy, had further unfortunate consequences when he mentioned Rommel's name during an interrogation while enduring Gestapo torture. Hofacker was tried on 30 August and executed in Plötzensee on 20 December. Ulrich Wilhelm Graf Schwerin von Schwanenfeld, a reserve officer, was arrested at the Bendlerblock on 20/21 July. He had opposed Hitler since the mid-1930s, and in 1941 had been appointed adjutant to Generalfeldmarschall von Witzleben, liaising between Yorck von Wartenburg and military members of the resistance in Berlin and the Feldheer in the west. Always at the centre of the conspiracy, he had been particularly appalled by the activities of the SS-Einsatzgruppen on the Eastern Front, and at his trial before the Volksgericht on 21 August he took the opportunity to condemn these atrocities in open court. Sentenced to be executed, he was hanged at Plötzensee prison on 8 September. So the litany of arrests and killings continued. In the midst of all these suicides, executions and imprisonments, there was a grim irony in the fate of Generaloberst Fromm, the former commander of the Ersatzheer who had done so much to frustrate the activities of the conspirators on 20 July. Despite all that he had done to distance himself from the events of 20 July, the general was eventually tried on a charge of cowardice, and subsequently shot by firing squad in Brandenburg prison on 12 March, 1945.

A particularly important victim in the aftermath of the July bombing was Generalfeldmarschall Rommel, whose opposition to Hitler had been negligible and who had certainly not been aware of or involved in the assassination attempt, despite Hofacker having revealed his name under interrogation. However, his views on the futility of the situation on the Western Front after the Allies had broken out from Normandy had become known, together with his involvement in various discussions about opening up that front to the Western Allies in order to forestall the Russian advance into Germany from the east. In October, while Rommel was convalescing at his home at Herrlingen bei Ulm after sustaining serious injuries in an Allied air strike in France, Hitler communicated to him that he had the option either of being tried for treason by the Volksgericht – the outcome of which was pre-determined, with potentially dire consequences for his family – or of committing suicide and receiving a state funeral with full military honours. It is likely that Martin Bormann had urged Hitler to take this action, although the Führer was in any case becoming increasingly wary and jealous of the widespread popularity that Rommel enjoyed by 1944. On 14 October, two generals – Burgdorf and Maisel – appeared at Rommel's home while SS troops surrounded the area. A short time later, Rommel left with the pair, having decided he had little choice other than to take the poison they had brought with them. The last words he said to his family as he left the house were: 'I'll be dead in a quarter of an hour.' No postmortem was permitted, and thereafter Hitler always maintained that Rommel had simply succumbed to his war wounds.

Remarkably, some members of the resistance and others who had been associated with them still managed to escape the attentions of the Gestapo, although not all survived the war. Among these were Generalmajor von Gersdorff, who had agreed to carry out a suicide bombing to kill Hitler in 1943 and was a close associate of von Tresckow. Meanwhile, Generalfeld-marschall von Bock, whose own association with von Tresckow and others might well have condemned him despite his refusal to join the conspiracy, also escaped the post-20 July purges. He died in an Allied air raid in May 1945.[211] Major von dem Bussche, another of the resistance's very few volunteer suicide bombers, avoided arrest after 20 July and survived the war. Against the odds, so did Leutnant Ewald Heinrich von Kleist-Schmenzin, who had also volunteered to blow himself up with Hitler early in 1944, as well as having served as adjutant to the conspirators in the Bendlerblock on 20 July. He remained under investigation until mid-December and was then posted to a front-line unit; he managed to survive the war (unlike his politically active father, who was executed in April 1945). In September 1938, Oberstleutnant Friedrich Wilhelm Heinz had stood ready to lead a force into the Chancellery and shoot Hitler, an intended assassination and coup that had been forestalled by the Munich conference. On 20 July 1944, Heinz had been assigned a similarly prominent task and spent much of that day at the Bendlerstraße headquarters awaiting the order to deal with SS or other Nazi officials as necessary. In the aftermath of the coup's collapse, he managed to evade capture and then successfully remained in hiding in Berlin during the remaining months of the war. Probably one of the luckiest conspirators was Leutnant Fabian von Schlabrendorff, who had acted as a contact between Army Group Centre and the military and civilian resistance groups in Berlin. He was arrested shortly after 20 July, subsequently held in the concentration camps at Flossenbürg and Dachau, and eventually brought to trial by the Volksgericht on 3 February, 1945. Part way through these proceedings, a US air raid destroyed the courtroom and most of the documents, as well as killing the court's president Roland Freisler. As a result, von Schlabrendorff's case was adjourned and then dismissed in March, although he remained in custody during the final weeks of the war.

In addition to the many military victims of Himmler's investigation and purge during the weeks and months after 20 July, the civilian resistance was also decimated. Among the better-known civilian members who were eventually arrested, tried and executed were von Moltke, Goerdeler, Hans-Bernd von Haeften, von Hassell, von Helldorf, Professor Jens Peter Jessen, Ewald von Kleist-Schmenzin, Julius Leber, trade union leader Wilhelm Leuschner, Professor Adolf Reichwein, von der Schulenburg, von Trott zu Solz, Josef Wirmer, Yorck von Wartenburg, Father Alfred Delp, Pastor Dietrich Bonhoeffer and his brother-in-law Hans von Dohnányi, lawyer Carl Langbehn, and Johannes Popitz. Throughout Himmler's ruthless campaign of retribution, the families, friends and work colleagues – military and civilian alike – of anyone found guilty of involvement in the conspiracy were also liable to be arrested and summarily imprisoned or dispatched to a concentration camp simply because of who they were or who they knew, rather than as a consequence of any actual complicity in the conspiracy. Estimates vary, but probably as many as 200 people, military and non-military, were executed as a direct result of the events of 20 July. Significantly greater numbers suffered persecution, retribution, detention and other sanctions during the remaining nine months of the war as the full force of the SS, SD and Gestapo was brought to bear against any remaining signs of dissent or disaffection with the Nazi regime. As the end of the last full year of the war approached, Allied forces were already pressing hard from the west, south and east, with the Fatherland, the Third Reich and the Wehrmacht moving inexorably towards a deepening abyss of destruction.

14

Into the Abyss

1944–1945

The July bomb plot, its execution and especially its aftermath, finally destroyed most of the remaining status and authority of the general staff and its ability to influence events at the operational level. It had lost its ability to do so at the strategic level as long ago as the winter of 1941, as a result of Hitler's policy direction that the OKH should be responsible solely for operations on the Eastern Front while the OKW dealt with all other theatres of operation. Although the OKH organization continued physically in being, and many general staff officers continued to serve in a whole range of staff posts throughout the Wehrmacht, the July 1944 bomb plot and its consequences effectively marked the end of the German general staff that had served the Third Reich. The residual organization was largely impotent and necessarily acquiescent to the orders of the Nazi leadership. With so many senior army officers and general staff officers of all ranks implicated and accused of involvement in the assassination attempt (justifiably or not), virtually the entire general staff was deemed by the Nazi leadership to be guilty of treason, directly or indirectly or simply by association. Amidst the turmoil, Himmler's SS moved adroitly to fill the various power and organizational vacuums left by those who had been arrested, imprisoned or executed, while also exploiting the senses of shock, fear, uncertainty and despondency that pervaded much of the army in the weeks and months following 20 July. Even within the army, many officers who were by no means supporters of the Nazis were nevertheless appalled by what they regarded as the disloyalty and treasonable nature of the act perpetrated by officers who had deliberately chosen to abrogate their oath of loyalty, obligation and absolute duty to their Führer.

In July 1944, Hauptmann Siegfried Knappe had been attending pre-general-staff training at the panzer training school at Bergen-Hohne, north of Celle, when the assassination attempt was carried out. He recalled:

> 'The next several days were total chaos throughout Germany. Nobody knew what would happen next or who would be arrested next. The government and the army were both in a constant state of uproar; there were endless rumours, whispered names, and some announcements on the radio. It was at least a week before the situation showed any signs of abating … Immediately, everybody in the general staff was under suspicion. The Nazi party leaders were particularly vocal and vicious in accusing general staff officers …We thought that at best the General Staff College would be abandoned, we would all be reassigned to the front, and there would be no more general staff. Many of our instructors at the General Staff College were concerned for their lives, because they knew some of the convicted general staff officers. It was a very critical time for general staff officers, especially those who had been in general staff work for some time. An officer could be arrested [simply] because a friend or relative had been arrested …even some junior officers were arrested because they had been on an implicated general's staff for some time and had become confidants of the general … Everybody knew someone who had been arrested. And with the Nazis' system of holding a man's family responsible if he did something wrong, even families were arrested and sent to concentration camps.'[212]

The repercussions of the 20 July bombing and the failed coup, together with the appointment of Guderian as chief of the general staff, produced a number of changes in parts of the army high command and general staff. Soon after his appointment, Guderian's experience matched that of his predecessors when he was unable to persuade Hitler of the merits of creating a properly constituted general staff for the Wehrmacht as a whole, to be headed by von Manstein. He was, however, gratified by the appointment of competent panzer officers to two important general staff posts: General Walter Wenck[213] was appointed Chef des Führungsstabs (literally, 'head of the leadership command staff', a new post which replaced the former Oberquartiermeister I post), and Oberst Bogislaw von Bonin[214] was appointed head of the army general staff's operations department. Von Bonin's new deputy was Oberstleutnant von dem Knesebeck. Responsibility for the military intelligence branch dealing with the Eastern Front ('foreign armies east') was taken on by Generalmajor Reinhard Gehlen, an officer who already enjoyed a formidable reputation as an intelligence operator.[215] However, by that stage, even sound general staff officers such as these could do little to affect the course of the war. In the meantime, Himmler's appointment as commander of the Ersatzheer ensured that the army high command could never regain its former control of the organization upon which it relied to reinforce and train the Feldheer, while at the same time the shadow of the SS began to fall across parts of the army that had previously avoided its unwelcome influence. At the OKW, General August Winter replaced Walter Warlimont (by now a General) as deputy chief of the Wehrmachtführungsstab in September, when Warlimont – who had been present in the Lagebaracke when the 20 July bomb exploded – asked to be relieved due to an increasing incidence of dizzy spells. General Schmundt had been one of the few fatally wounded in the explosion that day, and in October he was replaced as Hitler's principal Wehrmacht adjutant and head of the army's personnel office by the committed Nazi, General Wilhelm Burgdorf – one of the two generals who contrived Rommel's suicide on the 14th of that month.

Despite the unwelcome situation in which the general staff now found itself, the training of the army's general staff corps officers continued. Despite the seismic political events following the July plot and the deteriorating military strategic situation during the second half of 1944, Hauptmann Siegfried Knappe's training course still proceeded more or less as planned. Nevertheless, the very fact that this instruction was being conducted at Hirschberg, in the Sudeten mountains of Silesia, rather than at the general staff college in Berlin, was a telling indication of the devastating impact of Allied bombing attacks against the German capital by that stage – during December 1943 and January 1944 some 22,000 tons of bombs had been dropped upon the city. By mid-1944 Hirschberg was not particularly secure or safe either, as the advancing Russian ground forces continued moving steadily westwards.

Although defence and fighting withdrawals were by then the operations most frequently executed by the army – the Ardennes offensive in December 1944 being a notable exception – the instruction at Hirschberg followed the standard curriculum of the general staff training course. Only the ever-present urgency of the strategic situation and therefore the pressure of less time than usual to complete the course influenced the overall pace and content of this training, and limited some of the more traditional social aspects of the course that had been enjoyed by such students in former years. Knappe noted that, 'Our only social activity was a once-a-month event during which the whole [general staff college course] would have an evening in the ballroom, consisting of a cocktail hour and dinner.' Married officers could be accompanied by their families, with two-room accommodation provided to each family and a kitchen shared between four families, although all usually ate in the Officers Club in any case. Despite the unavoidable time constraints, the training programme was comprehensive, intensive, always demanding and in the best traditions of the old general staff. Knappe recalled:

'We learned to lead a division in different kinds of combat situations: attacking, retreating, conducting a rearguard action, attacking across a river, attacking in mountainous terrain, establishing a bridgehead, attacking a bridgehead, and so forth. All these different situations were played out with maps or in a sand box [sand table terrain model], with tests in between. The purpose was to make us capable of assisting a general in leading a division. We learned how to write orders, how to plan an attack, how to figure out the length of a column on a road, how long it would take the column to cross a bridge, how to group troops, how to arrange for reserves, how to defend against a massive attack by an enemy, how to conduct a massive attack against a defence line, how to position infantry, how to position artillery, where to put the engineers if there is a river in the attack line and when to move them forward. We also learned intelligence and counter-intelligence work: how to find out what kind of units were opposite us and what to do with that information – how to handle all these details for the general commanding the division. In war games, we would be given the situation we were in and what was happening. Then all of a sudden something unexpected would happen, which we would learn about in a report, a radio message, or a phone call. Then we would have to react to the new situation. In [routine day-to-day] training, we would get the information and have to work out the solution overnight or over the weekend.'[216]

The general staff training course continued into January 1945, but by the end of that month the strategic situation had deteriorated significantly, with the Russians already at the Vistula river, which was less than 100 kilometres from Hirschberg. Consequently, the course was terminated prematurely in order for the students – now fully qualified as general staff officers – to be assigned immediately to general staff appointments with the headquarters of front-line units and formations.

Siegfried Knappe's fairly positive experience at Hirschberg belied the rapidly changing and much abbreviated nature of the general staff training carried out in late 1944 and early 1945, as the system was forced to respond to the continuing attrition of staff officers in front-line formations. The purge of general staff officers after 20 July 1944 aggravated a situation already made difficult by the accelerating demand for trained general staff officers to fill staff posts in re-constituted divisions and in the headquarters of various new units (such as the Volksgrenadier 'peoples' divisions) created by Himmler after he assumed command of the Ersatzheer. As selection and training had always been the foundations upon which the professional excellence of the army general staff had been built, both of which elements were now being seriously affected, the further demise of that organization during the last months of the war was inevitable. By the end of 1944, some divisional headquarters had only a single trained general staff officer. Others, particularly Himmler's brand-new divisions, frequently had no trained staff officers at all. Necessarily, Knappe's training course had been curtailed, and this practice had become very much the norm, with young officers from front-line units attending truncated general staff training courses and then immediately being appointed to high-level, demanding staff posts. Many of these officers were well-selected and carried out their staff duties to good effect, but this was increasingly a result of their personal and intuitive military qualities rather than the comprehensiveness of their staff training. In the face of such pressure to qualify staff officers in sufficient numbers, the selection process inevitably fell short of that which had obtained in earlier times, while the much-reduced training courses provided an inadequate chance to rectify this or to prepare these young officers for the staff appointments they were destined to fill. The German historian Walter Görlitz encapsulated the problem that the general staff faced by late-1944, when he wrote:

'At best, many such young men continued to act with the dash, one might even say the *naïveté*, of a front-line officer, and made little effort to cultivate the cool objectivity of a General Staff officer of the old school. Many let themselves drown in the details of routine and lost their perspective over their problems as a whole. The true General Staff officer, whose heart belonged to the troops while his head belonged to his science, the man who could take responsibility and dared to have a mind of his own, became ever harder to find. As against this, the mere executors of orders, who desired nothing more than to remain what they were, multiplied exceedingly'.[217]

During the remaining months of the war in Europe, the OKH continued its task of directing operations on the rapidly crumbling Eastern Front and implementing Hitler's ever more unrealistic demands that the Wehrmacht should simply stand and fight rather than conducting aggressive withdrawals and delaying actions. The background to the final months of the existence of the general staff were characterized by a succession of personnel dismissals and replacements together with organizational changes largely occasioned by Hitler himself or by the wider repercussions of the July plot. Understandably, having being subjected to almost a decade of Nazi propaganda, many ordinary soldiers viewed the dismissal of senior officers as indicative of professional incompetence on the part of those who led them, rather than as a consequence of Hitler's own personality flaws and illogical obsessions – which was hardly conducive to maintaining morale in the Wehrmacht. All this was set against a steadily deteriorating operational situation on all fronts. In Italy, Generaloberst von Vietinghoff's Tenth Army and Generaloberst von Mackensen's Fourteenth Army withdrew steadily northwards, all the time imposing delays and casualties on the advancing Allies by means of a succession of well-prepared positions and defence lines: the 'Viterbo Line', the 'Trasimene Line' (also known as the 'Albert Line') , the 'Gothic Line', the 'Genghis Khan Line', the 'Adige' or 'Venetian Line', and the 'Alpine Line'. The 'Gothic Line' ran across Italy to the north of Pisa and Florence, and in the late summer of 1944 it was there that Generalfeld-marschall Kesselring effectively halted the advancing Anglo-US armies, although sporadic fighting continued and the British Eighth Army did manage to take Ravenna in December. In practice, following the success of the Allied landings in North-West Europe in June, any continuing necessity for the Anglo-US forces in Italy to advance beyond Rome was decidedly questionable. A holding campaign would have prevented any major redeployment of German forces from the Italian front to France, while at the same time the heavy casualties sustained during the fighting to overcome Kesselring's lines of defence could have been avoided. In any event, the occupation of the 'Gothic Line' signalled the end of the German army's year-long campaign of defence and fighting withdrawals along the length of Italy as the Italian campaign degenerated into a stalemate with the onset of the torrential rain, flooded rivers, occasional snow and ubiquitous mud that characterized the north Italian winter. Eventually the Allies mounted an offensive into the Po Valley in April 1945, subsequently striking north into the Alps towards the Brenner Pass and north-west towards Turin and Milan. By then, however, Germany's war had already been lost, and the remaining German forces in Italy, mainly Tenth and Fourteenth Armies and the paratroopers of two airborne corps, surrendered at Caserta on 29 April, with a general ceasefire being declared on 2 May.

In the meantime, almost a year earlier, and just six weeks before von Stauffenberg's abortive assassination attempt, the Allied invasion of occupied France at Normandy on 6 June 1944 had created yet another active front for Germany and its already hard-pressed army. The responsibility for this North-West Europe theatre of operations still lay with the OKW rather than the OKH. In overall command of the ground forces in France, Holland and Belgium was Generalfeldmarschall von Rundstedt, who was designated Oberbefehlshaber West (OB West). His forces included Army Group G (First Army and Nineteenth Army) and Army Group B (Seventh Army and Fifteenth Army). OB West also controlled a powerful armoured reserve, Panzer Group West. Army Group B was commanded by General-feldmarschall Erwin Rommel, in post since November 1943, with responsibility for the coastline from Brittany, through Normandy to Antwerp. Panzer Group West was commanded by General von Schweppenburg and was designated the OKW reserve, which could only be deployed on Hitler's personal authority. In the early spring of 1944 the German army in France comprised some 61 divisions, 11 of these armoured. From these divisions were drawn many of the units to defend the massive and elaborate conglomeration of obstacles, mines, concrete bunkers, underground tunnels, artillery emplacements and defensive positions that lined the coast of the European mainland from Scandinavia and along the north coast of the occupied Netherlands, Belgium and France. The quality of the forces defending the coastline varied widely, ranging from battle-seasoned armoured and infantry units to 'static divisions' comprised of 'stomach battalions' (medically downgraded troops) and even units of Russian 'volunteers' formed from prisoners-of-war taken on the Eastern Front. In planning their response to an Allied invasion, von Rundstedt and von Schweppenburg favoured holding the panzer divisions back, ready to strike the Allies as they moved inland from the beaches. But Rommel, mindful of his time as commander of the DAK and of the threat posed by the Allied air forces, believed that the sort of mobile operations employed by the army earlier in the war were no longer feasible. He argued that any Allied landing would need to be defeated within 24 hours if the Allies were to be denied a lodgement, and therefore urged strongly that the reserve panzer units should be positioned close to the beaches and placed under his direct command. Shortly after assuming command of Army Group B, Rommel, during a visit to the Normandy beaches and the German defences, had expressed his view that Normandy would be where the Allies would land and that it would be on those beaches that the fate of Europe would be decided. His assessment proved accurate and prophetic.

The Campaign in Normandy, June to August 1944

In some ways the events that followed the Allied airborne and seaborne landings in Normandy on 6 June are peripheral to the central story of the general staff and the catastrophic events that engulfed it during the late summer of 1944. However, they do serve to illustrate once again the fatal consequences of the split of command responsibility between the OKW and OKH, and the adverse impact of Hitler's direct influence upon matters that should properly have been left in the hands of operational commanders – and, ideally, to the general staff system: by mid-1944, however, the professional efficacy of this system was becoming little more than a distant memory.[218] By last light on D-Day, from Varreville in the west to Ouistreham in the east, the Anglo-US-Canadian and Free French forces had gained a foothold at the five landing beaches, codenamed by the Allies *Utah*, *Omaha*, *Gold*, *Juno* and *Sword*. By the evening of that day, five US, British and Canadian divisions, together with various independent brigades and other Allied and specialist units, were all safely ashore and setting about consolidating and exploiting their beachheads.

The OKW was soon receiving more and more reports of the deterioration of the situation in Normandy, together with ever more urgent requests for reinforcements. Well into 6 June, both Hitler (who was at the Obersalzberg and was not even briefed on the landings until the midday conference) and the senior staff at the OKW remained convinced that the landing in Normandy was merely a diversion – the main Allied assault would come across the Pas de Calais, the route that the Germans had intended for their invasion of England in 1940.

One of the most serious consequences of the OKW's assessment and resulting inertia was the failure to authorize the deployment of the reserve panzer divisions until that afternoon, by which stage it was too late for them to fulfil their mission of defeating the Allies on the beaches, an outcome that chief of the general staff Zeitzler had in any case already declared to be no longer achievable. Rommel's prediction proved all too accurate – Allied air power inflicted significant casualties upon the panzers as they drove northwards to join the battle, a move of as much as 160 kilometres in some cases. In one such air attack the entire headquarters staff of the commander of panzer forces were killed or severely wounded. As a result, these divisions were not committed to battle until 8 or 9 June, by which time they had already sustained significant losses of men and tanks. By 12 June, all five of the Allied landing beaches had linked up to form a single cohesive beachhead, while a huge fleet of cargo and troop-carrying vessels plied back and forth across the Channel bringing ever greater quantities of reinforcements and matériel to join the fighting in Normandy. This situation contrasted significantly with that of the Germans, all of whose available forces were already committed or still en route to the battle area. Even so, the army still managed to contain the Allied invasion through most of June and much of July, dealing successfully with two major Anglo-Canadian attempts to capture Caen.

While these momentous events had been taking place in Normandy, Zeitzler's time as chief of the general staff had finally drawn to a close. Despite his promotion to Generaloberst on 30 January, by June 1944 Zeitzler despaired of ever being able to carry out his duties properly in the face of Hitler's continued antagonism. Although he had originally seen the potential benefits of developing an effective OKW-OKH command structure, Zeitzler eventually refused to cooperate with the OKW in a vain attempt to indicate his growing frustration with the high-level management of the war and his virtual exclusion from that process. Not surprisingly, this approach simply exacerbated Hitler's displeasure, and so Zeitzler finally decided to remove himself from any further involvement with the war effort by voluntarily retiring from active duty – ostensibly on the grounds of ill-health. He was replaced by Generalleutnant Heusinger on 10 June, although as we have already seen, that officer's time as chief of the general staff was violently curtailed when he was wounded in the 20 July bomb explosion at the Wolfschanze. On 21 July, in the wake of that bombing, Guderian had become the third chief of the general staff to serve as such during 1944.

...ler and NSFO officers at the Wolfschanze, August 1944. He is accompanied by ...neralfeldmarschall Keitel and the head of the NSFO, General Georg Ritter von Hengl. The ...hly politicized NSFO organization increasingly undermined the general staff and the army ...ain of command during the war, especially after 20 July 1944.

...ff officers in the Foreign Armies East (FHO) intelligence branch of the OKH at the ...uerwald HQ, working on the enemy order of battle facing Army Group Centre, December ...44. A female staff assistant (Stabshelferin) is updating the organization board.

Staff officers of the Foreign Armies East (FHO) intelligence branch of the OKH at work in their bunker at the Mauerwald HQ, December 1944. The OKH intelligence staff enjoyed mix fortunes during the war, overestimating Anglo-French capabilities in 1939–40 and und estimating those of Russia in 1940–41.

On 6 March 1945, Generaloberst Guderian, the last significant chief of the army general st briefed German and foreign news correspondents in Berlin on the atrocities that were allege by then being committed by the Red Army as it advanced into East Prussia. Reich press ch SS-Obergruppenführer Dr. Otto Dietrich is sitting to the right. On 28 March, Guderian left t post of chief of the general staff, being succeeded by General Hans Krebs. By then German war had only a week to run.

EFS OF THE ARMY GENERAL STAFF
row, left to right: Generaloberst Johannes Friedrich
ns von Seeckt (as Reichswehr Chef des Truppenamtes
l Chef der Heeresleitung in the 1920s); Generaloberst
dwig August Theodor Beck (1933–8), who was
minent in the conspiracy against Hitler; and
neraloberst Franz Halder (1938–1942).
ntre row, left to right: Generaloberst Kurt Zeitzler
42–4); Generalleutnant Adolf Heusinger (1944), shown
e as a senior officer in the West German Bundeswehr in
1950s; and Generaloberst Heinz Wilhelm Guderian
44–5).
ht: General der Infanterie Hans Krebs (1945).

THE 20 JULY 1944 CONSPIRATORS
Top left: Oberst Claus Schenk Graf von
Stauffenberg. Top right: Generalmajor
Helmuth Stieff. Above left: Generalmajor
Hans Oster. Above: Generalmajor Herma
Karl Robert Henning von Tresckow. Left:
General der Nachrichtentruppe Fritz Eri
Fellgiebel. Opposite page, top left: Gener
der Infanterie Friedrich Olbricht. Opposi
page, top right: Oberst (later Generalmaj
Rudolph-Christoph Baron von Gersdorff.
Opposite page, bottom left: Oberleutnant
Werner von Haeften. Opposite page, bott
right: Oberst Mertz von Quirnheim.

Top row, left to right: Generaloberst Alfred Jodl and Generalfeldmarschall Wilhelm Keitel, the two principal staff officers at the OKW; and Generaloberst Werner Freiherr von Fritsch.

Centre row, left to right: Generalfeldmarschall Werner von Blomberg; Generaloberst Friedrich Fromm; and Generalfeldmarschall Heinrich Alfred Hermann Walther von Brauchitsch.

Left: Generalfeldmarschall Fritz Erich von Lewinski von Manstein.

Opposite page: Adolf Hitler with Reichsführer-SS Heinrich Himmler. Himmler's appointment to command the Ersatzhe in July 1944 significantly increased the involvement of the S in army affairs.

Adolf Hitler and Reichsmarschall Hermann Göring, whose political agendas as head of t[...] Luftwaffe often conflicted with the needs of the army ar[...] the general staff.

Below left: General [...] Artillerie Erich Marc[...] who produced the general staff's first p[...] for *Fall Otto* in 1940[...]

Below right: Major (later Generalmajor) Otto-Ernst Remer, whose actions on 20 July 1944 contribute[...] significantly to the failure of the attemp[...] coup in Berlin.

Hitler's uncertainty, procrastination, and poor judgement were all too evident in the crucial weeks during which the Anglo-US beachheads were consolidating and therefore still vulnerable to a decisive counterattack. It was not until 24 July that Hitler at last conceded that the landings at Normandy were not the precursor to a major landing at the Pas de Calais, at which time he authorized the redeployment of forces from that area against the Anglo-US beachhead. By then it was much too late. These armoured formations sustained heavy losses as they drove south, often in daylight and under skies dominated by Allied combat aircraft, against which the Luftwaffe was ineffective. Just a day later, the Allies broke out of the Normandy beachhead. Generalfeldmarschall von Kluge, who had succeeded von Rundstedt[219] in early July as commander of the forces combating the Anglo-US invasion, sought Hitler's approval for a general withdrawal to the River Seine, with a view to consolidating behind that natural obstacle before launching a major counterstroke. Instead, Hitler ordered an ill-conceived counterattack, thereby squandering the potential offered by the newly released armoured formations. The attack was launched by Fifth Panzer Army – a speedily assembled and disparate force of army and Waffen-SS units with just 120 tanks – on the night of 6 August. As the next day dawned, Allied air power again proved decisive, halting the attack virtually at its outset. During the succeeding days of heavy fighting up to 12 August, Seventh Army and Fifth Panzer Army were progressively encircled by US forces in the Mortain–Falaise–Argentan area. The Wehrmacht still managed to inflict very significant losses upon the Anglo-US forces opposing them, but, whereas the Allies could sustain such casualties and equipment losses, the Wehrmacht in northern France was now experiencing the sort of problems that had long existed during its war of attrition on the Eastern Front. The army's manpower losses were generally irreplaceable, while many of its matériel resources were now finite. Meanwhile the Nazi attrition of senior army commanders continued: on 17 August, Generalfeldmarschall Walter Model arrived unannounced at von Kluge's headquarters with orders from Hitler to relieve him. Von Kluge was to be dismissed and return to Berlin forthwith. In the aftermath of the 20 July bombing, such an order was virtually a death warrant, and on the way to Berlin in his staff car, while travelling towards Metz, he committed suicide by taking poison.[220]

Onslaught in the East, January to November 1944

While the OKW had been attempting to deal with the worsening situation in Normandy since June, the OKH had been trying to counter or mitigate the impact of a whole series of Russian offensives launched since the beginning of 1944. The 900-day siege of Leningrad was raised in January, Sevastopol fell in May, and Russian control of the Ukraine was fully restored by the late summer. It was in Belorussia that the Red Army chose to launch its main summer offensive (*Bagration*) on 22 June – three years to the day since the start of the German invasion of Russia. There, Generalfeldmarschall Ernst Busch's Army Group Centre, consisting of Fourth and Ninth Armies and Third Panzer Army, were defending a frontage of about 750 kilometres with just 34 divisions. The lines of supply and communication of these already weakened armies were frequently disrupted by strong and well-equipped partisan forces. On 22 June the Russians struck with a force of almost 200 divisions, supported by some 6,000 tanks and assault guns and no fewer than 7,000 aircraft. By the end of just twelve days of intense fighting, 25 German divisions had virtually ceased to exist, and most of Ninth and Fourth Armies became trapped between Minsk and the Byerezino River. Fourth Army lost 130,000 of its 165,000 men and was forced to withdraw – despite a period of confusion when Busch, mindful of Hitler's policy concerning such withdrawals, ordered it to retake the ground it had necessarily given up. Ten divisions of Third Panzer Army were lost, while Ninth Army lost several divisions; its commander, General Hans Jordan, was dismissed by Busch (an enthusiastic supporter of Hitler but ill-suited for Army Group command) for 'irresolute leadership' in the midst of the battle, being replaced by General Nikolaus von Vormann. Two generals were killed defending their headquarters as they were overrun, and in all as many as 300,000 men were killed or captured. Only about 15,000 troops escaped from what had become the 'Babruysk pocket'. On 28 June Busch was relieved of his command and replaced by Generalfeldmarschall Model, at the age of 53 the youngest field marshal in the Wehrmacht.

With Minsk, Vilnius and Vitebsk all in Russian hands by early July, the Red Army divisions drove rapidly on towards the River Vistula and East Prussia. Model retained his command of Army Group North Ukraine when he assumed that of Army Group Centre and as such became the most powerful commander on the Eastern Front. However, the northern German forces were now increasingly at risk of being cut off by the Russian advance, and Model sought to establish a new defensive line in Lithuania. In the meantime, forces were diverted from the Romanian front to reinforce formations in the centre and farther north. Hitler refused Model's requests for the Baltic area – specifically Estonia – to be evacuated and its troops sent to alleviate the ever more critical situation in the centre. Army Group South, commanded by Generaloberst Johannes Friessner, was gradually pressed back into southern Poland, Czechoslovakia and Galicia, and in these areas its 31 German divisions and 12 Hungarian light divisions or brigades eventually succumbed to a series of devastating Russian attacks in July and August. On 16 August 1944, Model was transferred to the Western Front, where he took over command of Army Group B from Generalfeldmarschall von Kluge shortly before the latter's suicide; Model's transfer from Russia was occasioned more by his strained relationship with Guderian (by then chief of the general staff) than by any professional failings.

In the late summer of 1944, the increasingly parlous state of Germany's situation on the Eastern Front was highlighted by a parade of 50,000 prisoners-of-war through Moscow. The parade took several hours to pass a given point, and the ranks of prisoners included no fewer than twelve generals. In the north, part of the German army became increasingly isolated as it was forced to withdraw towards the Courland peninsula and East Prussia. What now became the 'Courland Army Group' was commanded by Generaloberst Ferdinand Schörner. In August, Romania changed sides, and in September Bulgaria was occupied by the Red Army. By November, Russian forces in Hungary began a siege of Budapest.

While the fighting continued in the west, east and to the south, Himmler lost no time exploiting his appointment as commander of the Ersatzheer. A high priority amongst his various ideologically based aspirations was for the Waffen-SS to supplant the army as Germany's principal military force. Some twenty Waffen-SS divisions already existed, together with almost twenty regimental or brigade strength units. National Socialist dogma also envisaged a peacetime German defence force based upon a form of 'people's army', and Himmler now set about creating the foundation units of such a force with Volksgrenadier (People's Grenadier) divisions, to be supported by a people's artillery corps. In due course, these units also paved the way for Himmler's creation of the home-defence Volkssturm units that would fight some of the final, last-ditch battles in Germany itself. In reality, with replacement manpower for the Wehrmacht already in short supply, the combat effectiveness of these new organizations was always questionable, despite the use of veteran officers and soldiers (often the survivors of army divisions that had been decimated in combat) to provide the core of commanders and non-commissioned officers about whom these new divisions were built. With an actual manpower strength that rarely exceeded 10,000 (some 2,000 men less than in an army infantry division by 1944), the Volksgrenadier division relied upon an increased allocation of automatic weapons and man-portable anti-tank weapons (such as the Panzerfaust and Panzerschreck) to offset its reduced numerical strength. Army commanders might have a widely varying mix of Wehrmacht, Waffen-SS, and Volksgrenadier units under their command, with their different organizations, equipment, training and level of motivation all inviting a plethora of logistical and command and control difficulties.

Despite their limitations, Guderian perceived that the Volksgrenadier divisions could be usefully employed to assist with developing a strong defensive line on the Eastern Front, specifically in Poland, supplemented by a number of fortress artillery units manning some 2,000 captured heavy guns. He also proposed redeploying the more than 300,000 German troops of Eighteenth and Sixteenth Armies, some 30 divisions in total, that had become isolated on the Courland peninsula in Latvia and might now be much more usefully employed elsewhere on the Eastern Front. However, Guderian's proposals to Hitler once again fell on deaf ears. At the same time, he further reduced OKH operational authority in the east by directing that the development of these defences was henceforth to be the responsibility of the Nazi party officials who administered these occupied territories.[221]

Meanwhile, Volksgrenadier units were to be deployed to any and all fronts as necessary. The development of these units and Hitler's rejection of Guderian's suggestions served to underline yet again the increasing influence of Himmler and the Nazi party in the wake of 20 July 1944, as well as the Führer's determination to treat his new chief of the general staff just as dismissively as he had his predecessors.

Reverses in the West, August to December 1944

On the Western Front, the Allied armies in northern France had at last broken clear of the sunken lanes, dense hedgerows and patchwork of fields that characterized the bocage countryside of Normandy and advanced south and east across France and towards Belgium and the Netherlands. During August, the US Third Army had encircled most of Seventh Army and Fifth Panzer Army in the 'Falaise Pocket', where 60,000 troops, 500 armoured vehicles and thousands of other vehicles and quantities of equipment were trapped. On 21August the pocket was sealed, and as many as 10,000 German soldiers were killed in the battle that ensued before these beleaguered forces were finally forced to surrender.[222] Although there were almost ten million men fighting with the Wehrmacht by the beginning of August 1944, they were spread between three fronts – Eastern, Western and Italian – and with most of these troops already actively engaged there were few reserves available. On 15 August, part of the US Fifth Army from Italy landed on the French Riviera and advanced into southern France. Paris was liberated by the Allies on 25 August, Marseilles and Toulon fell on the 28th, and Amiens on the 31st. Dieppe and Rouen were lost on 1 September, Antwerp, Brussels and Lyons on 3–4 September, and just over a week later the US troops who had landed in southern France linked up with those who had landed in Normandy. On 12 September, elements of the US First Army at last crossed the border into Germany. By then, Generalfeldmarschall von Rundstedt, ably assisted by his chief of staff General Siegfried Westphal, had been reappointed as commander-in-chief in the west and had begun to stabilize the front. A vital element of the western defence was the formidable line of concrete bunkers, wire and anti-tank obstacles that stretched from Luxembourg in the north to Switzerland in the south. The proper title of this defence line was the 'West

Wall'; the Allies dubbed it the 'Siegfried line'. In a further snub to Guderian and the OKH, which was by then desperately trying to hold back the Russian armies on the Eastern Front, Hitler now directed that the fortress artillery units destined to defend the occupied territories in the east should instead be redeployed to man the West Wall defences. With no alternative Wehrmacht troops available to man the defences being urgently constructed under the supervision of the local Nazi authorities in Poland and elsewhere, most of these part-completed strongpoints, obstacles, bunkers and defensive earthworks became redundant.

The Anglo-US political-strategic decision to allow the Russians to capture Berlin, while the Anglo-US forces conducted a steady advance eastwards on a broad front (instead of adopting British commander Field Marshal Montgomery's plan for a rapid, potentially decisive strike towards the German capital), provided the Wehrmacht with a welcome respite and opportunity to consolidate its battered forces in the aftermath of the defeat in Normandy and the Falaise disaster. During the two months following the Allied landings in Normandy, as many as 53 German army divisions had been destroyed, with 22 corps and divisional commanders killed, seriously wounded or captured. After the fall of Paris, the first signs of a breakdown in discipline had appeared: 'Lorries loaded with officers, their mistresses and large quantities of champagne and brandy contrived to get back as far as the Rhineland, and it was necessary to set up special courts martial to deal with such cases'.[223] Such disciplinary measures, and the presence of the flying court martial teams, Feldjägerkorps (army special units established to apprehend and deal with deserters), Feldgendarmerie (military police) and Geheime Feldpolizei (secret field police) units that carried them out, rapidly became an everyday feature of the army's rear areas. More and more Wehrmacht officers and soldiers were being shot or hanged for desertion, dereliction of duty, and various other offences now deemed to warrant summary execution. Any officer encountered behind the front line risked suffering such action if he could not produce written orders from his commander to justify his presence there. In October alone, some 44,955 soldiers were sent for trial by court martial, many of whom received long sentences at hard labour or were dispatched to serve in the army's penal battalions, to which units tens of thousands of soldiers were consigned during the final six months of the war.[224] During the final month of the war, the newly qualified general staff officer Major Siegfried Knappe was organizing the rail move of his corps headquarters from Löbau, Saxony, in the operational area of Generalfeldmarschall Schörner's army group, to join Twelfth Army in Generaloberst Heinrici's army group in the Harz mountains. Knappe noted: 'Schörner had issued orders that anyone caught behind the lines without [written] orders was to be put in front of a tribunal and hanged if found guilty of desertion. Because of Schörner's orders, no soldier or officer dared to be seen in the cities behind the front, even when on [legitimate] duty.'[225] Nevertheless, at the lower levels of command recognition of the authority of the general staff clearly still persisted even in such turbulent times, as Knappe added, 'I was safe only because of the red [carmine] general staff stripes on my trousers.'

While there was a certain inevitability about the gradual demise of the German war effort in the face of the huge commitment of military-industrial might by the Allies on three major fronts,[226] the determination of the Wehrmacht to defend the Fatherland was still very evident as the Allied advance was forced gradually to slow down, with its lines of communication and supply growing ever longer as the Anglo-US forces approached the major obstacle of the River Rhine. In mid-September the Germans also inflicted an important reverse upon the Allies at Arnhem, when an attempt by an Anglo-US airborne corps of First Allied Airborne Army to seize a crossing over the Rhine in mid-September ended in a decisive defeat at the hands of Waffen-SS armoured units that had by chance just been deployed in the Arnhem area for rest and refurbishment. Arnhem illustrated very vividly that, although the Allies were approaching the very heart of the Third Reich, and despite the fact that on all fronts the Wehrmacht was being forced to give ground, the German army was by no means ready to accept a defeat on terms that every soldier knew would be 'unconditional'. Nevertheless, the sheer weight of military power now deployed against the Wehrmacht could only be held off for limited periods of time. The city of Aachen surrendered on 21 October, and on 9 November US forces crossed the River Moselle, with Free French units capturing Strasbourg on 24

November. Everywhere the German forces were withdrawing, and as the harsh winter weather swept across northern Europe the Allied high command discounted the possibility of any new counteroffensive by the Germans before 1945.

During the months following the Allied breakout from Normandy, Hitler's focus had switched from the Eastern Front to the west, and he had openly acknowledged to Jodl that Germany could afford to lose some of the occupied territory in the east, but not in the west. He still entertained a belief that victory in the west was achievable, and that once the Anglo-US forces – but those of Britain especially – had been defeated, the Wehrmacht could resolve matters on the Eastern Front. This belief was clearly unsustainable, but most of the officers who knew full well that the Russians posed a much greater threat than that faced by the troops in the west were serving in the OKH, and by late 1944 Hitler was hardly interested in the views of those general staff officers. As early as 19 August he had put in hand the initial planning work for a new offensive in the west, despite even the OKW advising him that the Wehrmacht was no longer capable of mounting major offensive operations. During that month alone the army had lost almost 500,000 men, with almost three and a half million casualties incurred over the previous six months. None the less, Hitler believed that an offensive in the west would achieve significantly more strategically than could an equivalent-scale operation on the Eastern Front. He also believed that the American soldiers were generally of poor quality, with potentially fragile morale, and were therefore vulnerable to a decisive counterstroke delivered as a complete surprise once they had over-extended the lines of supply upon which they depended. Accordingly, at a staff meeting on 16 September he announced operation *Wacht am Rhein* ('Watch', or 'Guard on the Rhine'), declaring that it would be launched into the Ardennes, which was perceived to be a weak link in the US defence line.

Wacht am Rhein: The Ardennes Offensive, December 1944 to January 1945

The operation's objective was to split the Anglo-US forces by crossing the Meuse, seizing Antwerp, then striking towards Brussels, finally precipitating 'another Dunkirk'. In addition, the offensive would gain time for the development, mass production and deployment of Germany's potentially devastating new V-weapons (Vergeltungswaffen or 'reprisal weapons'), which were increasingly being presented as the means by which Germany would regain the strategic initiative and finally win the war.[227] The principal formations conducting the offensive were to be Fifth Panzer Army, commanded by General Hasso von Manteuffel, Seventh Army, commanded by General Erich Brandenberger, and Sixth Panzer Army,[228] commanded by SS-Oberst-Gruppenführer und Generaloberst der Waffen-SS 'Sepp' Dietrich. Although the OKW was the responsible headquarters and von Rundstedt was in overall command of the Western Front, the concept of *Wacht am Rhein* was primarily Hitler's own idea, and in November he transferred his field headquarters from the Wolfschanze to the Adlerhorst ('eagle's nest') at Ziegenberg near Nauheim in Hessen. At the same time, the chief of the general staff transferred to the Maybach bunker complex at Zossen to the south of Berlin; his physical displacement from Hitler and the area of the forthcoming offensive highlighted his lack of direct involvement in this important undertaking.

Although the OKH suffered the removal of some of its units from the Eastern Front to boost the forces required for this new offensive, together with the diversion of much-needed ammunition, fuel and equipment to the Ardennes, OKH involvement with *Wacht am Rhein* was relatively limited. Irrespective of the strategic wisdom of the enterprise, it would undoubtedly have benefited from proper general staff analysis and planning at the operational level. The amounts of ammunition and fuel provided for *Wacht am Rhein* were inadequate – less than a quarter of the required fuel was provided – while the whole operation depended upon bad weather closing down Allied air supremacy. As the army had already learned in 1940 and 1941, close air support was essential to the success of any Blitzkrieg-type operation, and the Luftwaffe had long since lost the ability to defeat Allied air power. Meanwhile, the need for absolute security in order to guarantee surprise meant that the scope of all pre-briefings was strictly limited, which meant that the application of the doctrine of Auftragstaktik – by 1944 already somewhat problematical – was unavoidably constrained.

At dawn on 16 December the troops of the US First Army were awakened by a tremendous artillery bombardment, followed soon after by the sound of advancing tanks, assault guns and troop carriers. Masses of German armour and infantry burst out of the misty, snow-laden woods and valleys of the Ardennes as the Wehrmacht's last major offensive gathered momentum. The attacking forces included some of Himmler's newly-created Volksgrenadier divisions as well as Waffen-SS and army units. Initially, the battle later dubbed the 'Battle of the Bulge' by the Allies caused widespread panic among the surprised American units that bore the brunt of the initial assault, notably those of the US VIII Corps. Their consequent disarray and a series of precipitate withdrawals at first threatened the whole Allied situation in the west, and the attackers achieved a number of tactical successes. But the continuing lack of resources (especially fuel) and reserves to sustain and exploit these early victories meant that the offensive eventually lost momentum and ground to a halt. The winter weather had covered the early deployment of the ground forces very effectively, but when the mist and cloud finally lifted neither the already depleted Luftwaffe nor the German ground forces were able to counter the overwhelming weight of Allied air power that was rapidly launched against them. Eventually, the resolute defence of Bastogne by the 101st US Airborne Division, the eventual stabilization of US First Army, which had borne the brunt of the initial assault, the sheer weight of Allied air power, and finally the strong counterattacks launched by the British from the north and the Americans from the south enabled the Allies to restore the situation in the Ardennes. While 26 December marked the high-water-mark of the German offensive, *Wacht am Rhein* ended on 16 January, with those German units that had managed to escape the Allied counteroffensive and fighter bombers having already withdrawn back into Germany.

Although the Wehrmacht had inflicted enormous casualties upon the US forces, with 10,276 dead, 47,493 wounded and 23,218 missing, the Americans were well able to replace these losses. The German army's casualties during the offensive were at least as great as those of the Americans and may have numbered as many as 120,000 dead, wounded and missing. These were simply irreplaceable, as were the hundreds of armoured vehicles that had been destroyed or abandoned during the offensive. In that same month, another bizarre example of the perverse nature of military prioritization in Hitler's Third Reich occurred with the release on 30 January of a German film, *Kolberg*, which told the story of the heroic defence by the garrison and citizens of Kolberg against the French in 1807. This film was a spectacular production to which a range of military resources and more than ten thousand Wehrmacht troops had been committed as extras on virtually a full-time basis throughout 1943 and 1944, but who could undoubtedly have been much more usefully employed on one of Germany's several front lines by that stage of the war. With the failure of *Wacht am Rhein* and the Wehrmacht hard-pressed on all fronts in January 1945, the propaganda and morale boosting impact of this epic but now largely irrelevant film fell well short of that which had been envisaged at the time of its inception in 1943.[229]

Defence on the Rhine, January to April 1945

In the wake of *Wacht am Rhein*, the OKW had little choice but to base its main defence in the west upon the natural obstacle provided by the River Rhine. For Hitler, the only small consolation to emerge from *Wacht am Rhein* was the near-fracturing of Anglo-US relations on 30 December, stemming from Field Marshal Montgomery's forthright demand to the Allied supreme commander, General Eisenhower, that he should henceforth assume overall operational command of all the Allied forces in North-West Europe while at the same time reviving his plan for a speedy advance into Germany on a narrow front. Fortunately for the Allies, a potentially disastrous rift was averted, due primarily to the efforts of Montgomery's chief of staff, Major General de Guingand, in his placatory dealings with Eisenhower's headquarters.

The Allies resumed their advance on a broad front in February 1945, when an Anglo-Canadian attack into the Reichswald forest area on 8 February was soon confronted by General Alfred Schlemm's First Parachute Army. Schlemm's paratroopers showed yet again that the Wehrmacht was still capable of mounting a successful and spirited defence. First of all they utilized to very good effect a maze of well-prepared positions, bunkers and obstacles within the forest, coordinated with positions in the nearby towns of Goch and Cleve, to halt and delay the Allied advance. They then conducted a successful fighting withdrawal across the Rhine but incurred losses of as many as 90,000 men killed, wounded or missing in the process. To the south, the American advance was delayed by bad weather until 23 February, with further delays due to flooded roads and waterlogged countryside once the formations were again on the move. Despite these difficulties, troops of the US Ninth Army reached Düsseldorf on 1 March.

Farther south the US 12th Army Group drove on towards the Rhine, and on 7 March troops of the 9th US Armored Division seized more or less intact the weakly-defended railway bridge over the Rhine at Remagen, between Köln (Cologne) and Koblenz. The four German army officers responsible for the security and demolition of the bridge were summarily court martialled and executed on Hitler's orders – a fairly routine occurrence by that stage of the war. Shortly thereafter, on 10 March, von Rundstedt was replaced as commander-in-chief in the west by Generalfeldmarschall Albert Kesselring, whose command responsibility was extended at the end of April to include south and south-west Germany and those areas still occupied by the Wehrmacht in the adjacent countries. By March the Allied armies had all closed up to the Rhine, and on 23 March Field Marshal Montgomery's 21st Army Group crossed the river in a set-piece assault at ten places between Rheinberg and Rees, centred on Wesel. This combined ground and airborne assault by some 80,000 men supported by more than 2,000 guns and an aerial bombardment quickly overwhelmed the thinly-spread German defenders. There were by then no significant reserves available to launch a counterattack. By the end of the month the British had some twenty divisions and more than 1,000 tanks east of the Rhine, driving on towards Hamburg and the River Elbe at Magdeburg, and still poised to strike for Berlin if so ordered. However, the Allied leaders held firm to their decision that Hitler's capital would be left for the Russians to capture, and that the Anglo-US armies would not move east beyond the Elbe. Accordingly, the Western Allies advanced steadily onwards into the Netherlands, southern Germany, and towards the industrial Ruhr. There, between 25 March and 18 April, they gradually enveloped and then forced the collapse of Army Group B within the 'Ruhr Pocket' where as many as 325,000 troops and 30 generals were captured. At the same time, Germany's industrial heartland was devastated. After four days evading Allied patrols, the erstwhile commander of Army Group B, Generalfeldmarschall Model (who had earlier stated that 'a [German] field marshal does not become a prisoner. Such a thing is just not possible'[230]) committed suicide in the forest near Duisburg on 21 April. Throughout, Model had continued to believe Hitler's pronouncements that V-weapons would yet save the day, provided that the army bought enough time for their deployment, but by April 1945 the field marshal's faith in the Führer was exhausted.

By the end of April, despite some determined counterattacks and resolute last-ditch defensive actions, the army had lost the war in the west, and very many German soldiers now met their fate as casualties or prisoners-of-war while fighting in the devastated villages, towns, cities, fields and forests of the Fatherland itself. In January 1945 a British intelligence report derived from interviews with a number of German prisoners-of-war in the west assessed that, 'Few thought that Germany had any hope of final victory; most had had their fill of fighting and recognized the futility of continuing the struggle. Nevertheless, they all fought hard. The deduction would seem to be that no matter how poor the morale of the German soldier may be, he will fight hard as long as he has leaders to give him orders and see that they are obeyed.'[231] By implication, this testament to the quality of the German soldier was also an acknowledgement of the effectiveness of the German military system in former times, of which the general staff had for so long been architects, implementers and overseers.

Defeat in the East, January to April 1945

While the Anglo-US campaign in the west was approaching the limit of exploitation that had been agreed with Stalin, the tempo of the fighting on the Eastern Front was gaining in intensity. On 12 January 1945, a major Russian offensive struck towards Warsaw, the River Oder and Berlin. Within the first few days, Fourth Panzer Army was destroyed and Army Group A was penetrated so deeply that Russian armour broke right through its rear area and into the hardly defended area beyond. Despite Guderian's plea not to dismiss the very able army group commander, Generaloberst Josef Harpe, Hitler cited the Russian breakthrough as a failure and replaced him with Generaloberst Schörner. Harpe's removal was but one in a flurry of ill-judged and precipitate dismissals of first-rate army commanders by Hitler against Guderian's advice during the first two months of 1945. Generaloberst Georg-Hans Reinhardt was dismissed from Army Group Centre, General Friedrich Hossbach from Fourth Army, and Generaloberst Erhard Raus from Third Panzer Army. The Russian offensive also resulted indirectly in the removal of two more junior general staff officers on 16 January, when Oberst von Bonin, head of the OKH operations branch, and his principal staff officer, Oberstleutnant von dem Knesebeck, were arrested after von Bonin ignored a direct order by Hitler and authorized a withdrawal by Army Group A from Warsaw. Guderian attempted to mediate with Hitler on behalf of these two officers but without success. His intervention also attracted the unwelcome attention of Ernst Kaltenbrunner, head of the RSHA, leading to the chief of the general staff suffering the indignity of being required to submit to a formal examination by Kaltenbrunner. Later, Guderian's suggestion to Hitler that Generalfeldmarschall von Weichs should be appointed to command Army Group Vistula was roundly rejected by the Führer when he instead appointed Himmler – a man with no useful operational experience – to fill that important command post. This situation was further exacerbated by Himmler's refusal to accept more than one general staff officer (a lieutenant colonel) within the operations branch of his headquarters, while relying upon an SS-Brigadeführer (major general) as his chief of staff and principal military adviser.

Linked to Guderian's proposal of von Weichs to command Army Group Vistula was a plan for this army group to be reinforced by the forces still in Courland and by Sixth Panzer Army from the west to create a powerful army group of up to 40 divisions and as many as 1,500 tanks. Guderian's proposal envisaged this force striking into the Russian's northern flank, forcing the Red Army back across the Vistula thereby disrupting and delaying its advance towards Berlin. In fact Hitler did choose to adopt a modified version of this plan, but without authorizing the essential reinforcing troops specified by Guderian. The attack was scheduled to begin on 15 February. During the preceding few days, Guderian lobbied strongly for his own deputy, General Walter Wenck, to be appointed as chief of staff in Himmler's army group, and just two days before the offensive, Hitler suddenly agreed to this proposal. However, this proved a hollow victory for Guderian, as Wenck was injured in a car accident just before the operation commenced. Predictably, Himmler entirely mismanaged the attack, which quickly dissolved into a total failure that also opened the way for the Russians to strike northwards in strength. At that stage Himmler took himself away from the front, pleading an attack of influenza. This development did, however, provide an opportunity for Guderian to visit Himmler where he was recuperating at the SS-run sanatorium of Hohenlychen in Brandenburg, when the Reichsführer-SS proved very amenable to Guderian's persuasion that he should immediately hand over his short-lived command of the German forces on the Oder – by then based upon Ninth Army (General von Manteuffel) and Third Panzer Army (General Theodor Busse) – to Generaloberst Gotthard Heinrici.[232] This damage limitation in the wake of the Army Group Vistula débâcle was the last matter that Guderian could cite as a success during his time as chief of the general staff.

Ever since 21 July, virtually the only visibility for the general staff at the highest level had been provided by Guderian, and it had proved a thankless and at times potentially precarious task. Despite the constant rebuttals, personal frustration and frequent humiliation, while all the time risking Hitler's wrath, this unlikely chief of the general staff nevertheless fulfilled what he saw as his professional duty to represent to the Führer what were in his estimation the most appropriate operational solutions. Hauptmann Gerhard Boldt, a staff officer at the Führerhauptquartier, described the relationship between Hitler and Guderian thus:

'Their mutual hostility was partly due to basic differences of opinion about military tactics; but a strong additional factor, and one which will always redound to Guderian's credit, was the way in which the general mustered the courage, time and again, openly to contradict and warn Hitler. He was one of the very few men in Hitler's entourage who stood by his own views and who was bold enough to contradict the Führer without restraint at that time.'[233]

The end of Guderian's short and turbulent time as chief of the general staff came on 28 March, when he once again found himself defending a field commander who had in Hitler's view failed to achieve his mission. On this occasion the officer was General Busse, whose attempt to relieve Kustrin had been unsuccessful. The specific argument, which took place in the Führerbunker beneath the Reich Chancellery, rapidly broadened and became more and more animated, with Guderian robustly criticizing Hitler's military leadership and his negligence in failing to provide an adequate defence for the German people in the east. Hitler rapidly lost his temper, condemning the general staff, the whole officer corps and the generals. The Führer was verging on launching a physical assault against Guderian, and some of the others present at the meeting had to intervene. Remarkably, Guderian survived what might well have been Hitler's even more severe wrath, although his time as chief of the general staff was effectively over: the Führer ordered him to take six weeks' leave, beginning immediately, on the grounds of his very evident 'physical ill-health'. In practice, Guderian's dismissal probably served him well by removing him from the main focus of activity during the final weeks of the war.[234] During Guderian's few weeks of enforced sick leave, Hitler would die, Germany would be in ruins, the Wehrmacht would surrender unconditionally, and the war in Europe would finally end. On 1 April, Generaloberst Hans Krebs, a member of the Nazi inner circle and operational assistant to Guderian, was appointed as the last chief of the army general staff.

Budapest fell in mid-February, while in the area of Lake Balaton in south-west Hungary the Germans launched their last significant offensive of the war, when most of the remaining Waffen-SS panzer divisions were annihilated in the desperate fighting that ensued.[235] This defeat enabled the Red Army to advance into Austria – Vienna fell on 6 April – and on to Prague. Shortly before the fall of Vienna, the SS who were responsible for the defence of the city uncovered a plot by members of the general staff within the main army headquarters to overthrow the Nazi administration in Vienna, using a number of units, including artillery troops and part of the elite Reich Grenadier Regiment 'Hoch- und Deutschmeister'. The leaders of the conspiracy were Major Sokol, who was the principal operations staff officer to General Brünau, the city commandant, and Oberleutnant Huth. The SS response was swift. Every general staff officer in the operations department was arrested, Sokol and two other officers were hanged on the Florisdorf bridge in the city, while the other twelve general staff officers who had been arrested were summarily shot in a courtyard of the old imperial war ministry. This was the last such planned concerted action by a group of general staff officers against the Nazi regime, albeit that it was specifically focused only upon Vienna and Austria, and only at a stage when the final outcome of the war was hardly in doubt. In the meantime, behind the lines on all fronts the SS, the military police and 'flying court martial' teams ranged far and wide with renewed vigour, sweeping up and summarily executing large numbers of deserters, 'defeatists', and officers who had ordered withdrawals against orders or who were perceived to have failed the Third Reich in any other way, together with anyone suspected of 'undermining fighting morale'.[236] Typical of such draconian measures was the execution of Oberst Graf von Rittberg, a general staff officer shot for having expressed the view that the war was lost.[237]

For almost a decade, Hitler had undermined and finally persecuted, humiliated and purged the general staff. Now, during the last few months of the war, the Red Army was also destroying part of the cultural and traditional foundations upon which the general staff and the army had relied and from which it had drawn its ethos during some three centuries, as the Russian tanks rampaged across East Prussia and into eastern Germany. This part of the country – Prussia and Brandenburg – had been at the very heart of Prussian and later German militarism and military achievement for so long, its aristocratic families providing a continuing succession of some of Germany's greatest military commanders, statesmen, diplomats and general staff officers. But now this area and many of the great estates of its most famous families were laid waste as the Russians inflicted a savage retribution for *Barbarossa* and all that had followed on the Eastern Front. The German historian Walter Görlitz wrote:

Many old Prussian families who had already made heavy sacrifices of blood in the war, had also been the victims of persecution following the plot of July 20th ... Where they either could not escape or elected not to do so, they were deported, or failing that, tortured, shot or hanged. Many preferred not to survive the end of their world, and took their own lives. A few died defending their lands and houses, displaying to the end that obstinate pride which had always marked them as an order, and forcing as many of their enemies as they could to share their death.[238]

The devastating consequences of Hitler's war for just two of the great families of Prussia exemplified the experience of many such noble German families – as well as providing a poignant reminder of the conflict of duty and conscience that was ever-present during the Nazi era. As the Russians swept westwards, the extended family of Generaloberst von Arnim lost 98 of its estates and farms. Thirty of this family's sons had already fallen in battle during the course of the war, one had died in a concentration camp, two were shot by the Russians, three were transported, and eight committed suicide. A second example was that of the von der Schulenburg family. Over time, this family had produced three field marshals and 35 generals. However, two prominent von der Schulenburgs took part in the 20 July plot and were duly executed. Meanwhile, fourteen other family members died on the battlefield and another seven committed suicide as the Russians overran the family's 23 estates in Prussia and eastern Germany.

Several of the various ways in which the wider officer corps had sustained its losses since 1939 were unique to the unwelcome circumstances in which the army high command and general staff had eventually found themselves in the Nazi era. Of the army's field marshals, only three remained: Keitel, Busch and Schörner. Von Witzleben had been executed for his part in the 20 July conspiracy. Rommel, von Kluge and Model had all committed suicide. Von Bock had died in an Allied fighter ground attack. Paulus was a prisoner of the Russians. Von Brauchitsch, von Leeb, von Manstein, von Kleist, von Küchler, List and von Weichs had all fallen into disfavour with Hitler and been forced into retirement. Meanwhile, of the 36 officers who had attained the rank of Generaloberst by or after September 1939, seven had died as a result of enemy action, three had been executed as a consequence of the 20 July bombing, two had been dismissed from the army, and a further twenty-one had been dismissed in disgrace (including Halder, who had subsequently been imprisoned in a concentration camp). Overall, of some 800 general staff officers of all ranks who did not survive the war, as many as 150 had died as a consequence of their opposition or alleged opposition to Hitler and the Nazi regime that their duty and the soldier's oath had obliged them to serve.[239]

Götterdämmerung: The Battle for Berlin, April to May 1945

Ever since the Allied decision to allow the Russians to capture Berlin, the German capital had been the Red Army's final and most important objective. Its offensive to gain control of the eastern approaches to the city began on 16 April, when almost 200 divisions launched their attack against Generaloberst Heinrici's much weakened army group on the Oder, which by then comprised no more than about 50 German divisions, supplemented by various Hitler Jugend and police units, with some 200 tanks. Despite a desperate defensive battle by the Germans, the outcome of the attack was never in doubt, and Russian armoured forces broke through Ninth Army and Third Panzer Army some 72 hours later. On 21 April, the remaining general staff officers in their headquarters at Zossen were forced to evacuate the bunker complex as the Russian tanks drew ever closer, reaching the autobahn that ran to the south of the capital the very next day. The OKW and Wehrmachtführungsstab, including Keitel and Jodl, had already decamped to an alternative headquarters site deep in the woods at Fürstenberg in Mecklenburg-Vorpommern, about sixty kilometres north of Berlin. On 23 April the drive for Berlin began in earnest, as three Russian armies struck from the east and south-east in a developing assault which would eventually draw one and a half million Russian troops into the battle, together with some 5,000 tanks, 2,000 guns and 5,000 aircraft. By that stage, the city was defended by just 45,000 Wehrmacht and Waffen-SS troops with no more than 60 tanks, plus about 40,000 young, old, disabled and infirm Volkssturm soldiers. A further 2,000 Waffen-SS troops of the regiment Leibstandarte

'Adolf Hitler' were deployed specifically to defend the Reich Chancellery and the central government area. From the north, three more Russian armies attacked into the outer suburbs, while from the south-west two more gradually fought their way into the city. Farther to the south-west, yet another army struck northwards towards Potsdam.

By then Hitler and many of his immediate entourage were already closeted deep in the Führerbunker adjacent to the Reich Chancellery and the Brandenburg Gate at the very heart of Berlin. In that bunker, remote from the reality of what was happening not only across Germany but even from the destruction and wholesale slaughter taking place in the streets of the city above, the Führer played out a surreal game of strategy on operational maps that were routinely out of date and grossly misrepresented the operational and tactical situation, with few of the military forces shown being either still in the locations indicated or at anything like the combat strength suggested by their designations. Yet another series of changes of commanders was ordered by Hitler, this standard response to adverse operational situations being something with which the army high command had become all too familiar during the previous few years. On 28 April, Keitel encountered Heinrici's troops moving north towards Neubrandenburg to counter a Red Army breakthrough, instead of to Berlin as had been ordered by Hitler. Consequently, a day later Keitel dismissed Heinrici and offered the army group to von Manteuffel, who promptly refused it and also protested at Heinrici's treatment. Accordingly, General Kurt von Tippelskirch was temporarily appointed to command the army group, pending the arrival from the Netherlands of Luftwaffe Generaloberst Kurt Student as its commander. However, Student was captured by British forces before he could do this. In the meantime, Hitler had divided the Reich into a Northern Command, with Admiral Dönitz as its commander, and a Southern Command, headed by Luftwaffe Generalfeldmarschall Kesselring. Hitler's appointment of an admiral and an air marshal (albeit that Kesselring had once been a soldier and had already successfully demonstrated his ability to command ground forces in Italy) to command the remaining armies of the Third Reich was a final snub to the army and the general staff as well as an indication of the perverse thinking that drove Hitler's approach to operational matters. In parallel with these largely irrelevant changes of commander, plans for the creation of new armies and for attacks to relieve Berlin were discussed daily, none of which were at all practicable. In mid-April, a new Eleventh Army was formed under SS-Obergruppenführer und General der Waffen-SS Felix Steiner to fight its way into Berlin, but in reality this force never amounted to more than a strong division of 15,000 men. In any case, Steiner had no intention of obeying the orders he had received from Hitler on 21 April to march his totally inadequate force to the relief of the beleaguered city, and the next day this 'army' retreated westwards in a bid to surrender to the Anglo-US forces rather than the Russians.

The last, forlorn hope for Berlin was General Walter Wenck's newly-formed Twelfth Army, which on 21 April was engaged with US troops. On 22 April, Wenck was ordered to disengage from the Americans, turn around, and attack eastwards to link up with Generaloberst Theodor Busse's Ninth Army, prior to launching a coordinated attack on the Russians from the south and west. At the same time XLI Panzer Corps (commanded by Generalleutnant Rudolf Holste) would attack the Russians from the north. Wenck made remarkably good progress at first, reaching the outskirts of Potsdam by 28 April, but the other two forces were soon halted by Red Army units. Then, on the night of 28 April, strong Russian pressure forced Wenck's Twelfth Army to withdraw along its entire front. At that point Wenck advised the OKW at Fürstenberg that any further attacks to relieve Berlin were no longer practicable.[240]

Within Berlin, the command and control chaos at the operational level was mirrored by that at the tactical level. A steady succession of officers were charged with the responsibility of defending Berlin, subsequently being relieved for incompetence, cowardice, or simply failing to carry out the impossible task set by Hitler. Among the several senior officers handed this unwelcome command as 'battle commandants' were Generalleutnant von Hauenschild, General Kuntze, Generalleutnant Reymann, and Generalmajor Kaether. When none of these achieved that which was required, a young NSFO officer who had impressed with 'the glow of his National Socialist convictions'[241] was promoted general and given the task. Eventually, General Weidling, an artillery general, became the last incumbent of this unenviable appointment. By that stage, the last week of April, bitter street fighting was taking place in the city, as the few remaining Wehrmacht, Waffen-SS, Volkssturm, and Hitler Jugend units fought a final series of hopeless battles against overwhelming odds. Bizarrely, in the midst of all this chaos, the SS were still hanging deserters and any other soldiers or civilians whose wholehearted commitment to resisting the Russians and supporting Hitler were in doubt.

On 29 April, with Russian assault troops almost at the gates of the Reichstag and the Brandenburg Gate, Hitler married his mistress Eva Braun and later dictated his last will and political testament. During the afternoon of 30 April the man most responsible for World War II put a pistol to his head and committed suicide. Eva Braun, Frau Hitler, lay dead beside the body of her new husband, having taken poison. Afterwards, both bodies were doused with petrol and burned by members of the Führerbunker staff in a shallow ditch close to the main entrance to the bunker. Some of the Nazis who had been with Hitler in the bunker to the end subsequently managed to escape, while several others chose to commit suicide. The Reichstag finally fell at 1.00 p.m. on 2 May, although at 10.50 p.m. on 30 April a group of three Red Army sergeants had made their way to a balcony at the front of the building and there unfurled a blood-red flag signalling Soviet Russia's final victory over the forces of the Third Reich. The remaining German troops in Berlin capitulated on 2 May, having inflicted about 100,000 casualties on the attacking Russians since 16 April.[242] The last positions to capitulate were Berlin's three huge Flakturms (massive, virtually indestructible, concrete towers mounting multiple anti-aircraft guns) at Friedrichshain, Zoo-Tiergarten, and Humboldthain. These flak towers had been the capital's principal air defence system during the war years, and at the end provided protective havens for countless Berlin civilians that not even the Red Army's firepower could penetrate or subdue.

At Reims, on 7 May, Generaloberst Alfred Jodl signed a document mandating the unconditional surrender of the German forces and on 9 May Generalfeldmarschall Wilhelm Keitel formally signed the instrument of the unconditional surrender of Germany with the Russians in Berlin.[243] The war that the Wehrmacht had fought from September 1939 to May

1945 was finally over, and the process begun when Hitler and the Nazis achieved power some twelve years earlier had also run its course. However, very many members of the general staff had not survived to see its end, whether succumbing as battle casualties or as a result of being condemned for their opposition to Hitler and National Socialism, while the once-prestigious and influential organization in which they served had seen its final demise in the punitive and vengeful aftermath of the abortive assassination attempt on 20 July the previous year. Among the senior army officers to die in the Berlin bunker during the final days of the Third Reich were General Wilhelm Burgdorf, one of the two generals who had overseen Rommel's suicide the previous year, and General Hans Krebs, the very last chief of the army general staff, both of whom committed suicide on or soon after 1 May 1945.[244]

15

Truths and Consequences

1935–1945

Contrary to many widely held and commonly accepted views of the 1939–45 conflict, the German general staff of that period was neither the warmongering instigator of German armed aggression nor did it experience the largely unqualified military success that has routinely been ascribed to it.

Indeed, the political and international circumstances of 1930s Germany were very different from those which general staff officers of the imperial era had experienced, and therefore a full restoration of the general staff's pre-1918 power and influence was always an unrealistic and unachievable aspiration for the army general staff that served the Third Reich. When Hitler enabled the transformation of the Truppenamt into the general staff in 1935, in parallel with the several other wide-ranging armed forces measures and expansions announced by him in March that year, General Beck's aim and vision as chief of the general staff was to re-create a general staff in the image of its pre-1918 predecessor. It would have commensurate levels of power and influence not only within the armed forces but as an apolitical counter-balance to any undesirable political or destabilizing influences within Germany, and always with the best interests of the nation at the forefront of its activities. This had long been the traditional role of the general staff and the army that it directed. But such aims ran directly contrary to those of Hitler and the National Socialist regime, which regarded the Wehrmacht merely as one of the several necessary tools by which Nazism would achieve its ideological and strategic destiny.

Despite the intellect of Beck, von Blomberg, von Fritsch and many other senior officers, the army high command and the general staff at best underestimated, and at worst totally misunderstood, the true nature of the revolutionary and reactionary political movement that had been allowed to gain control of Germany by 1933. A less charitable observation might also be that many of these officers had put a misplaced and parochial interpretation of patriotism – together with a desire to rehabilitate and restore the army and the officer corps to their former prestigious position in Germany – before the wider democratic best interests of the state itself. In any event, until 1918 the army had enjoyed the patronage of a succession of hereditary heads of state carefully schooled in the traditions and command of the army. These kings and kaisers provided a clear leadership and loyalty focus entirely separate from that of elected government leaders such as prime ministers or chancellors. Consequently, the subordination of the army to the whims and objectives of Hitler – an elected politician and former army corporal – after 1935 was a totally new and increasingly difficult and unsettling experience for many of the more traditional German army officers, especially those already holding senior rank and in positions of significant authority.

In fact, if viewed dispassionately and irrespective of any distaste the general staff and the officer corps might have had for the Nazi regime, or of their reservations concerning the strategic developments prior to 1939 and Hitler's subsequent conduct of the war itself, the general staff probably could have done much more to influence directly Germany's part in the war that Hitler had inflicted upon the world. That it did not (or was unable to) demonstrated the perverse consequences of von Seeckt's de-politicization policy for the Reichswehr in the 1920s and its continuance into the 1930s. Although ostensibly uninvolved in politics, the Reichswehr was in practice much involved in the often distasteful internal politics of the nation in the mid-1930s, wherever it saw an advantage to be gained or a position to be defended in its own interests. The Reichswehr's generally enthusiastic acceptance of the Nazis gaining power in 1933, its barely passive support for the suppression of the SA by the SS in 1934, and its adoption of the personal oath of loyalty to Hitler the same year were some of the more obvious instances of this. Accordingly, although well-intended, von Seeckt's policy distanced the army from many of the political realities of the time, especially those bearing upon strategic matters, while also stifling a realistic awareness and understanding of the international and domestic influences affecting Germany. Eventually, this actually resulted in a sort of narrow, self-centred, almost exclusively German-centric, political introspection within the army and among those who opposed Hitler, which served the German resistance groups particularly badly in matters such as their expectations of the likely responses of the Western Allies to their approaches once the war had started. This situation also provided a convenient excuse for army commanders at all levels frequently to overlook or distance themselves from the excesses carried out in the name of National Socialist ideology, such as the wholesale killings of Jews, Red Army commissars, gypsies and others by the SS-Einsatzgruppen on the Eastern Front.

No doubt Hitler found the army's wider political isolation and generally passive acquiescence helpful, with a potential obstacle to his ambitions effectively allayed, as neither the 'old army' officer corps nor the general staff were ever able to gain his trust or confidence in the years prior to 1944. Then, that year, the assassination attempt against Hitler confirmed all his suspicions, destroyed the last vestiges of general staff authority and finally enabled the virtually total domination by Himmler and the SS of the German nation and many aspects of the army itself. Indeed, however well-intentioned the resistance movement against Hitler, which culminated in the 20 July 1944 bomb attack, the combination of sheer bad luck, misjudgement and ineptitude that attended the several assassinations planned and attempted by army officers over a number of years hardly demonstrated the German general staff officer's legendary reputation for consummate professionalism and efficient planning! At the same time, the mental turmoil, uncertainty and crises of conscience displayed by many officers over their perception of an insoluble clash of loyalty, duty and honour to Germany, to Hitler, and to the army – aggravated considerably by the terms and significance of the 1934 soldier's oath of loyalty to the Führer – distracted and muddied what should have been the relatively straightforward matter of neutralizing or killing Hitler. Indeed, a number of plans for the army to remove Hitler were discussed and developed prior to 1939; such ideas became increasingly difficult to carry through once the war began. On the one hand, the power of Himmler's Gestapo and the SS grew ever greater, while on the other the very idea of removing the head of state once the nation was at war was anathema to many of those who had actively opposed Hitler in the pre-war years. In essence, Hitler's position as the embodiment of the German state, its Führer and supreme commander eventually left those opposing him with few if any alternatives other than to assassinate him.

It is noteworthy that Hitler chose to allow such clear opposition and dissent to exist within the army officer corps and the general staff for so long. This was particularly so in 1938 during the Czech crisis and its aftermath – when an army and general staff-led coup d'état was so very nearly brought to fruition. In the pre-war years, and indeed to late 1941, Hitler's lack of any decisive action to crush this opposition may be explained by the high level of popularity and support that the Führer enjoyed throughout Germany. This widespread acclamation only diminished briefly when his policy towards Czechoslovakia appeared to invite a war in Europe for which the army was still unprepared. In these circumstances, the dissenting views of numbers of army officers might reasonably be dismissed as being of little consequence – words rather than actions – and were in any case more easily monitored by the Gestapo and the SS where they were expressed fairly openly. However, Hitler's inaction in this matter also provided evidence of the continued importance of the general staff to manage and direct the army to achieve his strategic objectives. While Himmler and other Nazi leaders and pro-Nazi generals with more personal ambitions and agendas would quite happily have seen the army's general staff system dispensed with altogether, Hitler (quite correctly) understood that even with the various constraints imposed upon it by the Nazi regime, the general staff was still an indispensable part of the forces upon which he now relied. When the wholesale cull of the general staff and senior army officers took place in the aftermath of the July bomb plot, the war was already lost and its strategic impact upon the armed forces was therefore largely academic. However, such action in the late 1930s or indeed during the 'Blitzkrieg years' of 1939–41 would have severely prejudiced what was at that stage a series of very successful campaigns. Indeed, these campaigns showed that the army had trained too few general staff officers during the rearmament process, and once the anticipated short war became one of attrition the consequences of this original shortage of suitably qualified staff officers became more marked as the war proceeded. The Wehrmacht's early victories also raised the profile and public awareness of the army and various commanders to such an extent that it would in any case have been much more difficult at that stage for Hitler to justify the removal of large numbers of senior officers and successful battlefield commanders.

It may be argued that the general staff relied too much upon the continuance of its traditional role and its indispensability and therefore failed to adapt to the particular environment in which it was required to operate from 1935. This failure to adapt was also an important factor in the ultimate failure of the military resistance movement, which was widely regarded both beyond and also within parts of the army as representative of just a small group of privileged, intellectual and generally aristocratic officers. The lack of involvement of ordinary soldiers in the military resistance movement, and the overwhelmingly hostile attitude of most of the German civilian population to those who opposed Hitler, showed very clearly the real weakness of a movement that certainly did not enjoy popular support. While this might possibly have been won prior to 1939, it was probably always unachievable thereafter.

Once the war began, any officer in the resistance faced the dilemma of being obliged to carry out his professional duties to the best of his ability while simultaneously working to undermine and overthrow the legally established leadership of the nation that he served. General staff officers and the more senior army officers – particularly those who had served in the 1914–18 conflict and in the Reichswehr – were imbued with the German army's long-standing traditions of duty and obedience, so that for men such as von Stauffenberg and his co-conspirators it was unthinkable that the orders issued from the Bendlerblock on 20 July would not be carried out by subordinate commanders without question. Such flawed assumptions, the social and intellectual disconnection between these officers and the majority of the army and the civilian population, and the instinctive aversion of army officers to any sort of revolt or violent attack against the state – especially in wartime, when such action could not unreasonably be construed as treasonable – meant that the military resistance movement was probably doomed to failure almost from the outset, and certainly once the 1938 opportunity to launch a coup had passed. In the meantime, as the civilian resistance was necessarily dependent upon the military resistance, its whole concept of opposition to

Hitler was generally ill-judged, largely impracticable and therefore probably also a lost cause from its own beginning. However, in the years after 1945, as the story of the German resistance to Hitler gradually became known and its members properly acknowledged, the fact that this movement had existed at all undoubtedly provided a welcome opportunity for international recognition that – contrary to Allied propaganda during the war years – not every German had blindly followed the National Socialist path.

At the same time, in Western democracies such as the United Kingdom and the United States, the very idea that senior members of the military high command of a long-established and apparently civilized Western European nation could have actively conspired against its legally constituted government for almost a decade – including several attempts to assassinate its duly elected head of state – could barely be comprehended either during the war (as indicated by the rejection by London and Paris of the resistance's early overtures to the Western Allies) or in its immediate aftermath. In order to understand this in the context of the 1940s, the activities of the military members of the German resistance might possibly be equated with a hypothetical conspiracy by the then British imperial general staff to usurp British Prime Minister Winston Churchill and his war cabinet in order to secure a peace settlement with Germany; or with a hypothetical coup in which the US joint chiefs of staff in America might have plotted to overthrow US President Roosevelt and replace the US legislature with a new governing body that owed its primary allegiance to the US military, in order for the United States to prosecute the war against Japan rather than against Germany. Viewed in this way, the apparent inability of the Allies to relate to and capitalize upon the actions of Beck, Halder, von Brauchitsch, von Stauffenberg and many others between 1935 and 1944 becomes somewhat easier to comprehend.[245]

Viewed objectively, if the general staff had perhaps used less time and energy criticizing and opposing Hitler's strategic aims and objectives and actively played a broader political game in Hitler's Germany by using every means possible to gain the Führer's confidence and to diminish the authority of the OKW and SS in favour of the OKH and the army, the general staff might possibly have enjoyed a somewhat happier and more productive war. That it did not follow such a course (albeit that this would have been at odds with its traditional character and military culture) was undoubtedly fortunate for Germany's enemies, while at the same time it detracted from what might have been a greater strategic success for Germany during the war. Similarly, by fully embracing Hitler's war plans and accepting that the conflict might well develop into a war of attrition rather than being the short war for which the German general staff always strived and planned, some of the significant failings that contributed to Germany's defeat might have been avoided or alleviated. Of particular note among these were logistical shortfalls and the reliance as a matter of policy upon captured resources ranging from tanks, weapons and transport to oil, iron ore and other strategic raw materials. The army's inadequate preparation for the winter campaign in Russia in 1941 and the widespread use of horses and mules within what purported to be a modern, highly mobile army throughout the war provided two very obvious indicators of general staff planning failings at the operational level. Similarly, operational intelligence was often poorly managed, contrasting badly with the handling of this staff function in the old Prussian army and the German imperial army. Admittedly, the general staff was bounced into a war some three to four years earlier than it had judged to be feasible in 1935, but its failure to make effective provision for such an eventuality again demonstrated its inability to comprehend and anticipate the true nature of Hitler. Meanwhile, its lack of influence with the Führer meant that any pressure by the general staff to bring German industry fully on to a war footing (always a politically unpopular measure for the Nazi government) in order to support such a possibility was always minimal.

Quite apart from its direct impact upon the future of the army general staff, the failure of all concerned to develop the OKW as a supreme command organization for the Wehrmacht as a whole – as well as for the Waffen-SS – represented an omission and missed opportunity of almost incalculable significance. This failure may readily be explained and understood in the light of Hitler's own agendas, his divide-and-rule policy and his obsessive mistrust of the army general staff and OKH. The Führer's decision to allow the OKW to develop in the relatively powerless – but nevertheless intrusive and obstructive – manner in which it did, and with parallel rather than hierarchical command responsibilities, exemplified his perverse approach to the management of operational matters. Ideally, the OKW should have provided much needed strategic and operational direction, coordination and arbitration for and between all three branches of the Wehrmacht and the Waffen-SS at the highest level. It should also have provided the principal military-economic-civil interface concerned with the production of war matériel and dealing with matters of homeland defence. To fulfil this demanding and wide-ranging role, the OKW would necessarily have been staffed by the very best general staff officers from all of these branches or organizations – army, navy, air force and Waffen-SS – and have been headed by a Wehrmacht chief of staff of the calibre, intellect and professional competence of someone like von Manstein (who in March 1943 Guderian had acknowledged was 'our finest operational brain')[246] – in order to become, in modern military parlance, a truly 'joint' headquarters. At the same time, while probably maintaining a status of 'first among equals' to reflect the actual nature of Germany's war, the OKH could then have become the principal army headquarters alongside the OKL, OKM and SS-Führungshauptamt (SS main operational office), subordinate to the OKW but still retaining direct operational control of all ground operations. As we have seen, officers such as Guderian, Warlimont and others had such a vision for the OKW but were never able to translate it into a reality.

With the creation of the OKW and so much to occupy it internally – in addition to directing army operations in Russia from 1942 – the general staff allowed itself to become ever more inward looking as the war progressed, which mirrored a much wider German mindset that made it disinclined to take proper account of (or to acquire!) effective military allies. Apart from the quite disparate levels of support provided by Italy, Japan, Romania and a few other European military contributors to the Axis campaigns, Germany essentially stood alone and certainly regarded itself as the leader of the lesser Axis nations rather than as a member of a coalition of partners – such as that of the United States, Russia, France and Britain on the Allied side. The total failure of Germany and Japan to carry out the attack on Russia from the west and the east simultaneously, as a properly coordinated joint venture, exemplified the dysfunctional nature of a so-called strategic alliance in which the Japanese also failed to inform Hitler of their intention to strike Pearl Harbor, and Hitler effectively discounted any Japanese involvement in *Barbarossa*. The nearest that Germany had ever come to practising effective coalition warfare was probably the alliance formed by Prussia with Bavaria, Saxony and other German states to fight France in 1870. However, this hardly qualifies as a precedent, being essentially a coalition of Germanic and German-speaking nations, in a grouping that was indisputably dominated by Prussia. Apart from its close relations with Austria-Hungary – albeit that, here again, this ally was always viewed as a lesser comrade-in-arms – between 1914 and 1918 the German experience during World War I also tended to reinforce this criticism.

None of the foregoing should be allowed to diminish the quality of the operational-level work carried out by the general staff between 1939 and 1945, as well as the measures taken to restructure and expand the army prior to 1939, then to ensure its efficient mobilization and deployment, and to continue to train its soldiers thereafter. Much of this work was excellent, in the best traditions of its predecessors, and it achieved some remarkable results. This was particularly so prior to 1942, but there were also a number of successes thereafter, albeit that the strategic balance had by then begun to move irrevocably against Germany. It is undeniable that the German general staff resurrected in 1935 never regained the pre-eminent position, power and wider influence of its imperial predecessor, but realistically it could probably never have done so under a Nazi regime led by a Führer who mistrusted the general staff and the army officer corps throughout his political life, and probably ever since his military service in World War I. Hitler's centralized control, ideological obsessions and direct interference in operational matters undoubtedly contributed to various operational reverses and defeats, and also to the demise of the army's core doctrine of Auftragstaktik. In the case of Auftragstaktik, the diminishing effectiveness of this doctrine in the traditional form long-recognized by the general staff and the Kriegsakademie was in any case becoming irrelevant, as the sheer scale and nature of the World War II air–land battles, together with the extent and capabilities of modern military communications, progressively rendered that doctrine inappropriate once the war began – and Generaloberst Franz Halder had already recognized this in

January 1942. Arguably, Hitler's actions stifled initiative and discouraged the delegation of operational responsibility rather than being the main or sole cause of the demise of Auftragstaktik in World War II. Irrespective of the Führer's part in this matter, the concept of Auftragstaktik that was first a principle, then developed into a doctrine, had already reverted to the status of principle again during the early years of the 1939–45 conflict.

Many army officers had initially viewed Hitler merely as a useful means to an end, then as an inconvenient militarily unqualified purveyor of ill-judged and risky strategic plans who needed to be vigorously opposed, and finally as an ideologically obsessed and unbalanced leader whose continued existence so threatened Germany as to merit his assassination. Despite its eventual failure, the very direct involvement of the general staff of the Third Reich era in the opposition to Hitler also set it apart from any of its predecessors. Arguably, therefore, the later fortunes and ultimate fate of the general staff that served the forces of the Third Reich were set in train on the day that the Versailles treaty first disbanded the organization in 1919, subsequently lying more or less dormant and maintaining a low profile through the days of the Reichswehr and the Truppenamt, until the German general staff rose again like a phoenix in 1935, only to decline and eventually expire a decade later in the aftermath of the July plot in 1944 and the 'Götterdämmerung' of Germany's catastrophic military defeat in 1945. At the meeting of the 'Big Three' Allied leaders at Potsdam in July and early August that year, the victorious Allies once again sought finally to obliterate the German general staff, along with the whole military and paramilitary infrastructure of Nazi Germany, when they agreed that:

> all German land, naval and air forces, the SS, SA, SD and Gestapo with all their organizations, staffs and institutions, including the General Staff, the Officers' Corps, Reserve Corps, military schools, war veterans' organizations and all other military and quasi-military organizations, together with all clubs and associations which serve to keep alive the military tradition in Germany, shall be completely and finally abolished in such manner as permanently to prevent the revival or reorganization of German militarism and Nazism.[247]

However, having acquiesced to, and to varying degrees participated in, enabling the rise of Hitler in the 1930s, then playing a key part in the war that he inflicted upon the world from 1939, the general staff and the Wehrmacht could hardly have expected to evade the fate of the rest of the apparatus of aggression and oppression that characterized the Third Reich.

Perhaps the greatest irony of this 'twilight of the gods' is that Hitler – a man who ultimately relied so much upon assets such as new tanks, innovative Blitzkrieg tactics and the much-vaunted V-weapons in his quest to dominate Europe – deliberately denied himself the proper use and significant potential and capability of a tried and tested human asset that might possibly have enabled a military victory for Germany. At the very least, it could have managed, mitigated and modified the consequences of defeat, as well as limiting the worst excesses of the ideologically-driven Nazi state. That increasingly denigrated, ignored and finally alienated, officially discredited and persecuted asset was the German general staff, which, against all the odds and severe constraints and crises of conscience, still attempted to carry out its duty to serve the Fatherland to the best of its ability throughout the historical aberration that was Hitler's Third Reich.[248] Conceivably, a general staff with the sort of authority and influence it had enjoyed in much earlier times might even have forestalled or limited the extent of Germany's pre-war territorial acquisitions, with the possible exception of the Austrian Anschluß and of regaining some of the German territory lost at Versailles in 1919. Had it been in a position to fulfil this role, the general staff might have proved instrumental in preventing the onset of a world war in 1939 and the consequent destruction of Germany by 1945. On the other hand, however, it might be argued that if it had been able to fulfil its traditional duties unconstrained by Hitler's interference – so often driven by ideological and political agendas rather than strategic and operational logic – the general staff would at the very least have prolonged the war, while possibly bringing the conflict to a somewhat different conclusion.[249] Consequently, for the Allies and much of the wider world, it was perhaps fortuitous that from 1939 to 1945 Hitler deliberately chose to deny the German general staff the opportunity to do what it did best.

Acknowledgements

My thanks are due to all those who permitted me to quote passages from their own works. In some cases a source or copyright holder could not be contacted, despite every reasonable effort to do so, but all such material is, of course, fully credited where used, and in the bibliography where appropriate. I have once again included several quotations from George Forty's excellent study of the German infantryman 1939–45, and I am most grateful to him for permission to do so. In several areas, this book draws upon some of the wider but necessarily unused research for *Hitler's Army, 1939–1945* (Conway, Anova Books, 2009), and I must therefore acknowledge once again the assistance of the Bundeswehr Militär-historisches Museum at Dresden and the Deutsches Historisches Museum in Berlin, as well as that of the Gedenkstätte Deutscher Widerstand in Berlin. Also in Germany, I am yet again indebted to my friend and former professional colleague Oberstleutnant Peter Hellerling, recently retired from the German Bundeswehr. His assistance in checking the glossary, advising on German language usage and terminology, and providing a point of contact in Germany, were indispensable. He also established an absolutely essential liaison with the German Bundesarchiv at Freiburg, which ultimately enabled the selection and acquisition of most of the Bundesarchiv photos used in this book. In the United Kingdom, at Tiverton, this work has benefited from access to the formidable range of contemporary and near-contemporary military history and political works generously made available to me by Jeremy Whitehorn at Heartland Old Books; as well as from the opportunity kindly afforded to me by Carolyn Channing to draw upon source material in Michael Channing's extensive military history book collection. Keith Luxton of Twyford Print once again provided sterling support for a whole range of print, photocopying and graphics work requirements during the development and reproduction of various aspects of the work. As ever, I am most grateful to David Green, Terry Hughes and my wife Prue for carrying out the unenviable task of proofreading the early drafts; the final work has benefited enormously from their informed comments, suggested revisions and corrections. I was delighted that this project allowed me to resume my association with David Gibbons and Tony Evans of DAG Publications in London. It is always a pleasure to work with two such consummate professionals in the matter of processing a book through to publication, and whose own enthusiasm for military history matches my own. However, I am particularly indebted to David Gibbons for his often inspired and invariably constructive editing of the final manuscript. Any errors, misinterpretations, or misplaced assertions that might still exist in the work are therefore mine alone. Finally, I must once again record my appreciation of the unfailing support, enthusiasm and friendship of my publisher, John Lee, and the team at Anova Books in London.

Notes

1   Melvin, Mungo, *Manstein: Hitler's Greatest General*, p. 49.

2   'Wolf Redoubt' or 'Wolf Strongpoint', where 'Schanze' means 'redoubt', 'bastion', 'fortification' or 'entrenchment' when applied in a military context, although most US and English accounts interpret 'Wolfschanze' as 'Wolf's Lair', the name given to Hitler's forward headquarters in East Prussia 1941–4 (also shown as 'Wolfsschanze' in some sources).

3   Schlieffen, *Die Taktisch-Strategischen Aufgaben* (1901), p. 84.

4   Due to the outbreak of war in 1914, the course of 1913 was curtailed, with the officers subsequently continuing to learn their trade as general staff officers while actually occupying staff positions in headquarters as well as in various combat units.

5   Arguably, the 'development' of Auftragstaktik might more accurately be described as 'refinement', as examples of its existence and practice may readily be found in Prussian army campaigns as early as those conducted by Frederick the Great.

6   In the early 1980s, on the direction of Lieutenant General (later Field Marshal) Sir Nigel Bagnall, the 1st British Corps in West Germany also embraced Auftragstaktik, based mainly upon studies of the German campaign in Russia 1941–4. The understanding, assimilation and practical adoption of Auftragstaktik both in 1st British Corps and later in the wider British army was not an easy process and took many years before it achieved widespread recognition and a qualified acceptance. In a British army that had long practised delegation of responsibility and applauded initiative, Auftragstaktik was widely viewed as a gimmick of doubtful practical relevance, which served to complicate rather than improve the command function. The concept was also studied and adopted in various forms by parts of the US Army during the Cold War period, although here also its practicalities, application and relevance were widely misunderstood and misrepresented. Accordingly, any effective application of Auftragstaktik in the modern age remained problematical, while an almost obsessive desire to teach and apply the principle – often cited as a 'force multiplier' in a period when defence budgets were particularly vulnerable – at the lower levels of tactical command from the mid-1980s, demonstrated a fundamental misunderstanding of the true place and context of Auftragstaktik in the wider history and business of war-fighting. See also Citino, pp. 302–3 and 310–11.

7   Such ploys were adopted during Operation *Wacht am Rhein* in the Ardennes offensive of December 1944: German soldiers who were captured in the Allied rear areas wearing US Army uniforms and using captured US Army vehicles were summarily executed by the US military authorities.

8   This view was again in evidence in the German attitude to, and treatment of, partisans and resistance groups in Russia and the occupied territories during 1939–45. However, by that stage these exclusively military guides to conduct had become increasingly conflated with Nazi political ideology concerned with the elimination of Jews, gipsies and other specified groups by the SS and some units of the Wehrmacht.

9   The 'stab in the back' phrase was allegedly adopted for the first time by Ludendorff during a meeting with a senior British officer, Sir Neill Malcolm, in Berlin in late 1918. Ludendorff had accused the German government and people of having abandoned and betrayed the army, at which point Malcolm asked Ludendorff: 'Are you endeavouring to tell

me, general, that you were stabbed in the back?' Apparently then Ludendorff replied, 'That's it! They gave me a stab in the back – a stab in the back!' Subsequently, von Hindenburg, Ludendorff and the high command actively promoted this as a concept to excuse or explain the army's final defeat on the Western Front in 1918.

10   Quoted by Melvin, p. 39.

11   The republic was so named following the government's relocation from Berlin to the small Thuringian town of Weimar in February 1919, by which time the deteriorating security situation in the capital had made its continued presence there untenable.

12   Rosinski, Herbert, *The German Army*, p. 177.

13   Rosinski, p. 180.

14   Görlitz, Walter, *The German General Staff: Its History and Structure 1657–1945*, p. 227.

15   Rosinski, pp. 185–6.

16   Nevertheless, following the resurrection of the general staff in 1935, the Army List of 1938 showed that of 187 general staff officers in post, no fewer than 50 were titled (e.g., 'von', 'Graf von', 'Freiherr von', 'Baron von', etc.). However, in 1938 the percentage of titled officers in the wider army was just ten per cent. See Görlitz, p. 293.

17   Quoted in Kurowski, Franz, *Infantry Aces: The German Combat Soldier in Combat in WW II*, p. 485.

18   Quoted by Melvin, p. 47.

19   In 1922, Berlin and Moscow signed a secret military agreement in parallel with the Rapallo agreement, by which Germany agreed to train the Red Army and to pay an annual amount to the Soviets, in return for which the Soviet Union put an extensive range of military and industrial facilities at the disposal of the Reichswehr for it to develop and train with those weapons prohibited by Versailles. This arrangement was a defining moment in the development of the Reichswehr, and it was well complemented by armaments production and training facilities that had already been made available to Germany by Spain and Sweden. It also provided numbers of senior German officers and staff officers the opportunity to travel secretly to the training areas in Russia to view projects and training in progress, as well as to observe Red Army manoeuvres. Both Soviet Russia and Germany still regarded the main Western Allies of 1914–1918 – France, Britain and the United States – as unfriendly and potentially hostile powers. These perceptions were based upon Versailles in Germany's case, while Soviet antipathy towards the former Western powers stemmed from the counter-revolutionary interventionist expeditions they had launched into Russia from 1917.

20   Görlitz, p. 227.

21   In 1925, von Hindenburg became president of Germany, and a period of relative stability ensued within Germany during the next few years. With much of his work accomplished, von Seeckt's power and influence declined in the new era of political rather than military activity. In late 1926 the minister of war, Gessler, forced his resignation after he allowed the Crown Prince of Prussia's son – a member of the politically unacceptable Hohenzollern royal family – to take part in military manoeuvres as a temporary officer. General Hans von Seeckt, architect and principal creator of the Reichswehr, died in 1936, having spent much of the ten years of his retirement actively involved in politics and in writing his memoirs, as well as for a short time as a military adviser to Chiang Kai-Shek.

22   Nevertheless, there were numerous instances of friction between the Reichswehr and the SA. In his biography of Generalfeldmarschall von Manstein, Melvin mentions (p. 63) a violent encounter between SA men and soldiers of the then Major Erich von Manstein's Jäger battalion of the 4th Infantry Regiment at Kolberg, when von Manstein observed with some satisfaction that 'the SA men and not [my] light infantrymen took a beating.'

23   In the spring of 1935 Hitler effectively terminated the Soviet-German military cooperation that had been agreed at Rapallo in 1922 and which had so benefited the Reichswehr during the following decade.

24   Anti-Semitism was by no means unique to Germany during the 1930s – such prejudice and anti-Jewish sentiments were also evident in very many other countries at that time.

25   The consequences of the collapse of the Wall Street Stock Exchange in October 1929 (the 'Wall Street Crash') were severe throughout Europe, but in Germany the event proved to be absolutely catastrophic. By the summer of 1931 the extent of this economic disaster was evident throughout the country, as business confidence collapsed and foreign investment fell away. The country's once-booming manufacturing industry swiftly disintegrated while trade and overseas markets stagnated and then crumbled, which in turn produced mass unemployment. Banks foreclosed, there was rampant inflation, and the nation's financial system was in turmoil.

26   From 17 February 1934 the black-white-red shield helmet decal was also taken into use, while instructions for the wearing of the spread-eagle and swastika national emblem on the uniform jacket were issued on 30 October 1935, although the national insignia had already been widely taken into use from early 1934. Uniform regulation references for these changes are quoted in Davis, p. 10, and Hormann (volume II), p. 23. Keith Simpson also states (p. 123) that, 'in February 1934 … Blomberg ordered that the Nazi Party's emblem … was to be worn on the uniforms of all members of the armed forces'.

27   Quoted by Le Tissier, *Berlin Then and Now*, p. 54.

28   Goebbels designated Tuesday 21 March the 'Day of the National Rising', also known as the 'Day of Potsdam', because, in addition to the formal events in Potsdam, on that day the state opening of the new Reichstag took place in Berlin – marking the true birth of the Third Reich. This date was not chosen by chance: 21 March 1871 was the day on which the inaugural Reichstag of the German Second Reich had been opened by Chancellor Otto von Bismarck after the Franco-Prussian War. In the meantime, the selection of Potsdam by Goebbels and

Hitler as the location for these ceremonies took full account of that town's historical and Prussian military symbolism and thus its propaganda value. It also reflected Hitler's growing belief that he was a leader in the same mould as Frederick the Great (Potsdam having been the residence of the Prussian kings), and he frequently sought to identify historical parallels between himself and that particular eighteenth-century ruler during his time in power.

29   Görlitz, p. 288.

30   Fest, Joachim, *Plotting Hitler's Death: The German Resistance to Hitler, 1933–1945*, p. 40.

31   Fest, p. 38 (both von Blomberg's own first-hand statement and the supplementary remark).

32   The Waffen-SS should not be confused with the Allgemeine SS, the 'general SS', which was the over-arching organization of the SS and included full-time, part-time and honorary members to carry out a multiplicity of political, security, concentration camp guarding, paramilitary and other tasks.

33   The German text of the Soldier's Oath introduced from 2 August 1934 is as follows: 'Ich Schwöre bei Gott diesen heiligen Eid, dass ich dem Führer des Deutschen Reiches und Volkes ADOLF HITLER, dem Obersten Befehlshaber der Wehrmacht, unbedingten Gehorsam leisten und als tapferer Soldat bereit Sein will, jederzeit für diesen Eid mein Leben einzusetzen.'

34   Roberts, Andrew, *The Storm of War: A New History of the Second World War*, p. 585.

35   The rivalry between such well-known officers as Guderian and von Kluge, Zeitzler and von Manstein was quite open, as was the way in which Jodl and (especially) Keitel were universally despised by most of the other senior army officers. Of the World War II armies, the Germans hardly had a monopoly on such high-level discord, but in their case it did diminish the ability of the high command to present its reservations and opinions to Hitler with a united voice.

36   Görlitz indicates (p. 313) that Hitler had already been made aware of this

allegation in 1935 and had ordered the 'evidence' destroyed. However, Himmler had chosen to retain the documents on file for future use if and as necessary.

37   At the von Fritsch trial it was alleged that, in addition to Schmidt having been coerced into perjuring himself, the Gestapo had intended to murder von Fritsch beforehand, making his death appear to be suicide, this intention only being frustrated by the provision to von Fritsch of a bodyguard of young officers, together with the presence of a company of infantry close at hand during his formal interview by the Gestapo. Much of the defence evidence was provided by Admiral Canaris, who was head of the Abwehr and also opposed to Hitler. See Görlitz, pp. 319 and 324.

38   Fest p. 61.

39   Von Blomberg and Eva Gruhn left Germany and went into voluntary exile in Capri, taking no further part in German military affairs. However, his previous work to enable Hitler's military aspirations was recalled by the Allies at the end of the war, and he died in a US military prison at Nuremberg on 4 March 1946. Meanwhile, von Fritsch was acquitted of any wrongdoing on 18 March (this event being largely overshadowed by the Austrian Anschluß with which his acquittal coincided) and publicly rehabilitated on 11 August 1938. He remained in Germany, fulfilling various military duties. In August 1939 he assumed command of Artillery Regiment No. 12 in East Prussia immediately prior to the Polish campaign. Then, during the third week of the invasion of Poland, he was killed by Polish machine-gun fire in open ground on the outskirts of Warsaw on 22 September 1939. Von Brauchitsch (who replaced von Fritsch as army commander-in-chief) had indicated that he would take up von Fritsch's case once the latter had been acquitted, but in the event he failed to do this – or more likely found that, despite his earlier good intentions, he was unable to do so against the pressure exerted by the Nazi leadership.

40   Simpson, William, *Hitler and Germany: Documents and Commentary*, p. 136.

41   Quoted by Brett-Smith, p. 43. Extract from a directive dealing with officer training, issued on 18 December 1938.

42   The post of war minister effectively disappeared with von Blomberg's departure, being subsumed into the OKW and by Hitler himself as Führer and supreme commander. In fact, Göring had aspired to replace von Blomberg, and his involvement in von Blomberg's dismissal was therefore by no means lacking in self interest. However, Hitler never intended to give Göring such power over the whole armed forces, and his appointment as Reichsmarschall by Hitler was largely as compensation for denying his long-standing National Socialist colleague and supporter what would have been a much more powerful and substantive position within the government.

43   The identifying numbers of Wehrkreise and Wehrbezirke were usually designated by Roman numerals, as were army corps, although this practice was not mandatory.

44   A suitably modified and updated version of *Die Truppenführung* is still used in the modern German armed forces.

45   In 1935, the Wehrmachtsamt department headed by Jodl was in effect an 'armed forces operations staff'. It also assumed control of the national war industries staff and the secret service (which at that time was headed by Admiral Canaris). On 1 October 1935, Generalleutnant Walther von Reichenau was succeeded as head of the Wehrmachtsamt by Generalmajor (later Generalfeldmarschall) Wilhelm Keitel, who, together with Jodl, was one of the senior army officers who remained closest to Hitler throughout the war years.

46   Melvin states (p. 74) that the Truppenamt expanded from five to thirteen branches in 1935, rather than the four to twelve indicated in other sources. Although this one additional staff branch is not identified, it could well be the Central Branch (which was not allocated a branch number) of the army general staff, which was responsible for the selection, training, posting and promotion of all general staff corps officers until March 1943, when this function passed to Branch P3 of the Army Personnel Office.

47   Görlitz, p. 294.

48   Görlitz, p. 293.
49   Guderian, General Heinz (Tr. Constantine Fitzgibbon), *Panzer Leader*, p. 30.
50   The creation of an army airborne capability followed the successful formation of a parachute infantry battalion from the Landespolizeigruppe 'General Göring' in January 1936. This battalion had been part of the Luftwaffe from 1 October 1935, and overall command of all of the German parachute forces was transferred to the Luftwaffe in January 1938, when any army parachute units were also subsumed into it. The Luftwaffe had already gained control of the army's air defence artillery units in 1935. The decision to transfer these units from the army to the Luftwaffe was political rather than operational and reflected Göring's considerable influence with Hitler at that time, rather than military commonsense – both the airborne forces and the anti aircraft artillery should logically have been part of the German ground forces rather than the air force.
51   See Stone, *Hitler's Army, 1939–1945: The Men, Machines and Organisation*, pp. 53–63 and 146–52. Given the fundamental divergence of ideology between Bolshevist Russia and what was then republican Germany, the Rapallo agreement signed between Russia and Germany in 1922 was in many ways an unlikely alliance – as well as ironic, in light of the later events of June 1941 with Operation *Barbarossa*. However, in the post Versailles era both Russia and Germany needed that which only the other could provide.
52   US War Department, *Handbook on German Military Forces*, TM-E 30-451, p. 1-2.
53   This understanding was later formally reinforced by the so-called 'Pact of Steel' in May 1939. Japan's disinclination to sign that pact weakened its wider international impact, in spite of the fact that Japan had signed the Anti-Comintern Pact with Italy and Germany in November 1936. Later the Tripartite Pact of 27 September 1940 would fully establish the Rome-Berlin-Tokyo Axis, with Hungary, Romania and Slovakia joining it in November 1940, Bulgaria in March 1941 and Croatia on 15 June 1941.
54   Oberst Hossbach was Hitler's adjutant (Wehrmachtadjutant) and head of the central department of the OKW, with the key task of acting as the army's personal representative to Hitler. Hossbach's notes made on 5 November 1937 were included with the evidence considered at the post-war trials conducted by the Allies at Nuremberg.
55   Görlitz, p. 328.
56   Görlitz states that the meeting took place at von Brauchitsch's home; others indicate that it was at the OKH offices at the Bendlerstraße.
57   Görlitz, p. 329.
58   27 August 1938 is quoted as the date of Halder's actual appointment as chief of the general staff in some sources.
59   During the summer of 1938, Oberstleutnant Hans Oster (the general staff officer who had unsuccessfully lobbied senior officers on behalf of von Fritsch at the time of his contrived dismissal earlier that year) became directly involved with a succession of secret overtures to London and Paris by several prominent civilian emissaries of those who opposed Hitler and hoped to prevent another war with Britain and France. They sought to persuade the British and French to issue clear statements of their intent to go to war in support of the Czechs. However, all these diplomatic approaches failed. This was due primarily to the fundamental misunderstanding by the French and British authorities (but especially by British Prime Minister Neville Chamberlain) of the true nature of Hitler and the danger he posed. Equally, the German envoys were poorly prepared and inadequately briefed, in that they failed to understand that the deliberately confrontational approach they were advocating conflicted directly with the Anglo-French desire to avoid war at all costs; a desire exemplified by the British government's formal adoption of a policy of appeasement.
60   Aspects of the creation, organization, activities and scope of the wider opposition groups and resistance

movement in Germany from 1933 to 1944 are provided in Chapter 12, together with the development of its links with the general staff from 1943, which culminated in the July plot of 1944.

61   Quoted by Fest, p. 81 (from Rainer Hildebrand, *Wir Sind die Letzten* (Neuwied und Bern 1949), p. 92).

62   Von Witzleben, Beck and Halder were agreeable to Hitler being detained and dealt with by due legal process, but not to his assassination. In late September a hard-core faction of younger officers, students and others, led by Hauptmann Friedrich Wilhelm Heinz, persuaded Oster that it would be too risky placing Hitler on trial in light of his popularity following the Austrian Anschluß and that he should therefore be shot while resisting arrest (or during a similarly contrived incident) at the Reich Chancellery. Apparently, Beck subsequently heard about this proposed modification of the coup plan and convinced Oster that Hitler's summary execution or murder would besmirch and entirely discredit the coup. It remains unclear whether those carrying out the arrest would have followed the original plan or chosen to adopt Heinz's more extreme solution. See also Fest, pp. 88–92.

63   Görlitz, pp. 334–5.

64   Görlitz, p. 338.

65   Görlitz, p. 338.

66   Görlitz, p. 338.

67   Sources vary on the extent of von Brauchitsch's commitment to, involvement in and knowledge of the 'Halder plot'. Certainly Halder discussed the matter with him, and in light of his own misgivings with regard to Hitler it is inconceivable that he was unaware of what was going on. However, while he did not oppose Halder's plans and was apparently prepared to acquiesce in them, the sudden change in the diplomatic situation over Czechoslovakia probably provided a most welcome solution to his crisis of loyalty and conscience.

68   Heydrich was later appointed Deputy Reich Protector for Bohemia and Moravia. On 29 May 1942, Czech resistance fighters ambushed his car on the outskirts of Prague, fatally wounding him. The German reprisals that followed were savage, with some 1,255 Czechs executed and the village of Lidice obliterated, all of its inhabitants being killed or displaced.

69   Quoted by Dennis Whitehead in *The Gleiwitz Incident* (*After the Battle* No. 142, 2008), p. 3).

70   Görlitz, p. 350.

71   See Dennis Whitehead, *The Gleiwitz Incident*, pp. 3–23.

72   In 1939 Poland maintained the fifth largest armed forces in the world, its standing army numbered about 300,000, but on mobilization this could be reinforced by about three million reservists. The front-line strength of the forces that directly opposed the German invasion was probably about one million men, with many more sited in depth and deployed in fixed fortification defences. The Polish air force had some 400 aircraft, including fifteen fighter squadrons; however, these were no match for the Luftwaffe. While the Polish army's overall order of battle and organization are fairly clear, sources concerning the total manpower strength of the Polish forces mobilized and actually committed in September 1939 do vary.

73   Görlitz, p. 359.

74   Görlitz, p. 367. Of the several sources consulted, the account of Himmler's decree appears only in Görlitz, where the divisional commander involved is named as 'Lieutenant-General Groppe'.

75   Quoted by Brett-Smith, Richard, *Hitler's Generals*, p. 209: conversation between von Stülpnagel and General Geyr von Schweppenburg.

76   Inevitably, the total numbers of divisions and panzer divisions allocated to the armies and to the OKH operational reserve shown in various drafts of the general staff plan for *Fall Gelb* during October 1939 differed, being subject to much modification during the planning and discussion process triggered by Hitler's *Directive No. 6* in early October. Eventually, the first OKH plan for *Fall Gelb*, produced on 19 October, showed Army Group A with 27 divisions, Army Group B with 37, Army Group C with 25, and an OKH reserve of 9 divisions. Overall, 10 panzer divisions were available for the offensive as at October 1939, and this relatively small total number was still

unchanged when the final plan was produced in February 1940. In October 1939, Eighteenth Army was shown deployed to the north of Army Group B, with 3 divisions assigned to secure that northern flank. However, the command status of this army (which would be required to launch an attack into the Netherlands, if necessary, in support of the main *Fall Gelb* offensive) remained flexible, being shown variously both as a fourth army subordinate to Army Group B and as a separate army, but with forces detached to carry out the flank security mission.

77 Fest, p. 127.

78 The Elser bombing was thoroughly investigated by the SS and Gestapo. Under interrogation Elser, who held strong socialist and anti-war views, admitted having planned and prepared the assassination attempt over a twelve-month period. He had also been motivated by a desire for personal revenge, as his brother, a communist, had earlier been consigned to a concentration camp by the Nazis. Although Elser in fact acted entirely alone, Himmler and Walter Schellenberg, a senior counter-intelligence officer in the SD, tried to implicate the British secret service in the assassination attempt and did so with some success by linking the bombing with the unrelated entrapment and arrest of two British agents (Captain Payne-Best and Major Stevens) at Venlo the following day. Elser spent most of the war in the Sachsenhausen and then Dachau concentration camps and was executed by the SS in April 1945. The two British agents remained in prison and were eventually liberated by US forces at the end of the war. One unfortunate consequence of the Elser incident was a general British reluctance thereafter to become involved with the activities of the German resistance movement against Hitler. Several accounts of the Elser incident and these related matters exist, including an article by Peter Marriott published in *Military Illustrated* MI/258, November 2009, pp. 40–5. In Max Hasting's *Sunday Times* autumn 2010 review (*Culture* magazine, p. 46) of Keith

Jeffery's book *MI6: The History of the Secret Intelligence Service* (Bloomsbury, 2010), he notes that, 'SIS operations on the Continent never recovered from the kidnapping of its key men in Holland, Stevens and Best, in 1939. The prisoners told Berlin everything they knew.'

79 Rudolf Schmundt was a committed Nazi who managed to retain the trust and confidence of both the army and the Nazi leadership until his death as a result of the severe injuries he sustained in the 20 July 1944 bomb attack against Hitler. Schmundt became an army adjutant to Hitler in 1937, was chief adjutant of the Wehrmacht from 1937 and became the Führer's principal adjutant in January 1938. He was not promoted major general until 1942, when he became head of the army personnel office while also continuing to serve as Hitler's adjutant. Prior to his promotion to Generalmajor, his power and influence had consistently exceeded his actual rank of Major (1937), Oberstleutnant (1938) and Oberst (1939). He was promoted Generalleutnant in 1943 and General der Infanterie in 1944. In addition to enjoying Hitler's confidence, he numbered men such as Göring, Model, Zeitzler, Canaris, von Tresckow and Rommel, together with other Wehrmacht senior officers, among his friends and associates, as well as Waffen-SS commanders such as Dietrich and Hausser.

80 Melvin provides a comprehensive account of the process by which the von Manstein concept for the attack in the west was developed and came to be adopted (pp. 136–55). Based upon the evidence he presents, it may reasonably be concluded that the original operational plan for the Blitzkrieg of 1940 was entirely von Manstein's and that Halder's principal contribution was defending the concept against its critics within the OKH and making it fit for purpose as an operational plan, with account taken of the direction provided by Hitler following the 17 February 1940 meeting in Berlin. However, during an interview in 1967, Halder asserted that his own was the principal part played in developing 'the plan for the French campaign – as it was

executed – [and that it] did not come from [von Manstein]'. (Quoted by Melvin, p. 154).

81   See Görlitz, p. 373. A telephone conversation between the Belgian ambassador to the Vatican and the government in Brussels inferred that the plan had been disclosed by a German source. Meanwhile, Abwehr head Admiral Canaris – always implacably opposed to Hitler – had sent his chief of staff, Oberstleutnant Hans Oster, to give a last warning to the Dutch military attaché in Berlin of German intentions in the west.

82   Eighteenth Army, with responsibility for potentially being required to launch an offensive against the Netherlands, was sometimes also shown as a fourth army of this army group.

83   The term 'Blitzkrieg' was probably first used by a *Time* magazine journalist in late 1939 to describe the German campaign in Poland, subsequently being used extensively by both the German and the Allied forces to describe the all-arms operations and tactics used by the German army during the war. Some sources attribute the first use of the term to Hitler himself.

84   Some of the total numbers of divisions finally deployed for *Fall Gelb* shown in some other sources (such as Macksey, Shepperd and Keith Simpson) vary slightly. For example, Shepperd shows Army Group A with 45 divisions, Army Group B with 29 divisions, and Army Group C with 19 divisions, while Simpson's figures for these army groups are 45½ divisions, 29½ and 17 respectively. However, these minor variations and increases generally reflect the *Fall Gelb* order of battle as at 10 May 1940 rather than the figures shown in the OKH plan as at 24 February 1940, any increases usually being achieved by reducing the original number of reserve divisions in order to reinforce the first echelon forces.

85   Statistical information drawn primarily from John Williams, *France: Summer 1940*, Macdonald & Co. (Publishers) Ltd., London, 1969, pp. 16–17.

86   Quoted by Görlitz, p. 375.

87   Tucker-Jones, Anthony, *Hitler's Great Panzer Heist: Germany's Foreign Armour*

in Action 1939–45, p. 29.

88   Bartov, Omer, *Hitler's Army*, p. 64.

89   See Pallud, Jean Paul, *Blitzkrieg in the West Then and Now*, pp. 354, 428–9, 439–41.

90   Pallud, pp. 476 and 479.

91   Pallud, p. 566.

92   Görlitz, p. 379 and Brett-Smith, p. 175.

93   By August 1940, Hitler's attention – and that of the OKW and OKH – was already becoming increasingly focused on the army's next great enterprise in the east, the defeat of the Soviet Union. Numbers of troops had already been redeployed from France in preparation for this, while that same month Hitler ordered that the army should increase its strength to 180 active divisions. The number of panzer divisions was doubled (to 20), and no less than 205 divisions had been created by June 1941, but the requirement set out for the army in *Directive No. 17*, dated 1 August 1940, was generally achieved only by splitting up and weakening its existing formations. Consequently, the actual increase in capability was negligible and its strategic impact illusory.

94   Quoted in *Mit Den Panzern In Ost Und West*, published in Germany in 1942 and re-published in English (tr. Prof. Alan Bance) as *Blitzkrieg In Their Own Words* by Pen & Sword Books in 2005.

95   Guderian, pp. 459–60.

96   Guderian, p. 460.

97   Guderian, p. 460.

98   This account is concerned primarily with the general staff and therefore only with regular officers. For full details of the selection, training, lifestyle, casualty rates and other matters relating to regular, reserve and specialist officers and officer-status administrative officials, see Stone, *Hitler's Army 1939–1945*, pp. 78–84, 92 and 250–4.

99   Senior officers were regularly in the forward battle areas. Between 1939 and 1942 more than 25 German army generals died in action, while as many as 80 had died in action by May 1945. The campaign in Russia increased the toll of officer casualties dramatically: 1,253 officers died in action between September 1939 and May 1941, but from June 1941 to March 1942 at least 15,000 officers were killed in action, and although there were 12,055

Leutnante (lieutenants) in the army in July 1941, by March 1942 the records showed only 7,276. See Bartov, p. 39.

100 Stoddard (p. 42) states that in June 1940 Göring had proposed a very different course of action against the British: a German occupation of Spain, followed by landings in North Africa and the defeat of all British forces in the Mediterranean. However, such action would have run contrary to Hitler's overall strategy and totally alienated Franco – a man still regarded as a potential Axis ally. Nevertheless, Göring's suggestion did perhaps recognize the Wehrmacht's lack of amphibious warfare experience and capability, together with the Luftwaffe's inability to guarantee air superiority over the English Channel in mid-1940. In any event, Jodl apparently prepared an outline campaign plan to seize Gibraltar, North Africa and the Suez Canal. Although Göring's proposal was quickly rejected and Jodl's work came to naught, it is noteworthy that the suggestion enjoyed the wholehearted support of General Guderian, who urged Hitler to delay concluding an armistice with the French so that his panzer units could strike across the Spanish border and seize Gibraltar. Guderian's support for Göring in June 1940 was later reciprocated by the Reichsmarschall's own support for Guderian, including on the occasion of his appointment as chief of the general staff on 21 July 1944.

101 Wheatley, Ronald, *Operation Sea Lion: German Plans for the Invasion of England 1939–1942*, pp. 35–6. *Führer Directive No. 16* dated 16 July 1940, 'Preparations for a Landing Operation against England'. The need to neutralize Britain (described as 'das englische Mutterland' in the original document) as a base from which future operations could be launched against Germany should be viewed in the context of Hitler's apparent reluctance to precipitate the collapse of the British Empire, or indeed to commit forces that would be required in the east from mid-1941 to a potentially costly invasion and long-term occupation of the British Isles.

102 Kershaw, Ian, *Hitler, 1936–1945: Nemesis*, pp. 303–4.

103 Stoddard, Brooke C., *World in Balance: the Perilous Months of June–October 1940*, p. 79.

104 Had the Luftwaffe high command realized it, the RAF had actually deployed its last reserves to counter the attacks of 15 September. However, the German losses that day were significant, and, in the absence of intelligence to the contrary, the OKW had no reason to believe that subsequent attacks by the Luftwaffe would not suffer the same fate.

105 Quoted by Brett-Smith, p. 25.

106 Quite apart from more obvious practical and strategic considerations, Hitler's reluctance to launch *Seelöwe* has frequently been attributed to his declared pre-war admiration for the British Empire, which implied a consequent reluctance to inflict a major military defeat against it on the British homeland. In 1939 and 1940, Hitler discussed possible terms for a British surrender based upon total control of Europe by Germany, but with Britain retaining control of its existing overseas empire – in effect the creation of an 'Anglo-German Axis'. No doubt such an arrangement would also have involved a strong German representative and security or policing presence on British soil. However, while this highly subjective reason for the Führer's successive postponements of *Seelöwe* might possibly have been a contributory factor for him personally, it is unlikely that it would have prevented him from ordering the operation to go ahead in 1940 if the necessary levels of air and maritime security had been in place. The strategic need for Germany to avoid a war on more than one front was simply so vitally important – as the general staff had pointed out time and again, quoting historical precedent and straightforward military logic. The failure to defeat Britain in 1940 followed by the decision to invade Russia in 1941 was Hitler's greatest strategic misjudgement – one that validated the pre-war warnings of generals such as Beck, and the formal assessments that had been developed by the general staff.

107 In fact, Franco had been strongly advised against joining the Axis or directly

supporting the *Felix* and *Isabella* proposals by Admiral Canaris, head of the Abwehr. Somewhat remarkably, Canaris had actually been dispatched to Madrid (where he had been successfully employed as a German agent during World War I) as a German special envoy to discuss the necessary arrangements for setting these operations in train. However, Canaris was in practice a committed opponent of Hitler and his ambitions; the extent of the admiral's opposition was clearly and seriously underestimated by Hitler in late 1940.

108   Adolf Galland, *The First and the Last* (tr. Mervyn Savill), New York, 1954, quoted by Brett-Smith, p. 60.

109   Accounts of the extent of Freyberg's prior knowledge of *Merkur* vary. The biography by P. Freyberg, *Bernard Freyberg, VC* (London, 1991), suggests that General Freyberg was fully privy to this 'Ultra' intelligence but was ordered to take the line and course of inaction that he did in order to safeguard 'Ultra'. Other accounts suggest that Freyberg was provided with an edited 'Ultra' 'take' that omitted or underplayed the probability of a predominantly airborne assault.

110   Rommel's tactical instincts were almost always correct, including his assessment of the Allied intentions regarding their invasion of Normandy in June 1944 and the need to defeat the landings on the beaches rather than inland. At that time he was neither convinced by the Allied deception plans nor did he accept the OKW's assessment that the invasion could not take place anywhere other than at the Pas de Calais (a judgement that was still based in large part upon the general staff's assessment in 1940 concerning the German options for *Seelöwe*). Unfortunately for the Germans, Rommel's predictions concerning the importance of Normandy and the operational countermeasures he wished implemented in light of these were overruled by Hitler and the OKW in 1944 until the invasion had taken place and it was all too late.

111   Reinforcing units for the DAK later benefited from the experiences of those who had gone before, and Grafenwöhr in northern Bavaria was in due course designated the army's 'hot weather training area' during the summer months.

112   Hitler feared that Stalin was on the verge of supporting Great Britain against Germany. In fact, Churchill had indeed already secretly proposed this course of action to Stalin, but the Soviet ruler had ignored the British overtures (believing them to be a trap orchestrated by Churchill) and had then dutifully informed Hitler about them – which merely fuelled Hitler's existing suspicions! However, these suspicions were later reinforced by Stalin's reluctance to join Germany in the war against Britain when Hitler proposed this in November 1940, despite the Führer's offer to Stalin of a significant part of the British Empire's overseas territories once Britain had been defeated. Stalin also harboured many suspicions about Hitler. While the ever-pragmatic Soviet leader had no thoughts of embarking upon a war against Germany at that stage, he had already anticipated that such a conflict would probably take place not less than two years hence. He also suspected that Hitler's failure to launch the invasion of England in 1940 was indicative of a secret Anglo-German pact against the Soviet Union, with any Russian declaration of war against Britain providing an excuse for Germany to invade Russia immediately, in order to support a country that Stalin at that stage believed could well be a secret ally of Hitler. This view was given added credibility by the bizarre, unauthorized and ill-fated flight to Scotland by Hitler's deputy, Rudolph Hess, in May 1941. In any event, Stalin was convinced that Germany could not attack Russia in the short-term, and certainly not while Britain remained undefeated. In common with many members of the German general staff, he reasoned that a German attack on Russia would involve Germany in a war on two fronts and knew that this was contrary to all military logic in light of Germany's limited resources and inability to fight a widespread and potentially lengthy war of attrition.

113   Halder, *Kriegstagebuch*, II, pp. 32–3, 22 July 1940, quoted by Albert Seaton, *The Russo-German War, 1941–1945*, p. 52

(Arthur Barker, 1971).

114 Given Hitler's obsession with the Soviet Union and his consequent desire to advance the preparations for that operation, this admission provided yet another reason to abandon *Seelöwe*, although it remained (in theory) a live operational option long beyond that point.

115 This assessment resulted in winter clothing sufficient only for one fifth of the force being produced.

116 Quoted by Brett-Smith, p. 27.

117 Quoted by Beevor, *Stalingrad*, p. 15.

118 Differences between the various English translations of the Kommissarerlaß are very minor. The version used here is quoted by Snyder, p. 199 and accords with most English-language versions of this text.

119 When first formed, the 'Brandenburg' army units were trained on an estate near Brandenburg. They consisted of high-quality soldiers equivalent to the British Commandos or US Army Rangers of the time. Often multilingual and very familiar with the theatres and countries in which they were deployed, they operated in German uniform, or in civilian clothes or Allied uniforms (thus risking being shot as spies). Originally under Abwehr control, the Brandenburgers were first used to seize key points in Poland in September 1939. Subsequently, they were expanded into several independent companies (Sonderverband) from October that year. Next, these troops carried out similar tasks in advance of the 1940 Blitzkrieg into Belgium and the Netherlands, where they secured bridges ahead of the German advance. In October 1940 the Brandenburgers were expanded into a regiment-sized unit. During the North Africa campaign, Sonderverband 288 conducted a particularly successful series of sabotage operations and raids, mirroring the activities of the Allies' Long Range Desert Group. Unsurprisingly perhaps, these non-SS special forces attracted the jealousy and hostility of the SS, who feared the success of the Brandenburg units would detract from that of the Waffen-SS special forces (the SS-Jagdverbände, commanded by SS-

Standartenführer Otto Skorzeny).

120 Lucas, James, *German Army Handbook*, p. 98.

121 The precise figures for the forces involved vary between sources; those quoted in the main text reflect a reasonable consensus. Pimlott (pp. 65–7) quotes 600,000 vehicles, 3,580 tanks, 7,184 guns and 1,830 aircraft, and a total 120 divisions; Keith Simpson suggests a total 145 divisions 'in the east' (p. 150), but a number of these were almost certainly not involved in the initial campaign. Bartov (pp. 14–15) quotes 3,600,000 troops, 3,648 tanks and 2,510 supporting aircraft. Some sources also quote an overall manpower figure of 'three million', while others quote 'four million'. Beevor in *Stalingrad* quotes 3,050,000 German troops within the international total of four million. However, the best available information indicates that some three million German soldiers were committed on 22 June 1941, plus up to a million other Axis military, non-army and paramilitary forces.

122 Some sources also show this spelling as 'Wolfsschanze'. However, I have adopted the spelling 'Wolfschanze' as shown on the original documents and maps of the Führerhauptquartier Wolfschanze in the archives of the Gedenkstätte Deutscher Widerstand (the memorial and museum to the German resistance movement during World War II) in Berlin. As noted earlier, although the Wolfschanze is habitually termed 'Wolf's Lair' in English language accounts, the precise meaning of 'Wolfschanze' is 'Wolf Redoubt' or 'Wolf Stronghold', where use of the word 'Schanze' has a specific meaning in a military context.

123 The Mauerwald bunker complex lay on the Rastenburg–Angerburg road about 35 kilometres north-east of the Wolfschanze. Its formal name was 'Oberkommando und Generalstabes des Heeres Mauerwald', and its codename was 'Anna'. About 1,500 personnel worked at this complex of about 200 bunkers and other buildings, including about 40 officers ranking as generals. Mauerwald was vacated in December 1944, when its functions were transferred to 'Maybach'

close to Zossen, to the south-east of Berlin.

124 Without Hitler's knowledge, his deputy, Rudolf Hess, had successfully flown solo to Scotland, where he parachuted safely to the ground and then announced that he wished to speak to the Duke of Hamilton (a former acquaintance). While Hess's actual intentions in May 1941 remain the subject of some debate, it is generally believed that he had hoped to negotiate a peace deal between Britain and Germany in advance of the invasion of Russia, thereby restoring his own waning power and influence within the Nazi government and gaining favour with Hitler as well as securing peace between what he regarded as 'the two principal Aryan nations of Europe'. It has been suggested that he had hoped the Duke of Hamilton would facilitate him making representations to King George VI, leading to Churchill's dismissal, and then to an alliance between Britain and Germany; or at least resulting in British neutrality. However, Hess was immediately interned and remained so for the rest of the war, eventually being arraigned before the Allied International Military Tribunal at Nuremberg in 1946 and then imprisoned at Spandau prison for the rest of his life.

125 Bastable, pp. 17–18.

126 Extract from Generaloberst Halder's diary in August 1941, quoted by Williamson Murray in 'Germany's Fatal Blunders' (article in *Military History*, Volume 26, No. 5, January 2010).

127 Görlitz, p. 397.

128 Guderian, p. 199. See also pp. 200–22 for details of Guderian's discussion with Hitler.

129 Knappe, Siegfried, and Brusaw, Ted, *Soldat: Reflections of a German Soldier, 1936–1949*, p. 201.

130 Knappe and Brusaw, p. 201.

131 Beevor, *Stalingrad*, pp. 16–17.

132 Beevor, *Stalingrad*, p. 16. Hassell was later implicated in the unsuccessful assassination attempt against Hitler on 20 July 1944 and was hanged at Plötzensee prison, Berlin, on 8 September 1944.

133 The decree was issued by Hitler on 7 December and (according to some sources) promulgated by Keitel on 12 December. Keitel justified it at the time by stating: 'Effective and lasting intimidation can only be achieved by capital punishment or by means which leave the population in the dark about the fate of the culprit.' The 'Nacht und Nebel Erlaß' was a telling aspect of the evidence brought against Keitel during his trial at Nuremberg after the war. However, true to the intended concept of the decree, the SD archive files recovered in 1945 included no record of those who had disappeared as a consequence.

134 Görlitz, p. 404.

135 Quoted by Citino, Robert M., *The German Way of War: From the Thirty Years' War to the Third Reich*, p. 305.

136 Quoted by Brett-Smith, p. 31.

137 Brett-Smith, pp. 80-81.

138 However, in the case of von Brauchitsch's removal on 19 December, the line between dismissal, replacement and retirement is very finely drawn. On 4 December, von Brauchitsch confided to Halder his desire to retire as commander-in-chief. No doubt the cumulative effect of the events of 1941 and his always stressful relationship with Hitler, together with the heart attack of 10 November, prompted this statement of intent. However, by that stage Hitler had effectively placed an embargo upon resignations by generals, so dismissal, severe incapacity or death were the only remaining practicable options for von Brauchitsch. Görlitz states (p. 404) that von Brauchitsch submitted a letter of resignation on 7 December, citing his worsening health, but his final removal by Hitler on 19 December was widely presented and viewed as a dismissal rather than as voluntary retirement. If he had not been dismissed in December 1941, it is unlikely that his ill-health would have allowed him to continue as commander-in-chief or indeed to survive the war. Despite his treatment by Hitler and the perceived stigma of his removal, von Brauchitsch remained loyal to the Führer, openly condemning those officers who later conspired against Hitler. During the last three years of the war he lived at the Tři Trubky hunting lodge in the Brdy mountains to the south-west of Prague.

He survived the collapse of Germany in 1945 and, although listed as a war criminal, never came to trial. Generalfeldmarschall Walther von Brauchitsch, the last professional commander-in-chief of the army of the Third Reich, died in Hamburg on 18 October 1948.

139 Halder, Franz, *Hitler as Warlord* (*Hitler als Feldheer*), Putnam, 1950, p. 49, with the final sentence from Görlitz, p. 406. Minor variations of Hitler's comments to Halder exist in various other sources, including 'What was wanted was political awareness and determination' in place of, or in amplification of, the specific phrase relating to the role of the commander-in-chief.

140 In late November, Oberstleutnant Bernhard von Lossberg (the army's representative in the Wehrmachtführungsstab at the OKW, and who had carried out a study of Generalmajor Erich Marcks' plan for *Fall Otto* for the OKW in September 1940) proposed merging the Wehrmacht's three separate general staffs into a single unitary organization, with a view to concentrating, coordinating and applying the best available talent of the army, the Luftwaffe and the Kriegsmarine. However, Jodl rejected this idea, anticipating that it would not find favour with Hitler.

141 Quoted by Citino, pp. 303–4.

142 The Wolfschanze was but one of fourteen static Füherhauptquartiere that were actually completed (a total of about twenty were planned). Of these, ten (including the Wolfschanze and the bunker complexes under the Reich Chancellery in Berlin and at the Berghof at Berchtesgaden) were used by Hitler. These were Fellsennest at Bad Munstereifel; Adlerhorst at Bad Nauheim, near the Ardennes; Anlage Sud at Strzyżów in Poland; Wolfschlucht I at Brûly-de-Pesche, near Couvin, Belgium; Wolfschlucht II at Margival, France; Tannenberg, near Freudenstadt in the Black Forest; and Werwolf at Vinnitsa in the Ukraine. Hitler also used a specially converted armoured railway train (Führersonderzug), which had the codename 'Amerika' (later redesignated

'Brandenburg') as a mobile headquarters. Although maintained ready for use throughout most of the war, and used by Hitler at various stages of the conflict, several of the permanent Führerhauptquartiere were only utilized for relatively short periods of time. The Wolfschanze, used from 1941 to 1944, was a notable exception.

143 See Görlitz, p. 407. Extracted from information provided by Jodl and Warlimont at Nuremberg after the war. On a day-to-day basis, Hitler's permanent 'intimates' within the inner zone of the Wolfschanze included his deputy, Martin Bormann, his SS, SA and Wehrmacht adjutants, his two doctors, his personal secretaries, his valets and his vegetarian chef.

144 From 1939, this armoured train was used for many other journeys within Germany and the occupied territories, including to Salzburg in Austria when conveying Hitler and members of his entourage to and from the Berghof. On 23 June 1941, Hitler used this train to travel from Berlin to the Wolfschanze on the day after the Wehrmacht launched Operation *Barbarossa*; this was his first visit to that headquarters in its fully operational form. The train also transported Hitler to the Führerhauptquartier near Bad Nauheim on 11 December, immediately prior to Operation *Wacht am Rhein* in the Ardennes. The final time on which 'Amerika' was used by the Führer was 15 January 1945, when he made his last journey from Rastenburg to Berlin: he remained there until his suicide in the Führerbunker on 30 April. Two separate supporting trains usually accompanied 'Amerika', one ahead and the other behind. This practice was well known to Polish saboteurs, who ambushed the railway in autumn 1941, having received intelligence that the Führer was travelling from Rastenburg to Berlin via Königsberg. 'Amerika' was by chance delayed while another train proceeded in its place. The resistance fighters detonated explosive charges, which derailed this train, killing some 430 German personnel, while 'Amerika' escaped the attack entirely. Belatedly, the Allied SOE organization

developed various plans to attack Hitler's train, but by the time these became viable in late 1944 the Führer had all but ceased travelling by this means. See also Peter Marriot, 'The Hitler Express', pp. 24–31, in *Military Illustrated* magazine, No. 252, May 2009.

145 Each of the Luftwaffenfelddivisionen numbered about 10,000 men when they were first formed. Following their transfer to the army in 1943, they were either disbanded or converted into 'Type 1944' army divisions. Unlike the Fallschirmjäger, the men in the Luftwaffe field divisions were never considered to be special or elite troops.

146 Manstein, Erich von, *Lost Victories*, p. 268–9.

147 The general staff's efforts to achieve a viable manpower situation was further compromised by a significant difference between what the general staff believed attainable in terms of properly manned divisions and what Hitler required. The general staff assessed that no more than 300 divisions could be manned, while Hitler required the army to field no fewer than 450. Over time, this would lead to a surfeit of divisional headquarters, commanding 'divisions' that were at best little more than reinforced regiments in size and combat power.

148 Hitler's policies for the mobilization of German industry were as flawed and changeable as his approach to military matters from 1941. Confident of the success of *Barbarossa*, he directed industry to revert to peacetime production levels in the autumn of 1941 (apart from aircraft production). Just a year later, armoured vehicles (but specifically tanks), U-boats and railway locomotives were allocated equal priority, with aircraft moving to second place. Meanwhile, also in 1942, several potentially war-winning scientific projects (such as jet aircraft, rocket motors and atomic weapons) were curtailed or halted by Hitler due to his misplaced anticipation of an early and favourable end to the war. Although these programmes would later be resumed, this pause and the consequent loss of Germany's technological advantage denied the Wehrmacht a technological force-multiplying effect that might well have proved decisive at a time when Germany's more traditional war-fighting capabilities were diminishing.

149 By that stage, von Kleist commanded 'Group Kleist', the successor to First Panzer Army, which consisted of that army plus part of Seventeenth Army. Although sometimes referred to as an 'army group', this force was in reality an enhanced panzer army and remained under the operational direction of von Bock's Army Group South.

150 Von Manstein had replaced Generaloberst Eugen Ritter von Schobert as commander of Eleventh Army on 12 September 1941, after von Schobert's Fieseler-Storch reconnaissance aircraft carried out a forced landing in what proved to be a Russian minefield and was totally destroyed.

151 Quoted by Brett-Smith, p. 217.

152 Görlitz, p. 418.

153 At the beginning of 1942, Zeitzler had still been a Generalmajor.

154 Simpson, Keith, p. 156.

155 Quoted by Brett-Smith, p. 218.

156 That Göring was still in a position to direct the Luftwaffe operationally by that stage of the war was remarkable and served to demonstrate Hitler's preference for a reliable, but militarily less competent, political ally over his professional adviser, the chief of the general staff. In 1940, Göring's air force had failed to destroy the Anglo-French forces at Dunkirk and proved unable to prevent the bombing of Berlin. Finally, it had lost the Battle of Britain, which meant that *Seelöwe* was non-viable. The Luftwaffe's inability to support Stalingrad effectively in 1942–3 was yet another huge failure on his part and did signal the beginning of a gradual diminution of Göring's power and influence during the remaining two years of the war.

157 Quoted by Görlitz, p. 419.

158 Schmundt was promoted Generalmajor on taking on this additional responsibility. He was later promoted Generalleutnant in 1943 and General in 1944.

159 Von Manstein was promoted Generaloberst on 1 January 1942 and Generalfeldmarschall in July, following his

successful operation to capture Sevastopol in June.

160 Bastable, p. 99.
161 Bastable, pp. 87–8.
162 Bastable, pp. 20–1.
163 Bastable, p. 208.
164 Bastable, p. 209.
165 Bastable, p. 207.
166 Bastable, p. 214.
167 The prisoners taken by the Russians included one Generalfeldmarschall and 22 other generals. Of the total 91,000 Axis prisoners-of-war, almost 50 per cent would be dead by the spring of 1943. Many were summarily shot by their captors, while even more – already weakened by fighting, with inadequate food, medical supplies and other resources throughout the winter – quickly succumbed to disease, starvation and the bitter cold. Many soldiers identified by their uniform or documents as members of the Waffen-SS were routinely shot on capture.
168 For a fuller account of the unconditional surrender issue, see David Stone, *War Summits: The Meetings That Shaped World War II and the Postwar World*, pp. 70–2.
169 In this case, the source was represented to Moscow as a highly-placed spy in the OKH, as the Russians were still officially unaware that the Anglo-US high command possessed a captured 'Enigma' machine and had broken its code system. It is probable that Stalin did in fact already know that his US and British allies had this capability but saw no advantage in disclosing this fact to them. The Germans were still unaware that the security of the 'Enigma' machine and code system had been compromised.
170 The relative strengths at Kursk quoted by different sources vary. These variations are generally not great, although Pimlott does suggest that as many as 5,000 tanks may have been available to the Russians at Kursk, rather than the 3,300 to 3,600 quoted in most other sources: Pimlott's higher figure might possibly have included self-propelled guns and tank destroyers. In any event, it is noteworthy that the Russian forces committed at Kursk were, if expressed as percentages of the total strength and capability of the whole of the Red Army in mid-1943, no less than 20 per cent of its men and guns, at least 33 per cent of its tanks, and 25 per cent of its combat aircraft.
171 The total number of tanks engaged in the core tank battle between Fourth Panzer Army and Fifth Guards Tank Army was probably no more than 850, with the balance of up to 1,400 or 1,500 deployed in the adjacent area. Some sources imply that as many as 1,000 (Pimlott) and 1,500 (Orgill) armoured vehicles were engaged in the central part of the battle.
172 Orgill, p. 121.
173 Görlitz, p. 444.
174 See also Görlitz, p. 448.
175 In any event, although Göring's power was diminishing by 1944, Kesselring would still have benefited from the personal support and protection of the Reichsmarschall as both head of the Luftwaffe and a very senior member of the National Socialist leadership.
176 Knappe and Brusaw, p. 245.
177 Knappe and Brusaw, p. 246.
178 See also Stone, *Hitler's Army, 1939-1945*, pp. 84–6.
179 In early 1938, Dr. Karl Friedrich Goerdeler (former mayor of Leipzig and Price Commissioner in the Nazi government) travelled to London to disclose Hitler's aggressive plans to the British and French authorities and make them aware that a resistance group already existed in Germany with the aim of displacing the Führer. In 1940, Christian Albrecht Ulrich von Hassell (former ambassador to Italy) sought to contact the British authorities via a British agent with a view to negotiating on behalf of the resistance movement. In the meantime, links with the US Office of Strategic Services (OSS) were also established via Switzerland. However, the wholehearted support of the Allies was never forthcoming, due in part to their mistrust of an organization that included general staff officers who professed their desire to end the war while still continuing to prosecute it to the best of their professional ability.
180 Issued on 21 March 1937 and titled *Mit brennender Sorge* (*With Deep Anxiety*).
181 The Weisse Rose group was exposed in

1943 in connection with a leaflet campaign denouncing Hitler. Its leaders and most prominent members, Hans and Sophie Scholl, Christoph Probst, Willi Graf, Alexander Schmorell and Professor Kurt Huber, were arrested and executed, and up to 100 others were arrested and detained.

182 Despite the service he had given to Moscow, Trepper was accused by the Russians of having colluded with the Gestapo and spent ten years in a Russian prison until he was eventually released following the death of Stalin. He was then permitted to emigrate to Israel.

183 Quoted in article 'Heroes of the moral resistance against Hitler' by Ben Mcintyre, *The Times*, 5 January, 2010, p. 26.

184 Oberst Stieff was promoted Generalmajor on 30 January 1944.

185 Apparently, the heater in the cargo hold of the aircraft had malfunctioned, and the most likely explanation for the bomb's failure was that the cold temperature in the hold had neutralized the volatility of the explosive, which was of a type sensitive to low temperatures. At least one account suggests that the detonator was defective and had therefore failed to ignite.

186 Görlitz, p. 434. Derived from Goebbels' diary entry in spring 1943.

187 The officers involved to varying extents in planned or aborted assassination attempts between the summer of 1943 and into 1944 included Generalmajor Helmuth Stieff, Major Joachim Kuhn, Oberleutnant Albrecht von Hagen, Oberst Joachim Meichssner, Leutnant Ewald Heinrich von Kleist, Hauptmann Eberhard von Breitenbuch, Hauptmann Werner von Haeften and Hauptmann Axel von dem Bussche. In every case these officers had been approached in the first place by Oberstleutnant (later Oberst) von Stauffenberg. A key interlocutor, who had close ties to the Kreisauer Kreis and also acted as an intermediary between various civilian and military resistance groups was Fritz-Dietlof Graf von der Schulenberg, a lawyer and lieutenant in the reserve. He was also responsible for introducing von Stauffenberg to von dem Bussche and von Kleist.

188 See Stone, *War Summits*, pp. 70–2. At best the German resistance movement was viewed as something with which the Allies felt unable to deal, while at worst it was regarded with open suspicion and mistrust, shaped by the bizarre perception (in the case of the British government) that it would be inappropriate for the foreign ministry to deal with people capable of committing treason!

189 Röhricht was promoted Generalleutnant with effect from 1 April 1943.

190 In March 1944, an NSFO staff branch was created to oversee and control the overall programme of NSFO activities and training throughout the army, and to issue directives to NSFO officers in the Feldheer units. Although based within the OKH, these staff officers were only attached to that headquarters, being directly subordinate to Hitler rather than to any superior army staff officer or commander.

191 Dr. Ferdinand Sauerbruch was the leading surgeon of the Third Reich, operating on President Paul von Hindenburg in 1934 and on several members of the Nazi leadership, including Hitler himself in 1940. Although originally a supporter of National Socialism, he later joined the German resistance movement against Hitler. Sauerbach survived the war and died in Berlin on 2 July 1951.

192 Fest, p. 215.

193 Fest, p. 215.

194 Numerous accounts of the events of 20 July 1944 exist, in some cases varying on minor points of detail. The works containing the accounts that have been used are included in the bibliography. However, the facts – times, actions, reactions – contained in the version of these events adopted in this work are based primarily upon the account provided by Fest, pp. 255–91, and Tony le Tissier (*Berlin Then and Now*), pp. 162–71, with these details confirmed, amended or expanded where necessary by reference to material from the Gedenkstätte Deutscher Widerstand in Berlin.

195 Stieff's presence is omitted from some accounts of these events, although he was certainly at the Wolfschanze that day, being arrested there on the evening of 20

July. The overall flight time of more than three hours indicates that the aircraft did indeed fly via Zossen.

196   Le Tissier, *The Third Reich Then and Now*, p. 397, and (by implication) Görlitz (p. 467) both indicate that the midday conference had been brought forward (rather than delayed) by half an hour in order to accommodate Mussolini's visit later that afternoon. However, the Deutscher Widerstand records do not appear to bear this out, and Fest's account (p. 255) of von Stauffenberg's meeting with Keitel shortly after his arrival at the Wolfschanze is quite clear. Furthermore, the fact that this conference routinely took place at midday, with this related to the time that it actually convened on 20 July and to all the other critical times thereafter, does tend to confirm that it was indeed delayed not advanced.

197   Fest provides details of the two bomb fuse timing mechanisms on p. 257. However, in the case of the ten-minute fuse it is noteworthy how many actions had to be carried out, and indeed took place, between the arming of the device and the eventual explosion. Given that the Gedenkstätte Deutscher Widerstand places the actual time of the explosion as 'between 12.40 and 12.50' (other sources variously quote the time of detonation as 12.41, 12.42, etc.), it seems likely that the time delay of the type of ten-minute fuse used was hardly precise and that it provided a minimum of ten minutes' delay and up to about fifteen or twenty minutes in practice, rather than detonation precisely at the ten-minute point. The bombs were activated by a fuse type that involved crushing a phial of acid, which then slowly dissolved the material about it and eventually set off the detonator.

198   The 'Lagebaracke' is also referred to as the 'Gästebaracke' ('guest' or 'visitors' barracks) in some accounts. In addition to Hitler and von Stauffenberg, the conference attendees included Generaloberst Jodl, Generalfeldmarschall Keitel, Generalmajor Warlimont, General Schmundt, Generalmajor Scherff, General Korten, Admiral von Puttkamer, Generalleutnant Heusinger, Oberst Brandt, General Bodenschatz, Oberst Borgman, Kapitän Assmann, Generalleutnant Buhle, Admiral Voss, Oberstleutnant von Freyend, Major Büchs, Oberstleutnant Waizenegger, Herr Sonnleithner, Oberst von Below, SS-Brigadeführer Fegelein, SS-Sturmbannführer Günsche, and a stenographer, Dr. Heinrich Berger.

199   Work to reinforce some of the Wolfschanze bunkers had begun in 1944 and was still ongoing in July. So the use of the Lagebaracke for the daily briefing was by no means unusual, and von Stauffenberg should have been well aware of this.

200   There are varying accounts of the events surrounding and immediately after von Stauffenberg left the Lagebaracke. Some omit any reference to von Stauffenberg's telephone call excuse, while others state that General Fellgiebel and von Haeften were already at the car, and that von Stauffenberg walked directly to the car park to join them there.

201   Quoted by le Tissier, *Berlin Then and Now*, p. 165, and other sources.

202   Von Stauffenberg or von Haeften had already telephoned Olbricht from Rangsdorf airfield as soon as they landed, to confirm that Hitler was dead. Görlitz states, on p. 468, that von Stauffenberg made the call, while le Tissier states, on p. 166, that von Haeften made it.

203   Hagen was a reserve officer. His civilian employment was as a department head within the propaganda ministry, and this fact no doubt prompted his approach to Goebbels.

204   Quoted by Fest, p. 277, and in other sources.

205   Some accounts suggest that the bodies were simply reburied in unmarked graves. A memorial to von Stauffenberg and the others executed on 20 July is today in place at the site of their initial interment at St. Matthäus church on Grossgörschenstraße, D-10827, Berlin. After the war, Bendlerstraße was renamed Stauffenbergstraße.

206   The loyalty of both the Luftwaffe and the Kriegsmarine was never in doubt, and in the west one senior naval officer, Admiral Krancke, even threatened to march on

Paris with a large force of sailors and the Waffen-SS unit Leibstandarte 'Adolf Hitler' to overcome General von Stülpnagel and his co-conspirators and re-establish Nazi control of the French capital.

207 A NSFO staff branch within the OKH had already been established in March 1944, attached to the army high command but directly subordinate to Hitler. NSFO activities and the transmission of directives to NSFO members with Feldheer units was coordinated by this staff branch.

208 Quoted by Beevor, *D-Day*, p. 337.

209 Although wounded in the 20 July explosion, Generalleutnant Heusinger had subsequently been implicated in the plot by General Stieff, who stated that he had told Heusinger what was about to happen on that day. However, at his trial on 7 August, Hitler accepted that he had not been involved and the case against him was dismissed.

210 Halder's rescue was very much a 'touch and go' affair. As the Allied forces overran what was left of the Third Reich, various groups of prominent people, many of whom had already been held in prisons or concentration camps for lengthy periods, and whom the Nazi leadership had decreed should not be allowed to survive Germany's defeat, were moved from camp to camp ahead of the advancing Allies. One such group was that which included Halder and von Falkenhausen, together with a former president of the Reichsbank, the French former prime minister and his wife, the last chancellor of Austria, the Hungarian former prime minister, several British military intelligence or secret service agents, a number of lesser diplomats and political figures, various generals who had served with the forces of nations that had originally been part of the Axis, and various family members of the 20 July conspirators. The group numbered about 139 (some sources state 160). On 24 April 1945, this group was moved from Dachau concentration camp, via Innsbruck (where a local labour centre refused to accept the prisoners), to Niederdorf/Hochpusteral, on the Austro-Italian border in the Tirol. They arrived at the village of Niederdorf, about seventy kilometres north-east of Bozen (Bolzano), in the late afternoon of 28 April. The disparate convoy of trucks and old buses was commanded by SS-Obersturmführer Edgar Stiller, assisted by SS-Untersturmführer Bader, and was guarded by about 88 SS and SD troops, with orders to kill the prisoners if there was any chance of them falling into Allied hands. In fact, Stiller had secret orders finally to take the group on into the nearby Pragser Wildsee valley, shoot all the prisoners, and dispose of their bodies in the Wildsee lake. However, while temporary accommodation was being arranged for the group in Niederdorf, Oberst Bogislaw von Bonin (one of the prisoners) managed to pass a message to three senior army officers who were accommodated in the village's hotel, apprising them of the status of the group and of their (well-founded) fear that they were shortly to be executed. Von Bonin's message was passed on to the army general staff at the headquarters in Bozen, where the area commander ordered Hauptmann Wichard von Alvensleben to look into the matter. However, on his own initiative, von Alvensleben acted immediately to protect the prisoners, quickly deploying the troops under his command to Niederdorf and then surrounding the village. At that point, with US forces also advancing rapidly towards the area, the SS and SD guards decided to make good their escape, leaving the prisoners free and to be accommodated at the Pragser Wildsee Hotel until the arrival of US Army units at Niederdorf on 5 May 1945. (Afternote: Wichard von Alvensleben was a much-decorated officer, having served in Poland, France, Russia, North Africa and Italy. He was also a Knight of the Order of Saint John and a deeply-committed Christian. He survived the war, but his wife, Cora von Erxleben, did not. The family owned extensive estates in the eastern part of Germany, and on 29 January 1945, just as the first Russian troops arrived at the von Alvenslebens' Tankow-Seegenfelde family estate, his wife chose to commit suicide rather than endure the outrages that she

anticipated would be committed by the Red Army.)

211 On 3 May 1945, von Bock had been travelling with family members to attend a tea party with the von Mansteins at what was by then the von Manstein residence at Gut Weissenhaus, near Oldenburg in Holstein on the Baltic coast. The two Generalfeldmarschall – both of them by that stage of the war no longer on active service – had intended discussing the imminent capitulation of Germany. Shortly before the von Bocks arrived at Gut Weissenhaus their car was strafed by RAF fighters, killing von Bock's wife and daughter instantly and fatally wounding the field marshal, who died a few hours later at Oldenburg hospital. Von Bock's last words to von Manstein were: 'Manstein, save Germany.' (Quoted by Melvin, p. 429, from an account of the incident provided by von Manstein's ADC, Leutnant Alexander Stahlberg.)

212 Knappe and Brusaw, pp. 254–5.

213 General Wenck was the army's youngest general during the war. In April 1945, he commanded Twelfth Army in its unsuccessful attempt to relieve Berlin.

214 Oberst von Bonin was arrested by the Gestapo on 19 January 1945 after authorizing the withdrawal of an army group, contrary to Hitler's orders. Imprisoned first at Flossenbürg and then Dachau concentration camps, he eventually found himself in the group of prominent prisoners that included Franz Halder in the Tirol in April 1945, where von Bonin played a key role in the survival and freeing of the group (see note 210).

215 After 1945, Gehlen worked for the CIA and other US military intelligence organizations against the Soviet Union throughout the Cold War, using to particular advantage the vast number of files on the Russian war machine and its key personalities that his organization had accumulated during the 1939–45 war. He had managed to secrete these files and records in the Austrian Alps and elsewhere during the final months of the war, all ready to be retrieved and used in the service of his post-war US employer.

216 Knappe and Brusaw, pp. 256–7.

217 Görlitz, p. 493.

218 Nevertheless, if the inevitability of the eventual defeat of Germany by mid-1944 is accepted, it may be argued that an Allied defeat at Normandy would merely have prolonged rather than changed the outcome of the war, and that this prolongation would then almost certainly have led to the use of the atom bomb against Germany. See the observation by Gerhard Weinberg, in *Military History*, volume 26, No. 5, in the article 'Germany's Fatal Blunders' (Williamson Murray), p. 35.

219 Von Rundstedt was reappointed commander-in-chief of the forces in the west by Hitler in September.

220 Although he could justifiably be described as a 'traditional German army officer', Generalfeldmarschall Günther von Kluge remained loyal to Hitler throughout the war. While aware of von Stülpnagel's commitment to the opposition movement, he was uninvolved in the July 1944 plot against Hitler and should have been able to avoid Hitler's retributive measures against the army general staff after 20 July 1944. However, an unfortunate set of circumstances in August 1944 persuaded the Führer that von Kluge had probably been involved in the opposition movement – and, much more specifically, that he had tried to negotiate a separate surrender with the Allied forces in the west. In fact he had not done this. His temporary disappearance and the loss of communications for a twelve-hour period during the fighting was due to his command group having been directly struck by an air attack. Hitler, already suspicious of von Kluge, chose to disbelieve him and ordered his dismissal and return to Berlin. Such an order post-20 July also implied a Gestapo investigation and his probable arraignment in connection with the July plot. Accordingly, despite his innocence, von Kluge chose to commit suicide and took poison while travelling in his staff car towards Metz on route to Berlin, rather than submit to the ignominy of investigation, trial, dishonour and almost certain execution. In advance of his departure from his headquarters in

France, von Kluge wrote a final letter to Hitler, reaffirming his loyalty and exhorting him to end the war in the event that the new V-weapons should not prove to be as successful as anticipated. During the war crimes trials at Nuremberg during 1945–6, Jodl stated: 'Hitler read this letter without comment, then passed it to [me] without saying a word.' (Brett-Smith, p. 86). Ignoring von Kluge's consistent loyalty prior to the events of August 1944 and ignoring the truth concerning the Allied air attack on von Kluge's command group in France, Hitler refused to allow the field marshal any military honours at his funeral.

221 Hitler's rationale for maintaining the Courland army group in place was its possible future use to launch an attack against the Allies' northern flank. However, strong lobbying by Admiral Dönitz also affected this matter, as he wanted a strong Wehrmacht presence in Courland to continue in order to secure the Kriegsmarine's U-boat training facilities and bases in the Baltic.

222 Görlitz states (p. 480) that the German losses at Mortain-Falaise were much higher – 1,500 tanks, 3,500 guns, 240,000 casualties and 210,000 prisoners-of-war. In practice, these figures reflect the wider losses sustained between the start of the abortive Mortain-Falaise offensive and the final collapse and surrender of the 'Falaise Pocket'.

223 Görlitz, p. 480.

224 Hastings, Max, *Armageddon: The Battle for Germany, 1944–45*, pp. 192–3.

225 Knappe, p. 287.

226 Although Allied strategic bombing had all but destroyed Germany's ability to manufacture the synthetic fuels needed to compensate for its reducing access to the eastern oilfields, national levels of armaments production were not only being sustained but even increased under Albert Speer's direction from 1942. During the first four months of 1944, equipment sufficient for some 130 infantry divisions and forty panzer divisions were produced by German factories and plants in the occupied territories. The Wehrmacht's most pressing problem, as ever, was its inability to replace its battle casualties, as the remaining finite pool of reserve manpower continued to dwindle. Neither could it afford to lose equipment on the sort of scale that could be absorbed by the Anglo-US and Russian forces.

227 The title 'reprisal weapon' provides an indication of Hitler's own view of the true function of the V-1 and V-2 rockets and other Vergeltungswaffen. Had these weapons been developed with a higher priority from the outset, entered service earlier and then been used in greater numbers and primarily for operational and strategic missions rather than as a form of terror weapon against civilian targets, their strategic impact might have been much more significant. Throughout the time it was used, there was no effective defence against the V-2 rockets other than by destroying them on their launch sites.

228 Sixth Panzer Army is also shown as Sixth SS Panzer Army in some documents.

229 Quoted by Melvin, p. 59.

230 Whiting, *Battle of the Ruhr Pocket* (1972), p. 145.

231 Public Records Office document PRO WO218/311, dated 17 January 1945 (also quoted by Hastings, *Armageddon*, p. 169.

232 Generaloberst Gotthard Heinrici should not be confused with General Sigfrid Heinrici. They were not related to each other, but Gotthard Heinrici was a cousin of von Rundstedt.

233 Quoted by Brett-Smith, p. 250.

234 Guderian surrendered to US Army troops on 10 May 1945 and was held as a prisoner of war until 17 June 1948. He was investigated as a potential war criminal but was not charged, his actions during the war being judged to have been consistent with the actions of a professional soldier. Thereafter he was heavily involved in the development of the West German Bundeswehr, in which one of his sons achieved the rank of general. Both of his sons had served in the Wehrmacht. Guderian died at Schwangau, Bavaria, on 14 May 1954 aged 65, and was buried in the Friedhof Hildesheimer Strasse at Goslar, in the Harz mountains region of Niedersachsen.

235 Subsequently Hitler ordered that the Waffen-SS officers who had fought at

Lake Balaton should be stripped of their decorations, an order greatly resented by the Waffen-SS. It also indicated that by that stage of the war Hitler had lost faith not only in the general staff and the army but also in even his most loyal fighting units.

236 During the war no fewer than 11,700 men were executed in this way, and there were possibly an even greater number of unrecorded executions; by comparison, during World War I just 48 German soldiers were executed for military offences.

237 Quoted by Görlitz, p. 488.

238 Görlitz, p. 489.

239 The statistics for senior and general staff officers are drawn primarily from Görlitz, p. 493–4, but with some figures updated and amended where appropriate. Although Generalfeldmarschall Kesselring began his career in the army, he had transferred to the Luftwaffe on 1 October 1933 and so is not included in the figure for army field marshals.

240 Subsequently, Wenck managed to bring Twelfth Army, together with the remnants (up to 25,000 men) of Ninth Army and as many as 250,000 civilian refugees, safely along a corridor and across the Elbe into territory occupied by the US forces.

241 Görlitz, p. 498.

242 Many of the German prisoners in the long columns that marched eastwards out of the ruined city of Berlin en route to captivity in Russian prisoner-of-war camps and special detention facilities would never see Germany again. In early May 1945 the Russians held 1,464,803 prisoners-of-war in Germany alone, while more than a million more had already been transported to Russia to join the several hundred thousand German soldiers who had been captured since 1941. Large numbers of these men remained in captivity within the Soviet Union for many years, with the last 9,626 survivors finally being released in 1955.

243 Jodl and Keitel were both condemned to death by the International War Crimes Tribunal at Nuremberg in 1946 and executed. In 1953 a German de-Nazification court exonerated Jodl posthumously of his conviction for war crimes.

244 Some accounts suggest that Krebs might have been taken prisoner by the Russians, with whom he did conduct some of the surrender negotiations in Berlin, although there is no evidence for this other than the lack of a specific record of the disposal of his body. Some listings of chiefs of the general staff do show Krebs occupying that post until 8 May 1945, the day of the final surrender.

245 The wider military culture, sense of duty, honour, ideological mores and obligations that shaped and determined the conduct and actions of the senior German army officer in National Socialist Germany in World War II meant that he had become much distanced from his predecessors (and very different from his British and American enemies) by the time Nazi Germany went to war in 1939, and increasingly so thereafter. A more extreme illustration of this was the relatively ready recourse to suicide – their personal Götterdämmerung – by some senior German officers, particularly during the final stages of the war, when the perceived shame of personal professional failure or despair at the prospect of the nation's defeat and the end of Hitler's dream of a 'thousand year Reich' proved intolerable. With the possible exception of matters of personal indiscretions and consequent dishonour, such extreme action was generally without precedent in the old Prussian and imperial German army, providing another indication of the perverse uniqueness of Hitler's Third Reich – undeniably an aberration in the overall history of Germany, its army and its people.

246 Guderian, p. 302. Ironically, von Manstein did finally come close to succeeding Keitel when, on 1 May 1945, Admiral Dönitz, who had by then succeeded Hitler as Führer, attempted unsuccessfully to contact von Manstein in order to offer him the post of head of the OKW. By then, however, this was an irrelevance. The Allies' insistence upon an unconditional surrender would undoubtedly have obviated any real opportunity for von Manstein to employ his reputation or his intellectual and practical skills in negotiating surrender terms with the Allied powers.

247   Quoted by le Tissier, *The Third Reich Then and Now*, p. 435. See also Stone, *War Summits*, pp. 237–63 for a full account of the Potsdam conference, its conduct, deliberations and decisions.

248   At Nuremberg on Saturday 31 August 1946, Generaloberst Jodl – who had by then already been condemned to death for war crimes – made a statement (quoted by Roberts, p. 580) to the International Tribunal in mitigation or defence of the German high command. He said that it had been 'confronted with an insoluble task, namely, to conduct a war which they had not wanted under a Commander-in-Chief whose confidence they did not possess and whom they themselves only trusted within limits; with methods which frequently were in contradiction to their principles of leadership and their traditional, proved opinions; with troops and police forces which did not come under their full command; and with an Intelligence service that was in part working for the enemy. And all this in the complete and clear realization that this war would decide the life and death of our beloved Fatherland. They did not serve the powers of Hell and they did not serve a criminal, but rather their people and their Fatherland.' While the sincerity and credibility of this statement – coming from one of Hitler's closest military supporters – must be treated with a considerable amount of caution, it none the less provides a fair summary of the views of many within the general staff and high command during the Third Reich period. However, it leaves unanswered the question why (if dissent and opposition were indeed so widespread and well-recognized), the armed forces still failed to remove Hitler when they still had good opportunities to do so. The answer almost certainly lies in the human frailty and personal ambitions of very many professional officers who, until 1942, still viewed compromise, acquiescence and the abandonment of traditional principles as an acceptable price to pay for a potentially historic German victory, with the return of the Fatherland to military and international pre-eminence.

249   This might even have included the use of atomic weapons in the European theatre. Any substantial prolongation of the conflict, an unresolvable strategic stalemate or a significant strategic reverse for the Allies (such as a defeat of the D-Day landings by the Germans in June 1944) could all have precipitated an Allied use of atomic weapons against Germany. In such circumstances, the pressure upon the British and US governments to avoid Allied casualties – albeit at the expense of mass casualties and unprecedented levels of destruction in Germany – could eventually have proved irresistible once these weapons became available. Witness the undoubted military and political logic of the Anglo-US decision to drop two atomic bombs on Japan in 1945, thus avoiding a potentially very costly (and almost exclusively US) invasion of the Japanese homeland. Finally, if the war had continued through and beyond 1945, another factor affecting the atomic issue would undoubtedly have been increasing Allied concerns about the true progress of Germany's own development of atomic weapons and long-range rockets, although the German atomic programme was in fact far behind that of the Allies by 1945.

Select Bibliography

Altner, Helmut, *Berlin Soldier*, Tempus Publishing, Stroud, 2007

Bance, Professor Alan (Tr.), *Blitzkrieg in Their Own Words*, Pen & Sword Military, Barnsley, 2005 (a literal translation of *Den Panzern In Ost Und West*, Germany, 1942)

Bartov, Omer, *Hitler's Army*, Oxford University Press, New York, 1992

Bastable, Jonathan, *Voices from Stalingrad: Nemesis on the Volga*, David & Charles, Cincinnati, USA, 2006

Beevor, Antony, *Stalingrad*, Penguin Books, London, 1999

– *Berlin: the Downfall 1945*, Penguin Books, London, 2003

– *D-Day*, Penguin Books, London, 2009

Bender, Roger James, *The Luftwaffe*, R. James Bender Publishing, Mountain View, California, 1972

— and Law, Richard D., *Uniforms, Organization and History of the Afrikakorps*, R. James Bender Publishing, Mountain View, California, 1973

— and Odegard, Warren W., *Uniforms, Organization and History of the Panzertruppe*, R. James Bender Publishing, San Jose, California, 1980

— and Petersen, George A., *Hermann Göring: from Regiment to Fallschirmpanzerkorps*, R. James Bender Publishing, San Jose, California, 1975

— and Taylor, Hugh Page, *Uniforms, Organization and History of the Waffen-SS*, R. James Bender Publishing, Mountain View, California, 1971

Biddiscombe, Perry, *The Denazification of Germany: A History, 1945–1950*, Tempus Publishing, Stroud, 2007

Blumentritt, Günther, *Von Rundstedt: The Soldier and the Man*, Odhams Press, London, 1952

Brett-Smith, Richard, *Hitler's Generals*, Osprey Publishing, London, 1976

Citino, Robert M., *The German Way of War: From the Thirty Years' War to the Third Reich*, University Press of Kansas, USA, 2005

Davis, Brian L., *German Army Uniforms and Insignia, 1933–1945*, Arms & Armour Press, London, 1971

Fest, Joachim, *Plotting Hitler's Death: The German Resistance to Hitler, 1933–1945*, Weidenfeld & Nicolson, London, 1996

Forty, George, *German Infantryman at War 1939–1945*, Ian Allan Publishing, Hersham, Surrey, 2002

Galland, Adolf (Tr. Mervyn Savill), *The First and the Last*, New York, 1954

Gill, Anton, *An Honourable Defeat: A History of the German Resistance to Hitler*, Heinemann, London, 1994

Görlitz, Walter, *The German General Staff: Its History and Structure 1657–1945*, Hollis & Carter, London, 1953

Guderian, General Heinz (Tr. Constantine Fitzgibbon), *Panzer Leader*, Futura Publications, London, 1979

Hassell, Ulrich von, *The Ulrich von Hassell Diaries: The Story of the Forces Against Hitler Inside Germany*, Pen & Sword Books (Frontline imprint), Barnsley, Yorkshire, 2011

Halder, Franz (Ed. Charles Burdick and Hans-Adolf Jacobsen), *The Halder War Diary, 1939–1942*, Novato, USA, 1988

— *Hitler as Warlord*, Putnam Press, 1950

Hanisch, Prof. Dr. Ernst, *Obersalzberg: The 'Eagle's Nest' and Adolf Hitler*, Berchtesgadener Landesstiftung, Bad Reichenhall, 1998

Hastings, Max, *Armageddon: The Battle for Germany, 1944–45*, Pan Macmillan Ltd., London, 2004

Haus Neuerburg, *Das Reichsheer und Seine Tradition*, Haus Neuerburg, Germany, c.1936

Hoffman, Peter, *German Resistance to Hitler*, Cambridge Press, Massachusetts, USA, 1988

Hormann, Jörg M., *Uniforms of the Infantry 1919 to the Present* (volume 2), Schiffer Publishing, Pennsylvania, USA, 1989

Keegan, John, *Waffen SS: the Asphalt Soldiers*, Macdonald & Co., London, 1970

Kershaw, Alex, *The Longest Winter*, Penguin Books/Michael Joseph, London, 2004

Kershaw, Ian, *The Nazi Dictatorship: Problems and Perspectives of Interpretation*, Arnold (Hodder Headline Group), London, 1993

— *Hitler: 1889–1936: Hubris*, Allen Lane, London, 1998

— *Hitler: 1936–1945: Nemesis*, Penguin Books, London, 2001

Knappe, Siegfried, and Brusaw, Ted, *Soldat: Reflections of a German Soldier, 1936–1949*, BCA with Airlife Publishing, London, 1993

Kolb, Eberhard (Tr. P. S. Falla), *The Weimar Republic*, Routledge, London, 1995

Kramarz, Joachim, *Stauffenberg: The Architect of the Famous July 20th Conspiracy to Assassinate Hitler*, New York, USA, 1967

Kurowski, Franz, *Infantry Aces: The German Combat Soldier in Combat in WW II*, Stackpole Books, Mechanicsburg, Pennsylvania, USA, 2005

Laffin, John, *Jackboot: The Story of the German Soldier*, Cassel & Company, London, 1965 (re-published by Sutton Publishing, Stroud, 2003)

Le Tissier, Tony, *Berlin Then and Now*, Battle of Britain Prints International, London, 1992

— *Blitzkrieg in the West Then and Now*, Battle of Britain Prints International, London, 1991

— *The Third Reich Then and Now*, Battle of Britain Prints International, London, 2005

Lucas, James, *German Army Handbook*, Sutton Publishing, Stroud, Gloucestershire, 1998

— *Kommando: German Special Forces of World War Two*, Cassell, London, 1985

MacDonogh, Giles, *Prussia: The Perversion of an Idea*, Mandarin Publishing, London, 1995

Mackenzie, Donald A. *Teutonic Myth and Legend*, Gresham Publishing Company, London, c.1930s

Macksey, Major K. J., *Afrika Korps*, Macdonald & Co., London, 1968

— *Panzer Division: the Mailed Fist*, Macdonald & Co., London, 1968

Manstein, Erich von, *Lost Victories*, Collins, London, 1958

Manvell, Roger and Fraenkel, Heinrich, *The Men Who Tried to Kill Hitler*, Skyhorse Publishing, New York, USA, 2008

Megargee, Geoffrey P., *Inside Hitler's High Command*, University Press of Kansas, Lawrence, Kansas, USA, 2000

Melvin, Mungo, *Manstein: Hitler's Greatest General*, Weidenfeld & Nicolson, London, 2010

Meyer, Kurt, *Grenadiers: The Story of Waffen-SS General Kurt 'Panzer' Meyer*, Stackpole Books, Mechanicsburg, Pennsylvania, USA, 2005

Moorehouse, Roger, *Killing Hitler: The Third Reich and the Plot to Kill the Führer*, Vintage, Random House, London, 2007

Neitzel, Sönke, *Tapping Hitler's Generals*, Frontline Books, 2007

Orgill, Douglas, *T-34: Russian Armour*, Macdonald & Co., London, 1970

Pallud, Jean Paul, *Battle of the Bulge Then and Now*, Battle of Britain Prints International, London, 1984

— *Blitzkrieg in the West: Then and Now*,

After the Battle Publications, Battle of Britain Prints International, London, 1991

Pimlott, Dr. John, *Wehrmacht: The Illustrated History of the German Army in WW II*, Aurum Press, London, 2001

Reibert, Oberstleutnant W., *Der Dienstunterricht im Heere*, Berlin, 1943

Reitlinger, Gerald, *The SS: Alibi of a Nation*, William Heinemann, London, 1957

Reynolds, Michael, *Sons of the Reich: II SS Panzer Corps, Normandy, Arnhem, Ardennes, Eastern Front*, Spellmount, Staplehurst, 2002

Roberts, Andrew, *The Storm of War: A New History of the Second World War*, Allen Lane, London, 2009

Rosinski, Herbert, *The German Army*, The Hogarth Press, London, 1939

Scheibert, Horst (Ed. Bruce Culver), *Panzergrenadier Division Grossdeutschland*, Squadron/Signal Publications, Warren, Michigan, USA, 1977

Schlabrendorff, Fabian von, *Revolt Against Hitler*, New York, USA, 1982

Schmidt, Heinz Werner, *With Rommel in the Desert*, Panther Books Ltd, London, 1968

Schrader, Helena, *Codename Valkyrie: General Friedrich Olbricht and the Plot Against Hitler*, J. H. Haynes & Co., London, 2009

Seligmann, Dr. Matthew, with Davison, Dr. John, and McDonald, John, *In the Shadow of the Swastika: Life in Germany under the Nazis, 1933–1945*, Spellmount, Staplehurst, 2003

Shepperd, Alan, *France 1940: Blitzkrieg in the West*, Osprey Publishing, London, 1990

Simpson, Keith, *History of the German Army 1648–Present*, Bison Books, London, 1987

Simpson, William, *Hitler and Germany: Documents and Commentary*, Cambridge University Press, Cambridge, 1991

Snyder, Professor Louis L., *Encyclopedia of the Third Reich*, Wordsworth Editions, Ware, 1998

Speidel, Hans, *Invasion 1944: Rommel and the Normandy Campaign*, Chicago, USA, 1950

Stahlberg, Alexander, *Bounden Duty: The Memoirs of a German Officer, 1932–1945*, New York, USA, 1990

Stoddard, Brooke C., *World in Balance: the Perilous Months of June–October 1940*, Potomac Books, Washington, D.C., 2010

Stone, David, *Fighting for the Fatherland: The Story of the German Soldier from 1648 to the Present Day*, Anova Books (Conway imprint), London, 2006

— *Hitler's Army, 1939–1945: The Men, Machines and Organisation*, Anova Books (Conway Imprint), London, 2009

— *War Summits: The Meetings that Shaped World War II and the Postwar World*, Potomac Books, Dulles, Virginia, USA, 2005

Strachan, Hew, *The First World War*, Simon & Schuster UK, London, 2003

Sweeting, C. G., *Blood and Iron: the German Conquest of Sevastopol*, Potomac Books, Dulles, Virginia, USA, 2004

Tucker-Jones, Anthony, *Hitler's Great Panzer Heist: Germany's Foreign Armour in Action 1939–45*, Pen & Sword Books, Barnsley, 2007

US War Department, *Handbook on German Military Forces*, TM-E 30-451 (15 March 1945), US War Department, Washington, 1945

Wheatley, Ronald, *Operation Sea Lion: German Plans for the Invasion of England 1939–1942*, Clarendon Press, Oxford, 1958

Whiting, Charles, *Battle of the Ruhr Pocket*, Pan/Ballantine, London, 1972

Williams, John, *France: Summer 1940*, Macdonald & Co., London, 1969

Woodman, Dorothy (Ed.), *Hitler Rearms: An Exposure of Germany's War Plans*, John Lane, The Bodley Head, London, 1934

Glossary

German	English
Abteilung	Branch (staff), unit, detachment; also used for some battalion-sized or equivalent units
Abwehr	Defence (but in the military organizational context it was the name of the national counter-espionage organization headed by Admiral Canaris prior to, and during most of, the war years
Adlerhorst	'Eagle's Nest', Hitler's forward field headquarters at Ziegenberg near Nauheim in Hessen
Afrikakorps	'Africa Corps', the principal German ground force formation in North Africa, commanded by Generalfeldmarschall Rommel 1941–3
Allgemeine	General (i.e., non-specialist)
Allgemeine SS	General SS (organization)
Allgemeines Heeresamt	General army office
Allgemeines Wehrmachtsamt	Armed forces general office
Amt	Office
Anschluß	Union (of Germany and Austria in 1938, Operation *Otto*)
Anwärter	Aspirant, candidate
Artillerie	Artillery
Aufklärung	Reconnaissance
Aufmarsch	Approach march immediately prior to tactical deployment
Auftragstaktik	Mission-led operational concept and doctrine focusing upon the wider aims and objectives rather than specifying in detail the means by which they should be achieved
Ausmarsch	Initial deployment on mobilization
Barbarossa, Fall	'Case Barbarossa', (literally Operation *Barbarossa*, the invasion of Russia in June 1941)
Baron	Baron (aristocratic title)
Bataillon	Battalion
Batterie	Battery (of artillery)
Befehlshaber	Commander
Bekenntniskirche	'Confessional Church', founded by Bonhoeffer and Niemoeller to promote Protestantism and resist the anti-religious policies of the National Socialist state
Berg	Mountain
Bewegungskrieg	Manoeuvre warfare, mobile operations
Blitzkrieg	'Lightning war'
Brigadeführer	SS rank equivalent to army major general
Chef der Heeresleitung	Chief of the Army High Command (the OKH)

Chef des Generalstabs des Heeres	Chief of the Army General Staff
Chef des OKW	Chief of the Armed Forces High Command (the OKW)
Chef des Truppenamtes	Adjutant-general (during the Reichswehr period)
Der Grüne Otto	'Green Otto', news sheet of the Neu Beginnen resistance group
Der Ring des Nibelungen	*The Ring of the Nibelungen,* Richard Wagner's famous opera based on the lays and legends of the Rhineland and the mythological Teutonic heroes of Germany (the Nibelungen were a mythological race of dwarves or elves)
Deutscher Widerstand	German Resistance [Movement]
Deutsches Afrikakorps (DAK)	German Africa Corps (see also Afrikakorps)
'Die Nacht der langen Messer'	The 'Night of the Long Knives' or the Nazi 'blood purge' of 30 June 1934
Dienst	Duty or service
Dolchstoß	The 'stab in the back' legend actively promoted from 1918 to support the perception that the army remained undefeated, and that Germany had lost the war through the country's political betrayal on the home front
Eilbeck Kameraden	'Eilbeck Comrades', social democrat resistance group formed in 1934 at Eilbeck near Hamburg (the town name changed to 'Eilbek' in 1946)
Einheit	Unit
Einjährig-Freiwillige	One-year period of voluntary full-time military service completed in the course of obtaining a reserve officer commission
Einsatzgruppen	Special task groups or task forces (usually used to refer to the 'SS-Einsatzgruppen')
Einsatzkommandos	Special units operating as 'killer groups'
Ersatz	Substitute or replacement
Ersatzabteilung	Replacement unit, which at different stages of the war comprised both a training element and a formed combat element or simply a training element
Ersatzeinheit	Replacement unit, comprising trained manpower immediately available to reinforce Feldheer units, but also able to operate as a combat unit in its own right
Ersatzheer	Replacement Army
Fahnenjunker	Officer cadet on active duty; also a non-commissioned officer aspirant
Fahrer	Horse handler(s) (in a field artillery unit)
Fall (Gelb, Grün, Otto, Weiß, Blau)	Case or situation (i.e., 'Plan' or 'Operation') (Yellow, Green, Otto, White, Blue, etc.)
Fallschirm	Airborne (i.e., delivered by parachute or glider)
Fallschirmjäger	Airborne (paratroop) infantry soldier
Fallschirmpanzerkorps	'Airborne armoured corps', a Luftwaffe armoured formation bearing the honour title 'Hermann Göring'

Fallschirmtruppe	Airborne (parachute) troops
Feld	Field
Feldartillerie	Field artillery
Felddivisionen	Luftwaffe field divisions employed as ground forces
Feldgendarmerie	Military police
Feldheer	Field Army
Feldjägerkorps	Special army units established late in the war to apprehend deserters and exercise summary justice in the field, including conducting 'flying courts martial'
Feldkommando	Field command post
Feldpost	Military field postal organization or office
Feldwebel	Warrant officer
Feldzeug	Ordnance
Felix	Codename for the intended German-Spanish operation against Gibraltar
Fernmelde (~bataillon)	Signals or communications (battalion)
Festung	Fortress
Flakturm	Flak tower
Fliegerkorps	Major Luftwaffe formation comprised of fighter and bomber aircraft
Flugabwehr (~regiment)	Air defence (regiment)
Flugabwehrkanone ('Flak')	Anti-aircraft ('Flak') gun
Freiherr	Baron or baronet (aristocratic title)
Freikorps	'Free corps' and variously used over time to describe local militia, irregular and other armed groups and paramilitary forces, including the post-1918 right-wing paramilitary groups raised by the post-World War I government
Fremde Heere Ost (FHO)	OKH intelligence staff branch dealing with foreign armies in the east
Fremde Heere West (FHW)	OKH intelligence staff branch dealing with foreign armies in the west
Friedhof	Cemetery
Fritz	Codename for the OKW version of the OKH's *Fall Otto* plans for the invasion of Russia, both of which were later superseded by the single codename *Barbarossa*
Führer	Any leader, vehicle driver etc.; also routinely applied when referring directly to Hitler and used instead of his name
Führer und Oberster Befehlshaber	Leader and supreme commander (of the armed forces): the title adopted by Hitler in February 1938
Führer-Begleit-Bataillon (FBB)	Führer Escort Battalion, an elite military security force of regimental rather than battalion size, providing personal security for Hitler and for the immediate area of his field headquarters (such as the Wolfschanze)
Führerbunker	Hitler's headquarters bunker beneath the Reich Chancellery building in Berlin
Führergehilfenausbildung	Leadership or commanders' assistants training

Führerhauptquartier(e)	Hitler's operational supreme headquarters (pl.)
Führerheer	Concept of the 'leadership-based army'
Führerstab, Führerstabsoffizier(e)	'Leadership or command staff' and 'leadership or command staff officer(s)': terms used to disguise the existence of a shadow general staff and general staff officers during the Reichswehr period
Führungshauptamt	Operational-level headquarters
Garde	Guard
Garnison	Garrison
Gästebaracke	Literally 'guest' or 'visitors barracks', the wooden building in which the 20 July 1944 bombing took place (see also Lagebaracke)
Gauleiters	Nazi leaders at district level; these party officials were appointed directly by Hitler
Gebirgs (~division)	Mountain (division)
Gebirgsjäger, Gebirgstruppe	Mountain infantry, mountain troops
Gefreiter	Junior corporal
Geheime Feldpolizei (GFP)	Secret Field Police
Geheime Staatspolizei ('Gestapo')	State Secret Police
General	General (UK), Lieutenant General (USA)
General der Infanterie, Panzer, Artillerie (etc.)	General of Infantry, Armour, Artillery (etc.)
Generale	General officers (as a group or category)
Generalfeldmarschall	Field Marshal (UK), General of the Army (USA)
Generalgouvernment	Government General (of Poland)
Generalleutnant	Lieutenant General (UK), Major General (USA)
Generalmajor	Major General (UK), Brigadier General (USA)
Generaloberst	Colonel General, ranked above General and immediately below Field Marshal (UK) and equivalent to General (USA)
Generalstab	General staff
Generalstab des Heeres	Army General Staff
General zur besonderen Verwendung	General officer appointment with no specific portfolio or designated specialist area of responsibility
Generalstabsoffiziere	General staff corps officers
Gleichschaltung	Concept and policy of grouping of all aspects of German life and activities into coordinated National Socialist entities
Götterdämmerung	'Twilight of the Gods' (derived from the final opera of Richard Wagner's four-opera Ring cycle Der Ring des Nibelungen with its cataclysmic closing scenes of death and destruction)
Graf	Count (aristocratic title)
Grenzschutz-Ost	Border troops on Germany's post-1919 eastern border
Grossadmiral	Grand admiral, the most senior officer rank in the Kriegsmarine

Grossdeutschland, Großdeutschland	Greater Germany, incorporating the Saarland, Rhineland, Austria and the Sudetenland; also the title of a specific elite army unit and formation
Großdeutsches Reich	Greater German Empire (concept of an expanded Germany incorporating all German-speaking and Germanic peoples into a single political entity)
Gruppe	Group
Gruppenkommando	(Army) group headquarters
Gut	Large farm or estate
Hakenkreuz	'Hooked cross', the principal symbol of the NSDAP and more usually termed 'Swastika'
Haltebefehl	'Stand fast' order
Haupt~	Head, main
Hauptmann	Captain (army rank)
Hauptquartier(e)	Headquarters (pl.)
Heer, das	Army, the
Heeresgruppe	Army group (of two or more armies)
Heeres-Unteroffizier-Schule(n)	Army non-commissioned officer school(s)
Heereswaffenamt	Army Ordnance Office
Heimat	'Homeland', in Greater Germany
Heeresleitung	Army high command prior to creation of the OKH
Heldengedenktag	Heroes' Memorial Day, which was originally titled 'Volkstrauertag' (People's Day of Mourning) when it was instituted after World War I; it was subsequently changed to 'Heldengedenktag' on Hitler's direction after the Nazis gained power in 1933
Infanterie	Infantry
Inspecteur	Head of a specific arm or corps within the army, such as the infantry, the panzer troops, the artillery, etc., dealing primarily with its training, education, tactical and weapons development, organizational and administrative matters
Isabella	Codename for the intended German-Spanish operation to occupy Portugal
Jäger	Literally 'hunter', but used to indicate light infantry, chasseur, rifleman
Jugend	Youth
Kaiser	Emperor
Kaisermanöver	Large-scale military exercises conducted during the pre-1914 period, which were regularly attended by the Kaiser
Kaiserschlacht	The 'Kaiser's battle', the last great German offensive in 1918
Kampf	Battle, struggle, fight
Kampfgruppe	Battle group
Kampfwagen (Kpfw.)	Tank
Kanone	Cannon
Kapitän	Captain (navy)

Karmesin	Carmine-red colour of uniform embellishments identifying general staff officers during the Third Reich period (see also Waffenfarbe)
Kaserne	Barracks
Kavallerie	Cavalry
Kettenkraftrad, Kettenkrad	Part-tracked light motor or motorcycle vehicle
Kommando	Special task detachment
Kommissarbefehl	Commissar order, by which the Kommissarerlaß was promulgated to the field army commanders
Kommissarerlaß	'Commissar Decree' (issued March 1941), which directed the summary execution of Red Army political commissars if captured
Kompanie	Company (military)
Königstiger	'King Tiger', the Pz.Kpfw. VI Tiger II tank
Kraftfahrabteilung(en)	Motor transport unit(s)
Kreisauer Kreis	Influential resistance group formed in 1933 at the city of Kreisau, also shown as the 'Kreisau Circle' in various English-language references
Krieg	War
Kriegsakademie	Military higher-level staff training academy or 'war college'
Kriegsheer	Field army in wartime (see also 'Feldheer')
Kriegsmarine	German Navy (1935–45)
Kriegsministerium	Ministry of War
Kriegsschule	Military training or 'war school'
Kriegsspiel	Literally 'war game', or military training exercise for commanders with or without troops deployed
Lagebaracke	Wooden building in which the 20 July 1944 bombing took place (see also Gästebaracke)
Lager	Camp, base, depot, storage depot
Landespolizei	Regional paramilitary police
Landser	Descriptive term for ordinary German soldier
Landsturm	Secondary reserve, home guard or local defence force (men aged over 45)
Landwehr	Reserve or militia force (men aged 35–45)
Lebensraum	'Living space', the territory Hitler wished to incorporate from countries on Germany's eastern border – notably Poland and western Russia – in order to enable his expansionist policies
Lehr~	Instruction or training
Leib (~standarte 'Adolf Hitler')	'Life' or 'lifeguard', but used in the military context to indicate 'bodyguard regiment', e.g., Leibstandarte-SS 'Adolf Hitler'
Leicht, leichter	Light, lightweight
Leutnant	Junior or 2nd lieutenant
Luftflotte	Air fleet
Luftwaffe, die	German air force, the (1935–45)
Luftwaffenfelddivisionen	Division of ground troops formed from Luftwaffe personnel

Major	Major (rank)
MAN (Maschinenfabrik Augsburg-Nürnberg AG)	MAN engineering and manufacturing firm with plants at Augsburg, Nuremberg and Gustavsburg
Marine, (oder Kriegsmarine), die	German Navy, the (1935–45)
Marita	Codename for the German intervention operation in the Balkans in April 1941
'Meine Ehre heißt Treue'	'My Honour is Loyalty' (the Waffen-SS motto)
Mein Kampf	'My Struggle', the title of Hitler's book written in 1923 and 1925–7, setting out the ideology and policies upon which the NSDAP was founded, including those concerned with race and ethnicity
Merkur	'Mercury', codename for the airborne invasion of Crete in May 1941
Nachrichten	Signal communications
Nachrichtentruppe	Signal communications troops
'Nacht und Nebel Erlaß'	'Night and Fog Decree' of December 1941, by which those suspected of acting against the state could be arrested and simply disappear without being subjected to due legal process, with no record of their arrest, imprisonment or summary execution being maintained or disclosed to their friends or family
Nationalsozialistische Deutsche Arbeiterpartei (NSDAP)	National Socialist German Workers Party (Nazi party)
Nationalsozialistische Führungsoffizier(e)	National Socialist Leadership Organization officer(s)
Nationalsozialistische Führungsorganisation (NSFO)	National Socialist Leadership Organization, established within the army to promote Nazi ideology, and loyalty and commitment to the Führer
Nationalsozialistischer Führungsstab des Heeres	National Socialist Leadership Staff of the Army, a staff branch formed within the OKH in March 1944
Nebel	Fog, mist, artificial smoke
Nebeltruppen	Smoke (including chemical (i.e., gas) warfare troops)
Nebelwerfer	Smoke shell or rocket-projector or rocket-launcher
Neu Beginnen	'New Beginning', a social democrat resistance group formed in 1934 and active in Berlin and the Ruhr
Nun danket alle Gott	'Now thank we all our God', a well-known traditional chorale or hymn much favoured throughout Prussia and Germany and their armies since the nineteenth century
Oberbefehlshaber	Commander-in-chief
Oberbefehlshaber des Heeres	Supreme commander (or commander-in-chief) of the army
Oberfähnrich	Advanced officer candidate
Oberfeldwebel	Senior warrant officer
Oberführer	SS rank equivalent to army brigadier
Obergefreiter	Corporal
Obergruppenführer	SS rank equivalent to army general

Oberkommando des Heeres (OKH)	High command (HQ) of the Army
Oberkommando der Luftwaffe (OKL)	High command (HQ) of the Air Force
Oberkommando der Kriegsmarine (OKM)	High command (HQ) of the Navy
Oberkommando der Wehrmacht (OKW)	High command (HQ) of the armed forces
Oberleutnant	Senior or 1st lieutenant
Oberquartiermeister	(General staff) senior quartermaster(s), who functioned as deputy chief(s) of staff
Oberquartiermeister I	Head of the operations branch within the general staff
Oberst	Colonel
Oberstleutnant	Lieutenant colonel
Obersturmbannführer	SS rank equivalent to army lieutenant colonel
Obersturmführer	SS rank equivalent to army senior or 1st lieutenant
Offizier	Officer
Offizieranwärter	Officer candidate
Offizierkaste	Officer class (as a social or hierarchical group)
OKH Heeres- verwaltungsamt	OKH administration office
Oldenburg	Codename for the economic and industrial plans for the exploitation of western Russia following the German invasion in June 1941
Ostfront	Eastern Front
Ostpreußen	East Prussia
Otto	Codename originally allocated to the general staff plans for invasion of Russia; later superseded by the codename *Barbarossa*
Panzer	Tracked armoured vehicle, usually referring to a tank or to describe an armoured formation or unit primarily comprised of tracked armoured fighting vehicles
Panzerabwehrkanone (PAK)	Anti-tank gun
Panzerarmee/~korps/ ~division/~brigade	Armoured or tank army, corps, division, brigade
Panzerfaust	A single-shot, disposable, rocket-propelled anti-tank grenade launcher, also known as the Faustpatrone
Panzergrenadier	Armoured infantry(man)
Panzergrenadierdivision/ ~brigade	Armoured infantry division, brigade
Panzergruppe(n) (Pz.Gp.)	Panzer group(s), an armoured formation usually comprised of two or more panzer corps
Panzerkampfwagen (Pz.Kpfw. or PzKw.)	Armoured vehicle, usually referring to a tank
Panzerschreck	'Tank terror', a hand-held anti-tank weapon projecting a rocket-propelled anti-armour missile (also known as the Raketenpanzerbüchse)

Panzertruppe(n)	Panzer or armoured forces or troops
Panzerwagen	Armoured vehicle, including wheeled armoured cars
Pioniere	Pioneer or engineer, including combat engineer
Plötzensee	The prison in Berlin in which many of the 20 July 1944 conspirators and others were executed
Polizei	Police
Propagandatruppen	Propaganda troops
Quartier	Military accommodation, quarters or billets
Reich	National state, empire
Reichsarbeitsdienst (RAD)	(German) National Labour Service
Reichsbahn	(German) National Railways
Reichsführer-SS (RF-SS)	National leader of the SS (Heinrich Himmler)
Reichsführung-SS	High command (headquarters) of the SS and Waffen-SS
Reichsheer, das	National Army, the (1920s and to 1935)
Reichskanzlei	Reich Chancellery building in Berlin
Reichskokarde	National cockade insignia (black/white/red)
Reichsmark (RM)	German national unit of currency (in early 1945, RM 1.00 was approximately equivalent to US$ 0.40)
Reichstag	Germany's central legislative assembly or parliament
Reichswehr, die	National Armed Forces, the (1920s and to 1935)
Reichssicherheits- hauptamt (RSHA)	SS central (main) security office, incorporating and controlling the merged Security Service (SD), Secret State Police (Gestapo) and Criminal Police (Kripo) from September 1939
Reserveoffizier(e)	Reserve officer(s)
Ritter	Knight (aristocratic title)
Ritterkreuz, Ritterkreuz des Eisernen Kreuzes	Knight's Cross of the Iron Cross
Rittmeister	Rank of army captain in a cavalry unit
Rote Kapelle	'Red Orchestra', a communist spy network operating within Germany, the title being that given to it by the German counter-espionage security organization
Schützenpanzerwagen	Armoured personnel carrier
Schutzstaffel (SS)	Elite guard of the Nazi movement during the NSDAP and Third Reich period
Seelöwe	'Sea Lion', the codename for the intended cross-Channel invasion of England in 1940
Sichelschnitt	Sickle-cut, term used to describe the concept for the sweeping deployment and advance of the panzer forces during the Blitzkrieg in the west in 1940
Sicherheitsdienst (SD)	SS security service
Sicherung	Security
Sieg	Victory
Sonder~	Special
Sonnenblume	Sunflower, codename for the deployment of German forces to North Africa in 1941
Sperrkreis	Secure, security controlled or prohibited area
SS-Führungshauptamt	Principal operational office of the SS

Stab	Staff
Stabsoffiziere	Field-grade officers (as a group or category)
Stabsquartier	Headquarters
Stellungskrieg	Positional warfare
Stoßtruppen	Shock troops, the assault detachments developed by the army during World War I
Stuka (Sturzkampfflug-zeug)	'Dive bomber', but usually used to refer to the Junkers 87 (Ju 87)
Sturmabteilung(en) (SA)	Storm trooper(s) paramilitary organization during the NSDAP and Third Reich period, also known as the 'Brownshirts'; also means 'assault unit' when used separately from the NSDAP context
Sturmbannführer	SS rank equivalent to army major
Swastika (Hakenkreuz)	Emblem or symbol adopted by the NSDAP in the 1920s, but already in use by various right-wing groups
Stahlhelm	German steel helmet introduced in 1916; also subsequently adopted as the name of the post-1918 veterans' association
Taifun	Typhoon, codename for the German plan for the attack on Moscow in September-October 1941
Totenkopf	Death's head (insignia widely used by the SS and by the army Panzer forces)
Truppenamt	Military office established in 1919 to administer and exert command over the army
Truppenübungsplatz	Military training ground or manoeuvre area
Untermenschen	Subhuman (derogatory term adopted by the Nazis relating to race or ethnicity)
Unteroffizier	Non-commissioned officer (typically sergeant)
Untersturmführer	SS rank equivalent to army junior or 2nd lieutenant
Walküre, Walküre I, Walküre II	Valkyrie, title of the contingency plan(s) for the internal security operation to deal with an uprising by foreign workers within Germany
Vaterland	Fatherland
Vergeltungswaffen	'Reprisal weapons', such as the V-1 and V-2 rockets
Verteidigung	Defence (position)
Verwaltung	Administration
Volksgericht, Volksgerichtshof	The People's Court in Berlin, which was established primarily to deal with those accused of activities against the Third Reich
Volksgrenadierdivision	'People's grenadier division', presented as an honour title when introduced in late 1944; these divisions were often second-rate and poorly equipped, especially in respect of major equipment items and mobility deficiencies
Volkssturm	Home Guard or 'people's army' created and employed during the final year of World War II
Von	Literally 'of', usually used as an important part of an officer's traditional family name or aristocratic title
Wachbataillon	Guard battalion
Wacht	Guard

Wacht am Rhein	'Watch on the Rhine', the codename given to the Ardennes offensive launched in December 1944
Waffe(n)	Weapon(s), also arm or branch of service
Waffenfarbe	System of distinctive coloured shoulder and collar insignia embellishments identifying arm or branch of service
Waffenschulen	Special service technical training schools
Waffen-SS, die	Armed SS, the
Wehrkreis(e), Wehrbezirke	Military district(s) (within Germany); usually identified by Roman numerals
Wehrkreiskommando	Military district headquarters
Wehrmacht, die	(German) Armed Forces, the (1935–45)
Wehrmachtadjutanten	Hitler's Wehrmacht adjutants, who were members of his personal military staff
Wehrmachtakademie	Name given to the Kriegsakademie when it was re-opened in 1935, although this new title was rarely used hereafter
Wehrmachtführungsstab	Operations staff branch at the OKW
Wehrmachtsamt	Armed forces office within the war ministry
Weisse Rose	'White Rose', a student resistance group in the early 1940s based primarily in Munich
Werwolf	'Werewolf', codename for Hitler's forward field headquarters in the Ukraine
Weserübung	Codename for the invasion of Denmark and Norway in April 1940
Widerstand	Resistance (as in 'resistance movement')
Wolfschanze	'Wolf Redoubt' or 'Wolf Strong-point', where 'Schanze' means 'redoubt', 'bastion', 'fortification' or 'entrenchment' when applied in a military context, although most US and English accounts interpret 'Wolfschanze' as 'Wolf's Lair', the name given to Hitler's forward headquarters in East Prussia 1941–4 (also shown as 'Wolfsschanze' in some sources)
X-Uhr	X-hour, the planned or actual start time for any military operation
Zitadelle	'Citadel', codename for the attack into the Kursk salient in 1943

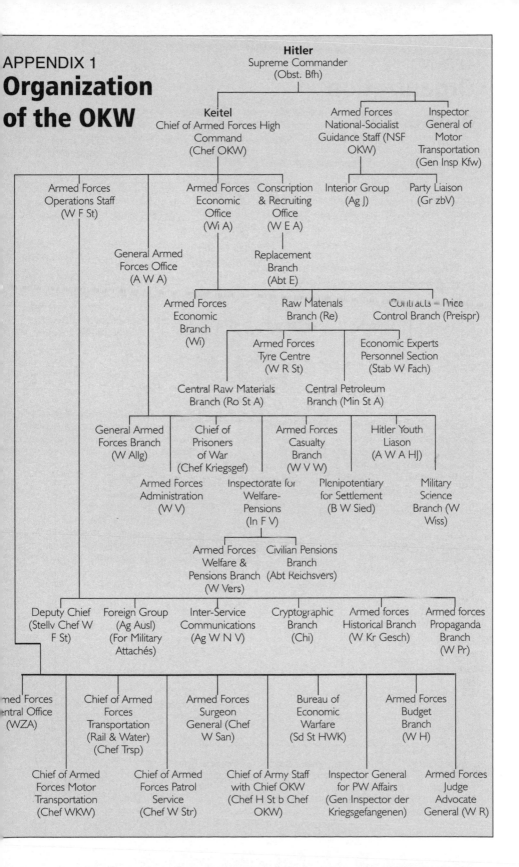

APPENDIX 1
Organization of the OKW

Hitler
Supreme Commander
(Obst. Bfh)

Keitel
Chief of Armed Forces High
Command
(Chef OKW)

Armed Forces
National-Socialist
Guidance Staff (NSF
OKW)

Inspector
General of
Motor
Transportation
(Gen Insp Kfw)

Armed Forces
Operations Staff
(W F St)

Armed Forces
Economic
Office
(Wi A)

Conscription
& Recruiting
Office
(W E A)

Interior Group
(Ag J)

Party Liaison
(Gr zbV)

General Armed
Forces Office
(A W A)

Replacement
Branch
(Abt E)

Armed Forces
Economic
Branch
(Wi)

Raw Materials
Branch (Re)

Contracts – Price
Control Branch (Preispr)

Armed Forces
Tyre Centre
(W R St)

Economic Experts
Personnel Section
(Stab W Fach)

Central Raw Materials
Branch (Ro St A)

Central Petroleum
Branch (Min St A)

General Armed
Forces Branch
(W Allg)

Chief of
Prisoners
of War
(Chef Kriegsgef)

Armed Forces
Casualty
Branch
(W V W)

Hitler Youth
Liason
(A W A HJ)

Armed Forces
Administration
(W V)

Inspectorate for
Welfare-
Pensions
(In F V)

Plenipotentiary
for Settlement
(B W Sied)

Military
Science
Branch (W
Wiss)

Armed Forces
Welfare &
Pensions Branch
(W Vers)

Civilian Pensions
Branch
(Abt Reichsvers)

Deputy Chief
(Stellv Chef W
F St)

Foreign Group
(Ag Ausl)
(For Military
Attachés)

Inter-Service
Communications
(Ag W N V)

Cryptographic
Branch
(Chi)

Armed forces
Historical Branch
(W Kr Gesch)

Armed forces
Propaganda
Branch
(W Pr)

med Forces
entral Office
(WZA)

Chief of Armed
Forces
Transportation
(Rail & Water)
(Chef Trsp)

Armed Forces
Surgeon
General (Chef
W San)

Bureau of
Economic
Warfare
(Sd St HWK)

Armed Forces
Budget
Branch
(W H)

Chief of Armed
Forces Motor
Transportation
(Chef WKW)

Chief of Armed
Forces Patrol
Service
(Chef W Str)

Chief of Army Staff
with Chief OKW
(Chef H St b Chef
OKW)

Inspector General
for PW Affairs
(Gen Inspector der
Kriegsgefangenen)

Armed Forces
Judge
Advocate
General (W R)

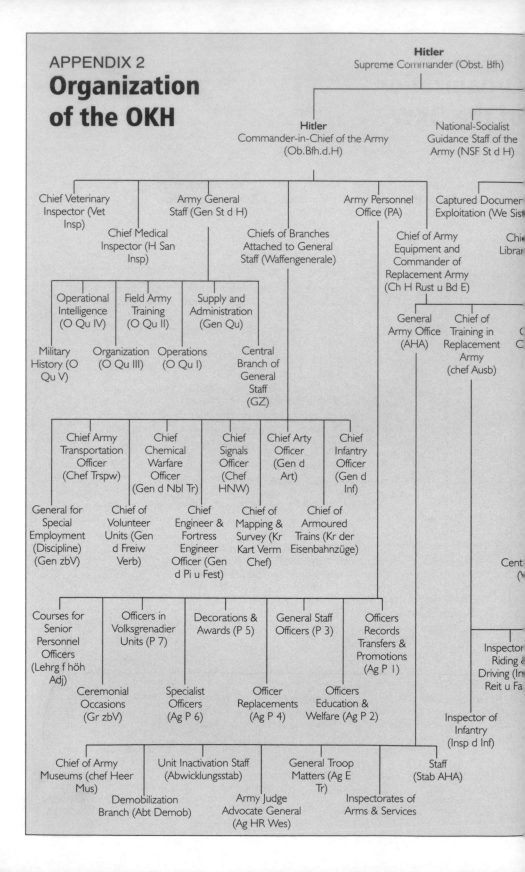

APPENDIX 2
Organization of the OKH

Hitler
Supreme Commander (Obst. Bfh)

Hitler
Commander-in-Chief of the Army
(Ob.Bfh.d.H)

National-Socialist
Guidance Staff of the
Army (NSF St d H)

Chief Veterinary
Inspector (Vet
Insp)

Army General
Staff (Gen St d H)

Army Personnel
Office (PA)

Captured Documer
Exploitation (We Sisi

Chief Medical
Inspector (H San
Insp)

Chiefs of Branches
Attached to General
Staff (Waffengenerale)

Chief of Army
Equipment and
Commander of
Replacement Army
(Ch H Rust u Bd E)

Chie
Librar

Operational
Intelligence
(O Qu IV)

Field Army
Training
(O Qu II)

Supply and
Administration
(Gen Qu)

General
Army Office
(AHA)

Chief of
Training in
Replacement
Army
(chef Ausb)

Military
History (O
Qu V)

Organization
(O Qu III)

Operations
(O Qu I)

Central
Branch of
General
Staff
(GZ)

Chief Army
Transportation
Officer
(Chef Trspw)

Chief
Chemical
Warfare
Officer
(Gen d Nbl Tr)

Chief
Signals
Officer
(Chef
HNW)

Chief Arty
Officer
(Gen d
Art)

Chief
Infantry
Officer
(Gen d
Inf)

General for
Special
Employment
(Discipline)
(Gen zbV)

Chief of
Volunteer
Units (Gen
d Freiw
Verb)

Chief
Engineer &
Fortress
Engineer
Officer (Gen
d Pi u Fest)

Chief of
Mapping &
Survey (Kr
Kart Verm
Chef)

Chief of
Armoured
Trains (Kr der
Eisenbahnzüge)

Cent
(V

Courses for
Senior
Personnel
Officers
(Lehrg f höh
Adj)

Officers in
Volksgrenadier
Units (P 7)

Decorations &
Awards (P 5)

General Staff
Officers (P 3)

Officers
Records
Transfers &
Promotions
(Ag P I)

Inspector
Riding &
Driving (In
Reit u Fa

Ceremonial
Occasions
(Gr zbV)

Specialist
Officers
(Ag P 6)

Officer
Replacements
(Ag P 4)

Officers
Education &
Welfare (Ag P 2)

Inspector of
Infantry
(Insp d Inf)

Chief of Army
Museums (chef Heer
Mus)

Unit Inactivation Staff
(Abwicklungsstab)

General Troop
Matters (Ag E
Tr)

Staff
(Stab AHA)

Demobilization
Branch (Abt Demob)

Army Judge
Advocate General
(Ag HR Wes)

Inspectorates of
Arms & Services

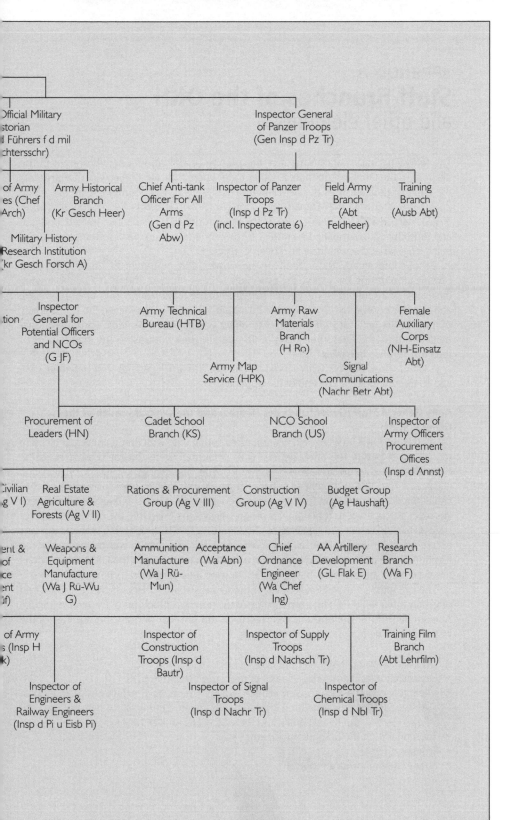

Official Military
storian
Führers f d mil
chtersschr)

Inspector General
of Panzer Troops
(Gen Insp d Pz Tr)

of Army
es (Chef
Arch)

Army Historical
Branch
(Kr Gesch Heer)

Military History
Research Institution
kr Gesch Forsch A)

Chief Anti-tank
Officer For All
Arms
(Gen d Pz
Abw)

Inspector of Panzer
Troops
(Insp d Pz Tr)
(incl. Inspectorate 6)

Field Army
Branch
(Abt
Feldheer)

Training
Branch
(Ausb Abt)

tion

Inspector
General for
Potential Officers
and NCOs
(G JF)

Army Technical
Bureau (HTB)

Army Map
Service (HPK)

Army Raw
Materials
Branch
(H Ro)

Signal
Communications
(Nachr Betr Abt)

Female
Auxiliary
Corps
(NH-Einsatz
Abt)

Procurement of
Leaders (HN)

Cadet School
Branch (KS)

NCO School
Branch (US)

Inspector of
Army Officers
Procurement
Offices
(Insp d Annst)

Civilian
g V I)

Real Estate
Agriculture &
Forests (Ag V II)

Rations & Procurement
Group (Ag V III)

Construction
Group (Ag V IV)

Budget Group
(Ag Haushaft)

ent &
of
ce
ent
if)

Weapons &
Equipment
Manufacture
(Wa J Ru-Wu
G)

Ammunition
Manufacture
(Wa J Rü-
Mun)

Acceptance
(Wa Abn)

Chief
Ordnance
Engineer
(Wa Chef
Ing)

AA Artillery
Development
(GL Flak E)

Research
Branch
(Wa F)

of Army
s (Insp H
k)

Inspector of
Engineers &
Railway Engineers
(Insp d Pi u Eisb Pi)

Inspector of
Construction
Troops (Insp d
Bautr)

Inspector of Signal
Troops
(Insp d Nachr Tr)

Inspector of Supply
Troops
(Insp d Nachsch Tr)

Inspector of
Chemical Troops
(Insp d Nbl Tr)

Training Film
Branch
(Abt Lehrfilm)

Staff Branches of the OKH
and other elements

The following information amplifies the outline organizational details shown in the diagram of the OKH in Appendix 2. Other than where indicated otherwise, it represents the OKH organization as at late 1944 and early 1945, as documented by the Allied intelligence staff (US War Department, *Handbook on German Military Forces*, TME-E 30-451, dated 15 March 1945), from which this information has been extracted, updated and reproduced in simplified summary form. Some minor errors of terminology found in the original document have also been corrected.

Despite the steady diminution of the power and influence of the general staff organization during the war years, especially from early 1942 and then again following the events of 20 July 1944, the overall structure of the organization 'on paper' might still appear to be comprehensive and quite formidable. However, this belied the actual ability of many of its general staff branches to affect wider policy, strategic and operational matters during the final three years of the war, in stark contrast to the experiences of their forerunners in earlier times.

A list of those officers who served as chief of the army general staff between 1933 and 1945 is included at the end of the appendix.

Army General Staff (Generalstab des Heeres) and the Central Branch of the General Staff

Located at the OKH forward field headquarters during war, with only a small rear element remaining in Berlin, the army general staff personnel were the main advisers to the commander-in-chief on all matters concerning operations, intelligence, supply, organization and policy. The OKH army general staff was originally intended to consist of twelve branches (Abteilungen) grouped under five senior general staff officers (Oberquartiermeister). However, the operations function was progressively subsumed into the operations staff of OKW, while the extent and significance of several other OKH general staff branch functions also reduced or were transferred to OKW from early 1942. As the war progressed, some functions were also delegated to other specialist branches within the OKH, while others devolved on to the Germany-based Ersatzheer soon after hostilities commenced.

The breadth of the responsibilities of the Generalstab des Heeres that the OKH had originally intended is evident from a listing of the principal functions of the twelve original Abteilungen of the Generalstab des Heeres in the pre-war period (the number of the responsible Abteilung is shown in brackets):

- Operations, tactical and warfare policy (1).
- Organization and authorized scales of men and equipment (2).
- Intelligence on eastern foreign armies (Soviet Union, lower Balkans, Scandinavia, Africa, Far East; this Abteilung also originally covered the western hemisphere until Pearl Harbor and the US entry into the war in December 1941) (3).
- Training within the operational theatre (4).
- Transport (5).
- Rear-echelon administration (6).

- Military history (7).
- Technical services (8).
- Topography (9).
- Large-scale manoeuvres and operational planning (10).
- Military schools and officer training (11).
- Intelligence on western foreign armies (Great Britain, upper Balkans, and (from January 1942) the Western Hemisphere) (12).

The Central Branch of the General Staff was responsible for the selection, training, posting and promotion of all General Staff Corps officers until March 1943, when this task passed to Branch P3 of the main Army Personnel Office.

Supply and Administration Groups (Quartiermeister-Gruppen)

A powerful and wide-ranging OKH staff branch headed by the chief of supply and administration (Generalquartiermeister), this organization consisted of a number of supply sections or groups (Gruppen) that dealt with the following functions (the number or other designation of the responsible Gruppe is shown in brackets):

- Overall planning and organization of supply to and within the field army, lines of communication and supply, control of service troops not allocated to specific army groups or armies (1).
- Civil affairs policy in the rear areas, including exploitation of resources, evacuation measures, prisoners of war, and the collection, control and exploitation of plundered military and non-military matériel (2).
- Coordination and processing of army group and army requisitions for combat supplies and engineer equipment (3).
- Personnel and security matters (IIa).
- Legal administration, jurisprudence and military law in the field (III).
- General administrative matters, including personal equipment, billeting, rations, pay and other financial matters, and the control of administrative personnel throughout the Feldheer (IVa).
- Control of all medical matters and personnel throughout the Feldheer (IVb).
- Control of all veterinary matters and personnel throughout the Feldheer (IVc).
- Control of all mechanical transport maintenance troops throughout the Feldheer and in Germany, as well as for general matters of mechanical transport availability and utilization (V).
- Non-military matters affecting civil administration of occupied areas within theatres of operations ('Section Z', with Gruppe II and Gruppe III).
- Control of all general headquarters supply troops (in collaboration with Gruppe III).
- All matters relating to army postal services in the Feldheer (FP).
- Organization and employment of technical troops in the Feldheer (no Gruppe number was allocated).
- All matters pertaining to the organization and employment of military police in the Feldheer (no Gruppe number was allocated).

Branch Chiefs attached to the General Staff

The following specialist senior officers were attached to the OKH army general staff, representing the combat arms and providing advice to the commander-in-chief on the organization, training, equipment and tactical employment of these arms in the field (amplifying detail is only provided where appropriate):

- Chief Infantry Officer (General der Infanterie).
- Chief of Armoured Trains (Kommandeur der Eisenbahn-Panzerzüge).
- Chief Artillery Officer (General der Artillerie).
- Chief of Mapping and Survey (Chef des Kriegskarten und Vermessungswesens).
- Chief Signals Officer (Chef des Heeresnachrichtenwesens).
- Chief Engineer and Fortifications Officer (General der Pionere und Festungen).
- Chief Officer of Smoke/Fog Forces (General der Nebeltruppen). ('Nebel' translates literally as 'fog' and refers here to chemically generated and projected smoke, as well as to the weapons, projectors and other equipment associated with the use of this capability on the battlefield.)
- Chief of Volunteer Units (General der Freiwilligenverbände). This section or branch was formed in January 1944, from when this officer and his staff dealt with the organization, equipment, training and employment of units formed from Soviet prisoner-of-war volunteers. In 1942 this branch was called General der Osttruppen (Chief of Eastern Forces) with an inspector of the 'turkvölkischen Verbände'. In 1944, a branch merger created the General der Freiwilligenverbände.
- Chief Army Transportation Officer (Chef des Transportwesens).
- General for Special Employment (Discipline) (General zur besonderen Verwendung). This section or branch was responsible for counter-espionage, discipline, penal matters and legal matters throughout the Feldheer in the field. As such, it overlapped and supplanted aspects of the responsibilities of Supply and Administration Gruppe III.

Chief Medical Inspector (Heeres-Sanitätsinspekteur)
Directed and advised medical and surgical matters as appropriate within the Feldheer, and controlled medical matters in the Ersatzheer.

Chief Veterinary Inspector (Veterinärinspekteur)
Directed and advised veterinary matters as appropriate within the Feldheer, and controlled veterinary matters in the Ersatzheer.

Army Personnel Office (Heerespersonalamt)
Consisted of seven main groups (Amtsgruppen) and branches (Abteilungen) and two special sections, most of which were based with the OKH rear headquarters element in wartime, with a representative presence at the field headquarters to facilitate speedy decision-making on important personnel issues. The Heerespersonalamt dealt only with military personnel and with certain non-military officials who were none the less categorized as military officers. In summary, the Heerespersonalamt dealt with the following matters:

- Amtsgruppe P1 was responsible for all officer records, appointments, postings, promotions and personnel policy. Its seven Abteilungen (numbers shown in brackets) dealt with policy and inter-service transfers (1); infantry and cavalry officers (2); panzer and supply troops officers (3); artillery and chemical warfare officers (4); engineer and signals officers (5); reserve officers and officers recalled to active duty (6); specialist (e.g., veterinary, medical, ordnance, mechanical maintenance) officers (7), until the responsibility for this particular category of officers passed to Amtsgruppe P6 in early 1944.

- Amtsgruppe P2 was responsible for officer education and welfare, including (from August 1942) the ideological, or political, training of officers. Its three Abteilungen (numbers shown in brackets) dealt with policy, education, officer corps honour issues, political matters, and any non-specific issues affecting senior officers (1); final decisions on individual officers concerning behaviour, courts martial and breaches of the code of honour (2); officer representations and complaints, Aryan ancestry issues, marriage, welfare and related matters concerning officers and their families (3).
- Heeres-Personalabteilung P3 was responsible for the selection, training, posting and promotion of all general staff corps officers (in place of the army general staff central branch from March 1943).
- Heeres-Personalabteilung P4 was responsible for officer replacements and related policy directives.
- Heeres-Personalabteilung P5 was responsible for decorations and awards.
- Amtsgruppe P6 was formed in May 1944, taking on the responsibility for the specialist officers formerly administered by Amtsgruppe P1. It now also dealt with administrative officers (Intendanten) and judge advocates (Wehrmachtsrichter). Its four Abteilungen (numbers shown in brackets) dealt with specialist officers (7); general policy and directives concerning those officers administered by the Amtsgruppe (8); other specialist categories of officer and (from May 1944) those former armed forces officials (Wehrmachtsbeamten) who had been accorded military officer status (Truppensonderdienst) (9 and 10).
- Heeres-Personalabteilung P7 was formed in October 1944 and was responsible for all army officers employed within Feldheer units under the control of Reichsführer-SS Heinrich Himmler. This principally concerned the Volksgrenadier formations created late in the war.
- Gruppe zbV was a special purpose section responsible for managing the physical distribution of decorations and awards, and for other ceremonial functions.
- The Lehrgänge für höhere Adjutanten administered the army personnel office's in-house six- to eight-week specialist courses on personnel policy, management and organization provided to senior personnel officers.

Chief of Army Equipment and Commander of the Replacement Army (Chef der Heeresrüstung und Befehlshaber des Ersatzheeres)

A powerful and wide-ranging organization that dealt within Germany, the 'zone of the interior', with personnel conscription, replacement and training; procurement, storage and provision of equipment; and the military administration of the territory, including control of the OKH rear headquarters elements (apart from the Army Personnel Office). Originally intended to be the deputy to the army commander-in-chief in wartime, the post of Chef der Heeresrüstung und Befehlshaber des Ersatzheeres became even more significant when Hitler dismissed Generalfeldmarschall von Brauchitsch in December 1941 and assumed direct command of the armed forces. However, the Ersatzheer came increasingly under SS control after Himmler was appointed as its commander by Hitler, following the failed July 1944 assassination attempt against the Führer; in the wake of which its former army commander, General Fromm, was executed in March 1945.

General Army Office (Allgemeines Heeresamt)
In practice the secretariat and coordinating organization for the OKH, miscellaneous branches and inspectorates, and various agencies in the Feldheer and within Germany including direct support for the commander of the Ersatzheer.

Staff (Stab)
Approved and issued publications such as manuals, equipment and organization tables, army regulations, clothing and uniform directives, and technical publications.

Inspectorates (Inspektionen) of Arms and Service Branches (Waffenabteilungen)
The separate OKH inspectorates included those for the infantry, horse riding and driving, artillery, anti-aircraft artillery, engineers, fortifications engineers, panzer troops (transferred to a separate newly created panzer troops inspectorate after 1943), signals (with three sub-branches), supply, chemical warfare and air-raid protection, railway engineers, technical troops, motor transport (with two sub-branches), medical (with three sub-branches), veterinary, and ordnance. Arms inspectors in the OKH were usually accorded the title 'General der ...'

General Troop Matters (Amtsgruppe Ersatzwesen und Allgemeine Truppenangelegenheiten)
Had a similar role to that of the army personnel office but dealt with enlisted personnel issues, policies and directives as opposed to those for officers. Its work was conducted on a general basis, rather than dealing with individuals. It had three sub-branches. The first dealt with all aspects of the regulations for troop postings, promotions, welfare, personal issues, non-commissioned officer matters, penal affairs, and German prisoners of war held by the Allies. The second was responsible for army chaplains, the third dealt with requisitioning accommodation and training areas for military use.

Army Judge Advocate General's Group (Amtsgruppe Heeresrechtswesen)
Consisted of the Judge Advocate's branch and a supporting legal staff section.

Unit Deactivation Staff (Abwicklungsstab)
A special-purpose staff element created in 1943 to resolve the affairs (including any residual financial matters) of the units destroyed with Sixth Army at Stalingrad at the beginning of that year. It also dealt similarly with the units of Heeresgruppe Afrika and the Afrikakorps after their surrender to the Allies in May 1943. From mid-1944 this staff element assumed responsibility for deactivating army units destroyed in any theatre of operations.

Demobilization Branch (Abteilung Demobilisierung)
Dealt with policies and directives concerning projected demobilization issues and associated arrangements.

Chief of Army Museums (Chef der Heeresmuseen)
Responsible for policy and providing direction affecting army museums.

Chief of Training in the Replacement Army (Chef des Ausbildungswesens im Ersatzheer)
This important post was created in October 1942, with the incumbent immediately

subordinate to the commander of the Ersatzheer. Through, and assisted by, the inspectors of arms and services, the Chef des Ausbildungswesens im Ersatzheer was responsible for controlling all training conducted within the Ersatzheer apart from that of the specialist medical, veterinary, ordnance and motor maintenance troops. The principal subordinate arm and service inspectors were those for the infantry, horse riding and driving troops, artillery troops, anti-aircraft troops, engineers and railway engineers, construction troops, signals troops, supply troops and chemical troops.

Training Film Branch (Abteilung Lehrfilm)
Controlled the production, distribution and archiving of army training films and the training of film projectionists and production staff.

Army Ordnance Office (Heereswaffenamt)
This sizeable office comprised eight major groups, most of which controlled numerous sub-sections and branches, and it had overall responsibility for the design, testing, development, proving and acceptance of all ordnance equipment. Its staff cooperated closely with the ministry of armament and war production (Reichsministerium für Bewaffnung und Kriegsproduktion), which also maintained representatives at the Heereswaffenamt.

* The sub-sections and branches of the Central Group (Zentral-Amtsgruppe des Heereswaffenamts) dealt with organizations, administration, plant efficiency, regulations, ordnance premises and their security.
* The many separate branches of the Development and Testing Group (Amtsgruppe für Entwicklung und Prüfung) dealt with all types of ballistic ammunition, infantry weapons and equipment, artillery weapons and equipment, engineer and railway engineer equipment, fortress engineer equipment, panzer and motorized equipment, signals equipment, optical survey, meteorological, artillery fire-control, and cartographic printing equipment, gas (chemical warfare) protection research and equipment, special equipment (such as some of the V-weapons developed late in the war), and the control of the various proving grounds on areas under military control (such as military training and manoeuvre areas).
* The Group for Weapons and Equipment Manufacture (Amtsgruppe für Industrielle Rüstung – Waffen und Gerät) dealt with all ordnance material except ammunition, including placing orders with industry. Its seven separate branches consisted of those that dealt with general equipment (including medical and veterinary), weapons, engineer, railway engineer and fortress engineer equipment, tanks and tractors, signals equipment, optical and precision instruments, and motor vehicle equipment.
* The Group for Ammunition Manufacture (Amtsgruppe für Industrielle Rüstung (Munition)) comprised five branches, each dealing with separate aspects or natures of ammunition manufacture and procurement.
* The Acceptance Group (Amtsgruppe für Abnahme) had three sub-branches, and these were responsible for ensuring that all ordnance material met the required specifications, and subsequently for accepting it for army service.
* The Chief Ordnance Engineer Group (Amtsgruppe Chefingenieur) controlled six branches, each of which dealt with the technical design, development and manufacture of various types of ordnance equipment.

- The Group for Anti-aircraft Artillery Development (Amtsgruppe für Flakentwicklung) controlled five branches, each of which dealt with a separate aspect of anti-aircraft artillery defence.
- The Ordnance Research Branch (Forschungsabteilung) carried out or directed additional research tasks as and when required.

Army Administration Office (Heeresverwaltungsamt)

The Heeresverwaltungsamt bore overall responsibility for the procurement of pay, rations, accommodation and clothing for the army. Until May 1944 much of this work was carried out by uniformed armed forces officials (Wehrmachtsbeamten), but from that time these (together with the army judge advocates) were re-categorized as special duty troops (Truppensonderdienst) and accorded military officer status, being administered thereafter by the army personnel office, although their duties with the Heeresverwaltungsamt continued as before. This office comprised five main groups, each with various sub-sections, branches and departments:

- The Group for Officials and Civilian Workers (Amtsgruppe Allgemeine Heeresbeamten-, Angestellen-, Arbeiter- und Kassenangelegenheiten) had seven branches and dealt with salaries, terms of employment, financial accounting, and administration of these personnel.
- The Group for Real Estate, Agriculture and Forests (Amtsgruppe Liegenschaften, Land- und Forstwirtschaft) had three branches, which dealt with the procurement of garrison real estate and quartering, the administration of manoeuvre areas, and army forestry matters.
- The Rations and Procurement Group (Amtsgruppe Heeresverpflegungs- und Beschaffungswesen) had three branches, each dealing with various aspects of ration procurement, inspection and supply.
- The Construction Group (Amtsgruppe Bau) had two branches, and these together dealt with matters affecting all army construction activities.
- The Budget Group (Amtsgruppe Haushalts- und Besoldungswesen) was created within the Heeresverwaltungsamt in February 1944, when the overall responsibility for army pay, general finance and budgetary matters were removed from the commander of the Ersatzheer. The group included four sub-branches.

Inspector General for Potential Officers and Non-commissioned Officers (Generalinspekteur für den Führernachwuchs des Heeres)

Originally, this organization and appointment was that of the Inspector of Army Training and Education, before its remit was broadened and its name was changed in March 1944. This important, politically sensitive and influential appointment was subordinate to the commander of the Ersatzheer, and the incumbent was responsible for the recruitment, training and National Socialist ideological instruction of all potential officers and non-commissioned officers. He also bore responsibility for all officer candidate (i.e., officer cadet) and non-commissioned officer schools, including course content, methods of instruction used, and the political training included. To achieve this he controlled four branches:

- The Branch for the Procurement of Leaders (Abteilung Heeresnachwuchs) was placed under the control of this office early in 1944 and represented the army in all matters affecting the procurement of potential leaders.

- The Cadet School Branch (Abteilung Kriegsschulen) administered all of the army officer candidate schools.
- The Non-commissioned Officer School Branch (Abteilung Unteroffiziervorschulen u. -schulen) administered all of the army non-commissioned officer schools.
- The appointment of Inspector of Officer Procurement (Inspekteur der Annahmestellen für Offizierbewerber des Heeres) was originally established in 1943 within the Army Personnel Office, and was subsequently transferred to the Generalinspekteur für den Führernachwuchs des Heeres in 1944. It controlled the officer candidate selection and acceptance centres in each German Wehrkreis.

Signals Communications Branch (Nachrichten-Betriebsabteilung des Ch H Rüst u. BdE)

Subordinate to the commander of the Ersatzheer, this independent organization comprised a telegraph company, a signals exploitation company, a radio transmission centre and a telephone operating company.

Army Raw Materials Branch (Heeres-Rohstoffabteilung)

Subordinate to the commander of the Ersatzheer, this independent agency procured raw materials for the OKH.

Army Cartographic Service (Heeresplankammer)

Subordinate to the commander of the Ersatzheer, this independent agency held stocks of foreign-area maps and produced all sorts of mapping for OKH as required.

Army Technical Bureau (Heerestechnisches Büro)

Subordinate to the commander of the Ersatzheer, this independent organization provided specialist engineer expertise to OKH.

Women's Auxiliary Corps (Nachrichtenhelferinnen-Einsatzabteilung)

The female members of this corps were organized into battalions (Einsatzabteilung) and deployed to provide communications, administrative and clerical support within OKH and the higher-level headquarters of the Feldheer and the Ersatzheer.

National Socialist Guidance Staff of the Army (Nationalsozialistischer Führungsstab des Heeres)

Established in March 1944, the members of this staff organization were attached to the army high command but were directly subordinate to Hitler. Their task was to oversee and control the overall programme of National Socialist ideological indoctrination within the army, and to develop and issue appropriate directives to National Socialist Guidance Officers (NSFO) assigned to units in the field.

Führer's Official Military Historian (Der Beauftragte des Führers für die militärische Geschichtsschreibung)

Established in 1942 to record the military history of the war, this appointment was attached to the OKH but remained directly subordinate to Hitler. It controlled five sub-branches, which included the Army Historical Branch (Kriegsgeschichtliche Abteilung des Heeres), Military History Research Institute (Kriegswissenschaftliches Institut), Chief of Army Archives (Chef der Heeresarchive), Chief of Army Libraries (Chef der Heeresbüchereien) and the Captured Documents Exploitation Centre (Wehrmacht-Sichtungs-stelle).

Inspector General of Panzer Troops (Generalinspekteur der Panzertruppen)

This most important post and supporting staff organization was established in 1943 when the OKH responsibility for panzer troops was separated from that originally borne by the Chief of Mobile Troops (General der Schnellen Truppen) within the army general staff organization. The Generalinspekteur der Panzertruppen was directly subordinate to Hitler but remained attached to the OKH, with responsibility for the organization, training and replacement of all panzer troops – including those of the Waffen-SS and Luftwaffe panzer units. To fulfil this extensive remit there were four branches:

- Chief Anti-tank Officer for All Arms (General der Panzerabwehr aller Truppen), who was appointed in November 1944 with responsibility for anti-tank tactics throughout the Wehrmacht and liaison on panzer matters with the Army General Staff.
- Inspector of Panzer Troops (Inspekteur der Panzertruppen), who (unlike the other OKH arms inspectors) carried out this function independently of the chief of training of the Ersatzheer.
- The Field Army Branch (Abteilung Feldheer) was responsible for liaison between the Generalinspekteur der Panzertruppen and the Feldheer, and for the evaluation and development of the panzer arm's organization, training and tactics in the light of combat experience.
- The Training Branch (Ausbildungs-Abteilung) was created early in 1944, when it assumed responsibility for administering the training of all panzer troops – a function previously carried out by the panzer branch of the General Army Office's Inspectorates of Arms and Services. The Ausbildungs-Abteilung also produced as a training publication a monthly account of the combat experiences of the panzer troops.

Chiefs of the German Army General Staff and Army High Command (OKH) 1933–1945

During the Third Reich period, the following senior officers served as chief of the army general staff:

Generaloberst Ludwig Beck, 1 October 1933 to 31 August 1938 (who actually resigned on 18 August, although Hitler refused to accept his resignation until 21 August, or to announce it until 31 August)

Generaloberst Franz Halder, 1 September 1938 to 24 September 1942

Generaloberst Kurt Zeitzler, 24 September 1942 to 10 June 1944

Generalleutnant Adolf Heusinger, 10 June 1944 to 21 July 1944

Generaloberst Heinz Guderian, 21 July 1944 to 28 March 1945

General Hans Krebs, 1 April 1945 to 30 April 1945 (some sources show 8 May 1945, the day of the German official surrender, but Krebs had almost certainly died a week earlier).

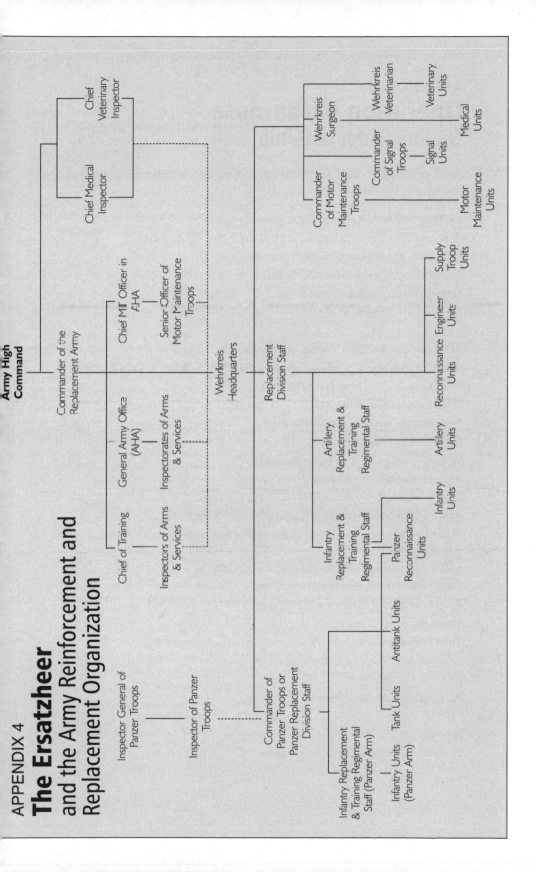

APPENDIX 4

The Ersatzheer
and the Army Reinforcement and Replacement Organization

APPENDIX 5
Operation Barbarossa
Outline Order of Battle

The deployment of German army groups and armies are shown from north to south and include Axis Allies.

ARMY GROUP NORTH (Generalfeldmarschall von Leeb)

(3 panzer divisions; 2 motorized divisions; 24 infantry divisions)

Eighteenth Army (Generaloberst von Küchler)

Panzer Group 4 (Generaloberst Höpner)

Sixteenth Army (Generaloberst Busch)

Air support: Luftwaffe Air Fleet 1

ARMY GROUP CENTRE (Generalfeldmarschall von Bock)

(9 panzer divisions; 6 motorized divisions; 33 infantry divisions; 1 cavalry division)

Panzer Group 3 (Generaloberst Hoth)

Ninth Army (General Strauss)

Second Army (General von Weichs)

Fourth Army (General von Kluge)

Panzer Group 2 (Generaloberst Guderian)

Air support: Luftwaffe Air Fleet 2

ARMY GROUP SOUTH (Generalfeldmarschall von Rundstedt)

(5 panzer divisions; 3 motorized divisions; 34 infantry divisions; 14 Romanian divisions; 1 Hungarian army corps)

Sixth Army (Generalfeldmarschall von Reichenau)

Panzer Group 1 (Generaloberst von Kleist)

Seventeenth Army (General von Stülpnagel)

Hungarian Army Corps

Third Romanian Army

Eleventh Army (Generaloberst von Schobert)

Fourth Romanian Army

Air support: Luftwaffe Air Fleet 4

Reserves

22 divisions, including 2 panzer divisions

Map Section

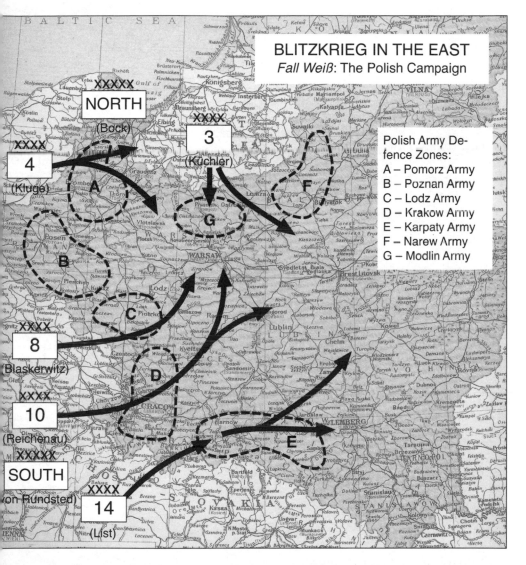

The general staff's plan (August 1939) for the invasion of Poland was subsequently carried out between 1 September and 6 October 1939. This was the first such Blitzkrieg. It then paved the way for the development of *Fall Gelb* and *Fall Otto*, as well as providing the Wehrmacht with access to the concentration areas close to the Russian border that would be so vital to the success of Operation *Barbarossa* in June 1941.

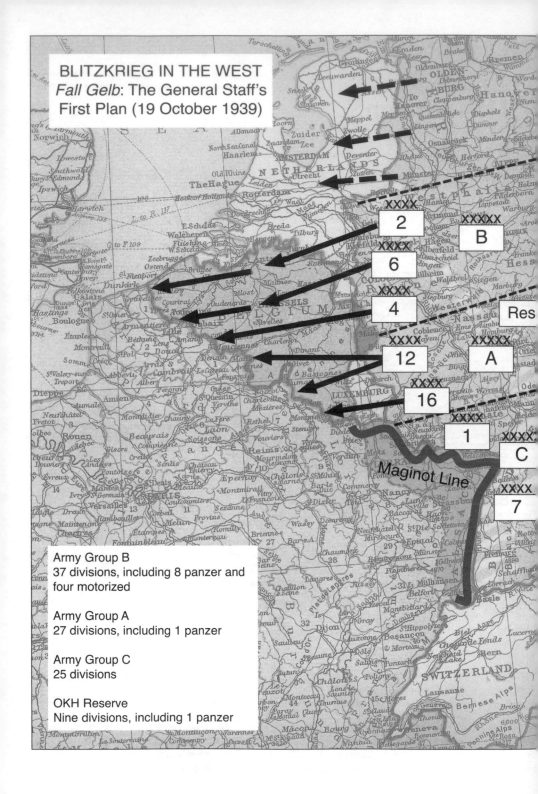

BLITZKRIEG IN THE WEST
Fall Gelb: The General Staff's
First Plan (19 October 1939)

Army Group B
37 divisions, including 8 panzer and
four motorized

Army Group A
27 divisions, including 1 panzer

Army Group C
25 divisions

OKH Reserve
Nine divisions, including 1 panzer

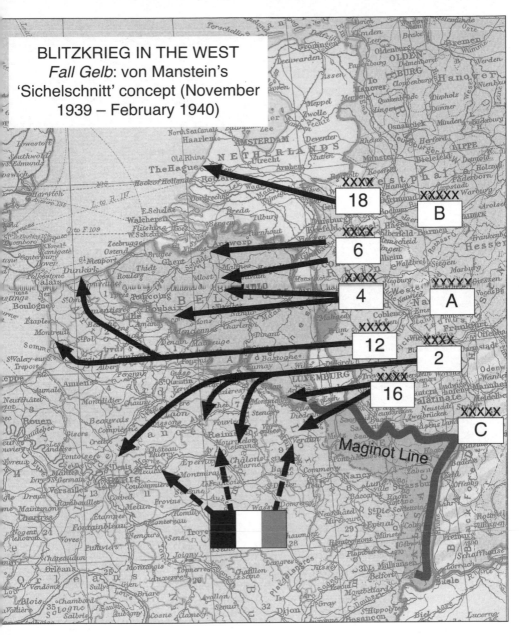

BLITZKRIEG IN THE WEST
Fall Gelb: von Manstein's 'Sichelschnitt' concept (November 1939 – February 1940)

he original concept was posited upon a German offensive being launched in response to a pre-
mptive or imminent French attack. The possibility of avoiding a violation of Belgian neutrality or
an advance into the Netherlands as shown in von Manstein's original plan had been largely
scounted by February 1940. In memorandums dated 6 December 1939 and January 1940, von
anstein set out the need for mobile armoured forces in Army Group A; also for that Army Group
have 40 divisions to carry out the main attack, with four more in reserve. The need to re-balance
e armoured forces was formally identified during a Kriegsspiel (war game) at HQ Army Group
, Koblenz, on 7 February 1940. The majority of panzer and motorized divisions remained
oncentrated within Army Group B instead of Army Army Group A until after von Manstein's
eeting with Hitler on 17 February 1940. There was an assumption that the French would
unch a strong counter-offensive against the left flank of Army Group A.

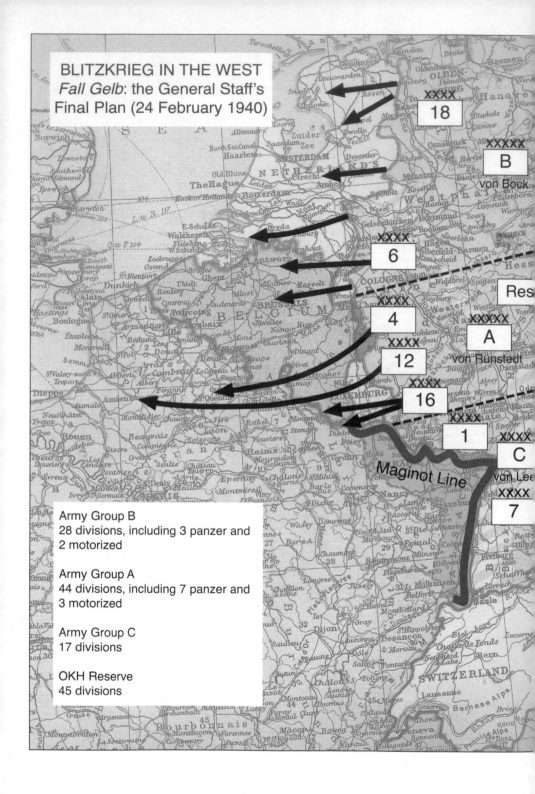

BLITZKRIEG IN THE WEST
Fall Gelb: the General Staff's
Final Plan (24 February 1940)

XXXX
18

XXXXX
B
von Bock

XXXX
6

Res

XXXX
4

XXXXX
A
von Runstedt

XXXX
12

XXXX
16

XXXX
1

XXXX
C
von Lee

Maginot Line

XXXX
7

Army Group B
28 divisions, including 3 panzer and
2 motorized

Army Group A
44 divisions, including 7 panzer and
3 motorized

Army Group C
17 divisions

OKH Reserve
45 divisions

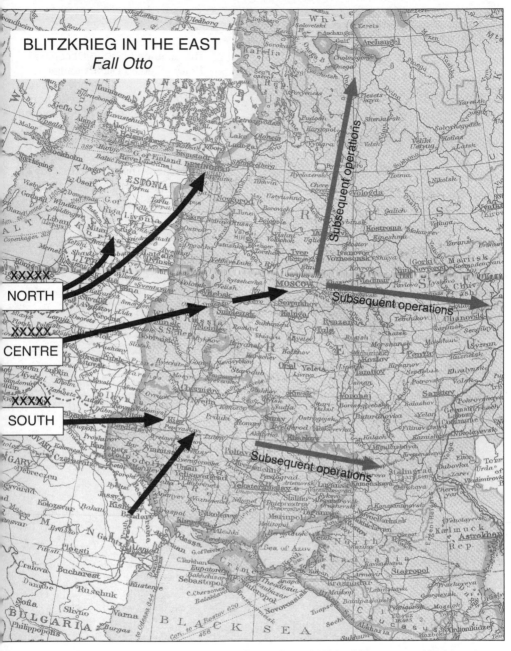

BLITZKRIEG IN THE EAST
Fall Otto

e general staff's first plan (developed June – December 1940) had Moscow and its important
l hub as the priority objective, while forcing the Red Army into a major battle to protect the city.
wever Hitler dismissed the assessed importance of Moscow, citing the greater importance of
ningrad and its adjacent port of Kronstadt on the Baltic coast, as well as the economic
portance of the Ukraine and the Black Sea ports in the south.

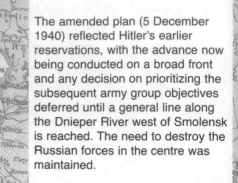

BLITZKRIEG IN THE EAST
Fall Otto

The amended plan (5 December 1940) reflected Hitler's earlier reservations, with the advance now being conducted on a broad front and any decision on prioritizing the subsequent army group objectives deferred until a general line along the Dnieper River west of Smolensk is reached. The need to destroy the Russian forces in the centre was maintained.

XXXXX
NORTH

XXXXX
CENTRE

XXXXX
SOUTH

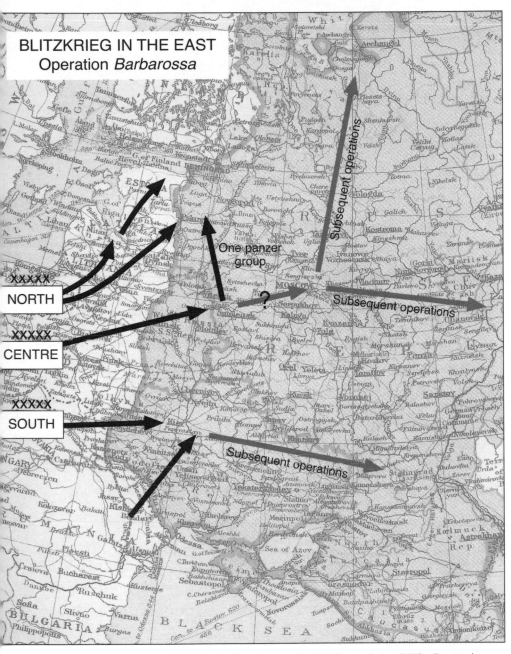

BLITZKRIEG IN THE EAST
Operation *Barbarossa*

XXXXX
NORTH

XXXXX
CENTRE

XXXXX
SOUTH

One panzer group

?

Subsequent operations

Subsequent operations

Subsequent operations

updated plan, in accordance with Hitler's directive no. 21 (18 December 1940) allocated
ority to the capture of Leningrad and Kronstadt. Once Smolensk was reached, Army Group
entre would halt and send a panzer group to reinforce Army Group North, while also standing
ady to reinforce Army Group South's advance into the Ukraine. Any further advance on
oscow would depend upon the capture of Leningrad by Army Group North, although both Hitler
d the OKH still agreed the need to destroy the Red Army as far to the west as possible.

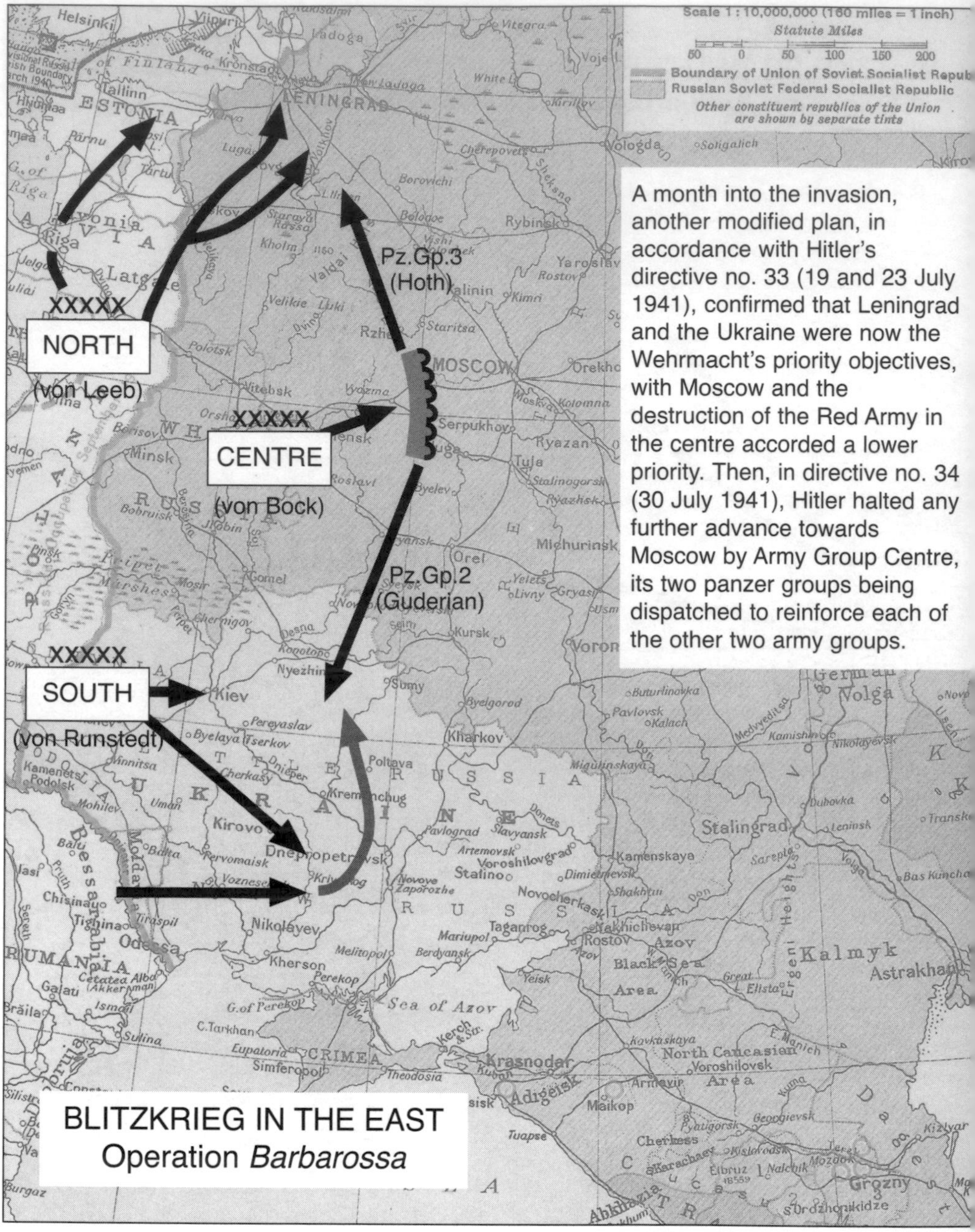

Scale 1 : 10,000,000 (160 miles = 1 inch)
Statute Miles
Boundary of Union of Soviet Socialist Republics
Russian Soviet Federal Socialist Republic
Other constituent republics of the Union are shown by separate tints
A month into the invasion, another modified plan, in accordance with Hitler's directive no. 33 (19 and 23 July 1941), confirmed that Leningrad and the Ukraine were now the Wehrmacht's priority objectives, with Moscow and the destruction of the Red Army in the centre accorded a lower priority. Then, in directive no. 34 (30 July 1941), Hitler halted any further advance towards Moscow by Army Group Centre, its two panzer groups being dispatched to reinforce each of the other two army groups.
XXXXX
NORTH
(von Leeb)
XXXXX
CENTRE
(von Bock)
XXXXX
SOUTH
(von Runstedt)
Pz.Gp.3
(Hoth)
Pz.Gp.2
(Guderian)
LENINGRAD
MOSCOW
Kiev
Stalingrad
BLITZKRIEG IN THE EAST
Operation *Barbarossa*

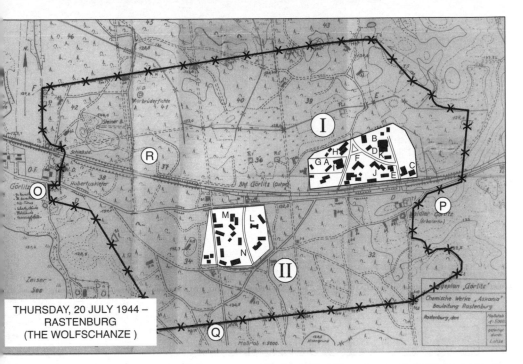

THURSDAY, 20 JULY 1944 –
RASTENBURG
(THE WOLFSCHANZE)

ap and diagram of the area of the Führerhauptquartier 'Wolfschanze' near Rastenburg in East
ussia. The site of the bomb explosion and other key locations within the secure areas (I and II)
e shown overlaid on to a contemporary sketch map. Note the description of the Wolfschanze
ea on this map as Chemische Werke 'Askania – which was used to conceal the true purpose
Sperrkreis (secure area) I during its construction. Before the war, a Kürhaus (residential health
a) occupied the north-west part of Sperrkreis II, to the south of the railway line. Sperrkreis I
mprised all of the key command bunkers and facilities, as well as the restricted access
hrersperrkreis compound (buildings A, G and I). Sperrkreis II comprised the headquarters'
ministrative and support facilities. The outer security perimeter of the Wolfschanze is shown
us –x–x–x–x–.

JILDINGS AND FACILITIES

Lagebaracke (site of the bomb explosion)
Hitler's bunker
Göring's bunker
Bormann's bunker
Keitel's bunker
Signal communications bunker
(overseen by General Fellgiebel)
Sicherheitsdienst (SD) facility
Guard detachment commander
Gästebunker

J Officers' club and dining facility
K Club and 'tea house' facility
L Guard detachment command post
M Area commandant's facilities
N Main telephone exchange
O Security checkpoint (west)
   (von Stauffenberg's entry point)
P Security checkpoint (east)
Q Security checkpoint (south)
   (von Stauffenberg's exit point)
R Rastenburg – Angersburg railway line

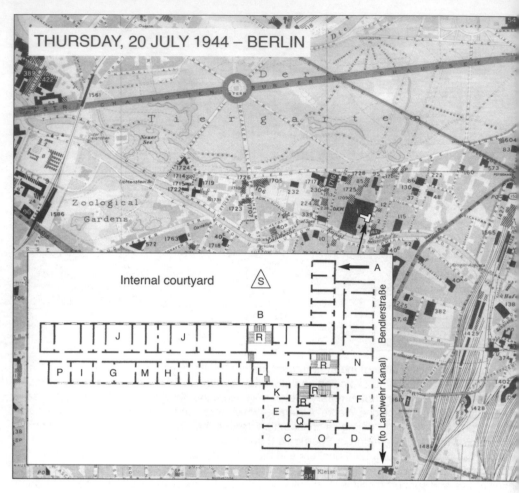

THURSDAY, 20 JULY 1944 – BERLIN

Map and diagram of part of the OKW building at the Benderstraße, which lay close to the Grossadmiral von Holtzendorf bridge on the Landwehr Kanal. Within this building, the main offices from which Oberst von Stauffenberg and his co-conspirators launched Operation *Valkyrie* and attempted to carry through their coup on 20 July 1944 are highlighted on the main map and shown in detail on the diagram. The building's internal courtyard is that in which Oberst von Stauffenberg, Oberst Mertz von Quirnheim, General Olbricht and Leutnant Haeften were shot later that night.

KEY TO DIAGRAM

A Vehicle entrance through archway from Bendlerstraße.
B Access to stairway from courtyard.
C Commander Ersatzheer (Generaloberst Fromm).
D Chief of Staff Ersatzheer (Oberst von Stauffenberg).
E Aide to Commander Ersatzheer.
F Outer Office, Chief of Staff Ersatzheer.
G Chief, General Army Office (General Olbricht).
H Chief of Staff, General Army Office (Oberst Mertz von Quirnheim.

I Aide to Chief, General Army Office.
J General Army Office offices.
K Chief Clerk.
L Clerical Staff.
M Secretaries.
N Duty Officer's offices.
O Map Room.
P Documents Registry.
Q Waiting room.
R Stairway.
S Pile of builder's sand in courtyard.

Index